Studies in Diplomacy and International Relations

Series Editors
Donna Lee
International Organisations and
International Political Economy
Manchester Metropolitan University
Manchester, UK

Paul Sharp
University of Minnesota
Duluth, USA

Marcus Homes
College of William & Mary
Williamsburg, USA

More information about this series at
http://www.palgrave.com/gp/series/14471

Linda Frey • Marsha Frey

The Culture of French Revolutionary Diplomacy

In the Face of Europe

Linda Frey
Department of History
University of Montana
Missoula, MT, USA

Marsha Frey
Department of History
Kansas State University
Manhattan, KS, USA

Studies in Diplomacy and International Relations
ISBN 978-3-319-71708-1   ISBN 978-3-319-71709-8   (eBook)
https://doi.org/10.1007/978-3-319-71709-8

Library of Congress Control Number: 2017964615

© The Editor(s) (if applicable) and The Author(s) 2018
This work is subject to copyright. All rights are solely and exclusively licensed by the Publisher, whether the whole or part of the material is concerned, specifically the rights of translation, reprinting, reuse of illustrations, recitation, broadcasting, reproduction on microfilms or in any other physical way, and transmission or information storage and retrieval, electronic adaptation, computer software, or by similar or dissimilar methodology now known or hereafter developed.
The use of general descriptive names, registered names, trademarks, service marks, etc. in this publication does not imply, even in the absence of a specific statement, that such names are exempt from the relevant protective laws and regulations and therefore free for general use.
The publisher, the authors and the editors are safe to assume that the advice and information in this book are believed to be true and accurate at the date of publication. Neither the publisher nor the authors or the editors give a warranty, express or implied, with respect to the material contained herein or for any errors or omissions that may have been made. The publisher remains neutral with regard to jurisdictional claims in published maps and institutional affiliations.

Cover illustration: Photo 12 / Alamy Stock Photo

Printed on acid-free paper

This Palgrave Macmillan imprint is published by Springer Nature
The registered company is Springer International Publishing AG
The registered company address is: Gewerbestrasse 11, 6330 Cham, Switzerland

To our family, always with us.

Acknowledgments

It is a truth universally acknowledged that authors want to mention those who have expedited or improved their work, although it is impossible to thank adequately all those who have given so generously of their time and their expertise. Our research led us from the banks of the Seine, to the Thames, the Potomac, the Brandywine, the Itchen, the Liffey, and the Leith, to name but a few. We studied not only the official but also the private correspondence that often proved more revealing. What great fun! The documents are still magical, transporting us to another time and another place. Monetary assistance, but even more importantly moral support was provided by the Earhart Foundation, the Hagley Museum and Library, the International Center for Jefferson Studies at Monticello, and the Newberry Library. Our institutions: Kansas State University, the University of Montana, The Ohio State University, and the United States Military Academy at West Point offered us both time and resources as did invaluable librarians, particularly those at Interlibrary Loan. Our secretaries Diane Rapp and Shelly Reeves and an energetic student assistant, Aram Kokuzian aided us as well.

Archivists working in the same historical vineyard made this work possible. The Manuscripts Divisions of the British Library, the Library of Congress, and the New York Public Library unfailingly provided invaluable assistance as did individuals at the London Public Record Office, the National Archives (Washington, D.C.), the Archives nationales, the Archives du Ministère des affaires étrangères, the National Library of Ireland, the National Library of Scotland, the National Maritime Museum, and the Public Record Office in Northern Ireland.

We were encouraged and heartened by those toiling in regional archives who had an unrivaled knowledge of their collections. This manuscript is grounded in material in the Centre for Kentish Studies, the Derbyshire Record Office, the Devon Record Office, the Hampshire Record Office, the Historical Society of Pennsylvania, the Lewis Walpole Library, Yale University (who knew you could play croquet in the winter?), the Lincolnshire Archives, the Merton College Library, Oxford, the Somerset Heritage Centre, the New York State Historical Society, the University of Virginia Alderman Library, and Duke University Library. The experiences there graced our lives and warmed our hearts.

Our readers: David Bell, James Friguglietti, Thomas Kaiser, Renaud Morieux offered us insightful comments as did the anonymous reviewers for the press. The work is certainly stronger for their comments, although on a number of occasions we could sympathize with the readers of Abelard's *Sic et Non*. We must thank those at Palgrave/Macmillan in particular Sarah Roughly for graciously and expeditiously steering the manuscript through the shoals of publication. This work would not have been possible without the unfailing support of our family and the dogged tolerance of our canine crew.

Contents

1 Introduction — 1

2 Mise en Scène: The Indictment — 23

3 The Enemy Within: The Attack on Diplomats — 65

4 The Revolutionary Theater of Power: Precedence and Etiquette — 97

5 Instruments of the Revolution: Language and Dress — 141

6 "Empire of Images": The Deployment of Symbols — 177

7 "Quite in the Clouds": French Emissaries Abroad — 219

8 Conclusion: Return to the Old — 259

Index — 287

Archival Sources

Archives nationales   A.N.
Archives du Ministère des affaires étrangères   A.A.E.
British Library   B.L.
Centre for Kentish Studies
Derbyshire Record Office
Devon Record Office
Hagley Museum and Library
Hampshire Record Office
Historical Society of Pennsylvania
The Lewis Walpole Library, Yale University
Library of Congress
Lincolnshire Archives
Merton College Library, Oxford
Monticello, International Center for Jefferson Studies
National Archives   N.A.
National Library of Ireland
National Library of Scotland
National Maritime Museum
Newberry Library
New York Public Library
New York State Historical Society
Public Record Office, London   P.R.O.
Public Record Office, Northern Ireland   P.R.O.N. I.
Somerset Heritage Centre
University of Virginia, Alderman Library, Special Collections

CHAPTER 1

Introduction

Georg Forster (1754–1794), a German Jacobin who helped establish a republic in Mainz and who went to Paris in 1792, wrote to his wife that "I must eat, live, and dress like a *sans-culotte*, and whatever is left over is dead and useless … In this revolution in thought lies the power of the republic."[1]

That revolution in thought encompassed foreign relations and extended to the French representatives abroad from 1789 to brumaire 1799, when a significant shift in the revolutionary dynamic occurred. Our book examines how that revolution in thought influenced the French revolutionaries sent abroad, negotiations, and thus the possibility of peace. Other French revolutionary studies have focused on the army, the navy, and even the engineering corps. None have examined the diplomatic corps and the creation of a new theater of power. We ask specifically how these diplomats responded to the demands of ideological conformity and to the challenges posed by contingency. These men were hardly puppets of revolutionary discourse but were independent actors who could and often did sabotage the government's agenda. This work underscores the importance of the creation of a new symbolic deployment and how rituals helped forge a revolutionary community. The French Revolution defied the international order just as the eschatalogical expectations of the French changed the nature of war. The French challenged the assumptions that had guided the European international order; they emphasized the importance of ritual

© The Author(s) 2018
L. Frey, M. Frey, *The Culture of French Revolutionary Diplomacy*,
Studies in Diplomacy and International Relations,
https://doi.org/10.1007/978-3-319-71709-8_1

and gesture not just as declarations or reflections of ideology but as tools in the reconstruction of diplomacy. That challenge and that vision echo throughout the diplomatic correspondence.

These dedicated revolutionaries could have argued, just as Trotsky did later, that we "do not belong to the diplomatic school. We ought rather to be considered as soldiers of the revolution."[2] The French revolutionaries saw themselves as soldiers fighting for a cause and thought they were not bound by the constraints of traditional diplomacy. In their fervor they discarded all diplomatic conventions and rejected the system as a whole. To do otherwise would have compromised the Revolution itself. The dictates of revolutionary ideology molded both the private and public face of republican France. Revolutionaries attempted to transform the public sphere by radically altering the insignia, dress, and rhetoric so inextricably associated with the *ancien régime*. The noble code of conduct had to be displaced and replaced by a revolutionary one[3]: one "theater of power" erected on the ruins of another.[4] Not surprisingly, Burke saw the revolutionary challenge as "acting on the moral theatre of the world."[5] The diplomatic corps thus transformed helped to precipitate war, prolong the conflict, and ultimately trigger the collapse of the republic.

The early revolutionary governments, although preoccupied with domestic concerns, had to perforce deal with diplomatic issues. The years from 1789 to 1792 witnessed a struggle over control of the diplomatic system with a few and as time went on even fewer diplomats of the old order still in place. When the Nootka Sound Controversy erupted in the spring of 1790, the Assembly abandoned the *pacte de famille* with Spain and in effect the European alliance system.[6] The abortive and aborted flight of the royal family to Varennes in the spring of 1791 changed the nature of the international arena, as did the declaration of war in the spring of 1792. At that same time, the Girondin ascendancy brought the imposition of more rigorous standards of ideological conformity to the diplomatic corps. The overthrow of the king and the constitution in August 1792 led many foreign governments to withdraw their representatives and to expel French diplomats. The king's execution in January 1793 created "an abyss that separated France from the rest of the world"[7] and isolated the revolutionary regime even further. The regicidal government and the Terror of 1793–1794 repulsed many and led more powers to expel French diplomats and the French to sever relations with most of Europe. In the autumn of 1794 the *tournant diplomatique* of the Thermidoreans was institutionalized by the reform of the Commission des Relations extérieures.

The decree of 7 fructidor, an III (24 August 1794) transferred the commission's political powers to the Committee of Public Safety. That committee was henceforth to reestablish ties with foreign governments and the commission to focus on commercial and cultural ties. Reciprocal interests, particularly commercial ones, would help recreate a diplomatic dialogue between agents of the republic and those of the kings. Martin argues that the Thermidoreans adopted a policy of cultural and diplomatic reconstruction in order to achieve a durable peace. Diplomacy thus served both as a political instrument and as a cultural vehicle.[8] The Thermidoreans moved away from the revolutionary diplomacy of the Terror to a "republican" diplomacy; they blamed the isolation of France from the rest of Europe on the "exaggerated bellicosity" and "frenzied propaganda" of the extremists. Through diplomacy France could reclaim her role in Europe.[9] These Thermidorean hopes of a rapprochement among peoples were undermined by the Directory's vision of French hegemony and of a glorious peace. The years of the Directory from 1795 to 1799 with its *politique de bascule* witnessed swings in both foreign and domestic policies. From 1789 to 1799, governments of whatever faction often responded to contingency (witness the agitation in Avignon) and military imperatives that overrode theoretical concerns. As the political sands shifted, so too did diplomacy, often seismically. Nonetheless, the determination to destroy the old diplomacy and replace it with a revolutionary one persisted and survived. The underlying theme—a rejection of the international order associated with the old regime—remained. Like a constant melody in polyphonic music with its various themes and changes in both tempo and meter, it retained a basic unity.

Steeped in the code of the *ancien régime*, the revolutionaries sought to replace it with another. The elaborate and punctilious, not to say litigious, attention to form and style that had characterized the *ancien régime* was echoed in the new. The revolutionaries could not concede this important representational ground and were then forced to adopt an alternative symbolic and visual system. As MacLeish argued in a later time and a later place: "A new world is not the same thing as a new land. A new land may be discovered. A new world must be created by the mind."[10] Those sent abroad were entangled in that symbolic deployment so integral to the revolutionary imagination and the revolutionary faith. Such men were to be revolutionaries, in Saint-Just's words, with "ardent hearts" and, in Marat's, with "warmth of soul."[11] Once appointed, these individuals were not free from scrutiny. The new order dictated that its representatives behave in ways befitting a republic: they had to take care not to adopt "diplomatic habits." Diplomacy was to be refashioned in the republican image. "French diplomacy ought to finally don the character of our revolution," Brissot intoned: "Our diplomatic style should be simple, laconic and clear."[12]

The new republican vision mandated if not the abolition, then the reform of the diplomatic system, so tainted by its association with the aristocracy and the *ancien régime*. In the new world envisaged by the revolutionaries, the secret machinations of the king would be replaced by the open negotiations of the people. The revolutionaries demanded nothing short of a change in diplomatic morals; in place of the "insidious manners" and the veiled or secret machinations of royal ambassadors they substituted the open and loyal policy of a free nation.[13] It would be a new diplomacy, a diplomacy which explicitly rejected many habits of the old. Was this mere bombast? Or even worse, a kind of rhetorical dressing designed to camouflage more sinister ends? Was John Quincy Adams right when he labeled French diplomacy a "Machiavellian mockery with which they have so long duped the world"?[14] Unconsciously, the revolutionaries, who were not even aware of this irony, adopted a system every bit as structured as the one that they had hoped to overturn. These men intended to replace the old aristocratic dress with the simple republican uniform, the deferential and circuitous language with a frank and direct speech, and the elaborate court etiquette with a simple, egalitarian style. Yet in doing so they reestablished the old practices with a new inflection. The republicans stressed how to speak, how to dress, and how to act, just as the aristocrats had.

The revolutionaries, advocates of a rationalist future, opposed "rite against rite, idol against idol," as Agulhon underscored, rather than adopting a "deritualized, desacralized, austere, transparent, and cold politics." This policy was inherently contradictory, for "scorn for the old cults is best expressed by refusing to copy them."[15] Cultural anthropologists, such as Geertz, however, have pointed out that such a course was not open to revolutionaries because they needed a cultural framework in which to legitimate their power.[16] Ideologies provided the "suasive images" by which politics could be grasped; they served as "maps of problematic social reality and matrices for the creation of collective conscience."[17] In a revolutionary upheaval such maps are desperately needed. They guide the individual, who, caught up in a political upheaval, finds himself, like a traveler on a journey to a strange country, confronted with the unknown. The French revolutionaries, following this interpretative schema, would be forced to invent a *mélange* of ceremonies and symbols to justify their existence and to consolidate their support.[18] Training in the law and familiarity with the classical tradition facilitated the forging of a common vision. French revolutionaries were not unique in investing symbols or language with such importance, for rituals also served as building blocks for the construction of a cultural and political framework in which to legitimate power. Such rituals served a vital role in forging a revolutionary community. In a state as ideologically driven as revolutionary France, rituals "create the experience of solidarity in the absence of consensus."[19]

Stites, looking at another and later revolution, that in Russia, emphasized the "culture building" apparent in dress, language, and gesture.[20] It may be, as Stites has argued, that "nowhere is the depth of a cultural revolution better revealed than as in what Brinton called the little things."[21] Some contemporaries realized just that. Burke, for one, perceptively noted that by such "little things" the revolutionaries "made a schism with the whole universe."[22] "Nothing in the Revolution, no, not to a phrase or a gesture, not to the fashion of a hat or a shoe, was left to accident."[23] Nor were these trivial issues. They were a facet of the creation of a revolutionary culture, part of that "total revolution in time, space, and personal relations."[24] The revolutionary tendency to rename months, streets, and children and to coin words indicates an attempt to erase the past and to remake the future.[25] These men articulated in their words and incarnated in their deeds the revolutionary attempt to reconstruct reality. Their actions illustrate another facet of the revolutionary attempt to tear down one world, in this case a diplomatic one, and to rebuild another. In that endeavor, predictably they were only partially successful. Diplomatic practice, recently relegated to the marginalia of revolutionary history, was as exemplary of the revolutionary order as the carefully staged festivals or the newly reconstructed calendar.[26] Just as the revolutionaries redesigned time, they also sought to redefine the relations among states.

The revolutionaries' vision of social reality as reflected in just such compelling images and idioms has attracted historians such as Furet, Agulhon, Ozouf, Hunt, Duprat, and Baecque who share a concern with the new political culture of the revolution, broadly defined.[27] For Furet, "the revolution was a collectively shared symbolic image of power" or "the process by which the collective imaginings of a society became the very fabric of its own history."[28] For both Hunt and Furet "the chief accomplishment" or the "real innovation" of the Revolution was the creation of a new political culture.[29] Others have followed the path they pioneered.[30] The diplomatic practices were one part or tessera of the mosaic of the Revolution. Revolutionary France furnishes excellent ground for such an investigation for the virulence of that social conflict intensified the identification with images and signs.[31] Supporters and critics alike testified to that intensity. Georg Forster, a few days before his death, compared the revolution to "a hurricane. Who can stop it?"[32] A British observer thought the French Revolution like "a shock of a tremendous earthquake, [that] has been felt from one extremity of the globe to the other."[33] Another thought it was "[b]edlam broke lose."[34]

The men examined were caught up in this earthquake of revolution and the tsunami of war. In this toxic atmosphere of mutual distrust, misperceptions, coupled with miscalculations, fueled the slide to war. "Denied reliable information and working from entirely different premises, the old-regime powers and revolutionary France held quite erroneous notions of each other's position and intentions."[35] As the historian Heidrich noted: the French revolutionaries and "their opponents no longer understood each other. They were breathing, as it were in different political atmospheres."[36] Faulty intelligence on both sides merged with a sense of invincibility. Ministers on both sides shared the anticipation that the war would be short and victory guaranteed. Note Bischoffwerder's advice to the Prussian officers: "Do not buy too many horses, the comedy will not last long …. we shall be home by autumn."[37] The "comedy" lasted almost 23 years.

Once begun, the eschatological expectations of the French changed the nature of war. Dumouriez's belief that "this war will be the last war"[38] was shared by many. Mirabeau had had the vision that "the time will no doubt come when we have only friends and no more allies, when … Europe will be one great family."[39] This vision of a new community was part of the Revolution's "intellectualized overestimation" of itself.[40] Still these hopes were important. Such expectations raised the stakes, glorified war, and demonized the enemy.[41] In the view of some contemporaries, revolution and war were not only "friends" but "two inseparable allies."[42] In this view, war was "constitutive, inevitable, and seminal," rather than "contingent, avoidable, and pernicious."[43] Belissa asks: "[W]as it [the Republic] not forced by its very nature to wage permanent war?"[44] Contemporaries such as Pierre Samuel Du Pont de Nemours noted this as well and deplored this "interminable war."[45] Others saw opportunities in the conflict. When Victor Du Pont asked Talleyrand for a position in the government, the minister assured him that there would be appointments "in the conquered territories," implicitly noting the inevitability of future conflicts.[46]

These revolutionary diplomats were operating in an era of what Bell, as well as Guiomar, has dubbed total war.[47] Blanning concurs: "It was not the French Revolution which created the modern world, it was the French revolutionary wars."[48] Furet, and even earlier Sorel, goes a step further in his contention that "the war conducted the Revolution far more than the Revolution conducted the war."[49] Increasingly, the cannon was "the great negotiator."[50] Martin noted that "[i]n 1792, the French Revolution was born in and of the war; in 1799, it died in and of the war."[51] The inability or the unwillingness of republican diplomacy to bring peace contributed to the destruction of the first republic.

Those Frenchmen sent abroad witnessed the costs of that war more immediately than many at home. These diplomats could not but be influenced by the hostilities as coalitions formed and reformed and peace remained chimerical. These men were sent to either former or potential belligerents, or both, and often found themselves passing through or near enemy territory. The isolation such men faced in hostile and suspicious courts only exacerbated their defensiveness.[52] Throughout their careers, war was the dominant note in the threnody of the age. Europe witnessed a war in which ideology was mixed with nationalism. It was a heady but deadly brew. As the war continued, cosmopolitanism became transformed into a crusade, the crusade into conquest. This evolution was hardly surprising given that the universalism had been leavened with a strong dose of xenophobia and an even stronger dose of ambitious nationalism. As Woolf has emphasized: "For some of its key ideas such as 'fraternity'—rapidly degenerated, at best into slogans, at worst into mockery, whether on the French political scene or in the territories 'liberated' by French armies; while others—such as liberty, equality or popular sovereignty—were to undergo deep and anguished redefinitions through the often fratricidal political struggle up to and beyond brumaire."[53] The ever-escalating needs of the French military also entailed more demands on the conquered and allied alike. The heavy burden of taxes and the weight of requisitions did nothing to endear the French to the local inhabitants whose voices "whether patriotic or desperate were rarely heard."[54] Nor did the systematic looting and the cultural piracy engaged in by the revolutionaries. The initial illusion that there would be "war to the *châteaux*, peace to the cottages" was soon shattered as the weight of war fell heavily on the conquered, poor and rich alike. The rhetoric of liberation did not hide the reality of expropriation.

The horrors of war were magnified by larger armies that were worse supplied and worse disciplined than in the past. The Prussian observer

Clausewitz noted that the French "sent their soldiers into the field and drove their generals into battle—feeding, reinforcing, and stimulating their armies by having them procure, steal, and loot everything they needed."[55] The demands of the revolutionary state too often conflicted with humanitarianism. It was no accident that many invoked a classical analogy, the Punic wars between Rome and Carthage, as an illustration of the conflict between Paris and London. Looting, levies, requisitioning, as well as rape and pillage, brought the brutality of the French Revolution into the lives of many who could not afford to flee as the armies approached. As Europe plunged into the maelstrom created by the lethal mix of revolution and war, no state escaped unscathed. Without clearly defined goals, the war, as Furet points out, could only end in "total victory or total defeat."[56] And it ended in total defeat. As Marx argued, Bonaparte "carried the Terror to its conclusion by replacing the permanent revolution with permanent war."[57]

The Revolution and the wars that ensued profoundly changed the nature of relations among European states. Moreover, this "fundamental rupture" had profound consequences and was reflected on the diplomatic parquet.[58] Not only were the former constraints that restricted war rejected, but so was the diplomatic system itself. Pierre-Marc-Gaston, duc de Lévis, could ask: "Are alliances more useful than harmful to France? Does a great people of 25 million men … need allies and alliance? Shouldn't it rather provide an example for that grand universal alliance that should unite all nations and all men?"[59] Diplomatic practice influenced and was influenced by ideology and war. The revolutionaries rejected the basic rules accepted by the powers of the *ancien régime*, such as the primacy of positive law in favor of the primacy of natural law, except in instances where treaty law served their ends. Edelstein and Bell note how the application of the law of nations escalated rather than moderated violence. French revolutionaries turned to natural law to condone "measures once condemned as barbaric."[60] Jacques-Antoine-Hippolyte Guibert contended that when a free state waged war "it will bring fire and steel to its enemy's hearth. In its vengeance, it will shock all the peoples who might have been tempted to disturb its peace. And let no one call barbarism, or a violation of the supposed laws of war these reprisals grounded in the law of nature."[61] Guibert dubbed the former conventions "the supposed laws of war" and invoked natural law to justify the formerly unjustifiable. In practice most of the conventions governing warfare were still observed as demonstrated by Morieux's work on prisoners of war.[62] Edelstein has noted that once the republic was conflated with nature, "almost any potentially subversive activity could be prosecuted as a crime against nature. The exceptional became terrifying normal."[63]

In this new vision of total war, the enemy was no longer an honorable adversary, a *hostis justus*, "but a criminal with whom there was no question of compromise," or an *hostis humani generis*.[64] Note again the classical allusion and the assumption that most of the deputies would have been familiar with it. Bertrand Barère could declare that "a sort of natural right known as the law of nations ... is unknown to the polished savages of Great Britain; that people is accordingly foreign to Europe, foreign to humanity; it must disappear."[65] The antipathy was often returned. Lord Robert Fitzgerald condemned "these monsters:" "Men who are become the agents of the devil and who openly disavow God and the truth and harden their hearts against everything that has hitherto been held sacred among men." "No honest man can deal with the villains who rule France."[66] Burke called the French "outlaws of humanity, an uncommunicable people."[67] "If your hands are not on your swords, their knives will be at your throats. There is ... no compromise with Jacobinism."[68] The revolutionary system of France is "in itself a declaration of war against mankind."[69] War was now more like a gladiatorial contest in which the loser was never spared rather than a duel in which one or both parties could delope. The revolutionaries also questioned the basic legitimacy of existing governments when they rejected the idea of dynastic sovereignty. This rejection made compromise impossible. Enmeshed in the rhetoric of natural law, struggling in the quicksand of revolutionary politics, stationed in the international arena, revolutionary diplomats repudiated the explicit and implicit conventions and assumptions of the international order.

This understanding (and mutual misunderstanding) is illumined by Wittgenstein's contention that everyone's "way of looking at things" takes place within the "scaffolding of our thoughts," that "all testing, all confirmation and disconfirmation [sic] of a hypothesis takes places with a system." Moreover, within the system "consequences and premises give one another *mutual* support." He explains that "the *questions* that we raise and our *doubts* depend on the fact that some propositions are exempt from doubt, are as it were like hinges on which those turn."[70] That certainty bedeviled both sides and made many of the interactions "dialogues of the deaf." It also made peace more elusive.

What did their most prominent antagonist, the British, think of the possibility or desirability of peace? The difficulties of forging a coalition in a divided Europe dominated the tenure of William Wyndham Grenville

(1759–1834), foreign secretary from 1791 to 1801. As early as September 1793, he thought the "destructive anarchy" of France "incompatible with the security of the other countries of Europe." Their "principles and measures leave no hope of Peace while their power is suffered to exist."[71] By 1800 though "not an enemy of peace," Grenville could not advocate "an unstable or insecure peace." In these notes, he looked back to his earlier thoughts in 1794. At that time he argued that the war must be continued because the French did not indicate any desire for peace and the only way to push the French toward it was to show a readiness to continue the struggle. Second, the "peculiar nature" of the war meant that reasonable terms could not be had. It would be dangerous if France kept her conquests and Britain should not renounce theirs. Third, no peace could be secure because of the permanent hostility of the revolutionary "system" and the instability of governments and personnel in France. A peace would only allow France to gain additional resources to wage war. Moreover, the French enjoyed the "advantage of always remaining armed from the very nature of their system." Peace would, however, only weaken the governments of Europe so that "all the usual advantages of peace would turn to the greatest evils." For example, mutual intercourse would mean the introduction of "innumerable emissaries to promote sedition." Britain must remain armed and that entailed expense, inconvenience, and the risk of renewing hostilities. In short, the usual advantages of a peace would not be reaped. Even if those now in power were supposedly committed to peace, the British could not rely on their word. Furthermore, they might lose power and a faction committed to war come to power. If the British felt it necessary to again resist "a system incompatible with the existence of any civilized society," it would be difficult to "reunite the powers of Europe in any common system." To prevent this danger, Britain must remain armed.

By 1800 his experiences with revolutionary France had only solidified his resolve. As long as "that system of aggression, ambition, and destruction … shall continue to prevail in France, we can have no security but in vigorous and determined resistance." France may have proclaimed her love of peace, but her actions contradict her words. France has been at war with most of Europe since 1792. She has waged war or committed "acts of aggression" against every power with the intent of conquest. How has France respected treaties and peace? Armistices violated, negotiations illusory and/or insulting (Paris, Lille, Rastatt), and peace treaties violated without exception. These actions "alone [were] sufficient to prove the nature of the government." A revolution in Paris only means "a new change of hands among the same set." If France continues to pursue the "same system ... No peace can be safe."[72] And so it proved.

This work focuses on the culture of revolutionary diplomacy, not the history of French foreign policy, except as it impinges on that diplomacy. It examines that culture as "a system of shared meaning, attitudes and values,"[73] thematically rather than chronologically through precedence and etiquette, language, dress, and images. Through these public expressions, revolutionary diplomats sought to remake the diplomatic world. The revolutionaries consciously, consistently, and deliberately attempted to extend their ideas to the international sphere. Undoubtedly they differed and the diplomatic face of France changed as factions rose and fell. The men of 1799 were not the dreamers and idealists of 1789. Nor does this work represent a triumph of form over substance. As Desch has argued: "Internal culture affects external outcomes because a state's culture provides its elite with a particular and quite limited way of organizing perceptions and actions; a state's freedom to choose among policies is limited in good part by its elite's set of assumptions, memories, values, norms, beliefs, and formal knowledge—factors that shape its collective understanding of the world."[74] We have attempted to examine these issues not just through the official injunctions and assessments of the French in Paris and abroad but also through the eyes of neutrals as well as enemies. Private correspondence in some cases was often more forthright and revealing than official memoranda. Memoirs, though sometimes problematic because they were composed in the light of subsequent events and often with retrospective *aperçus*, can still be used with caution.

Diplomats were hardly prisoners of discourse nor even of the directives from revolutionary governments; "republican diplomacy owed as much if not more to its practitioners, and to the information that guided their actions, as it did to the ideological positions of the decision-makers in Paris."[75] Assertion was one thing, implementation another. There was often a gulf between the publicly voiced intentions of Paris and the actions of the men in the field. Diplomats like other revolutionaries were embedded in networks of family, patronage, and friendship and often caught up in the viciousness of revolutionary factionalism. Personal, political, or increasingly military ends often prevailed. Witness the actions of Bernadotte in Vienna, Basville in Rome, or Sieyès in Berlin. As Soulavie in Geneva argued so trenchantly: "One does not negotiate for a cause one dislikes."[76] Tilly even ceased corresponding with the ministry of foreign affairs and wrote only to the deputies on mission.[77] "Indirectly the divergence between diplomatic discourse and ministerial instructions shaped the whole definition of the war waged by the Republic, and may also explain the failure of peace negotiations."[78] Virginie Martin has demonstrated how in the case of Italy "while the central government in Paris favoured negotiation, the diplomats were concerned only to extend the war."[79] Moreover, from 1792 the close ties between the diplomats and the military "steadily undermined the authority of Paris."[80] These were dangerous liaisons, for it meant the "defeat of the diplomatic by the military sphere."[81] Indisputably "republican diplomacy took shape in the service of the war, but was in the end completely taken over by the war."[82]

Diplomats, reluctant to engage in an international system they repudiated, proved even more reluctant to negotiate with those who represented a system and culture they rejected and a government they deplored. Revolutionary governments, moreover, tended not to appoint men skilled in the diplomatic arts, but those thoroughly imbued with revolutionary fervor. Predictably, those selected were often far from competent. Fonspertius, who served in the consulate in Charleston, illustrated the problem. He became known for his frivolous and scandalous conduct.[83] According to contemporaries, he drank all day and whored all night. He left the records in such disorder that a knowledgeable observer compared his successor's task to cleaning out the Augean stables.[84] There were of course such men appointed under the *ancien régime* but the revolutionaries too often valued ideological conformity over competence. When Victor Du Pont, consul at Charleston, astutely predicted that there would be "a diplomatic revolution," he lamented that "it is not possible that they will send able men."[85] Even worse these envoys often deliberately provoked and alienated their hosts; many flagrantly violated traditional social and diplomatic conventions and gloried in it. Their goal was to confront, not to negotiate. The actions of Genet in the United States, Mangourit in Madrid, and Bernadotte in Vienna leap to mind. One historian has argued that "Lacking the means or the ambition to become an instrument of negotiation, republican diplomacy was transformed instead into a vehicle of revolutionary propaganda."[86] Competence, skill, and hard work did not ensure success (witness the imprisonment of Otto who was associated with the Girondin faction) but rather commitment to the prevailing orthodoxy or alignment with the current faction. Those who did not or seemed not to conform to the prevailing orthodoxy lost their positions. The personal cost of these decisions can be seen in the heart-felt letter Theodore Charles Mozard, the former French consul at Boston, wrote to Victor Du Pont when he queried at the end of a long letter in French, in English: "What am I going to do?"[87] "This instability of places seems to me," Mozard complained, "a principle of the government."[88] Those who remained often found themselves surrounded by ideological enemies and feared being recalled.[89] These fears were not unfounded. The personnel of embassies and consulates shifted with the ideological winds and hardly bred consistency of policy.

The revolutionaries challenged Europeans' assumption of a common diplomatic culture, of a universal diplomatic language and most basically an international diplomatic community. Burke continued to underscore the importance of the "federative society, or in other words, ... the diplomatic republic of Europe."[90] To him France was to be "considered as expunged out of the system of Europe."[91] Gentz saw something even more invidious: "the fatal dissolution of all ancient ties, or all reciprocal attachment and fidelity."[92] Gentz and Burke realized that the revolutionaries in rejecting the tenets and practices associated with the traditional diplomacy fractured the ideological unity of the international order. Grenville noted that only those distant from and ignorant of the ramifications could admire "the development of this new diplomatic code."[93] In the context of another ideological struggle, the religious wars, Mattingly argued that "[t]he religious wars nearly wrecked the diplomatic institution with which Europe had been trying to adjust its quarrels.... As long as conflicts between states are about prestige or profit or power, grounds of agreements are always accessible to sane men. But the clash of ideological absolutes drives diplomacy from the field."[94] The assumptions and presumptions of those men, those voices from a distant and now muffled past, cast light on that challenge and the response.

NOTES

1. Quoted in Frederick C. Beiser, *Enlightenment, Revolution, and Romanticism: The Genesis of Modern German Political Thought, 1790–1800* (Cambridge, MA: Harvard University Press, 1992), 178.
2. Isaac Deutscher, *The Prophet Armed: Trotsky: 1879–1921* (London: Oxford University Press, 1954), 371. See David Armstrong, *Revolution and World Order: The Revolutionary State in International Society* (Oxford: Clarendon Press, 1993), for a discussion of the diplomacy implications of revolutionary states.
3. Linda and Marsha Frey, "'The Reign of the Charlatans is Over': The French Revolutionary Attack on Diplomatic Practice," *The Journal of Modern History* 65, no. 4. (December 1993): 707.

4. David Cannadine, "Introduction: Divine Rites of Kings," in *Rituals of Royalty: Power and Ceremonial in Traditional Societies*, edited by David Cannadine and Simon Price, 1–19 (Cambridge: University Press, 1987), 1.
5. Quoted in Frans De Bruyn, "Theater and Countertheater in Burke's Reflections on the Revolution in France," in *Burke and the French Revolution: Bicentennial Essays*, edited by Steven Blakemore (Athens, GA: University of Georgia Press, 1992), 28.
6. David A. Bell, *The First Total War* (New York: Houghton Mifflin, 2007), 87–89 and 109.
7. Frédéric Masson, *Le Département des affaires étrangères pendant la Révolution, 1787–1804* (Paris: E. Plon, 1877), 271.
8. Virginie Martin, "Les Enjeux diplomatiques dans le *Magasin encyclopédique* (1795–1799): du rejet des systèmes politiques à la redéfition des rapports entres les nations," *La Révolution française: Cahiers de l'Istitute d'histoire de la Révolution française* 1 (2012): 24, footnote 23.
9. Ibid., 5.
10. Quoted in Justin Hart, "Archibald MacLeish Rediscovered: The Poetry of U.S, Foreign Policy," *Historically Speaking: The Bulletin of the Historical Society* 8, no. 3 (January/February 2007): 21.
11. Quoted in Pierre Treilhard, *La Sensibilité révolutionnaire (1789–1794)* (Geneva: Slatkine reprints, 1967), 18.
12. Jacques-Pierre de Brissot de Warville, *Rapport fait à la Convention nationale au nom du comité diplomatique sur la négociation entre Genève et la République de France, et sur la transaction du 2 novembre 1792* (Paris: Imprimérie nationale, 1792), 5.
13. A.N., D XXIII, carton 2, dossier 34, Society of the Friends of the Constitution to the Diplomatic Committee, Nantes, 28 February 1791.
14. John Quincy Adams, *Writings* (New York: Macmillan, 1913–1917), 2: 211, to John Adams, 21 September 1797. See Marvin R. Zahniser, *Uncertain Friendship: American-French Relations through the Cold War* (New York: Wiley, 1975), 73.
15. Maurice Agulhon, "Politics and Images in Post-Revolutionary France," in *Rites of Powers: Symbolism, Ritual, and Politics since the Middle Ages*, ed. Sean Wilentz (Philadelphia: University of Pennsylvania Press, 1985), 194–195.
16. Clifford Geertz, "Centers, Kings and Charisma: Reflections on the Symbolics of Power," in *Rites of Power*, ed. Wilentz, 30.
17. Clifford Geertz, "Ideology as a Cultural System" in *Ideology and Discontent*, ed. David E. Apter (New York: Free Press of Glencoe, 1964), 63–64.
18. Geertz, "Centers, Kings and Charisma: Reflections on the Symbolics of Power," in *Rites of Power*, ed. Sean Wilentz, 30.
19. Edward Muir, *Ritual in Early Modern Europe* (Cambridge: University Press, 1997), 4.

20. Richard Stites, "Russian Revolutionary Culture: Its Place in the History of Cultural Revolutions," in *Culture and Revolution*, edited by Paul Dukes and John Dunkley (London: Pintner, 1990), 138.
21. Crane Brinton, *A Decade of Revolution, 1789–1799* (New York: Harper and Brothers, 1934), 142–150.
22. Edmund Burke, "Letters on a Regicide Peace" in *The Works of The Right Honourable Edmund Burke* (London: George Bell and Sons, 1893), 5: 215.
23. Ibid., 5: 208. Lotman called this "the poetics of every day behavior." Quoted in Peter Burke, *Varieties of Cultural History* (Ithaca, NY: Cornell University Press, 1997), 194.
24. Robert Darnton, "The French Revolution: Intellectuals and Literature," Lecture, University of Montana, June 1, 1989.
25. Ronen Steinberg, "Naming a Difficult Past after 9 Thermidor," paper presented at the Consortium on the Revolutionary era, 1750–1850, 24 February 2017.
26. The revolutionaries replaced the Gregorian calendar with a revolutionary one which was both rational and commemorative. It began on 22 September 1792, the first day of the Republic, thus 1 vendémiaire, year I. The ten-day *décade* displaced the seven-day week. The months with three *décades* were renamed according to a nature. Thus, nivôse (snow). Adopted in October 1793, it lasted until Napoleon abolished it in 1806.
27. Lynn Hunt, *Politics, Culture and Class in the French Revolution* (Los Angeles: University of California Press, 1984); Maurice Agulhon, *Marianne au combat: L'Imagerie et la symbolique républicaines de 1789 à 1880* (Paris: Flammarion, 1979); Mona Ozouf, *Festivals and the French Revolution* (Cambridge, Mass: Harvard University Press, 1988). For a more extended discussion of festivals, see James R Lehning, *The Melodramatic Thread: Spectacles and Political Culture in Modern France* (Bloomington, IN: Indiana University Press, 2007), in particular the introduction.
28. François Furet, *Interpreting the French Revolution* (Cambridge: University Press, 1981), 78 and 130.
29. Hunt, *Politics, Culture and Class in the French Revolution*, 15; Furet, *Interpreting the French Revolution*, 77.
30. See, for example, Stéphanie Roza and Pierre Serna, ed., "La Révolution ou l'invention de la femme et de l'homme nouveaux" *La Révolution francaise: Cahiers de l'Institute de la Révolution française*, 6 (2014).
31. Maurice Agulhon, "Politics and Images in Post-Revolutionary France," in *Rites of Power*, ed. Wilentz, 199.
32. Quoted in Beiser, *Enlightenment, Revolution and Romanticism*, 178.
33. Charles Popham Miles, ed., *The Correspondence of William Augustus Miles on the French Revolution 1789–1817* (London: Longmans, Green and Co., 1890), 2: 9, December 1792.

34. B. L., Add. Mss. 58980 fol. 21, Sir Sidney Smith to Grenville, 13 January 1795, quoting his brother Spencer.
35. T. C. W. Blanning, *The Origins of the French Revolutionary Wars* (London: Longman, 1986), 208, 73.
36. Quoted in ibid.
37. Quoted in ibid., 116.
38. Quoted in Bell, *The First Total War*, 1.
39. Philippe-Joseph-Benjamin Buchez and Prosper-Charles Foux, eds., *Histoire parlementaire de la Révolution française* (Paris: Paulin, 1834), 6: 77, 20 May 1790.
40. Ozouf, *Festivals and the French Revolution*, 10.
41. Bell, *The First Total War*, 115.
42. Calonne quoted in Marc Belissa, "Can a Powerful Republic Be Peaceful? The Debate in the Year IV on the Place of France in the European Order," in *Republics at War Republics at War, 1776–1840: Revolutions, Conflicts and Geopolitics in Europe and the Atlantic World*, edited by Pierre Serna, Antonio De Francesco, and Judith A. Miller (New York: Palgrave, 2013), 69.
43. Pierre Serna, "Introduction: War and Republic: 'Dangerous Liaison'" in ibid., 1.
44. Ibid., 65.
45. Hagley, W2-529, Pierre Samuel Du Pont de Nemours to Regnault de St. Jean d'Angély, 24 April 1798.
46. Hagley, W3-372, 7 vend n.y. [28 Sept 1798], Victor Du Pont to his wife.
47. Jean-Yves Guiomar, *l'Invention de la guerre totale, XVIIIe–XXe siècle* (Paris: Félin, 2004). This view is not without its critics such as Peter Paret in *The American Historical Review* 112, no. 5 (December 2007): 1489–1491.
48. Blanning, *The Origins of the French Revolutionary War*, 211.
49. Furet, *Interpreting the French Revolution*, 127.
50. Virginie Martin, "In Search of the 'Glorious Peace'? Republican Diplomats at War, 1792–1799" in *Republics at War*, ed. Serna and De Francesco, 46.
51. Ibid.
52. See the example of Alquier in Munich in Léonce Pingaud, *Jean de Bry (1760–1835)* (Paris: Librairie Plon, 1909), 87.
53. Stuart Woolf, *Napoleon's Integration of Europe* (London: Routledge, 1991), 9.
54. Ibid., 46.
55. Karl von Clausewitz, *On War*, edited and translated by Michael Howard and Peter Paret (Princeton, NJ: Princeton University Press, 1989), 332.
56. Furet, *Interpreting the French Revolution*, 127.
57. Karl Marx quoted in ibid., 129.
58. Marc Belissa, "Introduction," in *Acteurs diplomatiques et ordre international XVIIIe–XIXe siècle*, edited by Marc Belissa and Gilles Ferragu (Paris: Éditions Kimé, 2007), 8 and Marc Belissa, "Révolution française et ordre

international" in *Acteurs diplomatiques et ordre international XVIIIe–XIXe siècle*, ed. Marc Belissa and Gilles Ferragu (Paris: Éditions Kimé, 2007), 41.
59. Quoted in Bell, *The First Total War*, 98.
60. Ibid., 1.
61. Quoted in ibid., 79–80.
62. Reynaud Morieux, "Patriotisme humanitaire et prisonniers de guerre en France et en Grande-Bretagne pendant la Révolution française et l'Empire," in *La Politique par les armes: Conflits internationaux et politisation (XVe–XIXe siècle)*, edited by Laurent Bourquin, Philippe Hamon, Alain Hugon and Yann Lagadec, 299–314. Rennes: Presses universitaires de Rennes, 2013.
63. Dan Edelstein, *The Terror of Natural Right: Republicanism, the Cult of Nature, and the French Revolution* (Chicago: University of Chicago Press, 2009), 3–4. Edelstein bases his explanation of the terror on an intellectual formulation that cannot explain what is essentially an emotional and visceral response conditioned at last partially by the viciousness of revolutionary struggles. See Marisa Linton, *Choosing Terror: Virtue, Friendship and Authenticity in the French Revolution* (New York: Oxford University Press, 2013).
64. Marc Belissa, "Révolution française et ordre international" in *Acteurs diplomatiques et ordre international XVIIIe–XIXe siècle*, ed. Belissa and Ferragu, 41; Edelstein, *The Terror of Natural Right*, 30–32.
65. Quoted in ibid., 261.
66. B. L., Add Mss. 59020, fol. 112, Lord Robert Fitzgerald to Grenville, 13 January 1795.
67. Quoted in Emma Vincent Macleod, *A War of Ideas: British Attitudes to the Wars against Revolutionary France, 1792–1802* (Brookfield: Ashgate Publishing, 1998), 15.
68. Quoted in ibid., 16.
69. Quoted in ibid., 18.
70. Ludwig Wittgenstein, *On Certainty*, edited by G. E. M. Anscombe and G. H. von Wright, translated by Denis Paul and G. E. M. Anscombe (Oxford: Basil Blackwell, 1969–1975), 23, 13, 17, and 35. Thanks to Nicholas Capaldi for bringing this selection to our attention.
71. B. L., Add. Mss. 59094, fol. 5, Grenville to Sir M. Eden, 27 September 1793.
72. B. L., Add. Mss 59067A, fols. 5–35, 20 December 1794 and [1800].
73. Peter Burke, *Popular Culture in Early Modern Europe* (New York: Harper and Row, 1978), xi.
74. Desch quoted in Arthur M. Eckstein, *Mediterranean Anarchy, Interstate War, and the Rise of Rome* (Los Angeles, CA: University of California Press, 2006), 185.

75. Martin, "In Search of the 'Glorious Peace'? Republican Diplomats at War, 1792–1799" in *Republics at War*, ed. Serna and De Francesco Martin, 47.
76. Ibid., 59.
77. Ibid., 53.
78. Ibid., 51.
79. Ibid., 48. Also see Patricer Gueniffey, *Bonaparte, 1769–1802* (Cambridge, MA: Harvard University Press, 2015).
80. Ibid., 52.
81. Ibid., 58.
82. Ibid., 60.
83. Hagley, W3-261, Victor Du Pont to his family, 28 June 1795 and W3-262, Victor Du Pont his father Philadelphia 3 July 1795.
84. Hagley, W3-1058, Letombe to Victor Du Pont, 26 Sept 1795.
85. Hagley, W3-261, Victor Du Pont to his family, 28 June 1795, Philadelphia.
86. Martin, "In Search of 'Glorious Peace'? Republican Diplomats at War, 1792–1799" in *Republics at War*, ed. Serna and De Francesco, 47.
87. Hagley, W3-1149, Boston, 7 mesidor IV [25 June 1796].
88. Hagley, W3-1209, Mozard to Victor Du Pont, Boston, 26 frimaire, V [16 Dec 1796].
89. Hagley, W3-261, Victor Du Pont to his family, 28 June 1795, Philadelphia.
90. Edmund Burke, *The Works of the Right Honorable Edmund Burke* (Boston: Little, Brown and Company 1866), 4: 433, October 1793.
91. Edmund Burke, *The Speeches of the Right Honorable Edmund Burke in the House of Commons and in Westminster Hall* (London: Longman, Hurst, Rees, Orme and Brown, 1816), 3: 456.
92. Friedrich Gentz, *Fragments Upon the Balance of Power in Europe* (London: Golden Square, 1806), 93.
93. B. L., Add. Mss. 59041, fol. 106, Grenville to Stahremberg, Cleveland Row, 2 December 1797.
94. Garrett Mattingly, *Renaissance Diplomacy* (Boston: Houghton Mifflin, 1955), 195–196.

References

Adams, John Quincy. *Writings of John Quincy Adams*. New York: Macmillan Co., 1913–1917.

Agulhon, Maurice. *Marianne au combat: l'imagerie et la symbolique républicaines de 1789 à 1880*. Paris: Flammarion, 1979.

Armstrong, David. *Revolution and World Order: The Revolutionary State in International Society*. Oxford: Clarendon Press, 1993.

Beiser, Frederick C. *Enlightenment, Revolution, and Romanticism: The Genesis of Modern German Political Thought, 1790–1800*. Cambridge: Harvard University Press, 1992.

Belissa, Marc. "Can a Powerful Republic Be Peaceful? The Debate in the Year IV on the Place of France in the European Order?" In *Republics at War, 1776–1840: Revolutions, Conflicts and Geopolitics in Europe and the Atlantic World*, edited by Pierre Serna, Antonio De Francesco, and Judith A. Miller, 65–82. London: Palgrave, 2013.

———. "Révolution française et ordre international." In *Acteurs diplomatiques et ordre international XVIII–XIX siècle*, edited by Marc Belissa and Gilles Ferragu. Paris: Éditions Kimé, 2007.

Belissa, Marc, and Gilles Ferrague, eds. *Acteurs diplomatiques et ordre international XVIIIe–XIXe siècle*. Paris: Éditions Kimé, 2007.

Bell, David A. *The First Total War*. Boston: Houghton Mifflin Company, 2007.

Blakemore, Steven, ed. *Burke and the French Revolution: Bicentennial Essays*. Athens, GA: University of Georgia Press, 1992.

Blanning, T. C. W. *The Origins of the French Revolutionary Wars*. New York: Longman, 1987.

Brissot de Warville, Jacques-Pierre. *Rapport fait à la Convention nationale au nom du comité diplomatique sur la négociation entre Genève et la République de France, et sur la transaction du 2 novembre 1792*. Paris: Imprimérie nationale, 1792.

Buchez, Philippe-Joseph-Benjamin, and Prosper-Charles Roux-Lavergne, eds. *Histoire parlementaire de la Révolution française*. 40 vols. Paris: Paulin, 1834–1838.

Burke, Edmund. *The Speeches of the Right Honourable Edmund Burke, in the House of Commons and in Westminster Hall*. London: Longman, 1816.

———. *The Works of Edmund Burke*. Vol. 5. London: George Bell and Sons, 1893.

———. *The Works of the Right Honourable Edmund Burke*. 12 vols. Boston: Little Brown and Co., 1866–1867.

Burke, Peter. *Fabrication of Louis XIV*. New Haven: Yale University Press, 1992.

———. *Popular Culture in Early Modern Europe*. New York: Harper and Row, 1978.

Cannadine, David. "Introduction: Divine Rites of Kings." In *Rituals of Royalty: Power and Ceremonial in Traditional Societies*, edited by David Cannadine and Simon Price, 1–19. Cambridge: University Press, 1987.

Clausewitz, Karl von. *On War*. Edited and translated by Michael Howard and Peter Paret. Princeton, NJ: Princeton University Press, 1989.

Darnton, Robert Choate. "The French Revolution: Intellectuals and Literature." Lecture, University of Montana, June 1, 1989.

Deutscher, Isaac. *The Prophet Armed: Trotsky, 1879–1921*. London: Oxford University Press, 1954.

Eckstein, Arthur M. *Mediterranean Anarchy, Interstate War, and the Rise of Rome*. Los Angeles, CA: University of California Press, 2006.

Edelstein, Dan. *The Terror of Natural Right: Republicanism, the Cult of Nature, and the French Revolution*. Chicago: University of Chicago Press, 2009.

Frey, Linda, and Marsha Frey. "'The Reign of the Charlatans Is Over': The French Revolutionary Attack on Diplomatic Practice." *Journal of Modern History* 65 (December 1993): 706–744.

Furet, François. *Interpreting the French Revolution*. Cambridge: Cambridge University Press, 1981.

Geertz, Clifford. "Centers, Kings and Charisma: Reflections on the Symbolics of Power." In *Rites of Power: Symbolism, Ritual, and Politics Since the Middle Ages*, edited by Sean Wilentz, 13–38. Philadelphia: University of Pennsylvania Press, 1985.

———. "Ideology as a Cultural System." In *Ideology and Discontent*, edited by David E. Apter, 47–76. London: Free Press of Glencoe, 1964.

Gentz, Friedrich von. *Fragments Upon the Balance of Power in Europe*. London: Peltier, 1806.

Gueniffey, Patrice. *Bonaparte, 1769–1802*. Translated by Steven Rendall. Cambridge, MA: Harvard University Press, 2015.

Guiomar, Jean-Yves. *L'Invention de la guerre totale xviiie-xxe siècle*. Paris: Félin, 2004.

Hart, Justin. "Archibald MacLeish Rediscovered: The Poetry of U.S. Foreign Policy." *Historically Speaking: The Bulletin of the Historical Society* 8, no. 3 (January/February 2007): 20–22.

Hunt, Lynn. *Politics, Culture and Class in the French Revolution*. Los Angeles, CA: University of California Press, 1984.

Lehning, James R. *The Melodramatic Thread: Spectacles and Political Culture in Modern France*. Bloomington, IN: Indiana University Press, 2007.

Linton, Marisa. *Choosing Terror: Virtue, Friendship and Authenticity in the French Revolution*. New York: Oxford University Press, 2013.

Macleod, Emma Vincent. *A War of Ideas: British Attitudes to the Wars Against Revolutionary France 1792–1802*. Brookfield: Ashgate, 1998.

Martin, Virginie. "Les Enjeux diplomatiques dans le *Magasin encyclopédique* (1795–1799): du rejet des systèmes politiques à la redéfition des rapports entres les nations." *La Révolution française:Cahiers de l'Institut d'histoire de la Révolution française* 1 (2012): 1–30.

———. "In Search of the 'Glorious Peace.'" In *Republics at War, 1776–1840: Revolutions, Conflicts and Geopolitics in Europe and the Atlantic World*, edited by Pierre Serna, Antonio De Francesco, and Judith A. Miller, 46–64. London: Palgrave, 2013.

Masson, Frédéric. *Le Département des affaires étrangères pendant la Révolution, 1787–1804*. Paris: E. Plon, 1877.

Mattingly, Garrett. *Renaissance Diplomacy*. Boston: Houghton Mifflin, 1955.

Miles, William Augustus. *The Correspondence of William Augustus Miles on the French Revolution, 1789–1817*. Edited by Charles Miles Popham. 2 vols. London: Longmans, Green, and Company, 1890.

Morieux, Reynaud. "Patriotisme humanitaire et prisonniers de guerre en France et en Grand-Bretagne pendant la Révolution française et l'Empire." In *La Politique par les armes: Conflits internationaux et politisation (XVe–XIXe siècle)*, edited by Laurent Bourguin, Philippe Hamon, Alain Hugon, and Yann Lagadec, 299–314.Rennes: Presses universitaires de Rennes, 2013.

Ozouf, Mona. *Festivals and the French Revolution*. Translated by Alan Sheridan. Cambridge: Harvard University Press, 1988.

Pingaud, Léonce. *Jean de Bry (1760–1835)*. Paris: Librairie Plon, 1909.

Serna, Pierre, Antonio De Francesco, and Judith A. Miller, eds. *Republics at War, 1776–1840: Revolutions, Conflicts and Geopolitics in Europe and the Atlantic World*. London: Palgrave, 2013.

Stites, Richard. "Russian Revolutionary Culture: Its Place in the History of Cultural Revolutions." In *Culture and Revolution*, edited by Paul Dukes and John Dunkley, 132–141. London: Pintner, 1990.

Treilhard, Pierre. *La Sensibilité révolutionnaire (1789–1794)*. Geneve: Slatkine Reprints, 1967.

Wittgenstein, Ludwig. *On Certainty*. Edited by G. E. M. Anscombe and G. H. von Wright and translated by Denis Paul and G. E. M. Anscombe. Oxford: Basil Blackwell, 1969–1975.

Woolf, Stuart. *Napoleon's Integration of Europe*. London: Routledge, 1991.

Zahniser, Marvin R. *Uncertain Friendship: American-French Diplomatic Relations Through the Cold War*. New York: Wiley, 1975.

CHAPTER 2

Mise en Scène: The Indictment

France has collapsed and I doubt whether it will rise again—Joseph II[1]

The revolutionaries not only attacked the premises and functioning of the international order under the *ancien régime*, but also critiqued the demonstrable foreign policy failures of Louis XV and Louis XVI. The revolutionaries could draw upon a long tradition of criticism of the diplomatic system predating the *philosophes*. Alexis de Tocqueville astutely noted that "in fact, though nothing was further from their intentions, they [the revolutionaries] used the debris of the old order for building up the new."[2] The policies of Louis XIV, who had spent more than 65% of his reign at war and who had bequeathed a crippling war debt to his successors, spawned many critiques.[3] Vauban, a French military engineering genius who revolutionized the art of siege warfare, thought that war had "interest for its father, ambition for its mother, and for close relatives all the passions that lead us to evil."[4] The duc de Saint-Simon, a member of the old nobility and an acid critic of the king and his policies, had been more candid when he remarked that "reciprocal distrust" reigned between sovereigns: "Leurs ministres banissant toute bonne foie et se croyant habiles, selon qu'il savaient le mieux tromper."[5] Yet another critic of the king, the controversial French publicist Charles-Irénée Castel, abbé de Saint-Pierre (1658–1743), served as almoner to the duchesse d'Orléans and later as secretary to Melchior de Polignac, the French plenipotentiary at the Congress of Utrecht in 1713. In his chief work, *Le Projet de paix perpétuelle*, written in 1713 at the end

© The Author(s) 2018
L. Frey, M. Frey, *The Culture of French Revolutionary Diplomacy*, Studies in Diplomacy and International Relations, https://doi.org/10.1007/978-3-319-71709-8_2

of one of Louis XIV's most destructive wars, he argued that in the present system of Europe peace was impossible and perpetual war inevitable: "we have prevented private feuds only to fan the flames of public wars, which are a thousand times more terrible; in short mankind by gathering itself into groups, has become its own enemy."[6] European states should reduce the size of their armies so that all states, large or small, would have the same number of combatants.[7]

One of Louis' harshest critics was the highly regarded Archbishop François Fénelon (1651–1715), tutor to the Duke of Burgundy. The prelate wrote a letter to Louis (probably in 1694), criticizing the king and his ministers, especially the king's love of war and his careless, but increasingly predictable, disregard of treaties. In that letter, the archbishop condemned the king for "impoverishing" all of France and introducing a "monstrous and incurable luxury." "One no longer spoke of the state nor its rules but spoke only of the king and his pleasure."[8] Moreover, the king's ministers "had made his name odious and all the French nation insupportable to all its neighbors." France had not kept a single ally because all it wants is slaves. France had engaged in unjust wars for more than 20 years desolating Europe: "so much blood was spilled, so many scandalous acts were perpetrated, so many provinces sacked, so many towns and villages reduced to ashes."[9] By the seizure of cities, such as Strasbourg, to which he did not have "the least pretension," the king had "animated all of Europe against him."[10] Other European states preferred war to peace because they realized that no peace would ever be a true one. And in France? The people are dying of hunger, the cultivation of the fields is almost abandoned, the cities and villages are depopulated, and commerce is weakened. In short, the "realm is ruined." France has become "nothing more than a large desolated hospital without provisions."[11]

The most devastating critique of Louis, however, came from abroad. Leibniz, a brilliant philosopher and mathematician, condemned Louis' wars as a flagrant violation of not only international law but also Christian morality. In his *Mars Christianissimus* (1683) he savagely satirized Louis and his conquests, especially in the Holy Roman Empire. He noted that the French had adopted a resolution to recognize no judge "but the sword"[12]; they blatantly ignored international law and the canons of the church and "all scruples of conscience."[13] Christians should be grateful to France, for Louis has made them so miserable that the Germans would "go more willingly to heaven, leaving without regret this vale of miseries."[14] French actions, such as the ruin of Germany, the seizure of Lorraine's estates, or the violent taking of Strasbourg to name but a few, could not be justified. It was nothing but "unpardonable folly" to trust that France would keep the peace.[15]

Still later, under Louis XV, the idealistic and disillusioned former foreign minister, the marquis d'Argenson (1694–1757), who had played that dangerous game as foreign minister (1744–1747), had refused to cast aside all scruples and could only conclude that "[a] state should be always at the ready, like a gentleman living among swashbucklers and quarrelers. Such are the nations of Europe, today more than ever; negotiations are only a continual struggle between men without principles, impudently aggressive and ever greedy."[16] In his view, "[d]efensive treaties could not exist; every agreement made among states was implicitly offensive in nature."[17]

Yet another contemporary, Gabriel Bonnet de Mably (1709–1785), who had served briefly in the diplomatic corps (1742–1746) and who had penned a treatise on the *droit public*, contended that Europe would be free of "oscillations born of fraudulent practices" only after candor and justice had strengthened "the repose and alliance of all peoples."[18] He condemned the mania for secrecy as well as the Machiavellianism of *ancien régime* diplomacy and thought that a true policy would work toward the common good. He saw nothing useful in the "intrigues and petty chicaneries" which delighted the majority of diplomats. Treaties "instead of ending matters often only produce new divisions."[19] Charles Pinot (or Pineau) Duclos (1704–1772), a celebrated historian and literary figure noted for his clever *bon mots*, echoed the cynicism of many of his contemporaries: "treaties of peace are but truces…. Negotiations are carried on, alliances are sought, so as to get into a condition to resume hostilities with more advantage."[20]

Nor was Emerich de Vattel (1714–1767), the influential and widely read jurist, diplomat, and theologian, averse to criticizing, albeit indirectly, the international system. In his popular treatise, *Le Droit des gens*, Vattel defined the law of nations as "that system of right and justice which ought to prevail between nations or sovereign states."[21] Society, a "moral person," was "susceptible of obligations and rights."[22] The law of nations should not be confounded with the law of nature. He also went on to condemn those who rely on subtlety to outwit others; diplomats should not seek to craft treaties in "vague or equivocal terms," to slip in "dubious expressions" or to try to "entrap those with whom one treated,"[23] a reference no doubt to contemporary practice. For him Christian states were bound by absolute moral standards which should prevail. Even though such rubrics were not observed, Vattel's reliance on natural law gave his work a special resonance in the eighteenth century. Still his injunctions were widely ignored.

As one author astutely observed about the period: "Each nation … must be considered as the enemy of all others; or as disposed to be such."[24] Many in the eighteenth century suspected that what the ambassador and secretary of state, Vergennes, said of Frederick II was true of all European powers—namely that "[a]ny understanding with that power is impossible unless one is resolved to tread justice and humanity underfoot."[25] In the eighteenth century the basic choice countries faced was, as Blanning notes, simple: "to be predator or prey … If ever there was a time when war was the normal means of intercourse between states this was surely it."[26]

The *philosophes* shared these reservations. In *The Spirit of the Laws* Montesquieu noted that "the spirit of monarchy is war and aggrandizement."[27] "Let us not speak of the glory of the prince: his glory is his pride." When one speaks of glory "streams of blood will inundate the earth."[28] Furthermore, these unjust wars did not follow "the law of reason." Princes should not wage wars for frivolous reasons, such as treating ambassadors without respect.[29] In both his *Universal Monarchy* and *Persian Letters*, Montesquieu condemned offensive war.[30] He criticized what he saw as the ever-escalating arms race not only in France but also in Europe. This condition of "all against all" we "call peace,"[31] a "perpetual war of armed peace."[32] Indeed soon "by virtue of having soldiers, we will have nothing but soldiers, and then we will be like the Tartars."[33] For him this contagious distemper would bring nothing but "public ruin" and the "perpetual augmentation of taxes."[34] A tragic discordance prevailed between the needs of people and the policies of princes. Princes "always talk of their needs and never of ours."[35] Monarchies bred a spirit that longed for never-ending glory. Such a policy was doomed to fail. For "glory, when it is entirely alone, enters into the calculations of none but fools."[36] For many of the *philosophes*, including Montesquieu, all the principles of international law had been corrupted. In the *Persian Letters*, Montesquieu derided international law as a "science which teaches princes how far they can violate justice without injuring their own interests." These princes hardened their consciences "by trying to reduce iniquity into a system, by prescribing rules for it, by shaping its principles and deducing its consequences." This infamous art produced "monsters" and made "pliant the inflexibility of justice."[37]

Paul Henri Thiry, baron d'Holbach (1723–1789) was equally scathing. He criticized a system which equated expediency with "right" and which authorized the stronger to oppress the weaker.[38] For Holbach war was only just when it was necessary and it was only necessary "when the well being of a nation is really in danger."[39] "Their continual wars, their quarrels so often unjust and puerile, their thoughtless passions and their caprices to which these sovereigns sacrifice so lightly their happiness and that of their subjects," tell us that they are "the real cannibals."[40] For him the foreign policy of the *ancien régime* meant that nations were continually at war, "furious combats between peoples, enemies without knowing why."[41] Furthermore, he attacked the underlying rationale: conquest which he derided as "madness."[42]

Denis Diderot (1713–1784), who condemned this type of politics as unprincipled and insincere, exemplified the *philosophes*' critique of governments who "make alliances only in order to sow hatred. Incite war among my neighbors and try to prolong it. Always promise aid and never send it. Have no ambassadors in other countries but spies." Their aim in war is to take all they can and to destroy what they cannot.[43] Diderot equated diplomacy with duplicity and mocked the dispatches of envoys that contained "few important things embedded in many absurdities."[44]

In contrast, François Marie Arouet de Voltaire (1694–1778) thought that some wars like that of the Austrian Succession and the conflict with the Turks were necessary. The Turks in particular should be destroyed. It was not enough to humiliate them.[45] War, part of the human condition, could not be stopped. For Voltaire, "[i]t was as difficult to stop men from waging war as to stop wolves from eating sheep."[46] War to him was a necessity, a "scourge of heaven, frightful but necessary."[47] Nonetheless, he condemned war: "The combined vices of all ages and all places will never equal the evils produced by a single campaign."[48] Voltaire queried if politics was anything but the "right of lying at the right time?"[49] Their purpose is to deceive. Voltaire had little tolerance for peace plans envisaged by theorists, most notably that of the Abbé de Saint Pierre, whom he derided as "half *philosophe* and half fool."[50] This peace plan was nothing but a chimera which will no more exist between princes than between elephants and rhinoceroses or between rabbits and dogs. "Carnivorous animals will tear each other to pieces at the first opportunity."[51]

For Jean-Jacques Rousseau, one of the most bitter and caustic of the *philosophes*, the principal activities of diplomats were suspect, for treaties were nothing but "temporary alliances" and alliances only "preparations for treason."[52] Do not value alliances or treaties, Rousseau cautioned, for Christian powers "recognized no bonds except their own interests."

These interests were modified according to the passion of the moment, by the caprices of a minister.[53] Do not "expend your energies upon idle negotiations, or waste your substance upon the maintenance of ambassadors … or expect much from alliances and treaties. All that sort of thing is of no account when it comes to dealing with the Christian powers."[54] Secret negotiations only disguised personal ambitions. The art of negotiation relied on deceit to conquer and money to corrupt. The ambassador did not hesitate to foment revolts or revolutions to weaken the country where he was stationed.[55] Rousseau also derided the respect for and concern for forms and precedence.[56] General congresses took place when states sent representatives to an assembly to "say nothing."[57] Instead they deliberated on "whether the table should be round or square, if the room should have more or fewer doors … and thousands of other questions of similar importance."[58] How were differences resolved? "By the right of the strongest, that is to say of the state of uncivilization and war."[59] Rousseau noted that "one of the best props of the European system, as far as it goes, is the game of diplomacy, which almost always maintains an even balance."[60] Rousseau dismissed "what is commonly called international law" as "mere illusions."[61] In reality, Europe was "in a state of war" because the treaties between particular powers were nothing but "passing truces" rather than a true peace.[62]

For Rousseau war was triggered by irrational causes, selfish and self-seeking rulers, and the diplomatic system itself. Rousseau, who had worked as secretary of the French ambassador at Venice, condemned a system in which kings sought to extend their domination abroad and to render themselves more absolute within their territory. Everything served as a pretext to advance these mutually reinforcing goals: the subjugation of others. Rousseau notes "the perpetual dissensions, the brigandage, the usurpations…. To think of our fine talk and then of our horrible actions, so much humanity in principle, so much cruelty in deed … governments so moderate and wars so cruel … and this pretended brotherhood of the nations of Europe seems nothing but a term of derision to express ironically their mutual animosity."[63] Nations lived in a state of nature.[64] Because conquest was based on the law of the strongest, it had no moral basis. Rousseau noted the waste of war which "often loses what is allegedly gained." For even the "victor" the gain was Pyrrhic because he emerged "weaker than before the war." His only consolation was in "seeing the vanquished more enfeebled than himself." Because war involved the raising of vast sums and the establishment of armies, the condition of the conquerors was little better than the conquered. Conquests were "folly" which often "cost more than they are worth."[65]

Marie Jean Antoine Nicolas Caritat, marquis de Condorcet (1743–1794) (who ultimately died in prison during the Revolution), concurred and contended that treaties were not only useless but also dangerous because rulers relied on them to force their people into wars. He echoed the views of many *philosophes* and revolutionaries when he condemned alliances as both dangerous and useless. In his view it was better "to abolish them entirely in time of peace" because rulers exploited them to "precipitate" their states into wars,"[66] which were nothing more than relics of "barbarism." In his view even the most legitimate and the most just conflict inspired all men "with horror and repugnance."[67] Pierre Samuel Du Pont de Nemours (1739–1817), the noted physiocrat, condemned war whereby "each is ruined himself in the hope of ravaging others."[68]

Even worse from the perspective of the critics was to engage in war and fail. The geostrategic failures on land and sea[69] of Louis XV and Louis XVI underlay the attack on diplomats and the diplomatic system. The plummeting international reputation of France impacted the monarchy. The litany of defeats that Louis XV suffered greatly eroded France's standing and undermined the king. The revolutionaries were quick to indict not just the immorality of the foreign policy of the *ancien régime*, but also its disastrous results. In their view, the French ministers had not only sinned, but, perhaps even worse, they had failed. They had been outsmarted, outmaneuvered. During the debate on whether the nation should delegate to the king the right to declare war, Jérôme Pétion pointed out the consequences of giving power to men who were driven by "their ambition, their passion, their immoderate desire for vainglory; they attacked their neighbors; they believed themselves just when they were strong, they troubled the peace of all of Europe and poured out the gold and the blood of the French in great waves." Those policies had violated not only moral standards, but also the interests of France. Pétion saw only "a phantom of power" in France. Louis XV had "degraded" the nation.[70] Louis XVI followed in his footsteps by allowing his ministers to conclude dishonorable treaties. Many both in France and abroad "perceived (correctly) that the respect and authority that France had enjoyed in Europe's diplomatic affairs had all but disappeared in a hammering series of diplomatic retreats."[71] France was no longer able to project its power on the international stage. For many Frenchmen there was "no honor or dignity whatsoever in being a second-class power, even if only temporarily."[72]

By 1789, France, with its reputation on the international scene at a new low, faced and feared diplomatic isolation. As one minister morosely concluded, France "has no friend, no ally on whom it could count, and if it faced a war on the continent it would probably be left to its own resources."[73]

The all too perceptible failures of French foreign policy influenced the jaundiced perceptions of the revolutionaries. The costly war of the Austrian Succession (1740–1748) ended without advantage to France. In the words of one historian, "the only result of the war was the aggrandizement of Prussia."[74] Many thought that Frederick had played Louis XV for a fool.[75] Even worse, the war did not resolve the underlying issues and laid the basis for the next conflict, the more costly and disastrous Seven Years' War.[76] And then? "France, having played the game of Prussia in the War of the Austrian Succession, was to play that of Austria in the Seven Years' War…. She changed partners but remained the dupe."[77] France found itself enmeshed in yet another conflict, this time against their old ally, Prussia (1756–1763). France was defeated on the land, on the sea, in both Europe and the colonies. France lost not only in Europe but also in Africa, the Caribbean, India, and North America. The French navy faced such severe cutbacks that it was rumored that it could no longer afford to feed the cats deployed to reduce the rodent population in the naval yards. In the army the situation was arguably worse as not only defeat but also disorganization and poor leadership due in part to factions at court discredited and ultimately delegitimated the king.[78] Louis-Philippe, comte de Ségur, indicted the war as one "undertaken without reason, conducted without skill and ended without success."[79] The description of one battle—Rossbach (5 November 1757) in which the French outnumbered the Prussians two to one and initially enjoyed a superior strategic position yet still lost as a "rout and humiliation" seemed to contemporaries an equally apt, but devastating portrayal of the war as a whole.[80] This loss underscored the shortcomings of the French army: ineffective leadership at many levels, frequent alterations in strategy, severe financial constraints, and inadequate logistical support.[81] Strategically, the loss at Rossbach was not decisive but psychologically the disaster was devastating, especially in its effects on the French army and public opinion.[82] Cardinal de Bernis observed that the army, as well as the nation, was "completely demoralized." "Treachery and incompetence were the order of the day."[83] Yet another described it no less tellingly as "the signal for the approaching destruction of our monarchy."[84] The defeat at Vellinghausen in July 1761 further cemented that impression, for this had been a winnable battle in which the French outnumbered the Prussians three to two. The disasters on the European continent were replayed in the colonies: the British seized Louisbourg (1758) and French fortresses along the Ohio river as well as Quebec (1759), Montreal (1760), and Pondicherry (1761).[85]

France lost not only the war but also the peace. Ségur concluded, "France lost its influence in Europe"; "the French monarchy ceased to be a first rank power."[86] The Seven Years' War had been expensive, costing the monarchy approximately twice as much *per annum* as the War of the Austrian Succession.[87] France had to cede Canada and all lands west of the Mississippi to Great Britain and West Louisiana to Spain. France also lost Grenada, the Grenadines, and Senegal to Britain and most of French India. The French did retain St. Pierre and Miquelon off Newfoundland as well as Guadeloupe and Martinique, but only a remnant of their colonial Empire remained. Great Britain emerged as the preeminent maritime and colonial power. Some ingenuously blamed the disgraceful Peace of 1763 not on systemic problems but rather on "caprice" and "chance." Such speculations aside, for many the peace was both dishonorable and disadvantageous.[88]

The 1756 diplomatic alliance with Austria, never popular, even at its inception, faced an increasing barrage of criticism after the disastrous war.[89] Ironically, Louis XV's decision to ally with France's traditional enemy, Austria, was rooted in a core conviction, that the revolutionaries later shared, that the real enemy of France in Europe was Great Britain.[90] Louis XV's alliance was based on the age-old policy of preserving the status quo within the Holy Roman Empire but it was also founded on the new reality in mid-eighteenth-century Europe, the fear that not Austria, but Prussia would threaten the balance of power in the Holy Roman Empire and Europe. The revolutionaries saw it more simply: the traditional hostility to Austria had brought France prestige, its reversal disaster. It was a simple equation. The subtlety of diplomatic machinations and the rationale for dynastic reshuffling eluded the revolutionaries. Ignorant ministers had made France the dupe of Austria and had sacrificed France's prosperity and glory to Austrian interests. The court of Vienna was a leech on France. Retrospectively, the revolutionaries thought that the Austrian alliance had "rendered us null," especially in the Holy Roman Empire, where France was now treated with "insouciance" by some and "almost contempt" by others, namely, Brandenburg and Hesse.[91] Soulavie, among others, deplored the Austrian alliance for reducing France to the position of an "observing and passive power."[92] For him the decline of French prestige abroad dated from 1756.[93] In the view of some, only those who were "flatterers," "slaves of the court," defended the alliance with Austria as natural and necessary; others saw the results: the Seven Years' War, and an erosion of influence with the Turks, the Italians, and the princes of the Holy Roman Empire. In short, this entente had accelerated the political degradation of France.[94] A French diplomat and undersecretary of state for foreign affairs, Gérard de Rayneval, would later bemoan the deteriorating standing of France and observe that other nations by the end of Louis XV's reign "concluded that France no longer possessed strength or resources…. The envy … [had] degenerated into contempt…. Instead of being, as formerly, the hub of European policy, it became a passive spectator, whose approval or disapproval counted for nothing."[95]

The French alliance with Austria, which a recent historian has called a "squally marriage of convenience," only exacerbated a none-too-latent Austrophobia.[96] The French harbored an "insidious loathing" for the Austrians, which stemmed in part from the disastrous Seven Years' War but more importantly from a deep-seated "pathological distrust of the Habsburgs" as enemies of old.[97] In the words of Choiseul: "Vienna does not love us and would sacrifice us for its slightest interest."[98] Talleyrand, in commenting on the later alliance in 1798, noted that it would be impossible to have a solid amity between France and Austria or even between France and Britain because in both cases traditional hatreds and opposing interests would make such alliances impossible.[99] The "most conspicuous example"[100] of that compact, the queen, was committed to the Franco-Austrian alliance and acknowledged that it was "more precious to me than anyone."[101] The widespread, even if incorrect, perception that Marie Antoinette was willing to sacrifice her husband's interests for those of her brother discredited both her and the king. Her position became so perilous because of the conviction that her brother, Joseph II, pursued an aggressive foreign policy at French expense. The former foreign minister (1744–1747), D'Argenson, considered the alliance a diplomatic blunder, as did Maurepas, who left the ministry in 1749. He had no use for alliances, especially long-standing ones with either Austria or Spain, "everyone's friend and no one's ally." In his view France should rely only on what it could achieve on its own.[102] Some publicists argued that the alliance in essence subordinated French interests to Austrian ones by alienating that most traditional ally of France, the Turks, and betraying their other ally, the Poles.

The reality was far different. The Austrian alliance was no more than a "*fantôme*," as Montmorin, the foreign minister, candidly admitted to the Prussian representative.[103] The French had done little to aid their "ally": they had protested the Polish Partition; they had refused to support the emperor in the War of the Bavarian Succession; they had even threatened to intervene on the side of the Dutch against Joseph in the dispute over the opening of the Scheldt. The French failure to support Austria's annexation of Bavaria prompted Joseph II to remark that to have "a nominal ally who was a secret enemy was the worst of all possible worlds."[104] One French ambassador harbored the same view but from the other side, contending that since the inception of the alliance, the court of Vienna has acted "every day as if our old rivalries would revive on the next."[105] Many diplomats, including the Austrian ambassador, realized that the financial and political collapse of the monarchy made any alliance with the French worthless. Ultimately, the Franco-Austrian alliance ended "not with a bang but a whimper."[106] Although the Franco-Austrian alliance existed more in name than reality, that chimera did not prevent the revolutionaries from attacking it. Jean-Louis Carra typified many when he attacked the treaties with the Habsburgs as "moral and political calamities."[107] Early in the Revolution, in March 1790, Peysonnel concluded, quite incorrectly, that the Austrian alliance was the unique source of France's griefs and troubles.[108] Nor did the crisis in the Falklands in 1770–1771 salvage the monarchy's reputation, for Louis XV proved unwilling to aid his cousin in Spain and ally, only promising a "resounding and useful revenge."[109] That promise was still to be honored when the king died in 1774.

When Louis XVI came to power, his foreign minister, Charles Gravier, comte de Vergennes (1774–1787), deplored the diplomatic reverses that France had suffered: "the deplorable peace of Paris, the partition of Poland, and many other equally unhappy causes had profoundly undermined the consideration due the crown of France." France was no longer "the object of terror and jealousy." Now France suffered "the arrogance and insults" of others. Understandably, Vergennes, as he later told the king, was anxious to change a situation "so little compatible with the elevation of your soul and the grandeur of your power."[110] That he failed should not surprise. As France's geopolitical ambitions exceeded its grasp, France lost even more international credibility.

Some French officials myopically maintained the illusion that it was possible for France to regain "its natural place at the head of powers of the first order."[111] They seized the opportunity to act when the American colonists revolted from Great Britain. Many of the court nobility, who had served in the Seven Years' War, were humiliated by their losses and motivated to aid the Americans by a deep-seated Anglophobia rather than an inherent love of liberty. Lafayette clearly feared that a British victory would mean the loss of even more French possessions and the end "of our political existence."[112] French aid to the American colonies struggling for their independence against their old nemesis, Britain, garnered the French some satisfaction, but cost a great deal. One historian has estimated that these funds constituted the equivalent of ten years of the ordinary expenses of the state.[113] As Blanning has pointed out, even the French success in aiding the American revolutionaries was tainted with failure, in particular, the French naval defeat at Saintes and their inability to take Gibraltar. Yet again it appeared that France had expended a great deal and emerged with little: a share in the Newfoundland fisheries, a couple of West Indian Islands, and a few trading stations in Senegal and India. Spain, on the contrary, had expended little, but emerged with Minorca and Florida.[114] As Blanning has pointed out, if "the British had failed to win the war, they certainly won the peace."[115] As the British lost political control, they gained trade, which soon exceeded that before the war. The "brilliant interlude" of victory in 1783 proved all too ephemeral on the all too short but painful trajectory of French decline.[116] As Paul Schroeder has underscored, French triumph in the War of American Independence did little to weaken their foe: "Britain lost the war and France lost the peace."[117]

Even worse, France's abandonment of its traditional allies—the Poles, Turks, and the Swedes—underscored its impotence.[118] France stood idly by in 1764 when Catherine II imposed her former lover, Stanislaus Poniatowski, as king of Poland. More galling yet, in 1772 while Austria, Prussia, and Russia partitioned Poland, that "republic of anarchy,"[119] seizing over 29% of the land and four million people, France was not even consulted, prompting Horace Walpole to remark "that formidable monarchy is fallen, debased."[120] Comte de Mirabeau among others contended that it would be "impossible and reprehensible" to attempt to justify the partition, which had given Europe nothing but "a servile peace."[121] Jacques Mallet du Pan went further and labeled the partition "the horror of our age" and Broglie, the "tragedy of the North."[122]

Furthermore, France had betrayed the "most loyal of allies," the Turks. For the French the outcome of the Russo-Turkish conflict in 1774 was galling. They saw the poor performance of the Turkish army as a reflection on them, for France had provided military advisers. Nor could the French prevent the Turks from accepting a humiliating peace at Kutchuk-Kainardji in 1774.[123] Yet again the French did nothing from 1772 to 1775 when Joseph II brazenly annexed Bukovina, a quadrilateral of territory in northern Moldavia between Transylvania and Galicia of approximately 10,500 square kilometers that provided an important link with the newly acquired Polish territory.[124] This forced cession underscored the brutal nature of *Realpolitik* evident as well in the Polish Partitions. Nor could the Turks look to the French to prevent Russia's annexation of the Crimea in 1783.[125] How, one official queried, could the Turks save themselves when they were "abandoned by its old friends and completely sacrificed to the greed of its hereditary enemies?"[126] Still later, when the Turks faced yet another Russo-Austrian onslaught (the Russo-Austrian War against Turkey, 1787–1792), the French not only withdrew their military advisers, but also refused to sell their allies desperately needed ships. Instead, they pressured them to accept a peace that was far more advantageous to the Austrians and the Russians.[127] As John Frederick Sackville, third duke of Dorset, the British ambassador to France from 1784 to 1790, tellingly noted, the French stood only as "spectators of this important contest."[128] Cynically resolving that they did not have the means to aid their ally, the French went further and concluded that in order to conserve their position in the Levant, they should ally with Russia. Nor could the French stem the decline of their ally to the north, Sweden, or aid their allies in the Empire. When war broke out in June 1788 between Sweden and Russia, the French, who had signed a defensive treaty with the Swedes in 1784, did little but offer "their good offices." It was not France but Britain and Prussia who aided Gustavus III.[129] The French also had done little to support Bavaria and Cologne. When Austria imposed Joseph II's brother, Archduke Maximilian Franz, as Elector of Cologne, France could only watch. Joseph II's attempt to annex Bavaria (War of the Bavarian Succession, 1778) in exchange for the Austrian Netherlands merely underscored French weakness; when a number of states allied to stop Habsburg expansion, the coalition was headed not by France, but by Prussia. Admittedly, the French mediated the ensuing peace but its leverage in the Empire had clearly declined. As the comte de Ségur dismally noted: "What would happen to our old hegemony, our dignity, the balance of power in Europe and our own security if we ceased to be regarded as the protector of the weaker states against the three predators [Austria, Prussia, Russia]?"[130]

Even more shocking were treaties which committed France as well as other European nations to pay an annual tribute to the corsairs, who lived by murder and pillage. Can one believe, a contemporary queried, that "if the nation had exercised its rights, it would have been such an enemy of itself to squander its blood and its treasure in order to subscribe to humiliating treaties? Contemplate all these treaties or these political forfeits, and you will see each page dyed with the blood that the people have shed."[131]

Nor did the conclusion of the Eden Treaty in 1786 garner the king any credit. This treaty, which reduced the tariffs on grain, wine, and brandy exported to Britain and correspondingly those on British hardware and textiles exported to France, further discredited the king as contemporaries argued that it had benefitted Britain, but not France.[132] To many this treaty illustrated the "disgraceful French submission to British domination."[133]

France's reputation fell even further when they did not come to the aid of the Netherlands because of the impending threat of bankruptcy. Increasing ties between the French and the Dutch, traditional enemies, led in 1785 to an alliance, the preservation and effectiveness of which some, like Castries, thought was "France's single most important interest."[134] When the Prussian king, Frederick William II, invaded the Netherlands to restore William V and avenge the arrest, even though temporary, of his sister, the French, paralyzed by insolvency, stood by in "fuming impotence."[135] This refusal to act underscored French powerlessness[136] and shamed many, especially in the French military, who saw the decision as a matter of personal honor and the avoidance of war as either cowardly or shameful.[137] That decision prompted the resignation of both the Secretary of State for the Navy and the Secretary of State for War. That failure dealt yet another and telling blow to French prestige. The international indictment was telling. Joseph II concluded that "France has collapsed and I doubt whether it will rise again."[138] The Prussian envoy Ewald Friedrich Graf von Hertzberg could only concur and observed that France had lost not only the alliance with the Dutch but also "the remnants of her prestige in Europe."[139] To Soulavie, Louis XVI was now "a nullity."[140] Domestically, the criticism was just as harsh. Ségur, in commenting on this disaster, remarked that in a few days Montmorin had destroyed the work of 15 years in restoring the position of France and, he could have added, further undermined the authority of the king, for the "acid of patriotic frustration ate into domestic support for the Bourbon government."[141] In Blanning's words, this fiasco represented "the terminal humiliation of the old regime."[142]

In the midst of the Dutch crisis the French foreign minister, Vergennes, died. The king, believing that this minister had been one of the few whom he could rely upon to tell him the truth, regretted this loss. Vergennes had seen France's role as one of calming "the waves of ambition,"[143] but even that limited goal had eluded him. Many had criticized the minister, notably the war hero Charles Eugène Gabriel de La Croix Maréchal de Castries (1727–1801), who saw his policies as timid and pusillanimous, especially during the War of the Bavarian Succession and the Dutch crisis, and professed astonishment at his "strange complaisance" concerning Russia. Some thought that Vergennes had sacrificed his duty and his convictions in order to preserve his position; they criticized him as a man who lacked insight, foresight, activity, and energy, as one devoted to routine. His policy of calculated indecision led Frederick II to humorously label such tactics "the narcotic of Versailles."[144] Still Vergennes had had few options as France's international stature deteriorated. Vergennes' successor Armand Marc, comte de Montmorin (1745–1792), came to power in the midst of the Dutch crisis and ultimately suffered even more humiliation and savage critiques than his predecessor; he was imprisoned and later died in the September Massacres. During his ministry France's prestige and position in Europe plummeted. Montmorin realized the weakness of France's position. In a massive understatement, he candidly admitted to the British minister Dorset that the "present posture of the Affairs of France both at home and abroad" could only assure the English of France's good intentions.[145] Dorset's remarks only underscored the impotence of France by the 1780s. By 1790 Montmorin would write in despair that France "can influence nothing." "Instead of directing events, we face the painful necessity of following them."[146] The attacks against Montmorin were so toxic that some of those asked to serve as foreign minister subsequently refused, notably Demoustier and Ségur.[147]

By 1789 France found itself isolated in Europe. Mirabeau somberly noted that France had "lost its old friends" and that only Spain remained.[148] But Spain would soon be lost. The Spanish foreign minister, José Moñino y Redondo, conde de Floridablanca (1728–1808), somberly recalled that the French had broken so many treaties that "they could no longer be relied upon."[149] When the Nootka Sound crisis erupted in the spring of 1790 the Spanish bitterly learned that France would offer only "specious assurances of support"[150] and that, in the words of the famous orator Antoine Pierre Joseph Marie Barnave (1761–1793), the English could count on our "impotence."[151] Many criticized the *Pacte de famille* with Spain as merely a "League of Despots" which reflected the primacy of dynastic rather than national concerns. The Nootka Crisis provided a platform to criticize the diplomatic policies of both Louis XV and XVI. Both had suffered one diplomatic reverse after another and in the process discredited the institution of monarchy. Admittedly, the French did have isolated successes, most notably the acquisition of Corsica and Lorraine, but these were lost sight of in the general quicksand of decline.

The revolutionaries were not loathe to criticize. Brissot, for one, urged the Assembly to elevate its diplomacy to real heights. For him that meant rejecting in their entirety treaties "fabricated by ignorance and corruption," where the interests of the people were sacrificed to the interests of some individuals, treaties often broken as soon as they were signed, treaties which served as eternal pretexts for war rather than the foundation of peace. In short, he wanted to tear up the treaties which wound our constitution, particularly that of 1756 with Vienna.[152] Brissot, in particular, attacked Kaunitz and criticized Montmorin as a mannequin controlled by Vienna, who had sacrificed the interests of the nation to those of the royal family and of the house of Austria.[153] He also repudiated the alliance with Spain and argued that France should not aid an ally who had seized property claimed by Great Britain in Nootka Sound and, when threatened with war, had appealed to France. Brissot thought this agreement all too redolent of the *ancien régime* and should be repudiated.

Still others supported maintaining the alliances, especially the *Pacte de famille*, pointing out that it was based not only on family ties between the two houses of Bourbon but also on strategic and economic concerns and, as Spain underscored, on French honor and self-interest.[154] Others clearly saw the ramifications of such a refutation. An Italian in the service of Philip V disputed Sieyès' contention that the *Pacte de famille* was a pact only between relatives. Rather it was a real treaty concluded between sovereigns who acted as heads of state. Even when a country changes its form of government as France did from a monarchy to a republic, it was still bound by those agreements. The whole point of alliances was mutual succor and need. If France had the right to annul treaties with other powers, then so do those powers. Was it necessary then for France to give up all its acquisitions as these were gained in times past? Furthermore what about the real advantages France garnered from the commercial results of such treaties?[155]

Far more prevalent were those who indicted the diplomacy of the *ancien régime*. Those with the most diplomatic experience were often the most cynical. To Silas Deane (1737–1789), the American colonies' diplomatic agent to France in 1776, international relations was inherently evil. Princes subordinated the welfare of their people to considerations of glory. In his view, the rivalries among the European powers accounted for the numerous wars. Ironically, Louis XVI, who found himself and his ministers increasingly under attack, would have agreed with many of those who pilloried the international system. He had criticized it as well. He condemned the immorality of those who partitioned Poland and, even though a nominal ally of Austria, refused to support Joseph II's efforts to annex Bavaria, his attempt to open the Scheldt, and his annexation of Moldavia. Unlike many of his contemporaries, Louis believed in the observance of treaties and at the start of his reign had told his foreign minister that "honesty and restraint must be our watchwords."[156]

On 17 May 1790, Marquis Brulart de Genlis de Sillery urged the Assembly to free France from the sad consequences of the ambition of kings and the perversity of ministers. At the same time he condemned the king's indifference to our allies and in particular his failure to combat the brigandage of the three powers who partitioned Poland and to aid the Dutch. He pointed out—as others must undoubtedly have thought—the disparity between our constitution and the principles we have decreed and our conduct. In the debate over what, if any, action to take about the diplomatic crisis between Britain and Spain, he queried whether France had an obligation to repulse oppression and march against the aggressor. In rebuttal, the monarchist Pierre Victor baron Malouet (1740–1814) argued that a nation that wanted to be free should rid itself of insidious useless politics and not allow itself to engage in the quarrels of kings without its consent. Jérôme Pétion de Villeneuve articulated the widely held conviction that kings had a penchant for war: they attacked their neighbors, they troubled the peace of Europe, and they shed in streams the gold and blood of the nation. He summed up the case for the prosecution. Louis XIV not only breathed war, but waged it with barbarity and brought the realm to the brink of ruin. Louis XV engaged in a multitude of disastrous conflicts. Jérôme Pétion de Villeneuve then noted the disastrous, impolitic, and dishonorable treaties concluded during these reigns. In particular he deplored the loss of Canada and the pact with Austria which had exposed France to perpetual wars with numerous enemies. The consequence was predictable: France lost her ability to preserve the balance in Europe. She lost her consideration in Europe, she neglected her previous alliances, and she alienated her most faithful ally, the Turks. The pernicious and revolting treaty of 1756 in particular ruined commerce and manufacturing. France had been a perpetual theater of wars and of carnage. He had no use for the miserable sophism, often repeated, that kings promote the welfare of their people. Kings are men who were not always guided by reason and were often misled by passions. The love of domination, a natural penchant among men, is enhanced by the idolatrous homage they receive. The interests of a nation are better known, better investigated, and better conserved by an assembly rather than by a minister. With such a government, he ingenuously concluded, wars would be less frequent. A courtesy refused an ambassador, an indiscreet proposal, the ambition of a favorite, and the intrigues of a mistress would no longer cause wars that butcher millions. He erroneously and naively predicted that alliances would be more just and durable because France would abandon the ruses, the perfidies, and the obscure politics of courts. The Assembly should banish the politics of deceit and adopt that of loyalty and good faith and vow not to shed human blood in perpetual and senseless wars. France needed to abjure these archaic errors which have bloodied the land for centuries. Guillaume François Goupil de Préfelne (1727–1801) could only exult that "the reign of the charlatans is over."[157]

The revolutionaries leveled their critiques not only at the "charlatans," but also at the system as a whole. They would have concurred with a journalist, decrying the preceding 130 years of continuous warfare: "What has been the result of this bloody and stubborn struggle? Sterile success achieved by horrific calamities, a frightful effusion of blood, a general disorder in the finances in the majority of the states and a reciprocal and almost universal exhaustion?"[158] To avoid such debacles in the future the revolutionaries aimed to overturn the old order and everything associated with it—whatever in Tocqueville's words, "even bore, however faintly, [its] imprint."[159] The diplomatic system bore that imprint rather heavily. The ideological revolution in France meant the rejection of the norms and practices of classical diplomacy because the revolutionaries viewed the world in radically different terms than their predecessors. Jacques Pierre Brissot contended that "[w]e will not be tranquil until Europe, and all of Europe, is in flames."[160] Nor was he alone in that sentiment. Danton could propose on 28 September 1792 that "the National Convention should be a committee of general insurrection against all the kings of the universe."[161] Many revolutionaries had nothing but contempt for the old system of diplomacy.

Guillaume Bonne-Carrère (1754–1825), upon his appointment to the foreign ministry, exulted that the "idiom of liberty"[162] would replace the "rampant style of enslavement."[163]

The debate over the delegation of the exercise of the right to declare war and peace provided many an opportunity to attack the diplomatic system of the *ancien régime*. One journalist queried whether anyone could forget the passions of kings, the caprices of ministers, the ambitions of favorites, and the corruption and despotism of envoys not to mention the ruination, devastation, and depopulation of empires. For him the past was one of unjust wars and absurd treaties. Kings, by their nature, were more inclined to go to war to augment their prerogatives. The author lamented that a real *droit des gens* could only be established and universal peace secured if Europe treated people to people. In that eventuality politics would also become easier and simpler. However, because courts and cabinets conclude peace and wage war, it was also necessary to understand the intrigues, passions, and vices of cabinets and courts.[164] René Louis, marquis de Garardin, in an address of July 1790, argued against any engagement in foreign wars which would entail the destruction of France and would dishonor us in the eyes of the universe. The time, he argued, has come for us to be free. We should not reconstruct the edifice of despotism which we have destroyed at such cost. It was brigandage to engage in wars that were not purely defensive.[165]

Custine was not alone then in arguing that France would be successful if it no longer carried the imprint of those sordid intrigues which characterized the *ancien régime*.[166] Pétion, a lawyer, one-time mayor of Paris, and later member of the first Committee of Public Safety, argued that honest men shuddered at the thought of war, but kings and ministers did not.[167] All misfortunes could be attributed to the clandestine intrigues of ministers.[168] To revolutionaries such as Pétion, the public law of the *ancien régime* rested only on force. "Quel ordre, grand Dieu," Pétion cried, "that would subvert all morality and all justice."[169] To Antoine Pierre Joseph Marie Barnave (1761–1793), the gifted orator, the old order was a "false and perfidious system which dishonor[ed] nations" and only perpetuated reciprocal enmity.[170] One club complained that "nations have remained ... in this vulgar state of nature where force alone decides differences." States were not "bound by any law" but were "basically at the same level as African states, where kings wage war with slaves in order to get other slaves."[171]

Many revolutionaries argued that instead of seeking to enhance the nation's reputation abroad through wars and acquisitions France should instead concentrate on improving domestic conditions. Therein lay a nation's true glory. Furthermore, such a policy would enhance France's reputation abroad rather than leading to a "vain and sterile glory."[172] François-Jean, Marquis de Chastellux, for example, contended in 1774 in his *Essay on Public Happiness* that nations should "cherish the existence of public welfare and prosperity" and close "the wounds of humanity."[173] Still others during the Revolution, such as G. J. A. Ducher, advocated a "new diplomacy" which would remove obstacles to free trade. Friendship would replace conquest and expansion. For him there would be no "other diplomacy than the diplomacy of commerce which forms the natural bond among people."[174] The Revolution had "destroyed the old system of dynastic guarantees, of family alliances, of treaties of partition, of the balance of power.... This chain is broken."[175] Condorcet could speak of "a fraternity of mankind" or of "this fraternity of nations."[176] Some said it picturesquely. No stranger to hyperbole, Anacharsis Cloots prophesied in the summer of 1793 in an article in the *Moniteur* entitled "*Diplomatie révolutionnaire*": "We will dance together *la carmagnole*."[177] The *carmagnole*, fraternity, or commerce would unite a world formerly divided. Some even argued that the progress of equality in France would have as its logical counterpart "the destruction of inequality between nations."[178] Sincerity would replace double-dealing.

The revolutionaries did not doubt that they could disassociate themselves from the failures in foreign policy and the chicanery of the diplomatic system. Just as man could be shaped in the revolutionary mold, so could the relations between states. Reason, that talisman of the Revolution, would dominate, not the narrow interests of ministers or the selfish concerns of mistresses. In the words of one revolutionary: "Politics is known by all men with clear judgment and just hearts. The true policy is only the disposition of justice and of morals between all nations."[179] Many applauded the moderate Jean Jacques Régis Cambacérès when he juxtaposed the republican position based on nature and right with that of its opposite: "arrangements of cunning and convenience, artificial balances and indemnities."[180] For such men the diplomatic system was an artifact of a regime which followed false ideals and egoistic passions, a regime which divided a potentially united world. The new world which emerged from the carapace of the old order would be different.

The revolutionaries, like the *philosophes*, attacked "unjust aggression." Such wars had in the past been justified by sophistical notions about grandeur and dignity and acquisitions. Many concluded illogically that if all nations were free then there would be no more war. All states had the right to declare a defensive war but none had the right to declare an offensive one.[181] Such ahistorical utopianism led to the Assembly's celebrated, if short-lived, decree of 22 May 1790 that renounced the undertaking of any war with the idea of making conquests or employing forces against the liberty of any people.[182] Even Robespierre argued that the Revolution followed different principles and that men "content to be free" did not want to engage in war.[183] Still for some, such as Brissot, war was preferable to illusory and depressing negotiations. In his view a free people rarely has the advantage in cabinet negotiations. If France employs patriotic agents France is cheated (*trompe*), and if they employ ministerial agents they are cheated as well. That particularly the case when these men are easy to circumvent and seduce, when they are chosen by an executive power that is perhaps an enemy of liberty. What confidence can the people have in envoys who are creatures of the *ancien régime*, "valets" who still speak of the king, their master? This diplomacy is not frank, open, or simple. In war all is public; in negotiations all is mysterious and fraudulent. It is far better for a people who wishes to preserve its independence to assure its success by arms rather than by diplomatic finesse. There can be no sincere capitulation between tyranny and liberty.[184]

It was not much later that some, such as Custine, would argue that France had been "provoked by the unjust aggression of despots" who only existed to "satisfy their vain glory."[185] As late as 18 June 1793 in the midst of war, some revolutionaries ignored reality and argued that France no longer engaged in offensive warfare. Such disastrous wars were, in the words of one, the sole province of "the hereditary ambition of kings."[186] Saint-André concurred, pointing out that the French would never undertake such a war against their neighbors. The "national horror" that this would occasion would make such a conflict "impossible" in France.[187] Such idealism was not confined to the French. In the fourth year of the revolutionary wars, 1795, Immanuel Kant published his *Zum ewigen Frieden*. In this treatise he concurred with the Hobbesian view that states are in a state of nature and thus war. "States like lawless savages, exist in a condition devoid of right ... one of war."[188] He concluded that peace could only be secured by states with a republican constitution, for then the people, not the king, would decide on war or peace. Rulers, he pointed out, could "decide on war for the most trifling reasons, as if it were a kind of pleasure party."[189]

Some revolutionaries like Grégoire attacked—as did others, not only the old diplomacy but also the *droit public* as a "ridiculous and often monstrous scaffolding that the breath of reason has overturned."[190] For him the *droit public* was "an indecent and bizarre assemblage of both good and bad practices."[191] Such concerns prompted him to urge the adoption of a new *droit des gens* on 18 June 1793 and yet again on 26 April 1795. This resolution never passed because some regarded it as premature, even dangerous.[192] But these proposals, no matter how chimerical, reflect the revolutionary conviction that the ordinary laws of war and peace no longer existed and the hope the Revolution would see the birth of a new international law as well as new diplomatic practices.[193]

Some, such as Eschasseriaux the elder, also attacked what he termed the "sophisms" of diplomacy. In particular, the idea of an equilibrium or what others termed a balance of power was nothing but a chimera, "the pretext of all ambitions, the cause of all wars, the constant disaster of all peoples."[194] Eschasseriaux concluded, not surprisingly, that international tranquility depended on the maintenance of French power.[195] The establishment of this dominant French order would assure "peace to all."[196] He then goes on to indict the partition of Poland, the forced incorporation of Polish lands into Austria, Prussia, and Russia as an "outrage against humanity"; despotic governments had "devoured Poland and threatened Turkey." He, however, defended the reunions, that is, the forced incorporation of territories into France as being founded in nature, common interests, and legitimacy. Furthermore the new boundaries of France he regarded as essential for both the repose and the "political equilibrium."[197] Although ambition was the cause of all war, that was not the case with France, which "carries peace in its heart." It was not true that France wished to aggrandize itself through conquests. Rather, he sophistically concluded nature had fixed the boundaries of France—but outside the present perimeters.[198] Not surprisingly, neither he nor any other revolutionary argued for the establishment of natural borders *within* the present borders of France.

Even if the old diplomacy would not immediately grind to a halt, the revolutionaries could try to disentangle France from it. For example, Pétion contended that France should avoid involvement in the European state system, including the formation of alliances.[199] Even the far from radical, constitutional royalist Guillaume Thomas Raynal (1713–1796) claimed that alliances were only preparations for treason. He voiced a sentiment which many must have applauded. As Reubell argued, a great nation should have "no other allies but providence, its power and justice."[200] When the radical Charles François Dumouriez came to power as foreign minister in 1792, he intended to carry through a program he had enunciated earlier: "A great nation, a free and just nation is the natural ally of all nations and does not need to conclude particular alliances which tie her to the fate, the interests and passions of this or that nation."[201] This idealistic, and not incidentally isolationist, stance posed some problems.

In November 1792, the master opportunist, Charles Maurice de Talleyrand, found a clever way of reconciling the desire to avoid entangling alliances with the need to obtain the support of other nations. He distinguished between the ties that France could establish with other free nations and those with *ancien régime* governments. With free governments France could conclude "solemn treaties of friendship in which the interests of a common defense are established," but with other states only "temporary convention[s] concerning political and commercial interests" as circumstances dictated.[202] The citizens of Dieppe on 26 January 1792 phrased the question in terms dominated by revolutionary rhetoric. "What alliance," they asked, "could subsist between the people and kings, between a free nation and tyrants?" The question provided the answer. "Break off then as soon as possible the bonds that unite us to tyrants." "Call to our aid [those] who have preceded us in the conquest of liberty."[203] The Genevan Étienne Salomon Reybaz argued as early as 1792 that liberty, "the most precious of all bonds," made the inhabitants of free nations "fellow citizens"[204] Barère, on behalf of the Committee of Public Safety, argued in May 1793 that despotism can only have accomplices and liberty only friends.[205] Thus, revolutionaries could advocate strengthening the ties between France and her sister republics, namely, the United States and Switzerland, without violating the tenets of the Revolution.[206]

This policy reached its logical culmination after September 1793 when the Committee of Public Safety adopted the Hébertist war policy (*guerre à outrance*). At that time the French abandoned negotiations with the enemy and diplomatic relations virtually ceased. The committee dealt only with other democratic republics.[207] The revolutionary fervor drowned out the voices of those who thought that such a position would only prolong the war.[208] During the war and until the constitution was put into effect, France would not send ministers plenipotentiary or ambassadors to foreign powers other than to the United States and Switzerland. To others,

France would send only secret agents, secretaries of legation, and *chargés d'affaires*.[209] One historian has pointed out that "a regime so pure that it will entertain diplomatic relations only with other free peoples ... is a regime condemned to perpetual warfare."[210] And so it proved.

Notes

1. Quoted in T. C. W. Blanning, *The Culture of Power and the Power of Culture: Old Regime Europe, 1660–1789* (New York: Oxford University Press, 2002), 423.
2. Alexis de Tocqueville, *The Old Regime and the French Revolution*, translated by Stuart Gilbert (Garden City, NY: Doubleday, 1955), vii.
3. Jacques Bénigne Bossuet, both a prelate and a member of the court, described the old diplomacy as "a game where the clever player carries the day in the end." Quoted in Albert Sorel, *Europe and the French Revolution, The Political Traditions of the Old Régime*, trans. and ed. Alfred Cobban and J. W. Hunt (Garden City, New York: Anchor Books, 1971), 14, remarks that "never have more generous euphemisms disguised more unscrupulous tricks of policy."
4. Quoted in John A. Lynn, *The Wars of Louis XIV* (New York: Pearson, 1999), 72.
5. Quoted in Georges Lassudrie-Duchêne, *Jean-Jacques et le droit des gens* (Paris: Jouve, 1906), 43.
6. Charles Irenée Castel, abbé de Saint-Pierre, *A Project of Perpetual Peace, Rousseau's Essay* (London: Richard Cobden-Sanderson, 1927), 7. Although Saint Pierre's ideas influenced Jean-Jacques Rousseau, he remained skeptical of the *abbé*'s ideas, especially his desire to create a European federation and force, if necessary, others to join it. Rousseau did not think that a federative league could be created except by revolution. "Let us admire this plan," he concluded, but "console ourselves not to see it executed." Quoted in Claudius R. Fischbach, *Krieg und Frieden in französischen Aufklärung* (New York: Wasmann, 1989), 71. The renowned philosopher Gottfried Wilhelm, baron von Leibniz, thought Saint-Pierre's plan a "romance" and a fiction impossible to realize. He musingly observed that *Pax perpetua* only pertained to the dead who no longer fight, not to the living. Gottfried Wilhelm, Baron von Leibniz, *Political Writings*, Trans. and ed. Patrick Riley (New York: Cambridge University Press, 1988), 176–184.
7. Charles-Irénée Castel, abbé de Saint-Pierre, *Projet pour rendre la paix perpetuelle en Europe* (Utrecht: Antoine Schouten, 1713). Also see Gustave Molinari, *L'Abbé de Saint-Pierre: Sa vie et ses oeuvres* (Paris: Guillaumin et Cie Libraires, 1857); Édouard Goumy, *Étude sur la vie et les écrits de l'*

abbé de Saint-Pierre (Paris: Bourdier, 1859); Merle L. Perkins, *The Moral and Political Philosophy of the Abbé de Saint-Pierre* (Paris: Minard, 1959); and Sylvester John Hemleben *Plans for World Peace through six Centuries* (Chicago: University of Chicago Press, 1943), 58, 69.
8. François de Salignac de la Mothe-Fénelon, *Lettre de Fénelon à Louis XIV* (Paris: A Renouard, 1825), 11.
9. Ibid., 12–13, 14–15.
10. Ibid., 16.
11. Ibid., 17–18. See also Fischbach, *Krieg und Frieden in der Französiscen Aufklärung*, 19.
12. Leibniz, *Political Writings*, 123.
13. After concluding that "the empire was a name without power," they assumed it could "be vexed with impunity." Ibid., 125.
14. Ibid., 136.
15. Ibid., 143. For other critiques of Louis XIV, see William F. Church "Louis XIV and Reason of State," in John C. Rule, ed., *Louis XIV and the Craft of Kingship* (Columbus: The Ohio State University Press, 1969), 362–406.
16. D'Argenson quoted in Lassudrie-Duchêne, *Jean-Jacques Rousseau et le droit des gens*, 43.
17. See also Barry Rothaus, "The Emergence of Legislative Control over Foreign Policy in the Constituent Assembly (1789–1791)," unpublished Ph.D. diss., University of Wisconsin, 1968, 73.
18. Quoted in Lassudrie-Duchêne, *Jean-Jacques et le droit des gens*, 58.
19. Gabriel Bonnot de Mably, *Des Principes de négociations pour servir d'introduction au droit public de l'Europe, fondé sur les traités* (The Hague: n.p., 1767), 43. In Belissa's words, Mably sought to break the "vicious circle of treaties which settled nothing and carried the germs of future wars." Marc Belissa, "La Diplomatie et les traités dans la pensée des lumières: 'négociation universelle' ou école du mensonge." *Revue d'histoire diplomatique* 3 (1999): 291–317. Mably devastatingly criticized such past practices: "chance decides all." Mably, *Des Principes de négociations*, 67.
20. Charles Pinot Duclos, *Secret Memoirs of the Regency*, trans. E. Jules Meras (New York: Sturgic and Walton, 1910), 51.
21. Emerich de Vattel, *The Law of Nations; or, Principles of the Law of Nature, Applied to the Conduct and Affairs of Nations and Sovereigns*, 1863 Reprint (New York: AMS Press, 1982), vii, viii.
22. Ibid., xiii–xiv. See also Linda and Marsha Frey, *The History of Diplomatic Immunity* (Columbus, OH: The Ohio State University Press, 1999), 272.
23. Vattel quoted in Belissa, "La Diplomatie et les traités dans la pensée des lumières," 313.
24. Quoted in Bailey Stone, *The Genesis of the French Revolution* (Cambridge: University Press, 1994), 20. Frederick II, for example, had no qualms

about violating international law. For him "[l]egal distinctions are the business of ministers." The king put it even more graphically when he noted that: "It is the kingdom of heaven which is won by gentleness; those of this world belong to force." Stone, *The Genesis of the French Revolution*, 20. Also see M.S. Anderson, *Europe in the Eighteenth Century, 1713–1783* (New York: Holt Rinehart and Winston, Inc., 1961), 166.
25. Sorel, *Europe and the French Revolution*, 20, fn 48 quotes Vergennes. See also Ruddy, *International Law in the Enlightenment: The Background of Emmerich de Vattel's Le Droit des Gens* (Dobbs Ferry, New York: Oceana Publications, 1975), 45.
26. Blanning, *The Origins of the French Revolutionary Wars*, 37.
27. Quoted in Paul Rahe, *Soft Despotism, Democracy's Drift* (New Haven, CT: Yale University Press, 2008), 230.
28. Ibid., 211.
29. Charles Louis de Secondat, baron de la Brède et de la Montesquieu, *Persian Letters*, trans. George R. Healy (Indianapolis, IN: Bobbs-Merrill, Co., 1964), 157–158, letter XCV.
30. Rahe, *Soft Despotism, Democracy's Drift*, 40.
31. Quoted in Henry C. Clark, *Compass of Society: Commerce and Absolutism in Old-Regime France* (New York: Rowman and Littlefield, 2007), 94.
32. Émile Faguet, *La Politique comparée de Montesquieu, Rousseau et Voltaire* (Paris: Lecène, Oudin et cie., 1902), 242.
33. Quoted in Clark, *Compass of Society*, 94. See Charles Louis de Secondat, baron de la Brède et de la Montesquieu, *The Spirit of the Laws* (New York: Hafner Publishing Co., 1949), book 13, Chap. 17.
34. Montesquieu, *The Spirit of the Laws*, book 13, Chap. 17. See also Bertrand de Jouvenel, *On Power, The Natural History of its Growth* (Indianapolis, Ind: Liberty Fund. 1993), 9.
35. Quoted in Clark, *Compass of Society*, 94.
36. Ibid., 217.
37. Montesquieu, *The Persian Letters*, 155–156, Letter XIV. Much of his work was written at the time of the War of the Austrian Succession, which Montesquieu regarded as "wholly unnecessary, profoundly unjust and foolish in the extreme." Rahe, *Soft Despotism, Democracy's Drift*, 215.
38. Quoted in Lassudrie-Duchêne, *Jean-Jacques et le droit des gens*, 58.
39. Quoted in Fischbach, *Krieg und Frieden in der französischen Aufklärung*, 85.
40. Quoted in ibid., 86.
41. Théodore Ruyssen. *Les Sources doctrinales de l'internationalisme* (Paris: Presses universitaires de France, 1958), 2: 472.

42. Albert K. Weinberg, *Manifest Destiny, a Study of Nationalist Expansionism in American History* (Baltimore: The Johns Hopkins Press, 1935), 14.
43. Denis Diderot, *Oeuvres complètes*, 2: *Principes de politique des souverains* edited by J. Assezat (Paris: Garnier Frères, 1875), 478–479 for his view of Frederick II's principles. Also see Rothaus, "The Emergence of Legislative Control over Foreign Policy in the Constituent Assembly," 73.
44. Diderot cited in Belissa, "La Diplomatie et les traités dans la pensée des lumières," 301.
45. Quoted in Fischbach, *Krieg und Frieden in der französischen Aufklärung*, 52.
46. Quoted in ibid., 53.
47. Quoted in ibid., 55.
48. Quoted in Herbert H. Rowen, *The King's State: Proprietary Dynasticism in Early Modern France* (New Brunswick, NJ: Rutgers University Press, 1980), 128.
49. Quoted in Lassudrie-Duchêne, *Jean-Jacques et le droit des gens*, 57. Also see M. L. Perkins, "Voltaire's Concept of International Order," *Studies on Voltaire and the Eighteenth Century* 26 (1963): 1296.
50. Quoted in Fischbach, *Krieg und Frieden in der französischen Aufklärung*, 55, fn 152.
51. Quoted in ibid., 54.
52. Rousseau and Raynal quoted in Felix Gilbert, *The 'New Diplomacy' of the Eighteenth Century* (Indianapolis: Bobbs Merrill Reprints, 1951), 8.
53. "Rien n'est plus frivole que la science politique des cours." Quoted in Lassudrie-Duchêne, *Jean-Jacques et le droit des gens*, 127.
54. Jean Jacques Rousseau, *Considerations on the Government of Poland*, translated by W. Kendall (Minneapolis, MN: Minnesota Book Store, 1947), 66.
55. Lucien Bély, *L'Art de la paix en Europe: Naissance de la diplomatie moderne xvie–xviiie siècle* (Paris: Presses universitaires de France, 2007), 646.
56. Ibid., 646–647.
57. Jean Jacques Rousseau, "A Project of Perpetual Peace", trans. by Edith M. Nuttal (London: Richard Cobden Sanderson, 1927), reprint in M. C. Jacob, ed., *Peace Projects of the Eighteenth Century* (New York: Garland Publishing, 1974), 43.
58. Quoted in Belissa, "La Diplomatie et les traités dans la pensée des lumières," 307.
59. Rousseau, *A Project of Perpetual Peace*, 87.
60. Ibid., 33.
61. Quoted in Ian Clark, *Reform and Resistance in the International Order* (Cambridge: Cambridge University Press, 1980), 66.
62. Rousseau, *A Project of Perpetual Peace*, 21–25.

63. Ruddy, *International Law in the Enlightenment*, 38.
64. "All peoples have a kind of centrifugal force that makes them continually act one against one another, and tend to aggrandize themselves at their neighbors' expense ... thus the weak run the risk of being swallowed up; and it is almost impossible for any one to preserve itself except by putting itself in a state of equilibrium with all." Quoted in Michael W. Doyle, *Ways of War and Peace, Realism, Liberalism and Socialism* (New York: Norton, 1997), 148.
65. Rousseau, *A Project of Perpetual Peace*, 69.
66. Quoted in Rothaus, "The Emergence of Legislative Control over Foreign Policy in the Constituent Assembly," 78. Also see Jeremy Black, *British Foreign Policy in an Age of Revolutions, 1783–1793* (Cambridge: University Press, 1990), 525; Stone, *The Genesis of the French Revolution*, 20; Werner Bahner, "Der Friedensgedanke in der franzözischen Aufklärung," *Neue Beiträge zur Literaturwissenschaft* 1 (1955): 141–207.
67. Quoted in Rothaus, "The Emergence of Legislative Control over Foreign Policy in the Constituent Assembly," 48. See also J. Salwyn Schapiro, *Condorcet and the Rise of Liberalism* (New York: Octagon Books, 1963), 145–146.
68. Hagley, W2 4588.
69. Stone, *The Genesis of the French Revolution*, 61. See also 146.
70. *Réimpression de l'Ancien Moniteur* (Paris: Plon Frères, 1862) 4 (1790): 389–391, henceforth *Moniteur*.
71. Orville Murphy, *The Diplomatic Retreat of France and Public Opinion on the Eve of the French Revolution* (Washington, DC: Catholic University of America Press, 1998), 5.
72. Ibid., 10.
73. Quoted in Kaiser, "From Fiscal Crisis to Revolution" in *From Deficit to Deluge, The Origins of the French Revolution*, ed. Thomas E. Kaiser and Dale K. Van Kley (Stanford: University Press 2011), 155.
74. Sorel, *Europe and the French Revolution*, 286.
75. Montesquieu, appalled at French policy, opposed the conflict: "a war that I detest and which the princes of Europe would soon end, if they were prepared to listen to the requests of their faithful subjects." Quoted in Michael Sonenscher, *Before the Deluge: Public Debt, Inequality, and the Intellectual Origins of the French Revolution* (Princeton: Princeton University Press, 2007), 117.
76. Both Austria and Spain felt betrayed by their allies. Maria Theresa resented the British sanction of Frederick's ill-gotten gains in Silesia. The Spanish were furious over the French guarantee of the British possession of Gibraltar and Minorca and the reassertion of British commercial rights within their Empire without even the patina of consultation. The Spanish

were also disappointed at receiving only Piacenza, Parma, and Guastalla. Charles Emmanuel of Savoy was disgruntled at not acquiring either Piacenza or Finale. See M. S. Anderson, *The War of the Austrian Succession* (New York: Longman, 1995), 204–207. See also Reed Browning, *The War of the Austrian Succession* (New York: St. Martin's, 1993).
77. Sorel, *Europe and the French Revolution*, 286–287.
78. For excellent coverage of French disasters see Thomas Kaiser's unpublished paper, "Making War to Making Peace: Diplomacy, 'Patriotism' and Public Opinion in Choiseul's Grand Exit Strategy at the End of the Seven Years' War."
79. T. C. W. Blanning, *The Pursuit of Glory, Europe 1648–1815* (New York: Penguin, 2007), 587.
80. Saint-Germain on 5 November 1757 about the battle of Rossbach quoted in ibid. Also see Edmond Dziembowski, *Un nouvel patriotisme français, 1750–1770: La France face à la puissance anglaise à l'époque de la guerre de Sept Ans* (Oxford: Voltaire Foundation, 1998), 426–430.
81. Hamish M. Scott, *The Birth of a Great Power System, 1740–1815* (London: Longman, 2006), 102–103.
82. Jonathan R. Dull, *The French Navy and the Seven Years' War* (Lincoln: University of Nebraska Press, 2005), 100–102. The allies lost 10,000, while the Prussian casualties only numbered 550.
83. Quoted in Stone, *The Genesis of the French Revolution*, 55.
84. Colin Jones, *The Great Nation: France from Louis XV to Napoleon 1715–1799* (New York: Columbia University Press, 2002), 235. See also 238–239.
85. Jones, *The Great Nation*, 242–244.
86. Blanning, *The Origins of the French Revolutionary Wars*, 42. See also Stone, *The Genesis of the French Revolution*, 62.
87. Riley quoted in Stone, *The Genesis of the French Revolution*, 100.
88. Fischbach, *Krieg und Frieden in französischen Aufklärung*, 154. For the treaty of 1763 also see Thomas J. Schaeper, *France and America in the Revolutionary Era: The Life of Jacques-Donatien Leray de Chaumont, 1725–1803* (Providence, R.I.: Berghahn Books, 1995), 41.
89. Sven Externbrink, "Louis XV and Foreign Policy: A Reassessment," Unpublished paper, 6.
90. Ibid., 9.
91. France, *Recueil*, vol. 18: *Diète germanique*, 377.
92. Jean-Louis Soulavie, *Mémoires historiques et politiques du règne de Louis XVI* (Paris: Treuttel et Wuertz, 1801) 1: 8.
93. Ibid., 1: 4.
94. Blanc de Volx, *Coup d'oeil politique sur l'Europe*, 1: 15–24.
95. Quoted in Stone, *The Genesis of the French Revolution*, 62.
96. Blanning, *The Origins of the French Revolutionary Wars*, 41.

97. Munro Price, "The Court Nobility and the Origins of the French Revolution," in *Cultures of Power during the Long Eighteenth Century*, edited by Hamish Scott and Brendan Simms, (Cambridge: University Press, 2007), 276–277.
98. Thomas E. Kaiser, "The Austrian Alliance, the Seven Years' War and the Emergence of a French 'National' Foreign Policy, 1756–1790," in *The Crisis of the Absolute Monarchy: France from Old Regime to Revolution*, edited by Julian Swann and Joël Félix (Oxford: Oxford University Press, 2013), 171.
99. Paul Bailleu, ed. *Preusssen und Frankreich von 1795 bis 1807: Diplomatische Correspondenzen* (Osnabrück: Otto Zeller, 1965), 1: 173–174, 28 Feb 1798, interview with Talleyrand.
100. Thomas E. Kaiser, "Who's Afraid of Marie-Antoinette? Diplomacy, Austrophobia, and the Queen," *French History* 14 (2000): 247.
101. Kaiser, "From Fiscal Crisis to Revolution," in *From Deficit to Deluge*, ed Kaiser and Van Kley, 147.
102. John Hardman, *Louis XVI* (New Haven: Yale University Press, 1993), 97.
103. Blanning, *The Origins of the French Revolutionary Wars*, 44.
104. Scott, *The Birth of a Great Power System, 1740–1815*, 185.
105. Quoted in Kaiser, "From Fiscal Crisis to Revolution" in *From Deficit to Deluge*, ed. Kaiser and Van Kley, 147.
106. Munro Price, *Preserving the Monarchy: The Comte de Vergennes, 1774–1787* (Cambridge: University Press, 1995), 197.
107. Gary Savage, "Foreign Policy and Political Culture in Later Eighteenth-Century France," in *Cultures of Power*, ed. Scott and Simms, 312.
108. François-Alphonse Aulard, ed., *La Société des Jacobins*, 6 vols. (Paris: Librairie Jouast, 1889), 1: 26. The object of French policy under Louis XV and earlier had been "to play in Europe the superior role which suits its seniority, its dignity, and its grandeur." Stone, *The Genesis of the French Revolution*, 29. Such may have been the goal of Bernis in 1759 but it turned out to be an increasingly unrealistic one.
109. Stone, *The Genesis of the French Revolution*, 33–34.
110. Ibid., 111–112.
111. Quoted in Kaiser, "Who's Afraid of Marie-Antoinette?" 260.
112. Price, "The Court Nobility and the Origins of the French Revolution," in *Cultures of Power*, ed. Scott and Simms, 275.
113. Jacques de Saint-Victor, "Montmorin," in Lucien Bély et al., *Dictionnaire des ministres des Affaires étrangères* (Paris: Fayard, 2005), 199.
114. Blanning, *The Culture of Power and the Power of Culture*, 420.
115. Blanning, *The Pursuit of Glory, Europe 1648–1815*, 595.
116. Sorel quoted in Murphy, *The Diplomatic Retreat of France*, 2.
117. Paul W. Schroeder, *The Transformation of European Politics, 1763–1848* (Oxford: Oxford University Press, 1996), 38.

118. France, *Recueil*, 18: *Diète germanique*, 377.
119. Norman Davies, *God's Playground, A History of Poland* (New York: Columbia University Press, 1982), 1: 511.
120. Blanning, *The Pursuit of Glory, Europe 1648–1815*, 590. See also Peter J. Stanlis, "Edmund Burke and the Law of Nations," *American Journal of International Law* 47, no. 3 (July 1953): 407.
121. Davies, *God's Playground, A History of Poland*, 1: 525.
122. Ibid. Hardman, *Louis XVI*, 92–93. See also 94. Others depicted it as a crime against all nations and a dangerous precedent, a fundamental rupture of the existing order. Marc Belissa, "Les Lumières, le premier partage de la Pologne et le 'système politique' de l'Europe," *Annales historiques de la Révolution française*, 356 (2009): 58, 69, 80.
123. Stone, *The Genesis of the French Revolution*, 50–52.
124. Scott, *The Birth of a Great Power System, 1740–1815*, 169–170 and Murphy, *The Diplomatic Retreat of France*, 18–19.
125. Scott, *The Birth of a Great Power System, 1740–1815*, 189–190.
126. Quoted in Kaiser, "From Fiscal Crisis to Revolution," in *From Deficit to Deluge*, ed. Kaiser and Van Kley, 162.
127. Ibid., 158.
128. Centre for Kentish Studies, U269 Sackville Manuscripts, C 173, Dorset to Carmarthen Paris, 1 May 1788.
129. Murphy, *The Diplomatic Retreat of France*, 3.
130. Quoted in Blanning, *The Culture of Power and the Power of Culture*, 421.
131. *Moniteur*, 4 (1790): 389–391.
132. Stone, *The Genesis of the French Revolution*, 124–125.
133. Murphy, *The Diplomatic Retreat of France*, 75. See also 63–79.
134. Price, *Preserving the Monarchy*, 221. Also see 222.
135. Blanning, *The Pursuit of Glory*, 613. Also see Price, *Preserving the Monarchy*, 187–195.
136. Stephen M. Walt, *Revolution and War* (Ithaca: Cornell University Press, 1996), 47.
137. Murphy, *The Diplomatic Retreat of France*, 80–96.
138. Quoted in ibid., 423. For the English view see Centre for Kentish Studies, U269 Sackville Manuscripts, C 176, O150. and C190 throughout. See also Saint-Victor, "Montmorin," in Lucien Bély et al., *Dictionnaire des ministres des Affaires étrangères*, 199.
139. Quoted in Stone, *The Genesis of the French Revolution*, 146. See also 144.
140. Quoted in Murphy, *The Diplomatic Retreat of France*, 166.
141. Stone, *The Genesis of the French Revolution*, 140. See also Kaiser, "From Fiscal Crisis to Revolution," in *From Deficit to Deluge*, ed. Kaiser and Van Kley, 154–155. Hamish Scott, "A Model of Conduct from the Age of Chivalry?

Honour, International Decline and the End of the Bourbon Monarchy," in *The Crisis of the Absolute Monarchy*, ed. Swann and Félix, 181–204.
142. Blanning, *The Culture of Power and the Power of Culture*, 423. See Savage, "Foreign Policy and Political Culture in Later Eighteenth-Century France," in *Cultures of Power*, edited by Hamish Scott and Brendan Simms, 311.
143. Quoted in Murphy, *The Diplomatic Retreat of France*, 21–22.
144. Jean-François Labourdette, *Vergennes: Ministre principal de Louis XVI* (Paris: Edition Desjonquères), 284–290.
145. Centre for Kentish Studies, U269 Sackville Manuscripts, C 173, Dorset to Carmarthen, 11 December 1788.
146. Thomas E. Kaiser, "A Tale of Two Narratives: The French Revolution in International Context, 1787–1793," in *A Companion to the French Revolution*, edited by Peter McPhee (Malden, MA: Wiley-Blackwell, 2013), 169.
147. Armand Marc comte de Montmorin-Saint-Hérem, *Observations de M.de Montmorin, adressés à l'Assemblée nationale sur le discours prononcé par Mm. Gensonné et Brissot, dans la séance du 23 mai 1792* (Paris: Du Pont, 1792), 11.
148. Saint-Victor, "Montmorin," in Bély et al., *Dictionnaire des ministres des Affaires étrangères*, 201.
149. Quoted in Thomas E. Kaiser's unpublished paper, "Abandoning 'Dynasticism' and Imagining Counter-Revolution: The Nootka Sound Crisis and the Recasting of Foreign Policy in the Early French Revolution."
150. Ibid.
151. Antoine Barnave, *De la Révolution et de la Constitution* (Grenoble: Presses Universitaires de Grenoble, 1988), 181. See also Barry Rothaus, "The Emergence of Legislative Control over Foreign Policy in the Constituent Assembly," and Howard V. Evans, "The Nootka Sound Controversy in Anglo-French Diplomacy-1790," *Journal of Modern History* 46 (1974): 609–640.
152. Jacques-Pierre Brissot de Warville, *Discours de J.P. Brissot, député de Paris sur la necessité d'exiger une satisfaction de l'Empereur* (Paris: Imprimerie nationale, 1792), 19.
153. Jacques-Pierre Brissot de Warville, *Discours sur dénonciation contre le comité autrichien et contre M. Montmorin, ci-devant ministre des affaires étrangères prononcé à l'Assemblée Nationale à la séance du 23 mai 1792* (Paris: Imprimerie nationale, 1792). For Montmorin's defense see Montmorin, *Observations de M.de Montmorin*.
154. Jean-Barthélemy Le Couteulx de Canteleu, *Observations sur la réclamation faite au nom du roi d'Espagne par son ambassadeur à la cour de*

France, M. le Cte de Fernan Nuñez et communiquée à l'Assmblée nationale, le 26 février [1790] (Paris: Imprimerie nationale, n.d.).
155. [Cardinal Guilio Alberoni], L'Ombre du cardinal Alberoni sur le traité connu sous le nom de Pacte de famille et le situation de la France par rapport à l'Espange et aux autres puissances avec des observations dur le commerce d'Espagne et sur son importance (n.p., 1790).
156. John Hardman, *Louis XVI: The Silent King* (New York: Oxford University Press, 2000), 63.
157. *Archives parlementaires de 1787 à 1860*, edited by Jérôme Mavidal et al. (Paris: P. Dupont, 1879), (17 mai 1790) 15: 532–547.
158. Fischbach, *Krieg und Frieden in der französischen Aufklärung*, 180, cites an article in the *Journal de Genève*, 776.
159. Tocqueville, *The Old Regime and the French Revolution*, 20.
160. Quoted in Georges Michon, *Robespierre et la guerre révolutionnaire, 1791–1792* (Paris: M. Rivière, 1937), 129, letter of 26 November 1792.
161. Georges Jacques Danton, *Discours de Danton*, ed. André Fribourg (Paris: Cornély et cie, 1910), 203.
162. France, *Recueil, 28: États allemands, 1:l'Electorat de Mayence*, 282.
163. Barry Rothaus, "The Emergence of Legislative Control over Foreign Policy in the Constituent Assembly," 73.
164. *Journal de la Société de 1789*, 1 (5 juin 1790): 31–40.
165. Aulard, ed., *La Société des Jacobins*, 1: 200–202.
166. Adam Philippe, comte de Custine, *Le Général Custine au president de la Convention Nationale* (Cambrai: Defremery Frères et Raparlier, 1793), 7.
167. Quoted in Rothaus, *The Emergence of Legislative Control over Foreign Policy in the Constituent Assembly*, 119.
168. Quoted in Eric Thompson, *Popular Sovereignty and the French Constituent Assembly, 1789–1791* (Manchester: University Press, 1952), 144.
169. André Fugier, *La Révolution française et l'empire napoléonien*, vol. 4 of *Histoire des relations internationales* (Paris: Hachette, 1954), 25.
170. Buchez and Roux, eds., *Histoire parlementaire*, 6: 110, 21 May 1790.
171. A. N., D XXIII, carton 2, dossier 34, Society of the Friends of the Constitution, Nantes to Diplomatic Committee, 28 February 1791. See also David Bell, "The Culture of War in Europe, 1750–1815," in *The Crisis of the Absolute Monarchy*, ed. Swann and Félix, 147–165. For a later critique see Virginie Martin, "Les Enjeux diplomatiques dans le *Magasin encyclopédique* (1795–1799): du rejet des systèmes politiques à la redéfition des rapports entres les nations," *La Révolution française: Cahiers de l'Institut d'histoire de la Révolution française* 1 (2012): 1–30.
172. Quoted in Sonenscher, *Before the Deluge*, 163.
173. François-Jean, marquis de Chastellux. *An Essay on Public Happiness* (London: T. Cadella, 1774), 1: 414.

174. Quoted in Gilbert, *The 'New Diplomacy' of the Eighteeenth Century*, 36.
175. Quoted in Frederick L. Nussbaum, *Commercial Policy in the French Revolution: A Study in the Career of G. J. A. Ducher*, 1923 Reprint (New York: AMS Press, 1970), 104–106.
176. Marie Jean Antoine Nicolas de Caritat, marquis de Condorcet, *Oeuvres* (1847–1849, Reprint (Stuttgart: Friedrich Frommann Verlag, 1968) 16: 190 (*Esquisse d'un tableau historique des progrès de l'esprit humain*) and 16: 265 (*De l'esprit humain*).
177. Quoted in Masson, *Le Département des affaires étrangères*, 299, fn. 1.
178. Condorcet, *Oeuvres*, 16: 237 (*De l'esprit humain*).
179. *Moniteur* 4 (1790): 411, Menou on 20 May 1790.
180. Albert Sorel, *L'Europe et la Révolution française* (Paris: E. Plon Nourrit et cie, 1904), 4: 265.
181. Jacques Godechot, *La Grande nation: L'Expansion révolutionnaire de la France dans le monde de 1789 à 1799* (Paris: Aubier, 1956) 2: 699.
182. L. G. Wickham Legg, ed., *Select Documents Illustrative of the History of the French Revolution, The Constituent Assembly* (Oxford: Clarendon Press, 1905) 1: 226–227. Also see Godechot, *La Grande nation*, 2: 700 and Boris Mirkine-Guetzévitch, "La 'Guerre juste' dans le droit constitutionnel français" (1790), *Revue générale de droit international public* (1950): 226–250.
183. Quoted in Bély, *L'Art de la paix en Europe*, 649.
184. Brissot, *Discours de J.P.Brissot, deputé de Paris sur la necessité d'exiger une satisfaction*, 8–9, 12.
185. *Moniteur*, 14: 323, declaration of 24 October 1792 by General Custine.
186. Ibid., 16: 659, 18 June 1793.
187. Ibid., 16: 659, 18 June 1793.
188. Quoted in Doyle, *Ways of War and Peace*, 251.
189. Hemleben, *Plans for World Peace*, 89. See also Doyle, *Ways of War and Peace*, 280.
190. *Moniteur*, 24: 294, 26 April 1795. See also Sorel, *L'Europe et la Révolution française* 4: 299.
191. *Moniteur*, 24: 294, 26 April 1795.
192. Ibid., 24: 294, 26 April 1795. See also Linda and Marsha Frey, "Grégoire and the Breath of Reason: The French Revolutionaries and the *Droit des gens*," *Proceedings of the Western Society for French History* 38 (2010): 163–177.
193. Bély, *L'Art de la paix en Europe*, 648.
194. *Moniteur*, 27: 378–379, 7 February 1796.
195. Ibid., 27: 379, 7 February 1796.
196. Ibid., 27: 386, 8 February 1796.
197. Ibid., 27: 386, 8 February 1796, 594–595, 5 March 1796.
198. Ibid., 27: 394, 9 February 1796.

199. Pétion de Villeneuve in *Archives parlementaires* 15: 536–544, 17 May 1790. On 21 May 1790 Cazalès argued that France "should isolate herself from the political system of Europe." (Quoted in Gilbert, *The 'New Diplomacy' of the Eighteeenth Century*, 32.)
200. Quoted in Gilbert, *The 'New Diplomacy' of the Eighteeenth Century*, 33.
201. Quoted in ibid.
202. G. Pallain, ed., *Le Ministère de Talleyrand sous le Directoire* (Paris: Plon Nourrit et cie., 1891), xlix–xl.
203. Quoted in Bélin, *La Logique d'une idée-force*, 4: 123.
204. François-Alphonse Aulard, ed., *Recueil des actes du Comité de salut public avec la correspondance officielle des représentants en mission et le registre du conseil exécutif provisoire* (Paris: Imprimerie nationale, 1889) 1: 344, 9 December 1792.
205. *Moniteur*, 16 (7 May 1793): 312–313.
206. Decree adopted in fall of 1793 or beginning of 1794 (*Histoire parlementaire* 30: 247–248).
207. R. R. Palmer, *Twelve Who Ruled: The Years of the Terror in the French Revolution* (Princeton, NJ: Princeton University Press, 1941), 59.
208. Sorel, *L'Europe et la Révolution française*, 4: 214.
209. Aulard, ed., *Recueil des actes du Comité de salut public*, 7: 28–29, 24 September 1793.
210. T. C. W. Blanning, *The French Revolution in Germany: Occupation and Resistance in the Rhineland, 1792–1802* (Oxford: Clarendon Press, 1983), 72.

References

Alberoni, Cardinal Guilio. *L'Ombre du cardinal Alberoni sur le traité connu sous le nom de Pacte de famille et le situation de la France par rapport à l'Espange et aux autres puissances avec des observations sur le commerce d'Espagne et sur son importance.* S.l.: s.n., 1790.

Anderson, M. S. *Europe in the Eighteenth Century, 1713–1783.* New York: Holt Rinehart and Winston, Inc., 1961.

———. *War and Society in Europe of the Old Regime, 1618–1789.* New York: St. Martin's Press, 1988.

———. *The War of the Austrian Succession, 1740–1748.* New York: Longman, 1995.

Archives Parlementaires de 1787 à 1860. Series 1: 1789–1800. Vol. 15: *Assemblée nationale constituante du 21 Avril au 30 Mai 1790.* Edited by M. J. Mavidal and M. E. Laurent. Paris: Paul Dupont, 1883.

Aulard, François-Alphonse, ed. *La Société des Jacobins: Recueil de documents pour l'histoire du club des Jacobins de Paris.* 6 vols. Paris: Librairie Jouast, 1887–1897.

Bahner, Werner. "Der Friedensgedanke in der französischen Aufklärung." *Neue Beiträge zur Literaturwissenschaft* 1, no. 9 (1955): 141–207.
Bailleu, Paul, ed. *Preusssen und Frankreich von 1795 bis 1807. Diplomatische Correspondenzen*. Osnabrück: Otto Zeller, 1965.
Barnave, Antoine. *De la Révolution et de la Constitution*. Grenoble: Presses universitaires de Grenoble, 1988.
Bélin, Jean. *La Logique d'une idée-force: l'Idée d'utilité sociale et la révolution française*. Paris: Hermann et Cie., 1939.
Belissa, Marc. "La Diplomatie et les traités dans la pensée des lumières: 'negociation universelle' ou école du mensonge." *Revue d'histoire diplomatique* 3 (1999): 291–317.
———. "Les Lumières, le premier partage de la Pologne et le 'système politique' de l'Europe." *Annales historiques de la Révolution française*, 356 (2009): 57–92.
Bély, Lucien. *L'Art de la paix en Europe: Naissance de la diplomatie moderne XVIe–XVIIIe siècle*. Paris: Presses universitaires de France, 2007.
——— et al., *Dictionnaire des ministres des Affaires étrangères*. Paris: Fayard, 2005.
Black, Jeremy. *British Foreign Policy in an Age of Revolutions, 1783–1793*. Cambridge: Cambridge University Press, 1994.
Blanc de Volx, Jean. *Coup d'oeil politique sur l'Europe*. 2 vols. Paris: Dentu, 1802.
Blanning, T. C. W. *The Culture of Power and the Power of Culture: Old Regime Europe, 1660–1789*. Oxford: Oxford University Press, 2002.
———. *The French Revolution in Germany: Occupation and Resistance in the Rhineland 1792–1802*. Oxford: Clarendon Press, 1983.
———. *The Origins of the French Revolutionary Wars*. New York: Longman, 1987.
———. *The Pursuit of Glory: Europe 1648–1815*. New York: Viking, 2007.
Brissot de Warville, Jacques-Pierre. *Discours de J. P. Brissot, député de Paris sur la necessité d'exiger une satisfaction de l'Empereur*. Paris: Imprimerie nationale, 1792a.
———. *Discours ... sur les causes des dangers de la patrie et sur les mesures à prendre, prononcé le 9 juillet 1792*. Paris: Imprimerie nationale, s.d., 1792b.
———. *Discours de J. P. Brissot, député sur les dispositions des Puissances étrangères, relativement à la France, et sur les préparatifs de guerre ordonné par le Roi*. Paris: Imprimerie Nationale, 1791.
Browning, Reed. *War of the Austrian Succession*. New York: St. Martin's, 1993.
Buchez, Philippe-Joseph-Benjamin, and Prosper-Charles Roux-Lavergne, eds. *Histoire parlementaire de la Révolution française*. 40 vols. Paris: Paulin, 1834–1838.
Chastellux, François-Jean, marquis de. *An Essay on Public Happiness*. 2 vols. London: T. Cadell, 1774.
Church, William F. "Louis XIV and Reason of State." In *Louis XIV and the Craft of Kingship*, edited by John C. Rule, 362–406. Columbus: The Ohio State University Press, 1969.

Clark, Henry C. *Compass of Society: Commerce and Absolutism in Old-Regime France*. Lanham, MD: Lexington Books, 2007.

Condorcet, Marie Jean Antoine Nicolas Caritat (marquis de). *Oeuvres de Condorcet*. Paris: Firmin Didot frères, 1847–1849.

Custine, Adam Philippe (comte de). *Le Générale Custine au président de la Convention nationale*. Cambrai: Defremery frères et Raparlier, 1793.

Danton, Georges Jacques. *Discours de Danton*. Edited by André Fribourg. Paris: Société de l'histoire de la Révolution française, 1910.

Davies, Norman. *God's Playground, a History of Poland*. New York: Columbia University Press, 1982.

Diderot, Denis. *Oeuvres complètes de Diderot*. Edited by J. Assézat. Paris: Garnier Frères, 1875.

Doyle, Michael W. *Ways of War and Peace, Realism, Liberalism and Socialism*. New York: Norton, 1997.

Duclos, Charles Pinot. *Secret Memoirs of the Regency: The Minority of Louis XVI*. Translated by E. Jules Meras. New York: Sturgis and Walton, 1910.

Dull, Jonathan R. *The French Navy and American Independence: A Study of Arms and Diplomacy, 1774–1787*. Princeton, NJ: Princeton University Press, 1975.

Dziembowski, Edmond. *Un nouvel patriotisme français, 1750–1770: La France face à la puissance anglaise à l'époque de la guerre de Sept Ans*. Oxford: Voltaire Foundation, 1998.

Evans, Howard V. "The Nootka Sound Controversy in Anglo-French Diplomacy—1790." *Journal of Modern History* 46 (December 1974): 609–640.

Externbrink, Sven. Louis XV and Foreign Policy: A Reassessment. Unpublished paper.

Faguet, Émile. *La Politique comparée de Montesquieu, Rousseau et Voltaire*. Paris: Lecène, Oudin et Cie., 1902.

Fénelon, François de Salignac de la Mothe. *Lettre de Fénelon à Louis XIV*. Paris: A Renouard, 1825.

Fischbach, Claudius. *Krieg und Frieden in der französischen Aufklärung*. New York: Waxmann Münster, 1989.

France. Commission des Archives diplomatiques au ministère des affaires étrangères. *Recueil des instructions données aux ambassadeurs et ministres de France depuis les traités de Westphalie jusqu'à la Révolution française*. Vol. 18. *Diète Germanique*. Edited by Bertrand Auerbach. Paris: Félix Alcan, 1912.

———. Commission des Archives diplomatiques au ministère des affaires étrangères. Vol. 28. *États Allemands*, part 1: L'Electorat de Mayence. Edited by Georges Livet. Paris: Centre National de la recherche scientifique, 1962.

Frey, Linda, and Marsha Frey. "Grégoire and the Breath of Reason: The French Revolutionaries and the *Droit des gens*." *Proceedings of the Western Society for French History* 38 (2010): 163–177.

———. *The History of Diplomatic Immunity*. Columbus, OH: Ohio State University Press, 1999.

Fugier, André. *Histoire des relations internationales*. Vol. 4: *La Revolution française et l'empire napoléonien*. Paris: Hachette, 1954. http://research-repository.st-andrews.ac.uk/handle/10023/1881.

Gilbert, Felix. *The 'New Diplomacy' of the Eighteenth Century*. Indianapolis: Bobbs Merrill, 1951.

Godechot, Jacques. *La Grande nation: L'Expansion révolutionnaire de la France dans le monde de 1789 à 1799*. Paris: Aubier, 1956.

Goumy, Édouard. *Étude sur la vie et les écrits de l'abbé de Saint-Pierre*. Paris: Bourdier, 1859.

Hardman, John. *Louis XVI*. New Haven: Yale University Press, 1993.

———. *Louis XVI: The Silent King*. New York: Oxford University Press, 2000.

Hemleben, Sylvester John. *Plans for World Peace Through Six Centuries*. Chicago: University of Chicago Press, 1943.

Jones, Colin. *The Great Nation: France from Louis XV to Napoleon, 1715–99*. New York: Columbia University Press, 2002.

Journal de la langue françoise. Paris, 1791.

Journal de la Société de 1789, 1 (5 juin 1790): 31–40.

Kaiser, Thomas E. "Abandoning 'Dynasticism' and Imagining Counter-Revolution: The Nootka Sound Crisis and the Recasting of Foreign Policy in the Early French Revolution." Unpublished paper.

———. "The Austrian Alliance, the Seven Years' War and the Emergence of a French 'National' Foreign Policy, 1756–1790". In *The Crisis of the Absolute Monarchy: France from Old Regime to Revolution*, edited by Julian Swann and Joël Félix, 167–179. Oxford: Oxford University Press, 2013a.

———. "From Fiscal Crisis to Revolution: The Court and French Foreign Policy, 1787–1789." In *From Deficit to Deluge: The Origins of the French Revolution*, edited by Thomas E. Kaiser and Dale K. Van Kley, 139–164. Stanford, CA: Stanford University Press, 2011.

Kaiser, Thomas E. "Making War to Making Peace: Diplomacy, 'Patriotism' and Public Opinion in Choiseul's Grand Exit Strategy at the End of the Seven Years' War." Unpublished paper.

Kaiser, Thomas E. "A Tale of Two Narratives: The French Revolution in International Context, 1787–1793." In *A Companion to the French Revolution*, edited by Peter McPhee, 161–177. Malden, MA: Wiley-Blackwell, 2013b.

———. "Who's Afraid of Marie Antoinette? Diplomacy, Austrophobia and the Queen." *French History* 14 (2000): 241–271.

Labourdette, Jean-Francois. *Vergennes: Ministre principal de Louis XVI*. Paris: Edition Desjonquères, 1990.

Lassudrie-Duchêne, Georges. *Jean-Jacques Rousseau et le droit des gens*. Paris: Jouve, 1906.

Le Couteulx de Canteleu, Jean-Barthélemy. *Observations sur la réclamation faite au nom du roi d'Espagne par son ambassadeur à la cour de France, M. le Cte de Fernan Nuñez et communiquée à l'Assmblée nationale, le 26 février [1790].* Paris: Imprimerie nationale, n.d.

Legg, L. G. Wickham, ed. *Select Documents Illustrative of the History of the French Revolution: The Constituent Assembly.* 2 vols. Oxford: Clarendon Press, 1905.

Leibniz, Gottfried Wilhelm (baron von). *Political Writings.* Translated and edited by Patrick Riley. New York: Cambridge University Press, 1988.

Lynn, John A. *The Wars of Louis XIV.* New York: Longman, 1999.

Mably, Gabriel Bonnot de. *Des Principes des négociations, pour servir d'introduction au droit public de l'Europe, fondé sur les traités.* The Hague: n.p., 1767.

Martin, Virginie. "Les Enjeux diplomatiques dans le *Magasin encyclopédique* (1795–1799): du rejet des systèmes politiques à la redéfition des rapports entres les nations." *La Révolution française: Cahiers de l'Institut d'histoire de la Révolution française* 1 (2012): 1–30.

Masson, Frédéric. *Le Département des affaires étrangères pendant la Révolution, 1787–1804.* Paris: E. Plon, 1877.

Michon, Georges. *Robespierre et la guerre révolutionnaire, 1791–1792.* Paris: Rivière, 1937.

Mirkine-Guetzévitch, Boris. "La 'Guerre juste' dans le droit constitutionnel français." *Revue générale de droit international public* 54 (1950): 225–250.

Molinari, Gustave. *L'Abbé de Saint-Pierre: Sa vie et ses oeuvres.* Paris: Guillaumin et Cie Libraires, 1857.

Moniteur, seule histoire authentique et inaltérée de la Révolution française. 32 vols. Paris: Plon Frères, 1847–1863.

Montesquieu, Charles Louis de Secondat, baron de la Brède et de. *The Persian Letters.* Translated by George R. Healy. Indianapolis, IN: The Bobbs-Merrill Co., 1964.

Montmorin Saint Hérem, Armand Marc, comte de. *Observations de M.de Montmorin, adressés à l'Assemblée nationale sur le discours prononcé par Mm. Gensonné et Brissot, dans la séance du 23 mai 1792.* Paris: Du Pont, 1792.

Murphy, Orville T. *The Diplomatic Retreat of France and Public Opinion on the Eve of the French Revolution, 1783–1789.* Washington, DC: The Catholic University of America Press, 1998.

Nussbaum, Frederick L. *Commercial Policy in the French Revolution: A Study of the Career of G. J. A. Ducher.* New York: AMS Press, 1970.

Pallain, G., ed. *Le Ministère de Talleyrand sous le Directoire.* Paris: Plon, Nourrit et cie., 1891.

Palmer, R. R. *Twelve Who Ruled: The Year of the Terror in the French Revolution.* Princeton: University Press, 1941.

Perkins, Merle L. *The Moral and Political Philosophy of the Abbé de Saint-Pierre.* Paris: Minard, 1959.

Price, Munro. "The Court Nobility and the Origins of the French Revolution." In *Cultures of Power in Europe During the Long Eighteenth Century*, edited by Hamish Scott and Brendan Simms, 269–288. Cambridge: University Press, 2007.

Rahe, Paul A. *Soft Despotism, Democracy's Drift: Montesquieu, Rousseau, Tocqueville and the Modern Prospect*. New Haven, CT: Yale University Press, 2008.

Rothaus, Barry. "The Emergence of Legislative Control Over Foreign Policy in the Constituent Assembly (1789–1791)." Unpublished Ph.D. diss., University of Wisconsin, 1968.

Rousseau, Jean-Jacques. *Considerations on the Government of Poland*. Translated by W. Kendall. Minneapolis, MN: Minnesota Book Store, 1947.

———. "A Project of Perpetual Peace." Translated by Edith M. Nuttall. In *Peace Projects of the Eighteenth Century*. Edited by M. C. Jacob. New York: Garland Publishing, 1974.

Rowen, Herbert H. *The King's State: Proprietary Dynasticism in Early Modern France*. New Brunswick, NJ: Rutgers University Press, 1980.

Ruddy, Francis Stephen. *International Law in the Enlightenment; The Background of Emmerich de Vattel's Le Droit de Gens*. Dobbs Ferry, NY: Oceana Publications, 1975.

Ruyssen, Théodore. *Les Sources doctrinales de l'internationalisme*. Vol. 2. Paris: Presses universitaires de France, 1958.

Saint-Pierre, Charles Irénée Castel, abbé de. *A Project of Perpetual Peace*. London: Richard Cobden-Sanderson, 1927.

———. *Projet pour rendre la paix perpetuelle en Europe*. Utrecht: Antoine Schouten, 1713.

Savage, Gary. "Foreign Policy and Political Culture in Later Eighteenth-Century France." In *Cultures of Power in Europe During the Long Eighteenth Century*, edited by Hamish Scott and Brendan Simms, 304–324. Cambridge: University Press, 2007.

Schaeper, Thomas J. *France and America in the Revolutionary Era: The Life of Jacques-Donatien Leray de Chaumont 1725–1803*. Providence: Berghahn Books, 1995.

Schapiro, J. Salwyn. *Condorcet and the Rise of Liberalism*. New York: Octagon Books Inc., 1963.

Schroeder, Paul W. *The Transformation of European Politics, 1763–1848*. Oxford: Clarendon Press, 1994.

Scott, Hamish M. *The Birth of a Great Power System, 1740–1815*. London: Longman, 2006.

———. "A Model of Conduct from the Age of Chivalry? Honour, International Decline and the End of the Bourbon Monarchy." In *The Crisis of the Absolute Monarchy: France from Old Regime to Revolution*, edited by Julian Swann and Joël Félix, 181–204. Oxford: Oxford University Press, 2013.

Sonenscher, Michael. *Before the Deluge: Public Debt, Inequality, and the Intellectual Origins of the French Revolution*. Princeton, NJ: Princeton University Press, 2007.

Sorel, Albert. *Europe and the French Revolution: The Political Traditions of the Old Régime*. Translated and edited by Alfred Cobban and J. W. Hunt. New York: Anchor Books, 1971.

———. *L'Europe et la Révolution française*. 8 vols. Paris: E. Plon Nourrit et cie, 1897–1904.

Soulavie, Jean-Louis. *Mémoires historiques et politiques du règne de Louis XVI*. 6 vols. Paris: Treuttel et Wuertz, 1801.

Stanlis, Peter J. "Edmund Burke and the Law of Nations." *The American Journal of International Law* 47, no. 3 (July 1953): 397–413.

Stone, Bailey. *The Genesis of the French Revolution*. Cambridge: Cambridge University Press, 1994.

Swann, Julian and Félix Joël, eds. *The Crisis of the Absolute Monarchy: France from Old Regime to Revolution*. Oxford: Oxford University Press, 2013.

Thompson, Eric. *Popular Sovereignty and the French Constituent Assembly, 1789–91*. Manchester: University Press, 1952.

Tocqueville, Alexis de. *The Old Regime and the French Revolution*. Translated by Stuart Gilbert. Garden City, NY: Doubleday, 1955.

Vattel, Emerich de. *The Law of Nations: Or, Principles of the Law of Nature Applied to the Conduct and Affairs of Nations and Sovereigns*. New York: AMS Press, 1982.

Walt, Stephen M. *Revolution and War*. Ithaca, NY: Cornell University Press, 1996.

Weinberg, Albert K. *Manifest Destiny. A Study of Nationalist Expansionism in American History*. Baltimore, MD: The Johns Hopkins Press, 1935.

CHAPTER 3

The Enemy Within: The Attack on Diplomats

Your greatest enemies, Rome, are within your gates.[1]

The revolutionaries critiqued not only the international system but also the actors in it as "fools, rogues, personal enemies and rivals."[2] In the words of the journalist Louis Marie Prudhomme, these diplomats, "tainted by aristocracy," were spies, glib, dangerous, and ambitious intriguers who reveled in outward luxury and show.[3] Appointment remained problematic as the definition of loyalty constantly shifted during the Revolution. The vicious factionalism of the Revolution made the position of a diplomat particularly perilous. The revolutionaries attacked not only the diplomats but also the foreign ministry and the foreign minister himself and attempted to wrest control of foreign affairs. The critics had a long tradition to draw upon, including the sardonic seventeenth-century observer Jean de la Bruyère (1645–1696). A minister was, in his words, a "chameleon or a Proteus" who knows "how to assume any character most suited to his designs…. All his designs and maxims, all the devices of his policy, tend only to prevent his being deceived, and to deceive others."[4] During the Revolution many echoed such refrains.[5]

Some revolutionaries thought that in a reformed world, "based on reason, foreign policy and diplomacy would become unnecessary…. The new world would be a world without diplomats."[6] Brissot de Warville said much the same thing when he condemned the indecency of espionage.[7] As early in the Revolution as December 1791, Mercier urged that philosophical principles could rule better than diplomatic errors.[8] In a similar fashion, Charles Alexis Brulart, marquis de Sillery, comte de Genlis (1737–1793), a deputy to the National Convention, derided the function of the ambassador as "futile" and argued that "the reign of the protected spies is over."[9] These revolutionaries only articulated the view of Thomas Jefferson, who considered diplomacy "the workshop in which nearly all the wars of Europe are manufactured." Jefferson's strategy had been much the same as that of the revolutionaries when he came into the administration. He "dismissed one half of our missions and was nearly ripe to do so by the other half."[10] In the new world envisaged by the revolutionaries, permanent ambassadors by definition were not needed. For what purpose could they serve in the new order? Their very activities were discredited. The nobles' preeminent association with diplomacy, with what Mably denounced as "the art of intrigue,"[11] underlay the larger assault on privilege, on the international system of the *ancien régime*, and on diplomacy itself.[12] The revolutionaries even commissioned a report that considered whether resident ambassadors should be replaced by roving ones.[13] Pragmatism, however, ultimately prevailed. One revolutionary realistically noted that should France reduce the number of ambassadors it would be at a disadvantage in the courts of Europe. He instead suggested that France send more, not fewer ambassadors.[14] When the Executive Provisionary Council debated the vital question of prisoner exchanges with Great Britain, they concluded that the commissioners should ideally be adroit, circumspect, and politically knowledgeable. They should not, however, have any acquaintance with diplomacy.[15] So opprobrious did the word "diplomat" become that it was rarely employed during the Revolutionary era, although the words "diplomacy" and "diplomatic" were often used in the sense of negotiating with foreign powers.[16] Diplomacy continued to be so abhorred that the most guileless of revolutionaries would boast of their ignorance of such.[17]

Revolutionaries wanted to disassociate themselves from the chicanery of the international system but they feared that the ruinous iniquity of the old politics[18] and the miasma of the *ancien régime* lingered on. Even ministers of foreign affairs were not averse to leveling such criticism. François-Louis-Michel Chemin Deforgues condemned the "obscure intrigues" of diplomacy[19] and Dumouriez, its pride, machiavellianism, and artifice.[20] Brissot voiced the suspicion of many when he argued that the department of foreign affairs had been screened "from the influence of the revolution." He saw there "the same form, the same mystery, the same falsity of language." There only the king existed, not the National Assembly. Diplomats spoke of the king, not the nation. Brissot wondered, when will "the language of diplomacy purify itself?"[21] In 1790, Brissot attacked not only the minister of foreign affairs but also the *premier commis* whom he derided as "veterans of the aristocracy," "*comédiens de parade*," and argued that the people through its representatives should nominate its envoys.[22] Such concerns impelled the Assembly in July 1790 to create a diplomatic committee with Mirabeau as its *rapporteur*.[23] The Diplomatic Committee was charged with overseeing and regularly reporting to the Assembly on France's relations with foreign powers.[24] It lasted until June 1793. At that time Jeanbon Saint-André demanded its suppression.[25]

As the Revolution became more radical, the attack on the foreign minister accelerated, especially after the king's flight to Varennes in 1791. The Constitution of September 1791 provided that only the legislative body could ratify treaties of peace, alliance, and commerce. In 1792 the revolutionaries decreed that the minister of foreign affairs would be the last member of the *conseil exécutif provisoire* chosen, a clear indication of the changing emphasis of the new revolutionary government.[26] Charles Delacroix was later selected as minister of foreign affairs (1795–1797) in part because he had no diplomatic background. That appointment may have reflected the directors' desire to control foreign policy, but it also may have mirrored the revolutionaries' distrust of those who had served the *ancien régime* and of diplomacy.

Other revolutionaries launched their attacks indirectly by criticizing the expenses of the foreign ministry. They predicted, incorrectly as it turned out, that because the diplomacy of the republic was both simpler and more loyal than that of the *ancien régime*, it would be less expensive. Ducher condemned the diplomacy of the *livre rouge*; these ministers he regarded as both corrupters and corrupted. France should disdain the diplomacy of Pitt, the science of perfidies.[27] To counter such attacks, in 1790 Montmorin published a public explanation of the expenses of the Ministry of Foreign Affairs, listing the salaries of the ministers abroad as well as the subsidies paid to powers such as Saxony.[28] That publication predictably did not appease his critics.

The post of foreign minister was suspect, even when held by novices, as can be seen in the fate of those who occupied it from 1789 to 1794. Montmorin (foreign minister from 14 February 1787 to 12 July 1789 and then from 16 July 1789 to 20 November 1791), denounced as "the traitor ... this diplomatic spider,"[29] was killed in prison; La Vauguyon (12–16 July 1789) subsequently served as France's ambassador to Spain and prudently remained there after his recall; Lessart (November 1791–March 1792) was a victim of the September Massacres; Dumouriez (15 March–13 June 1792) fled; Chambonas (16 June–16 July 1792) sought refuge in London after August 1792; Bigot de Sainte-Croix (1–10 August 1792) fled to Great Britain; Lebrun (10 August 1792–21 June 1793) was executed; Deforgues (21 June 1793–2 April 1794) was imprisoned, but released in thermidor 1794. Some, such as Moustier, Ségur, Choiseul, and Narbonne, had been prudent enough to decline the poisoned chalice.[30]

Ever since the outbreak of the Revolution many castigated the Minister of Foreign Affairs for employing the agents and relying on the diplomatic methods of the *ancien régime*. They had "thrown themselves into excuses and apologies"; they had negotiated feebly and timidly. One underscored: "This incoherence between our vigorous constitution" and the "cowardly and timid" men who represent us in foreign courts."[31] Many revolutionaries thought that by January 1792 the relations with Europe had reached a crisis.[32] For the revolutionaries this conclusion was inescapable: "the false prudence of our ministry and our diplomatic agents" had achieved only our disparagement or debasement. Our "weakness" left us only enemies.[33] Others saw us not as weak but as threatening, "abettors of assassins."[34] In France some concluded that the only recourse France had was to recall all our envoys and cease all negotiation since such men had only attracted "contempt, hatred and war." At the very least France had to adopt a system of diplomacy "analogous to our constitution … [that] would deploy all the majesty of a great free and just nation."[35] Thus France would regain the influence as the premier power in Europe that she should never have lost. Diplomats accordingly had to adopt "the most courageous, the most prudent, the most frank, the most pure conduct." Only by so doing would the ministers of France be able to "conserve or regain consideration and confidence."[36] In this view, "all negotiation conducted by guile and based on the old forms would be fruitless."[37]

These critiques of the old diplomatic methods led some, such as Brissot, to demand the replacement of all French representatives abroad. In a scathing indictment not only of the foreign minister but also of some of the ministers abroad such as Choiseul-Gouffier, Desmoulins, implicitly comparing France to Rome, argued that "Your greatest enemies, Rome, are within your gates."[38] Such proposals, coupled with the drastic reduction in the budget of the ministry of foreign affairs proposed on 6 October 1789, reflected the increasing hostility of the Assembly. By January 1791 Mirabeau could credibly suggest that all French envoys be replaced. Although that suggestion was not followed, revolutionaries did not hesitate to criticize envoys proposed by the king because of their noble lineage and their questionable devotion to the Revolution. The abolition of noble status in June of 1790 reflected the revolutionaries' attitude as did the employment of the bourgeoisie.[39] Nobles would not play a prominent role in the diplomatic corps until Napoleon.

The mere mention of a profession so associated with the *ancien régime* as diplomacy tarred Barthélemy and others as well with the taint of treason for its purported virtues—reticence, formality, and deviousness—could only compare unfavorably with the frankness and openness of the ideal revolutionary. Many would have shared Samuel Johnson's castigation of the courtier and ambassador Lord Chesterfield (1694–1773) for his advice to his son to above all know how to please. That counsel was founded on "the morals of a whore and the manners of a dancing master."[40] Throughout the Revolution the people preferred not to deploy professional diplomats who were automatically suspect, but the Revolution's partisans.[41] As early as year II the Committee of Public Safety urged the hiring of revolutionary apostolates who displayed a republican spirit and a pronounced love of the country. France needed to be served not by men cold, egotistical, or indifferent to the Revolution but rather by men who loved France with as much passion as constancy. Those who wanted to be hired had to fill out a form asking for not only name and age but also their positions before and after the Revolution as well as their character, their work, and their abilities.[42] These simple citizens would disdain the old formulas and reject the hypocritical courtesies. The ministers of the republic would be pure and skillful and very different from those of the *ancien régime*.[43] The revolutionary man, according to Saint Just, was "inflexible, but he is sensible, he is frugal, he is simple without vaunting an excess of false modesty; the irreconcilable enemy of all lies, all indulgence, all affectation."[44] Compounding the difficulty of selection was the ever-changing view of what constituted a true revolutionary as the various factions vied for power.

As Jeremy Black somewhat wryly notes, although the revolutionaries intended to substitute the "parasites" of the *ancien régime* and the enemies of the new with men of "proven ability and loyalty" they rarely agreed on how to do so.[45] In both the diplomatic corps and the civil service the revolutionaries wanted to replace the servants of the *ancien régime* with men more noted for their probity and patriotism than their knowledge, experience, or machiavellianism.[46] In the Ministry of War Edmond Louis Alexis Dubois-Crancé made clear his goal of recruiting republicans. An employee in his view should be educated and hardworking but most importantly "a friend of the public good." An "ardent zeal" will sometimes serve instead of distinguished talent but nothing could supplant republican virtues. There were some who served the *ancien régime* and had not contracted unfortunate attitudes; they were "republicans" serving a tyranny. These men were precious; the "genius of liberty," he thought, could create extraordinary men.[47] Such patriots, however, were not easy to find. They too often resorted to men who had no experience in foreign affairs.[48] Victor Du Pont who had been appointed as French consul in Charleston lamented that "rogues, intriguers, Jacobins, and fools of the republic advanced and triumphed." The conduct of his predecessor was "disagreeable to the Americans and unsuitable to the dignity of France or of its interests."[49] He had even harsher words for Mangourit, a violent man known for his bonnet rouge, his revolutionary declamations and his respect for the supporters of the guillotine. An enthusiast without judgment, a *brouillon*, a revolutionary charlatan, a ranter without reason or measure, a terrorist in diplomacy.[50]

Although revolutionaries often referred to the necessity of removing the "gangrene" of aristocracy from the corps, they continued to grapple with the problem of appointing men loyal to the regime. Diplomats thus found themselves under increased surveillance. The revolutionary regimes tried to ensure revolutionary ardor by scrutinizing credentials for revolutionary sympathies and by imposing a succession of loyalty oaths throughout 1791–1793. Some predictably refused. After the abortive flight to Varennes in the spring of 1791, 50% of the ambassadors and 30% of the ministers resigned.[51] As the king's position became more precarious, still others left the service. Successive crises—the king's abortive flight in the spring of 1791, the outbreak of war in 1792, the Second Revolution of 10 August 1792, the proclamation of the republic in September 1792, and the king's execution in January 1793—saw the severance of relations with revolutionary France by many states and the reduction of French representatives abroad. For example, Emmanuel Marie Louis, marquis de Noailles, who represented Louis XVI in Vienna from 1783 to 1792, demanded that he be recalled. That demand was regarded as treasonous and he was incarcerated during the Terror, only to be saved by Robespierre's death.[52] He was but one of many. By January 1793 the foreign minister Lebrun had few experienced diplomats. A new elite arose, replacing the nobles. Political recommendations from either the assembly or the ministry replaced court favor. Increasingly, revolutionary governments chose younger men to serve; those, as Martin points out, who were "formed under the Revolution" and those who had "made the Revolution."[53]

The evisceration of the diplomatic corps would have been even more critical but for the increasing isolation of France within the European international order. By January 1793, of the 39 who had served the *ancien régime*, only 6 remained in the rank of *chargé* or higher. Those who had survived were from the second *couche* such as Barthélémy. Only one, Jean Frédéric Helflinger, served from 1771 to 1812 because of his ability to tack to the ever-changing political winds, his relatively low rank (chargé and later resident), and his comparatively obscure post, the Valais. Shifting definitions of loyalty, coupled with the rise and fall of various factions from the Reign of Terror to the Thermidoreans to the Directory, accounted for a number of the dismissals, purges throughout the period for still more, and expulsions by host governments the rest. The continuous turnover of diplomatic personnel directly impacted relations with other states. The Committee of Public Safety selected diplomats on the basis of revolutionary credentials and excluded all former nobles. As the formal diplomatic apparatus collapsed, the Committee of Public Safety sent ten agents abroad. Saint Just even asked whether France should maintain relations with neutral powers. We have accepted, he noted, "phantoms instead of realities" as we have opened "the veins of our treasury to insatiable and contemptible powers ... to buy their inertia, their cowardice, their perfidies ... it is time to end these ruinous follies."[54] After 5 September 1793, foreign relations virtually ceased; the French recalled all their representatives except those accredited to other republics. Excluding the Turks, France had relations only with the United States and republics in Italy (Genoa and Venice) and the Swiss lands (Geneva, the Valais, and the Helvetic Corps). France had eviscerated her diplomatic corps just at the time when she was waging war with most of Europe.

The few diplomats left found themselves in a precarious position because of the vicious factionalism. Saint Just in March 1794 asked the committee to at least send "true republicans." He wanted to replace those "imbecile diplomats," specifically those "ex-Brissotins."[55] After the attack on the Girondins, Genet and Otto were dismissed. Genet's fears of forced repatriation were not unfounded; Robespierre had attacked him in the National Convention for using "extraordinary means" to turn the United States against France.[56] Even extensive experience and impressive training in foreign languages and in law did not exempt one from political rancor. In 1779, Louis Guillaume Otto (1753?–1817) came to the United States as secretary to Anne César, chevalier de La Luzerne, the French minister plenipotentiary, and in 1785 was promoted secretary of the embassy. On a number of occasions he served as *chargé*. He returned to France at the end of 1792 and was appointed to the political division in the ministry of foreign affairs. The Girondin crisis led to his arrest on specious charges. After his return to France, Victor Du Pont, who had worked with and respected Otto, went to the ministry to see him. He was told brusquely by the guard that he was under arrest and another served in his place.[57] Among the accusers was Jean Antoine Joseph Fauchet, who would later be appointed as minister to the United States from 1794 to 1795. Fauchet found Otto's previous experience under the *ancien régime* and his social ties with the United States' elite suspicious. In a letter of January 1794 he condemned him as "a man without ability or spirit" whose talents were best suited to "taking coffee and tea." Fauchet admitted that Otto "chatters well enough to give the impression of understanding things, but his principles are absolutely opposed to the revolution."[58] This assessment of his revolutionary principles or lack thereof is independently confirmed by the British diplomat Sir George Jackson, who noted that he dined with Otto and his wife, who were "of the old school for they are exceedingly polite and unlike in manner what I should have expected to find citizens of either of the modern republics."[59] Otto, on his part, had disdained the revolutionary diplomacy, particularly as practiced in the United States. He escaped the guillotine only because of the fall of Robespierre.

Fauchet had also suspected Antoine René Charles Mathurin de la Forest, the consul general who had returned to Philadelphia in 1794, and placed spies inside the consulate. De la Forest was damned by association. Fauchet accused him of royalist sympathies and of fraternizing with *émigrés*, such as Talleyrand. He escaped the terror net only because of his absence from Paris.[60] Another caught up in the dragnet against the so-called Girondins was Félix Desportes (1763–1849), who had served in Zweibrücken from June to December 1792 and was arrested in April 1794. After the Girondin crisis of June 1793 he was suspect because of his ties with Dumouriez and Lebrun, his ostentatious living style, his expulsion from the Jacobins in June 1793, and his missions abroad. He was arrested and accused of negotiating with the prince of Zweibrücken without authorization. Moreover, he had been ill advised enough to have used titles in his correspondence, a practice contrary to revolutionary ideology. He was eventually cleared after Thermidor and, unlike many others, returned to his diplomatic career, serving in Geneva from 1794 to 1795 and again from 1796 to 1798.[61]

After the move against the Dantonists, François-Joseph Michel Noël (1756–1841) was dismissed. Noël, who had been a professor before the Revolution, had had no prior diplomatic experience. Shortly after the August 1792 Revolution he went to London on a short—and unsuccessful—mission. At the beginning of 1793 he went to The Hague as *chargé d'affaires* but again very briefly. In late 1793 the government sent him as minister plenipotentiary to Venice, where he remained until his recall in September 1794. His mission to Venice was also fraught with difficulties; the Senate refused to accept his letters of credence in the new republican form and in Paris he was denounced as a counter-revolutionary and a friend of Danton. His situation deteriorated to the extent that letters from Paris were sent not to him but to his secretary, prompting his resignation on 26 July 1794.[62] When the political sands shifted yet again and the Thermidoreans came into power, they recalled five of the seven representatives abroad. After the Reign of Terror just as the army was purged of its terrorists, so too the diplomatic corps was purged of radicals. The diplomatic corps also paralleled the army in its reinstatements. Just as many of the officers who had lost their positions in the Terror were reinstated, so too in the diplomatic corps. For example, Noël resumed his diplomatic career at The Hague as minister plenipotentiary in 1795. Still accusations of being too radical or too moderate could trigger a recall.

The Directory's *politique du bascule* influenced the diplomatic service just as it did the army. Only a complete commitment to the prevailing orthodoxy gained one an appointment. Cronyism also played a major role as friends or associates of the Directors were appointed. For example, Louis-Marie La Revellière-Lépeaux secured the appointment of a fellow botanist and a Girondin, Louis Augustin Guillaume Bosc (1759–1829), as vice-consul in Wilmington in 1797 and subsequently as consul to New York in 1798, where he did not serve because of the opposition of the United States. Of the 12 posted abroad when the Directors came to power, only 8 remained. The Directors recalled those on both ends of the political spectrum. For example, Louis-Grégoire Le Hoc had served under the *ancien régime* and the new. Arrested during the Terror, he was sent to Sweden by the Thermidoreans, but suspicions lingered and the Directory dismissed him. In year IV (1795–1796) the Directory decided to recall many of those with radical Jacobin leanings who had maintained unusually close relations with local revolutionaries. That group included Dorothée Villars, who had been sent to Genoa as envoy extraordinary and minister plenipotentiary ironically after Thermidor in October 1794. By November 1795 rumors were circulating that he was to be replaced and even arrested. Despite all his efforts and his previous service, he was relieved of his duties on 3 February 1796.[63] He was replaced by Guillaume-Charles Faipoult de Maisoncelle, an intelligent, honest man, a sincere republican, and an ex-noble who had been banished by the decree of 26 germinal, year II (16 April 1794). He was a *protégé* of Carnot with whom he attended engineering school but that connection meant his recall after fructidor 1797.

Like the army, the diplomatic service saw royalists ousted and Jacobins reinstated after fructidor 1797, a coup directed against the right. Eight diplomats were recalled. Friendships with men now discredited, accusations of moderation, aristocratic birth, relations who were *émigrés*, service in the *ancien régime*, general distrust or a lethal combination of the above led to dismissal. Now the criterion was a "dogmatic and proselytizing spirit."[64] The next revolutionary gale of 22 floréal (11 May 1798), this one against the left, led to a purge of radicals, including two diplomats who had gained their posts after fructidor. The coup of 30 prairial (18 June 1799) was a purge of the right and of two of the Directors, including La Revellière-Lépeaux. The most notable casualty in the diplomatic corps was Henri Maes de Perrochel (1750–1810). During the Revolution he had served as a volunteer in the army before his promotion to captain in 1793. Badly wounded at Martigny, he left the army. One of the Directors, La Revellière-Lépeaux, who knew him, had him appointed first secretary to Truguet at Madrid, where he also served briefly as *chargé* before being appointed minister plenipotentiary to Lucerne (1798–1799). After his dismissal, like his protector, he went into political retreat, never serving again.[65]

Given the virulence of revolutionary politics, diplomats, even more than other revolutionary officials, were not free from scrutiny. Brissot voiced the sentiments of many revolutionaries when he contended that "a free people can only conduct its affairs well … by agents exposed unceasingly to its attention."[66] He realized that that kind of scrutiny was impossible, but that did not mean that he and others did not try. Secret agents and not-so-secret commissioners were sent to ensure that its representatives behaved in ways befitting a republic.[67] The representatives found themselves walking the revolutionary tightrope and continually under pressure to prove their ideological credentials. The presence of numerous secret agents in London at a time of increasing tension could not have made Chauvelin's posting (1792–1793) easier and he had made it difficult enough. It certainly reinforced his tendency to employ a decidedly revolutionary rhetoric.[68] In Solothurn, Barthélémy (1792–1797) found himself under scrutiny from

Claude François de Payan, a secret agent and friend of Robespierre's.[69] In the midst of the Terror, in December 1793, Deforgues, the Minister of Foreign Affairs, wrote a letter to Barthélemy in which he described Payan as an "enlightened patriot," "inflamed" with "the most pure patriotism." He assured Barthélemy that he had the confidence of the Committee of Public Safety. Nonetheless, the problem with those sent abroad, he contended, was that "The progress of reason ... escapes them.... Surprised by events, they are in danger of judging them badly." Deforgues went on to explain that diplomats might have only "a vague and indeterminate attachment" to France, rather than an elevated "elan of republican virtues." Agents of the republic, he explained, must be not only honest but also "zealous" and the most "partisan of patriots." Those considerations led him to send "enlightened patriots, who ... carry with them the thermometer of the public spirit." Barthélemy could hardly have been reassured by these words.[70] The *ancien régime* had served as training ground for men like Barthélemy who came from the second *couche*. Barthélemy remembered his life in Vienna as legation secretary with "tenderness" and his interactions with Thugut with respect.[71] That training lingered on. Marzio Mastrilli, marchese di Gallo, the Sicilian representative to the Emperor, confided to Thugut that Barthélemy was "infinitely polite and obliging." If Europe only had to negotiate with such men whose politics were "wise and moderate," it would be "tranquil and secure for a long time." Barthélemy's success at concluding the Peace of Basel in 1795 was partly because he appealed to their interests and because he avoided confrontational rhetoric.[72] Still that background and his views made him suspect.

In addition to pressure from commissioners sent from Paris, Barthélemy was undermined by Jean Louis Giraud Soulavie (1751–1813), the resident at Geneva. Barthélemy alleged that Soulavie, a former priest, consorted with shady characters, acted in a disgraceful fashion, uttered gibberish and, in short, dishonored the republic. Barthélemy's accusations were seconded by the secretary of the Genevan embassy, Delhorme, and by the representative of Geneva's government, Étienne Salomon Reybaz. Soulavie's arrest was decreed in December 1793 with the support of Hébert, but it was never carried out because of Barère's intervention. After Thermidor, Soulavie was arrested in Geneva on the grounds that he was a supporter of Robespierre and interned until the amnesty of 1796. He was luckier than most; he escaped both the guillotine and later, after 18 brumaire, deportation.[73] Barthélemy faced another struggle in 1796 with the *chargé* at Basel, Pierre Claude, marquis de Poterat. Poterat had let it be known in Paris that he did not approve of either the principles or the conduct of Barthélemy and that were he there he would conduct affairs in a very different manner. This news only confirmed the assessment of the emperor's minister to Switzerland (1794–1797), Sigmund Ignaz Freiherr von Degelmann, that Poterat was "very presumptuous and even less discreet."[74] There was also dissension inside the mission. In Switzerland Barthélemy was forced to request authorization to hire two German-speaking aides in order to stop his first secretary, Bacher, from "re-wording some of their outgoing correspondence." Reubell's refusal signaled a decided setback for Barthélemy.[75] Despite these machinations, Barthélemy retained his position until 1797.

These pressures extended to consular officials. Victor Du Pont in Charleston believed that Bosc, the botanist and Girondin, had been sent to spy on him. He thought Bosc intended to intrigue against him, that he was "in league with the sans-culottes creatures of his infamous predecessor" and that Bosc hoped to replace him. Du Pont decided to befriend him and to be open and confident.[76]

The Revolution had its costs. The Directory continued to question the commitment of those diplomats who had served the *ancien régime* or those associated with a traitorous faction. That definition constantly changed. Even the *politesse* of François Barthélemy was in question. He was, one complained, "too smooth tongued, too humble." He went beyond "what is required in a republic."[77] His "coldness" did not go unremarked. "He speaks little," Paul-François Jean-Nicolas Barras wrote. "He is extremely formal. Diplomats are accustomed to believe that their silences, their reticences, their civilities are marks of genius. If that is correct, Barthélemy has all the characteristics of genius." This sarcastic critique was so devastating because it hinged on Barthélemy's language. His words discredited him, for they revealed that he was *du très ancien régime*.[78] Barthélemy, who had served in Sweden, Great Britain, and Switzerland, was subsequently condemned to deportation after the coup of fructidor.[79] The mere mention of a profession so associated with the *ancien régime* as diplomacy tarred Barthélemy and others as well with the taint of treason, for its purported virtues—reticence, formality, and deviousness—could only compare unfavorably with the frankness and openness of the ideal revolutionary.[80] The challenges Barthélemy faced illustrate how revolutionary ideology fostered a climate of mutual recriminations and denunciations.

That atmosphere poisoned other missions as seen in the enmity between the Jacobin Dorothée Villars at Genoa and the moderate François Cacault in Rome. In 1795 Villars was undermined by rumors of his recall and even of his arrest.[81] Ironically, Villars was recalled in 1796 because of his extremism and Cacault in 1797 because of his moderation. In Madrid, Dominique-Catherine de Perignon was undermined by the secretary of the embassy, Michel-Ange-Bernard Mangourit, an ardent revolutionary who condemned Perignon as "polite," a damning indictment during an era when politeness was equated with aristocracy. In the contest between the two, Perignon ultimately prevailed and Mangourit was recalled and dispatched first to Philadelphia and later to the court of Naples, which refused to receive him.[82]

This poisonous atmosphere extended even to the remote United States. In Charleston, where Victor Marie Du Pont served as consul, rumors spread that the legation was to be replaced with Jacobins.[83] Philippe-André-Joseph de Letombe, the French consul general and later minister plenipotentiary to the United States, assured Du Pont that "your letters marked 'tibi soli' were burned as soon as read."[84] Letombe also marked a number of his own letters "for you only." Letombe did not hesitate to caution Du Pont that it was "essential that you act like a diplomat, that is to say, with the greatest secrecy."[85] Charles François Bournonville, the secretary of Genet, confided to Du Pont that a consul who had conciliated the pretensions of a party and the prejudices of another could find himself in the position of Jean Baptiste Thomas Dannery (1744–1806), French consul in Boston, who said that it would be necessary to kill his father in order to be consul. He concluded these sober observations with the thought that "some days of dissipation were necessary from time to time to reanimate our courage in a career of public affairs."[86] In this atmosphere Pierre Auguste Adet, French representative to the United States, shared his happiness to be returning home; he could happily say "adieu to all diplomatic titles" and would be content if he could forget every day he held them.[87] Adet later noted that he did not know how to engage in intrigues and "only intriguers win."[88] Many shared this disenchantment. Letombe did not like "that one governs without principles."[89]

The Committee of Public Safety and the Directory often sent more than one agent to a given post in order to report on the other. The situation at the French legation in Constantinople, a house divided against itself, was not uncommon. Louis Marie Descorches, marquis de Sainte-Croix, had been one of the few nobles who had been exempted from the general interdiction of nobles filling public offices. He had served previously in Liège (1782–1791) and Poland (1792), from which he was expelled. As late as 1 frimaire, an II (21 November 1793), the Minister of Foreign Affairs praised his "patriotic reputation" and his "ardent love of liberty." His adherence to revolutionary principles did not save him from the accusation of treason. Rumors about his wife, who allegedly was sheltering the wife and sister of an *émigré*, led officials in Paris to place guards around the home. Those rumors coupled with his aristocratic background had already undermined his position. Descorches, who arrived in Constantinople on 7 June 1793, found himself betrayed by the *chargé*, Étienne Félix Hénin de Cuvillier.[90] Oddly enough Hénin was sent to Constantinople to take charge pending the arrival of the official envoy.[91] The men, both ex-nobles, disliked each other on sight. "Descorches was dumbfounded to discover that not only did Hénin's orders differ from his own, but that a third plenipotentiary was en route, reportedly carrying a new set of instructions." The third man, Sémonville, was arrested by the Austrians at Novale and imprisoned for 30 months.[92] Hénin, who had been sent to report on Descorches, soon began to plot against him. In his complaint to the Committee of Public Safety, Hénin begins his tirade with a defense of his own revolutionary conduct as that of "a republican." The implication was obvious. He then attacked Descorches as weak and claimed that "the least difficulties for him are insurmountable obstacles." Hénin accused him of being anti-republican: he had not immediately destroyed remnants of the *ancien régime* in the ambassadorial residence, such as the *fleur de lys* and portraits of the king and various aristocrats. In addition, Descorches had refused to live in the ambassadorial place, had not worn the cockade, had not visited the tree of liberty, and had been seen in the company of "enemies of France," aristocrats and merchants known for their royalism. And most damning, Descorches kept the "forms of the *ancien régime*."[93] Hénin undermined Descorches not only with the French government but also with the local French community.[94] The complaints against Descorches ranged from his being "an insolent aristocrat" to "an extravagant revolutionary." He was, according to other allegations, too modest, too obscure, and did not have sufficient "*éclat*" for a representative of the French republic.[95] Hénin scattered his charges widely. He also attacked the secretary, Gaudin, on the general charge of aristocratic sympathies, of consorting with *émigrés* and of not "being very well instructed" in the rights of man. The retired dragoman, Antoine Fonton, the previous *chargé*, he thought, was a "false patriot," who was suspect because of his hostility to the Jacobins and support for the *émigrés*. Fonton had supported Choiseul-Gouffier, who had opposed the Revolution. Hénin even leveled charges against the courier Duclos, who was accused of aristocratic and royalist sentiments.[96] To further compound this imbroglio, Descorches was authorized to act against Hénin.

The Committee of Public Safety dispatched three commissioners, but only two actually left and arrived in March 1794.[97] Their mission was to check on Descorches' activities and replace him, if necessary.[98] Their distrust meant that Descorches received few orders (he received only one dispatch from Paris from June 1793 to January 1794)[99] and never did conclude an alliance with the Turks. Saint Just condemned the main protagonists of this drama, Hénin and Descorches, as "scoundrels" and ex-nobles. The guillotine "alone," he argued, "ought to worthily recompense their services." He found both "craven rogues," who had engaged in "scandalous disputes."[100] Oddly enough, Descorches was abruptly recalled in 1795 on the allegation that he was a Robespierrist. Descorches, whom Hénin damned as a royalist, seems to have been guilty of being simultaneously insufficiently revolutionary and too revolutionary. Certainly the internal politics of the embassy had played an important role in Descorches' recall. Hénin, "a relentless enemy" of Descorches, was caught up in the Thermidorean dragnet and also recalled.[101] That post seemed particularly doomed. Under the Directory Carnot urged the recall of Descorches' successor, Raymond Verninac de Sainte-Maure (April 1795 to October 1796), lumping him with those "who had dishonored the French nation by the immorality of their character and the perversity of their conduct." Was Verninac, he asked, an "honorable choice for the premier nation of the universe?" Verninac, he alleged, was a dried-up intriguer, who had been seen dining with aristocrats.[102] These incidents provide just a glimpse of the venomous atmosphere. Moreover, the precariousness of their tenure can hardly have encouraged states to negotiate with men who were likely to be disavowed.

Nor was there only official scrutiny. The conduct of French representatives often incurred the wrath of the French abroad: sailors, merchants, and travelers.[103] Faced with the possibility of denunciation, not a few resorted to very public displays of revolutionary zeal, which smacked of propaganda rather than diplomacy. Hardouin, comte de Châlon, French ambassador in Portugal from 1789 to 1792, who had previously served in Venice and Cologne, was accused of failing to intervene when the Portuguese government had forbidden two French soldiers from wearing cockades and national uniforms. At least one person rallied to his defense, citing his habit of living simply and respectably surrounded by his family.[104] Another citizen denounced the chemist Pierre Auguste Adet, the envoy in Geneva in 1794, for spreading malicious falsehoods.[105] Adet faced other difficulties on his next post as he tried to avoid the wrath of various revolutionaries and to propitiate the local population. As French minister plenipotentiary to the United States 1795–1797, he had not hesitated to take the oath to respect the constitution,[106] but nonetheless still decided not to authorize the celebration of August 10 in order to avoid ridicule.[107] He found that he could please neither those he dubbed aristocrats nor the Jacobins. Often those who leveled complaints were disgruntled opportunists. In letters to the diplomatic committee of November 1791 Abbé Louis-Alexandre Expilly de la Poipe, the first constitutional bishop of France and not incidentally a member of the commission of twelve, charged with ferreting out traitors, stressed that at Genoa, where the government was theocratic/aristocratic, the representative must be superior to the priests. The post, he opined, required someone who was courageous, wise, and educated and not someone like the former representative who was "an imbecile." Echoing the complaints from a member of the National Assembly that the minister lacked civism, Expilly volunteered his services and requested a southern posting.[108]

Still others, perhaps less self-interested or better able to hide it, leveled charges about incompetence, malfeasance, or the failure to enforce revolutionary legislation, such as the law about issuing passports, in particular to *émigrés*.[109] The vice-consul at Charleston Antoine, Louis Fonspertius,[110] fell under the scrutiny of the Committee of Public Safety when he was accused of negligence, misconduct, embezzlement, and general ineptitude. Fonspertius had been the consul in the Canary Islands, but was expelled by the Spanish government and sent to Charleston to replace Mangourit.[111] The only-too-common complaints echoed by the French that Fonspertius dabbled in politics, was not restrained, and did not fulfill his duties resonated with many. Du Pont wrote his family that not only was Fonspertius incompetent but that his conduct was "scandalous"; he passed his days in bed and his nights gambling.[112] Adet concurred and complained that it was "dangerous" to leave him in his position because he "compromises … the interests and dignity of the French republic."[113] Letombe, the French consul at Philadelphia, referred to Fonspertius "of unfortunate memory" and noted that Victor Du Pont would find his task at Charleston akin to cleaning "the Augean stables." Mixing his ancient metaphors, he noted that the consulate there was "a labyrinth."[114] The report on Fonspertius' conduct was enlivened by tales of his alleged immorality: he stayed out until 3 am and then slept until noon, dressed ridiculously (in a short vest with two epaulettes and a large sabre), revealed secret affairs, and in general made "inexcusable errors." The authors of this accusation were not sure whether he was inept or ill-intentioned. But it was clear, or so they thought, that he had lost all influence. At least one praised his good heart and his patriotism, but noted his inability to keep accounts. At least one correspondent blamed his youth and his ignorance of men and affairs, his isolation, and his boredom. The official report concluded that a hardworking, active, capable, and honest functionary should be appointed in his stead.[115] Fonspertius' obvious unsuitability illustrates how very difficult it proved to find "pure" and "prudent" patriots, especially as the definition constantly shifted.[116]

Once found, those sent abroad faced certain difficulties unique to the Revolution. Miot de Melito at Turin noted that he assumed his post at a time of great difficulty when he could not know the real intentions of the Directory, divided, as it was into two factions, nor guess which of those factions would triumph. He decided to respect treaties and to refuse "all countenance to agitators, whatever the mask of patriotism they might assume."[117] Barthélemy recalled "the utter confusion of trying to learn what precisely had been discussed in any set of negotiations, because no one in the executive branch of government kept any systematic record."[118] As Napoleon's position strengthened, diplomats faced other challenges, for Napoleon was hardly one to mute his criticism. He condemned Lallement's behavior in Venice as either puny or felonious.[119] Periodic purges of the ministry worsened an already difficult situation. The turnover in personnel and the decision to appoint often inexperienced cronies worsened the difficulties inherent in a premodern diplomatic service, including communication.

Those stationed across the Atlantic found the situation even more challenging. In the United States, Ternant received no dispatches in eight months, Genet none in nine, and Fauchet none in a year. Fauchet justifiably complained about never receiving dispatches, letters, gazettes, or bulletins of decrees. "Never were agents in a more embarrassing position than ours." In contrast, he claimed the enemies' agents were regularly informed.[120] He juxtaposed the uncertainties and the negligence of the French with the activity and constancy of London. Moreover, the "versatile system by our cabinet under the republican regime" put the French representatives in an impossible position. His instructions were "absurd and perfidious." He continued to ask for new instructions, but suspected that his letters were never even read.[121] Upon his arrival back in France, he visited all the bureaus but could not accomplish anything despite precious time wasted in the antechamber, time better spent in study, he bemoaned. And then he underscores:

"Si l'on veut me entendre!"[122] Fauchet echoed what surely must have been a perennial grievance. Unfortunately his situation was not unique.

Diplomats, too often cut off from their governments, also faced hostility from an *émigré* community only too eager to undermine them. Such was the case with Genet in Russia, where Bombelles represented the king and Esterhazy the *émigrés*. Many French *émigrés* flocked to friendly courts where they served as functionaries.[123] At Coblentz, the French representative, Bigot de Sainte Croix, insisted on having loaded pistols to hand before admitting anyone. When he finally left, he did so secretly after taking the precaution of drafting a dispatch to be read the next day and ordering his servants to stay an additional 24 hours.[124] It was certainly a short mission; he presented his credentials on 30 December 1791 and left on 27 February 1792. At Madrid French representatives found themselves obstructed by a large *émigré* community. In 1796 Perignon complained that "[m]y open course is obstructed at each step by the hissing of these vipers."[125] Nor were these fears always unfounded. At Zante in Dalmatia, the house of the French consul was set on fire.[126]

French representatives also had to deal with the suspicions and hostility of British representatives. These problems began even before war broke out between the two. William Eden, Baron Auckland, who was stationed at The Hague from 1790 to 1793, sent frequent reports on a "very evil" person, Emmanuel de Maulde Hosdan, the French representative (May 1792 to January 1793). He found Maulde "guarded and plausible in society, but so incessantly and so malignantly occupied in conferences and correspondence with malcontents, libellers, and printers, whenever we lost sight of him, that it becomes necessary to make this place disagreeable to him." He even thought about denying him admission to his house when receptions were held.[127] Although Maulde became more "circumspect" and took pains to deny any intrigues despite evidence to the contrary, he was soon excluded from society.[128] The British view was reinforced by the Dutch. One Dutchman contended that Maulde was not very well known. His society was not sought because it was suspected that he saw only malcontents and spent all his time at an inn where perhaps he goes "to preach equality."[129] According to British intelligence, although Maulde's manners were "not unpleasant," he continued to be "indecently active" in cabals with disaffected individuals.[130] The British found him "a dangerous fellow, notwithstanding his ridiculous *patenlinage* (wheedling) and indiscretion."[131] That judgment was confirmed when Maulde's letters were intercepted, opened, and carefully resealed.

Tensions worsened when the two powers were at war. For example, Sir Richard Worsley in Venice tried to prevent the French representative Jean Baptiste Lallement from being received, and when that failed, he retired to the country rather than be present at his public entry.[132] Grenville instructed Worsley not only to "keep a watchful eye over the Proceedings of the French Minister," but also to "exert yourself to defeat every attempt" the latter made to circumvent the Venetian republic's "mask of its neutrality."[133] Worsley found the French minister "as violent a man and as warm a Republican as can be."[134] Despite Worsley's best efforts, Lallement encouraged conspiracies against the Venetian Republic.[135] In another case, Arthur Paget, envoy extraordinary 1798–1799 in Munich, thought that Alquier and the French mission in general are "doing as much mischief as possible,"[136] even inciting revolution. The Bavarians were watching him closely but, despite Paget's hopes, could bring no direct charge against him.[137] Munich, Paget reported, "swarms with Jacobins and Persons whom I am convinced are paid by the Directory." Paget was disturbed that "the government seems perfectly blind to this [threat] and [that] agents left and directed by Alquier perform this work unmolested."[138] Paget certainly thought that "the reigning evil has made much progress here." Some who had been banished as conspirators had returned and "breathe forth uncontrolled their fatal doctrines."[139] Whether efficacious or not, British representatives not only reported such activities but, as Paget vaunted, "continue to do as much mischief to their cause as lays in my power—my enemies are therefore without number."[140] It was certainly true that both sides attempted to intercept the other's correspondence. Adet, the French representative to the United States, alleged that the English attempted to seize both Joseph Fauchet, who was stationed in the United States from 1794 to 1795, and his papers while he was in American waters.[141] The British regularly intercepted the correspondence of both the French and neutral Americans.[142] Phineas Bond, the British consul general (1792–1812) and *chargé* (1795–1796) in the United States, corresponded with the British in Montreal who reported on Adet's attempts to disseminate French doctrines. In one case, Captain Alexander John Ball of the *Argonaut* noted that he intercepted bread casks stuffed with cockades.[143] In part because of such activities or even the suspicion of such, French diplomats abroad often found themselves in a precarious position in a hostile Europe. Those suspicions were only reinforced by the revolutionaries' attempt to change the rules under which diplomacy had been conducted.

Notes

1. Camille Desmoulins, *Révolutions de France and et Brabant*, no. 6 (1790): 275. This issue was an attack on Choiseul-Gouffier and Montmorin. Quoted in Kaiser, "From Fiscal Crisis to Revolution," in *From Deficit to Deluge*, ed. Kaiser and Van Kley, 162.
2. Sorel, *Europe and the French Revolution*, 18 quotes Cardinal Guillaume Dubois (1656–1723).
3. Louis Marie Prudhomme, *Révolutions de Paris*, no. 92, 16 April 1791.
4. Jean de la Bruyère, *The Characters* (New York: Brentano's, 1929), 254–258.
5. For Thomas Paine "the diplomatic character is of itself the narrowest sphere of society that man can act in. It forbids intercourse by a reciprocity of suspicion; and a Diplomatic is a sort of unconnected atom, continually repelling and being repelled." Thomas Paine, *The Rights of Man* in *Collected Writings* (New York: Library of America, 1955), 491–492.
6. Gilbert, *The 'New Diplomacy' of the Eighteenth Century*, 36.
7. Brissot de Warville, *Le Patriote François*, no. 600, 31 mars 1791.
8. Louis H. Kientz, *J. H. Campe et la Révolution française avec des lettres et documents inédits* (Paris: H. Didier, 1939), 34.
9. Quoted in Masson, *Le Département des affaires étrangères pendant la Révolution*, 153–154.
10. Jefferson did not expect that the United States would be driven "into completion of the a-diplomatic system." Jefferson to William Short, 23 January 1804, in *American Historical Review* 33 (July 1928): 833.
11. Gilbert, *The New Diplomacy of the Eighteenth Century*, 10.
12. James der Derian, *On Diplomacy: A Genealogy of Western Estrangement* (Oxford: Basil Blackwell, 1987), 165.
13. Ibid., 179.
14. *Moniteur* 12 (4 avril 1792): 33.
15. Aulard, ed., *Recueil des actes du comité de salut public* 4: 485–486, 8 June 1793. Intellectuals, such as Simon-Nicholas-Henri Linguet (1731–1794), who was later guillotined for his defense of the king, mused that if princes negotiated directly rather than relying on their agents, it would result in a "*une politique toute nouvelle.*" Linguet quoted in Bély, *L'Art de la paix en Europe*, 647. That strategy had of course been tried earlier and rejected partly because so many had died in the attempt.
16. Ferdinand Brunot, *Histoire de la langue française des origins à 1900*, 14 vols. (Paris: Armand Colin, 1905–1927, 9: part 2: 919.
17. Jacques-Pierre Brissot de Warville, *J.P. Brissot, Deputy of Eure and Loire to his Constituents* (London: John Stockdale, 1794), 83.
18. Aulard, *La Société des Jacobins*, 3: 622.

19. Masson, *Le Département des affaires étrangères pendant la Révolution*, 297.
20. Charles François Dumouriez, *Mémoire sur le ministère des affaires étrangères* (Paris: Imprimerie nationale, 1791), 5.
21. Jacques-Pierre Brissot, *Discours de J.P. Brissot, député sur les dispositions des puissances étrangères* (Paris: Imprimerie nationale, 1791?), 43–44.
22. Blaga, *L'Évolution de la diplomatie*.
23. Virginie Martin, "Le Comité diplomatique: homicide par décret de la diplomatie (1790–1793)?" *La Révolution française: Cahiers de l'Institut d'histoire de la Révolution française* 3 (2012): 1–33. See also Hamish Scott, "A Model of Conduct from the Age of Chivalry? Honour, International Decline and the End of the Bourbon Monarchy," in *The Crisis of the Absolute Monarchy*, ed. Swann and Félix, 201.
24. Géraud Poumarède, "Le Bouleversement des relations internationales pendant la Révolution française," in *Le Bouleversement de l'ordre du monde, Révoltes et révolutions en Europe et aux Amériques à la fin du 18e siècle*, ed. Jean Pierre Poussou et al. (Paris: Sedes, 2004), 410–412. For Professor Koch, a most distinguished jurist, see Jürgen Voss, "Christophe Guillaume Koch (1737–1813): Homme politique et historiographe contemporain de la Révolution, " *History of European Ideas* 13, no. 5 (1991): 531–532; Jean Richerateau, *Le Rôle politique du Professor Koch* (Strasbourg: Imprimerie Alsacienne, 1936) and Michaud, *Biographie universelle*, 22: 84–86.
25. *Archives parlementaires*, 66: 4, 3 June 1793.
26. Aulard, ed. *Recueil des actes du Comité de salut public*, 1: 1.
27. G. J. A. Ducher, *Douanes nationales et affaires étrangères* (Paris: Imprimerie nationale, n.d.), esp. 2–3.
28. Armand-Marc, comte de Montmorin, *Observations sur le chapitre VIII d'un imprimé ayant pour titre Livre Rouge* (Paris: Baudouin, 1790).
29. Masson, *Le Département des affaires étrangères pendant la Révolution*, 101.
30. C.-Alexandre Geoffrey de Grandmaison, *L'Ambassade française en Espagne pendant la Révolution (1789–1804)* (Paris: Plon, 1892), 67. Also see Virginie Martin, "La Révolution française ou'l'ère du soupçon 'Diplomatie et dénociation." *Hypothèse* 12 (2009): 131–140.
31. France, *Recueil*, 18: *Diète germanique*, 377–378, instructions to Marbois of 1 January 1792.
32. Ibid., 380.
33. Ibid., 378.
34. Ibid., 380. Burke, for example, thought—and he was not alone—that "a general spirit of treachery governed these ministers who intended the subversion of monarchies." See Centre for Kentish Studies, U269 Sackville Manuscripts, Mss C 186, Edmund Burke to Dorset, 11 September 1791.
35. France, *Recueil*, 18: *Diète germanique*, 378.

36. Ibid., 380.
37. Ibid., 378.
38. *Révolutions de France et de Brabant* 6 (1790): 275.
39. William Doyle, *Aristocracy and Its Enemies in the Age of Revolution* (Oxford: University Press, 2009), especially Chaps. 6 and 7.
40. Marc Belissa, "La Diplomatie et les traités dans la pensée des lumières," 297 and 302.
41. Brissot, *Discours sur la denonciation contre le comité autrichien et contre M. Montmorin*, 21.
42. *Le Comité de Salut public de la Convention nationale à la société populaire de la section de des droits de l'homme* (Paris, 23 brumaire, an II), 2.
43. Custine, *Le Général Custine au president de la Convention Nationale*, 7.
44. Louis de Saint-Just, *Oeuvres complètes* ed. Charles Vellay (Paris: Librarire Charpentier et Fasquelle, 1908) 2: 372, 26 germinal II.
45. Black, *British Foreign Policy in an Age of Revolution, 1783–1793*, 48.
46. Clive H. Church, *Revolution and Red Tape: The French Ministerial Bureaucracy, 1770–1850* (Oxford: Clarendon Press, 1981), 84.
47. Ibid.
48. Victor Du Pont complained that he found himself working next to a young man who had never worked in foreign affairs but who made considerably more than he did. Hagley, W3-238, 26 December 1794.
49. Hagley, W3-265, Victor Du Pont to his father, 1 thermidor, n.y. [19 July 1795].
50. Hagley, W3-202, Victor Du Pont to his father, Charleston, 10 brumaire, v [31 October 1796].
51. The data for these figures comes from Linda Frey and Marsha Frey, *"Proven Patriots": The French Diplomatic Corps, 1789–1799* (St. Andrews, Scotland: St. Andrew Studies in French History and Culture, 2011). Also available on line: http://research-repository.st-andrews.ac.uk/handle/10023/1881.
52. Sorel, *L'Europe et la Révolution française*, 2: 428–429.
53. Virginie Martin, "Devenir diplomate en Révolution: Naissance de la 'carrière diplomatique,'"*Revue d'histoire moderne et contemporaine* 63, no. 3 (2016): 110–135.
54. He scathingly attacked "neutral powers, inept ministers, scandalous expenses, ridiculous negotiations, deceptive promises, exhausted treasuries." Saint-Just, *Oeuvres complètes*, 2: 331–332.
55. Ibid., 2: 334–350.
56. A. A. E., C.P., États Unis, vol. 39 part v. The French consul in New York Alexandre Maurice Blanc de Lanautte, comte d' Hauterive, confided that if he were not given sanctuary in the United States, he would go live with the savages, rather than return to a sure death under the Terror. Frances S. Childs, "The Hauterive Journal," *The New York Historical Society Quarterly*, 33 (April 1949): 86, n. 32.

THE ENEMY WITHIN: THE ATTACK ON DIPLOMATS   87

57. Hagley, W3-240, Victor Du Pont to his wife, n.d.
58. Peter P. Hill, *French Perceptions of the Early American Republic, 1783–1793* (Philadelphia: American Philosophical Society, 1988), 11.
59. Sir George Jackson, *Diaries and Letters of Sir George Jackson*, K. C. H., ed. Lady Catherine Hannah Charlotte Jackson (London: Richard Bentley and Son, 1872), 1: 9, letter of 31 October 1801.
60. Hill, *French Perceptions of the Early American Republic, 1783–1793*, 8.
61. Édouard Chapuisat, *De la Terreur de l'annexation: Génève et la République française, 1793–1798* (Geneva: Edition ATAR, 1912), 93–94.
62. France, *Recueil*, 26: *Venise*, 316–317.
63. B. L., Add. Mss. 46832, fol. 326, 18 February 1796; fol. 328 20 February 1796; fol. 330, March 1796. Also see B. L., Add. Mss. 46830, fol. 161 Genoa, 9 November 1795; fol. 170, 24 November 1795.
64. André F. Miot de Melito, *Memoirs of Miot de Melito, Minister, Ambassador, Councillor of State*, ed. Wilhelm August Fleischmann (New York: Charles Scribner's Sons, 1881), 117.
65. Michaud, 32: 540–541; Otto Friedrich Winter, *Repertorium der diplomatischen Vertreter aller Länder seit des Westfälischen Frieden* (Graz: Verlag Herman Böhlaus, 1965), 3: 136, 137, 140.
66. Brissot, *Discours de J. P. Brissot député de Paris sur la nécessité d'exiger une satisfation de l'Empereur*, 8–9.
67. Guyot, *Le Directoire et la paix de l'Europe*, 87.
68. J. T. Murley, *The Origins and Outbreak of the Anglo-French War of 1793*, unpublished dissertation (Oxford, 1959), 82; Jeremy Black "From Pillnitz to Valmy: British Foreign Policy and Revolutionary France 1791–1792," *Francia: Forschungen zur westeuropäischen Geschichte* 21 (1994): 141.
69. Robespierre's support had garnered Payan the appointment to the committee of correspondence of the Committee of Public Safety in August 1793 and in September appointment to the Revolutionary Tribunal. He would die in Thermidor.
70. François Barthélemy, *Papiers du Barthélemy*, edited by Jean Kaulek, 4 vols. (Paris: F. Alcan, 1886–1910), 3: 263–4, Deforgues to Barthélemy, Dec 1793; Chapuisat, *De la Terreur de l'annexation*, 22. David A. Silverman, "Informal Diplomacy: The Foreign Policy of the Robespierrist Committee of Public Safety," University of Washington, Ph.D., unpublished dissertation, 1973, 148–149.
71. Hermann Hüffer, ed. *Quellen zur Geschichte des Zeitalters der französischen Revolution. Teil 2: Quellen zur Geschichte der diplomatischen Verhandlungen Erster Band: Der Frieden von Campoformio* (Innsbruck: Verlage der Wagner'schen Universitäts-Buchhandlungen, 1907), 52, Gallo to Thugut, Laufenbourg, 15 June 1796.
72. Blaga, *L'Évolution de la diplomatie*, 454.

73. Édouard Chapuisat, *La Suisse et la Révolution française: Épisodes* (Geneva: Edition du Mont-Blanc, 1945), 56–57; Marc Peter, *Genève et la Révolution* (Geneva: Alex Julien, 1950), 2: 29; Michaud, 39: 675–676.
74. Hüffer, ed. *Quellen zur Geschichte des Zeitalters der französischen Revolution*, part 2: vol. 1: 39, Degelmann to Thugut, Basel, 15 April 1796.
75. Thomas M. Iiams, *Peacemaking from Vergennes to Napoleon* (Huntington, New York: Robert E. Krieger, 1979), 104.
76. Hagley, W3-313, 19 nivôse V [7 January 1797], Victor Du Pont to family and W3-315, extract of letter to his colleagues [7 January 1797]. The revolution, he thought, was "not yet finished because France is still subject to an arbitrary and revolutionary government." Hagley, W3-320, Victor Du Pont to the family, 15 ventôse, V [3 March 1797].
77. Jean-Paul-Francois-Nicolas, vicomte de Barras, *Memoirs of the Directorate* (New York: Harper and Bros., 1895), 2: 497.
78. Adrien Fleury Dry, *Soldats ambassadeurs sous le Directoire, an IV-an VIII* (Paris: Plon, 1906), 1: 43.
79. Guyot, *Le Directoire*, 76–77.
80. After brumaire he returned to France and was chosen for the Senate. Louis XVIII made him a marquis in 1818.
81. B. L., Add. Mss. 46830, fol. 161, Drake Papers, 9 Octobre 1795.
82. Grandmaison, *L'Ambassade française*, 115–125.
83. Hagley, W3-288, Victor Du Pont to his family, 10 June 1796.
84. Hagley, W3-1360, Letombe to Victor Du Pont, 23 ventôse, VI [13 March 1798].
85. Hagley, W3-1359, Letombe to Victor Du Pont, Philadelphia, 23 ventôse VI [13 March 1798].
86. Hagley, W3-1259, Bournonville to Victor Du Pont, 12 floréal, V [1 May 1797].
87. Hagley, W3-1262, Adet to Victor Du Pont, Philadelphia, 15 floréal, V [4 May 1797].
88. Hagley, W3-1323, Adet to Victor Du Pont, 9 brumaire, VI [30 October 1797].
89. Hagley, W3-1296, Letombe to Victor Du Pont [22 August 1797].
90. Hénin had served in 1785 as secretary of legation at Triers, in 1786 as secretary of embassy at Venice, from 1788 to 1793 as chargé at Venice, and from 1793 to 1795 as chargé at Constantinople.
91. Iiams, *Peacemaking from Vergennes to Napoleon*, 128.
92. Ibid., 129.
93. Étienne-Félix Hénin de Cuvilliers, *Sommaire de correpondance d'Étienne-Félix Hénin, chargé d'affaires de la République française à Constantinople pendant la 1re 2e et 3e années de la République* (Paris: Imprimérie du dépôt des lois, an IV), 3, 12–13, 24–25, 33, 55, 68, 160.

94. Alphone Aulard, *Études et leçons sur la Révolution française*, (Paris: Félix Alcan, 1902), 240; Sorel, *L'Europe and la Révolution française*, 4: 66. At least one of those men urged the Committee of Public Safety to name a patriotic and Montagnard negotiator and to put Descorches under surveillance. Édouard de Marcère, *Une Ambassade à Constantinople: La Politique orientale de la Révolution française* (Paris: Félix Alcan, 1927), 1: 309–348.
95. Ibid., 1: 303–305.
96. Ibid., 2: 109–154.
97. They sent Jean Marie Claude Alexandre Goujon, a member of the Mountain (1766–1795), who never went, and two other commissioners, Charles François Dubois-Thainville and Fourcade.
98. Silverman, "Informal Diplomacy," 148–149.
99. Iiams, *Peacemaking from Vergennes to Napoleon*, 129.
100. Marcère, *Une Ambassade à Constantinople*, 2: 156–263.
101. Ibid., 1: 348.
102. Ibid., 2: 155–156.
103. Martin, "La Révolution française ou'l'ère du soupçon 'Diplomatie et dénociation,'" *Hypothèse* 12 (2009): 136.
104. [Philippe-Antoine Grouvelle], *Lettre à Monsieur le Rédacteur de la Gazette nationale, ou le Moniteur universel* [France, s.n., 1790?].
105. A. A. E., C.P., États Unis 44, 1795, fol. 275 report of 17 fructidor, year 3.
106. Frederick Jackson Turner, ed., *Correspondence of the French Ministers to the United States 1791–1797*, 2 vols. (New York: Da Capo Press, 1972), 2: 810, 18 April 1796. Also see Turner, 2: 771, 18 August 1795. The revolutionary governments tended to resort to oaths to try to guarantee the loyalty of those abroad. Hagley, W3-1095, Delacroix to Victor Du Pont, 1 pluviôse, iv [2 January 1796] and W3-312, Victor Du Pont to Letombe, Charleston, 18 pluviôse, an VI.
107. Ibid., 2: 771, 18 August 1795.
108. A.N., F. série administration générale de la France, F/7, Police générale, 4402 Comité de sûreté générale., comité diplomatique. Imprisoned in June 1793, he was released in August but that reprieve was short-lived. He again fell under suspicion and was executed in May 1794 after giving absolution to his fellow prisoners.
109. A. N., F. série administration générale de la France, F/7, Police générale, 4395 Comité de sûreté générale., 13 October 1792.
110. A. A. E., C.P., États-Unis, 44, 1795, part 2, fol. 176–182, Philadelphia, Adet and Lecombe to the Committee of Public Safety.
111. Turner, ed., *Correspondence of the French Ministers to the United States 1791–1797*, 1: 316 and 386.
112. Hagley, W3-261, Victor Du Pont to his family, 28 June 1795.

113. Turner, ed., *Correspondence of the French Ministers to the United States 1791–1797*, 2: 760–761.
114. Hagley, W3-1057, Letombe to Victor Du Pont, Philadelphia, 26 September 1795.
115. A. A. E., C.P., États Unis, 44, 1795, part 2, fols. 176–182, report of Adet and Lecombe. See also fols. 183–184 and 187–191.
116. Turner, ed. *Correspondence of the French Ministers to the United States 1791–1797*, 2: 390, Fauchet and Le Blanc to Minister of Foreign Affairs, 7 May 1794.
117. Miot de Melito, *Memoirs*, 98.
118. Iiams, *Peacemaking from Vergennes to Napoleon*, 95.
119. Lincolnshire Archives, Papers of Sir Richard Worsley, 17, fol. 96, 4 May 1797.
120. A. A. E., État Unis, C.P., vol. 41, part 5, fol. 332, Fauchet? 15 fructidor year 2.
121. Joseph Fauchet, "Mémoire sur les États-Unis d'Amérique," edited by Carl Ludwig Lokke, *Annual Report of the American Historical Association* 1 (1936): 118.
122. A. A. E., État Unis, C.P., vol., 44, part 4, fol. 450–452, Fauchet to citizen ministers of foreign relations, no date.
123. B. Mirkine-Guetzévitch, "L'Influence de la Révolution française sur le développement du droit international dans l'Europe orientale," *Recueil des Cours* 2 (1928): 299–456.
124. P.R.O., FO, 27/38, dispatch of 9 March 1792, Paris.
125. Grandmaison, *L'Ambassade francaise en Espagne pendant la revolution (1789–1804)*, 131.
126. Joseph-Henri Lasalle, *J. H. Lasalle à M. Mallet du Pan, sur la Révolution de Venise et les affairs d'Italia* (Paris: Chez les marchands de nouveautés, 1797), 7.
127. H. T. Colenbrander, *Gedenkstukken der Algemeene Geschiedenis van Nederland van 1795 tot 1840*. vol. 1: *Nederland en de revolutie, 1789–1795* (The Hague: Martinus Nijhoff, 1905), 283, 12 June 1792, Auckland to Grenville.
128. Ibid., 284, Auckland to Grenville, 15 June 1792.
129. Ibid., 177, Van de Spiegel aan Mevrouw d'Aelders, 14 July 1792.
130. Ibid., 284, Auckland to Grenville, 22 June 1792.
131. Ibid., 285, Auckland to Grenville, 6 July 1792.
132. Lincolnshire Archives, Papers of Sir Richard Worsley, 13, fol. 178 Worsley to Grenville, Venice, 31 October 1794 and 13, fol. 240, Worsley to George Baldwin, Venice, 12 December 1794.
133. Ibid., 14, fol. 1, Grenville to Worsley, Downing Street, 30 December 1794.
134. Ibid., fol. 4, Worsley to Grenville, Venice, 27 February 1795.

135. Ibid., fol. 171, Worsley to Grenville, Venice, 19 April 1797.
136. B. L., Add Mss. 48388, fol. 9 Paget to Grenville, 18 October 1798.
137. Ibid., fol. 32 Paget to Grenville, Munich, 28 February 1799.
138. Ibid., fol. 40, Paget to Grenville, Munich, 31 March 1799.
139. Ibid., fol. 44, Paget to Grenville, Munich, 16 April 1799.
140. Ibid., fol. 40, Paget to Grenville, Munich, 31 March 1799.
141. A. A. E, C.P., vol. 44, part III, fol. 253, Adet to Randolph, Philadelphia, 23 thermidor, year 3 and Turner, ed. *Correspondence of the French Ministers to the United States 1791–1797*, 2: 772, 25 August 1795.
142. For example, see the Historical Society of Philadelphia, 1454 Cadwallader Papers, series 5: Phineas Bond papers, box 205, particularly his correspondence with Captain Alexander Ball.
143. The Historical Society of Philadelphia, 1454 Cadwallader Papers, series 5: Phineas Bond papers, box 206, Thomas Forsyth to Phineas Bond, 11 February 1797, and box 205, Captain Ball to Phineas Bond, Halifax, 17 November 1795.

References

Archives Parlementaires de 1787 à 1860. Series 1: 1789–1800. Vol. 15: *Assemblée nationale constituante du 21 Avril au 30 Mai 1790.* Edited by M. J. Mavidal and M. E. Laurent. Paris: Paul Dupont, 1883.

Aulard, François-Alphonse. *Études et leçons sur la révolution française.* Paris: F. Alcan, 1902.

———, ed. *Recueil des actes du Comité de salut public avec la correspondance officielle des représentants en mission et le registre du conseil exécutif provisoire.* 27 vols. Paris: Imprimerie nationale, 1889–1923.

———, ed. *La Société des Jacobins: Recueil de documents pour l'histoire du club des Jacobins de Paris.* 6 vols. Paris: Librairie Jouast, 1887–1897.

Barras, Paul vicomte de. *Memoirs of Barras, Member of the Directorate.* New York: Harper and Brothers, 1895.

Barthélemy, François. *Papiers de Barthélemy, ambassadeur de France en Suisse, 1792–1797.* Edited by Jean Kaulek and Alexandre Tausserat-Radel. 6 vols. Paris: Alcan, 1886–1910.

Belissa, Marc. "La Diplomatie et les traités dans la pensée des lumières:'negociation universelle' ou école du mensonge." *Revue d'histoire diplomatique* 3 (1999): 291–317.

Bély, Lucien. *L'Art de la paix en Europe: Naissance de la diplomatie moderne XVIe–XVIIIe siècle.* Paris: Presses universitaires de France, 2007.

Black, Jeremy. "From Pillnitz to Valmy: British Foreign Policy and Revolutionary France 1791–1792." *Francia: Forschungen zur westeuropäischen Geschichte* 21 (1994): 129–146.

Blaga, Corneliu S. *L'Évolution de la diplomatie.* Paris: Pedone, 1938.
Brissot de Warville, Jacques-Pierre. *Discours de J. P. Brissot, député de Paris sur la necessité d'exiger une satisfaction de l'Empereur.* Paris: Imprimerie nationale, 1792a.

———. *Discours de J. P. Brissot, député sur les dispositions des puissances étrangères, relativement à la France, et sur les préparatifs de guerre ordonné par le Roi.* Paris: Imprimerie nationale, 1791.

———. *Discours sur la dénonciation contre le comité autrichien et contre M. Montmorin, ci-devant ministre des affaires étrangères, prononcé à l'Assemblée nationale à la séance du 23 mai 1792.* Paris: Imprimerie nationale, 1792b.

———. *J. P. Brissot deputy of Eure and Loire to his Constituents on the Situation of the National Convention.* London: John Stockdale, 1794.

———. *Le Patriote français, journal libre et impartial.* Paris, 1789–1793.

Brunot, Ferdinand. *Histoire de la langue française des origines à 1900.* 14 vols. Paris: Armand Colin, 1905–1927.

Chapuisat, Édouard. 1912. *De la Terreur de l'annexation: Génève et la république française, 1793–1798.* Geneva: Edition ATAR.

———. *La Suisse et la Révolution française: Épisodes.* Geneva: Editions du Mont-Blanc, 1945.

Childs, Frances S. "The Hauterive Journal." *New York Historical Society Quarterly Bulletin* 33 (April 1949): 69–86.

Church, Clive H. *Revolution and Red Tape: The French Ministerial Bureaucracy 1770–1850.* Oxford: Clarendon Press, 1981.

Le Comité de Salut public de la Convention nationale à la société populaire de la section de des droits de l'homme. Paris: n.p., 23 brumaire, an 2.

Custine, Adam Philippe, comte de. *Le Générale Custine au président de la Convention nationale.* Cambrai: Defremery frères et Raparlier, 1793.

Der Derian, James. *On Diplomacy: A Genealogy of Western Estrangement.* Oxford: Basil Blackwell, 1987.

Doyle, William. *Aristocracy and Its Enemies in the Age of Revolution.* Oxford: University Press, 2009.

Dry, Adrien Fleury. *Soldats ambassadeurs sous le Directoire, an IV-an VIII.* Paris: Plon, 1906.

Ducher, G.-J.-A. *Douanes nationales et affaires étrangères.* Paris: Imprimerie nationale, n.d.

Fauchet, Joseph. "Mémoire sur les États Unis d'Amérique." Edited by Carl Ludwig Lokke. *Annual Report of the American Historical Association* 1 (1936): 83–123.

France. Commission des Archives diplomatiques au ministère des affaires étrangères. *Recueil des instructions données aux ambassadeurs et ministres de France depuis les traités de Westphalie jusqu'à la Révolution française.* Vol. 18. *Diète Germanique.* Edited by Bertrand Auerbach. Paris: Félix Alcan, 1912.

———. Commission des Archives diplomatiques au ministère des affaires étrangères. *Recueil des instructions données au ambassadeurs et ministres de France depuis les traités de Westphalie jusqu'à la Révolution française.* 26: *Venise.* Edited by Pierre Duparc. Paris: Félix Alcan, 1958.

Frey, Linda, and Marsha Frey. *"Proven Patriots": The French Diplomatic Corps, 1789–1799.* St. Andrews: St. Andrew Studies in French History and Culture, 2011. http://research-repository.st-andrews.ac.uk/handle/10023/1881.

Gilbert, Felix. *The 'New Diplomacy' of the Eighteenth Century.* Indianapolis: Bobbs Merrill, 1951.

Grandmaison, Charles-Alexandre Geoffroy, de. *L'Ambassade française en Espagne pendant la Révolution (1789–1804).* Paris: Plon, 1892.

Grouvelle, Philippe-Antoine. *Lettre à Monsieur le Rédacteur de la Gazette nationale, ou le Moniteur universel.* France: s.n., 1790?

Guyot, Raymond. *Le Directoire et la paix de l'Europe: Des traités de Bâle à la deuxième coalition, 1795–1799.* Paris: Félix Alcan, 1911.

Hénin de Cuvilliers, Étienne-Félix. *Sommaire de correspondance d'Étienne-Félix Hénin, chargé d'affaires de la République française à Constantinople pendant la 1re, 2e and 3 années de la République.* Paris: Imprimérie du dépôt des lois, an IV.

Hill, Peter P. *French Perceptions of the Early American Republic, 1783–1793.* Philadelphia, PA: American Philosophical Society, 1988.

Hüffer, Hermann, ed. *Quellen zur Geschichte des Zeitalters der französischen Revolution. Teil 2: Quellen zur Geschichte der diplomatischen Verhandlungen. Erster Band: Der Frieden von Campoformio.* Innsbruck: Wagner, 1907.

Iiams, Thomas M. *Peacemaking from Vergennes to Napoleon: French Foreign Relations in the Revolutionary Era, 1774–1814.* Huntington, NY: Robert E. Krieger Publishing Company, 1979.

Jackson, Sir George. *The Diaries and Letters of Sir George Jackson, K.C. H.* Edited by Lady Catherine Hannah Charlotte Jackson. London: Richard Bentley and Son, 1872.

Jefferson, Thomas. "Jefferson to Short." *American Historical Review* 33 (1928): 832–835.

Kaiser, Thomas E. "From Fiscal Crisis to Revolution: The Court and French Foreign Policy, 1787–1789." In *From Deficit to Deluge: The Origins of the French Revolution,* edited by Thomas E. Kaiser and Dale K. Van Kley, 139–164. Stanford: Stanford University Press, 2011.

Kientz, Louis. *J.H. Campe et la Révolution française avec des lettres et documents inédits.* Paris: H. Didier, 1939.

La Bruyère, Jean, de. *The Characters.* New York: Brentano's, 1929.

Lasalle, Joseph-Henri. *J. H. Lasalle à M.Mallet du Pan, sur la Révolution de Venise et les affairs d'Italia.* Paris: Chez les marchands de Nouveautes ... an V de la république, 1791.

Marcère, Édouard, de. *Une Ambassade à Constantinople: La Politique orientale de la Révolution française*. 2 vols. Paris: Felix Alcan, 1927.
Martin, Virginie. "Le Comité diplomatique: homicide par décret de la diplomatie (1790–1793)?" *La Révolution française: Cahiers de l'Institut d'histoire de la Révolution française* 3 (2012): 1–33.
———. "Devenir diplomate en Révolution: Naissance dela 'carrière diplomatique'." *Revue d'histoire moderne et contemporaine* 63, no. 3 (2016): 110–135.
———. "La Révolution française ou'l'ère du soupçon 'Diplomatie et dénociation." *Hypothèse* 12 (2009): 131–140.
Masson, Frédéric. *Le Département des affaires étrangères pendant la Révolution, 1787–1804*. Paris: E. Plon, 1877.
Miot de Melito, Andre F. *Memoirs of Count Miot de Melito, Minister, Ambassador, Councillor of State*. Edited by Wilhelm August Fleischmann. New York: Charles Scribner's Sons, 1881.
Mirkine-Guetzévitch, Boris. "L'Influence de la Révolution française sur le développement du droit international dans l'Europe orientale." *Recueil des Cours* 2 (1928): 299–456.
Moniteur, seule histoire authentique et inaltérée de la Révolution française. 32 vols. Paris: Plon Frères, 1847–1863.
Montmorin Saint Hérem, Armand Marc, comte de. *Observations de M.de Montmorin, adressés à l'Assemblée nationale sur le discours prononcé par Mm. Gensonné et Brissot, dans la séance du 23 mai 1792*. Paris: Du Pont, 1792.
Murley, J. T. "The Origin and Outbreak of the Anglo-French War of 1793." Unpublished Ph.D. dissertation, Oxford, 1959.
Paine, Thomas. *Collected Writings*. New York: Library of America. 1955.
Peter, Marc. *Genève et la Révolution*. Geneva: Alex Jullien, 1921.
Poumarède, Géraud. "Le Bouleversement des relations internationales pendant la Révolution française." In *Le Bouleversement de l'ordre du monde: Révoltes et révolutions en Europe et aux Amériques à fin du 18e siècle*, edited by Jean-Pierre Poussou et al., 405–430. Paris: Sedes, 2004.
Prudhomme, Louis-Marie. *Révolutions de Paris*. Paris: n.p., 1789–1794.
Révolutions de France et de Brabant. Paris, 1790.
Richerateau, Jean. 1936. *Le Rôle politique du Professeur Koch*. Strasbourg: Imprimerie alsacienne.
Saint-Just, Louis de. *Oeuvres complètes de Saint-Just*. Edited by Charles Vellay. 2 vols. Paris: Librairie Charpentier et Fasquelle, 1908.
Scott, Hamish. "A Model of Conduct from the Age of Chivalry? Honour, International Decline and the End of the Bourbon Monarchy." In *The Crisis of the Absolute Monarchy: France from Old Regime to Revolution*, edited by Julian Swann and Joël Félix, 181–204. Oxford: Oxford University Press, 2013.

Silverman, David A. "Informal Diplomacy: The Foreign Policy of the Robespierrist Committee of Public Safety." Unpublished Ph.D. diss., University of Washington, 1973.

Sorel, Albert. *Europe and the French Revolution: The Political Traditions of the Old Régime*. Translated and edited by Alfred Cobban and J. W. Hunt. New York: Anchor Books, 1971.

———. *L'Europe et la Révolution française*. 8 vols. Paris: E. Plon Nourrit et cie, 1897–1904.

Turner, Frederick Jackson, ed. *Correspondence of the French Ministers to the United States, 1791–1797*. 2 vols. 1903. Reprint. New York: Da Capo Press, 1972.

Voss, Jürgen. "Christophe Guillaume Koch (1737–1813): Homme politique et historiographe contemporain de la Révolution." *History of European Ideas* 13 (1991): 531–543.

Winter, Otto Friedrich. *Repertorium der diplomatischen Vertreter aller Länder seit dem Westfälischen Frieden*. Vol. 3. Graz: Verlag Hermann Böhlaus Nachf., 1965.

CHAPTER 4

The Revolutionary Theater of Power: Precedence and Etiquette

"Those people are gravely mistaken who imagine that all this is mere ceremony."—Louis XIV[1]

The condemnation of the profession of diplomat inevitably entailed an attack on its practices and customs, particularly etiquette and precedence. The revolutionaries attacked politeness, which they did not regard as a "republican virtue."[2] Most who knew them could only agree. Rather they equated politeness with the "fatuous mannerisms of Versailles"[3] and with the aristocracy. The revolutionaries also wanted to avoid "ridiculous" disputes over etiquette, especially the question of precedence, for in theory they regarded all peoples as brothers. They would not have recognized these issues as ones of mere style, for such customs had validated the *ancien régime* and reinforced the aristocratic code. The revolutionaries rejected these minutely regulated ceremonies, part of what Duindam calls "the public presentation of power"[4]; they understood only too well what historians have come to recognize that "'symbolics of power' [were] not mere incidental ephemera."[5] The revolutionaries "resolved to destroy these aristocratic prejudices"[6] and repudiated that system with its implicit ideological underpinnings; they refused to become entwined in that "ghostly perpetuum mobile": the etiquette and the ceremonial of court society.[7]

Rousseau had seen its dangers. Civilized peoples, "happy slaves," cultivate "that delicate and refined taste on which you pride yourselves; that softness of character and urbanity of customs which makes relations among you so amiable and easy; in a word, the semblance of all the virtues without the possession of any."[8] In "this herd called society," man, whose soul had been corrupted, "no longer dares to appear as he is."[9] Such an individual followed the demands of propriety, of politeness, of usage, not his own inclinations. Everything is "reduced to appearances, everything becomes factitious and deceptive; honor, friendship, virtue…. We have only a deceitful and frivolous exterior, honor without virtue, reason without wisdom and pleasure without happiness."[10]

Rousseau's arguments found a receptive audience among the revolutionaries. In Sièyes' attack on that society, he noted that "the French person is not polite because he thinks he *owes* it to others, but because he thinks he *owes* it to *himself*. It is not the rights of others that he respects, it is himself and his own dignity."[11] These revolutionaries tore away what Rousseau called that "perfidious veil of politeness."[12] Burke condemned the change wrought in the diplomatic corps: "All elegance of mind and manners is banished. A theatrical, bombastick [sic], windy phraseology of heroic virtue, blended and mingled up with a worse dissoluteness, and joined to a murderous and savage ferocity, forms the tone and idiom of their language and their manners."[13] Revolutionaries explicitly rejected the aristocratic injunction that a gentleman only walks, never runs and that he enters a room *langsam und feierlich*, in a slow and solemn manner. Like the Quakers, they rejected phatic communication, that is, "greetings phrases, and gestures employed to convey general sociability rather than to transmit specific meaning,"[14] and that very rejection made them seem rude. The Revolution juxtaposed sincerity, transparency, authenticity against the insincerity, artificiality, and sublimation of emotions of the *ancien régime*.[15] Pichon, the French chargé to the United States, lauded Jefferson, who received individuals in informal dress "and without the least ceremony."[16]

Such things as manners were not insignificant; Burke argued that they were more important than laws. "Manners are what vex or soothe, corrupt or purify, exalt or debase, barbarize or refine us, by a constant, steady, uniform, insensible operation, like that of the air we breathe in. They give their whole form and colour to our lives."[17] Burke realized that changes in the power structure of a society affect conduct and taste.[18] "Taste and elegance," Burke argued, "though they are reckoned only among the smaller and secondary morals, yet are of no mean importance in the regulation of life."[19] Indeed, "[w]hen antient opinions and rules of life are taken away, the loss cannot possibly be estimated. From that moment we have no compass to govern us; nor can we know distinctly to what port we steer."[20] The French, he thought, were attempting "a regeneration of the moral constitution of man."[21] He glimpsed what historians today, such as Hunt, Furet, and Ozouf, call the creation of a political culture. We can find confirmation of this view from the opposite side of the political spectrum. Barère, at one time a member of the Committee of Public Safety, fulminated against the lack of revolutionary fervor. "Manners have now culminated into perfect politeness, always a sign of corruption."[22]

Louis XIV stressed that etiquette was an instrument of power: "Those people are gravely mistaken who imagine that all this is mere ceremony."[23] Even the nobility became caught in "the vicious circle of enforced ostentation," "imprisoned by their own ceremonial and etiquette,"[24] like an insect imprisoned in amber. This "incessant competition" meant that "everyone was running on the spot."[25] One had to cultivate the appropriate gestures, move in the rigidly mandated way, wear the right fabrics, and choose the correct shoes. A satire dating from the reign of Henri IV has one courtier explain to another the minutiae of dress (high heels, gilded spurs), what to say, when to laugh, how to move the head, when to fling the arms, when to shift from one foot to another, and so on.[26] The essayist Jean de La Bruyère (d. 1696) parodied the man who understood the court. He was "master of his gestures, of his eyes, of his face." He dissimulated: he smiled at his enemies, disguised his passions, and spoke and acted against his sentiments.[27]

A diplomat who was, nonetheless, not part of the courtly elite, François de Callières, condemned the "vain ceremonies," which he equated with a "play" in which the courtiers were "comedians."[28] They were comedians Shakespeare would have understood as he did that "idle ceremony."[29] *L'Encyclopédie méthodique* of 1784 opined that ceremony has introduced "a constraint which often jeopardizes the success of affairs. One negotiates badly when etiquette dictates each step and each word."[30] The revolutionaries would have applauded that sentiment. François Gabriel, comte de Bray (1765–1832), who served under Montmorin and was sent as French representative to the Diet of Ratisbon, was hardly sympathetic to the Revolution. He resigned in August 1792 and subsequently served Bavaria at various courts. Even he found the etiquette a "labyrinth," such that one cannot find one's way once one enters: the number of steps to advance or to retreat, the number of bows were counted and predetermined. When to put on one's hat and when to remove it was stipulated. "All this is almost as difficult to study as one of the most important rules of [the French mathematician] Bezout."[31] The magnificent clothing, the pompous ceremonial, the march that lasted two and a half hours, combined with visits, ceremonies, fêtes, and dinners, made him deplore the time lost. This is "an abominable business" with its "oppressive vanities." He deplored the five-hour ceremonial, the reception line that lasted three and a half hours, and the "fatiguing luxury." In short, he found this way of life "miserable."[32] Many would have applauded that sentiment.[33]

That stifling ceremonial reflected the absolutist and authoritarian *ancien régime* that encoded hierarchy in a representational system. The monarchy was adept at what Oresko described as the manipulation of "representational culture, the use of external signs, visual imagery, to express status and power."[34] Diplomats were particularly vulnerable because ceremonial niceties both reflected and determined the status of their state.[35] As members of the "distinctive diplomatic culture" that evolved in the long eighteenth century, they were part of an "independent society," so termed by an official of the foreign ministry, Antoine Pecquet, in 1737.[36] Drawn from an aristocratic elite, these individuals shared certain assumptions grounded in the court culture. Not incidentally, court and embassy reinforced ceremonial.

The diplomatic network was so "corrupted" by the *ancien régime* and so permeated by an aristocratic code that it proved difficult to act within that "perfidious and inept system" without compromising revolutionary ideals.[37] The integument of the aristocratic code proved difficult to cast aside, for the aristocratic *mentalité* had penetrated the structure itself. More than one patriot criticized Semonville, the French representative to Constantinople, for behaving like an ambassador of the *ancien régime*—a damning indictment. Semonville created a sensation because he traveled so slowly with such a numerous entourage and with such pomp and ostentation.[38] Such behavior was castigated because the revolutionaries explicitly rejected "the dazzling and minutely choreographed public rituals that … re-legitimat[ed] the old order as a whole."[39]

Nonetheless, the revolutionaries inherited the *ancien régime*'s obsession with such issues, while rejecting the underlying premise, the preeminence of royalty. In the *ancien régime*, states manipulated etiquette to advance social status, just as the aristocracy did. Not surprisingly, such discussions had dominated diplomatic manuals and legal treatises. In

Vattel's classic *The Law of Nations*, this well-known jurist noted that "at present kings claim superiority of rank over republics." The Roman Republic, he noted, had considered all kings beneath them but the monarchs of Europe "have refused to admit republics to equality."[40] This mentality was so pervasive that even Venice, the Republic of Saint Mark, claimed royal status not because of its commercial success, its independence, or its constitutional structure but because "it ruled or had at some time ruled over several kingdoms, namely Cyprus, Crete, and Euboea."[41] The French monarchy predictably had not accepted this argument as definitive. The republic of Genoa also claimed royal status on the grounds that it had proclaimed Our Lady as Genoa's royal queen.[42] This obsession was shared by others. In its quest for royal status, the house of Savoy began using a silver vessel with moistened napkins because of its association with sovereignty.[43] In their repudiation of royal culture, the French revolutionaries did not follow the path of either Venice or Genoa in their elision of royal and republican symbols or Savoy in its utilization of royalist paraphernalia.[44]

As Black has pointed out, diplomats used ceremonial and protocol "as a means of asserting and defending status and interests. It was perfect for a competitive world that wished to have an alternative to conflict."[45] Diplomats were ordered to engage in a kind of "ceremonial brinkmanship as they sought to defend and enhance the prestige of their masters."[46] Precedence was so vigorously contested because it reflected a state's power, what the Comte de Broglie called, the "interest of regard."[47] The courtiers were so obsessed with rank and with deportment because such maneuvering was "a zero-sum game: the gains of one entailed the other's losses."[48] Probably no one played that game as well as the French. Jean Baptiste Colbert, marquis de Torcy, the Secretary of Foreign Affairs under Louis XIV, an adept practitioner of the art, noted that these "trifles of etiquette" signaled the importance of a country, affirmed its power, and helped to establish its grandeur. When the king of Denmark announced that he would in the future receive the French envoys as Louis received his, that is, seated and covered, Louis XIV refused to accept this change. Torcy underscored that to accept an inferior rank or even to consent under the "pretext of politeness or equality and the suppression of all prerogatives" would be to "recognize and admit the decline of the country."[49] Through such ceremonial games Louis could inflict "political humiliation" and assert his *gloire*.[50] Nor were the revolutionaries adverse to playing such games.

We can get a good idea of the practical aspects of the new diplomacy from the General Instructions for diplomatic agents, drafted by the Girondin foreign minister, Charles François Lebrun, in June 1793.[51] On all occasions the agents were instructed to maintain the "dignity of the Republic and that of their personal character." As for the disputes about precedence that so preoccupied their predecessors, the agents of the nation declared that the French people regarded all peoples as brothers and equals. If, however, some state claimed some particular distinction, the French people would then reclaim the prerogatives they had always enjoyed. In such an instance, French representatives should observe that it was as heads of a great nation that the former kings of France had possessed certain rights of precedence, not in their capacity as monarchs. France was ready to abandon those rights, provided, of course, that the other powers also renounced their pretensions.[52]

Grégoire encapsulated the view of many revolutionaries that "nothing was more ridiculous than the worries concerning precedence."[53] The French representative to the United States, Edmond Charles Genet, who arrived in April 1793 was specifically instructed to avoid "as much as he can the ridiculous disputes about etiquette." Still the representatives of other powers could not pretend "to any particular distinction." If they did, the French representatives must "insist on all the prerogatives the French power has at any time enjoyed; the nation determining that in that case its ministers should defend those rights, being certain that the nation will make them respected."[54] In France, James Monroe, the US minister (1794–1796), had a practical demonstration of the new republican observance. In 1795 all the ministers were told to assemble at the home of the Minister of Foreign Affairs and proceed en masse. They were "presented without regard to precedence." The president then addressed the diplomatic corps, underscoring the cordiality of the welcome and contrasted present practice favorably with that of the court.[55]

Practical considerations in addition to ideological constraints led the revolutionaries to abandon precedence and protocol. The old etiquette stipulated that ministers of republics yielded place to those of kings. If they tinkered with the system, the French would open up a series of unresolved and probably unresolvable demands and complaints. On the other hand, if France followed the former usage, it would have to renounce the rank it had previously enjoyed. The revolutionaries, therefore, saw no alternative but to abandon it in its entirety, even had they had not been ideologically predisposed to do so.[56] Still the French republic paid particular attention to Vattel's caveat that if the form of government changes, nations still preserve the same honors and ranks.[57] Vattel's argument interestingly enough implied that kingdoms could not lose status, although those who became monarchies could gain it. The Directory, facing the consequences of a hostile Europe, sent a circular to its representatives, urging them to avoid any difficulties over etiquette. They were also instructed "to support with firmness the dignity of the French nation." It also provided general principles to guide their conduct: at all times the French agent should provide an "example of propriety and of the purity of morals." He should "respect the political, civil and religious laws of the country" and encourage them to respect those of the French. These injunctions were explicitly designed to "increase the number of friends of France."[58] Friends or not, Talleyrand, among others, cautioned the French representatives to remember that as long as the old etiquette persisted, they should demand the right to maintain all the prerogatives of the old monarchy for the new republic.[59]

French representatives followed Talleyrand's injunction. When Bernadotte was sent to Vienna in 1798, a special supplement to his instructions stressed this very point. At court, Bernadotte demanded and was accorded the same privileges that representatives of *ancien régime* France had enjoyed.[60] Sieyès, accredited as special envoy to Berlin from 1798 to 1799, did not hesitate to assert the primacy of France. At a reception celebrating the king's birthday, many ambassadors arrived early to claim first place but Sieyès entered last, an effective ploy. The chamberlain was hesitant to displace all the others, but Sieyès insisted that the first place be occupied by the representative of the French republic. Nor were these actions limited to the old world. In 1796 Pierre Adet, the French representative to the United States, demanded that a privately printed directory listing the British minister before the French be suppressed. His protests echoed concerns already voiced.[61]

Nor was Bonaparte reticent to push France's rights. He refused, he wrote to the Directors, to allow the Austrians "to put the Emperor before the Republic." He claimed to be "indifferent" to etiquette but thought that the Holy Roman Emperor should accord the French republic the same status as the kings of France had enjoyed.[62] In an interview with Johann Philipp von Cobenzl (1753–1809), the Austrian diplomat, Bonaparte did not disguise the fact that he intended to assert France's "ancient pretensions" and claim precedence over Russia. Cobenzl countered that at the emperor's court pell-mell had been established. This argument did not sway

Bonaparte, who retorted: "He did not know why a power that had always been victorious should cede precedence to those which had been constantly beaten"[63]—a pragmatic approach not appreciated by other states. When the Austrians instead offered to recognize the republic, Napoleon retorted that the Republic did not wish to be recognized: "It is in Europe what the sun is on the horizon; so much the worse for anyone who does not wish to see it and does not wish to profit from it."[64] At Campo Formio Napoleon provoked a procedural crisis by insisting on the privilege of signing his copy first. Not incidentally he had stationed his grenadiers around the negotiators. The Austrians insisted that the conferences would be held in a neutral place, "a farce," in Napoleon's words, "to which I have willingly lent myself to satisfy the puerile vanity of these people." This supposedly "neutral point" was surrounded on all sides by French troops.[65] Napoleon had also demanded that Vienna send an ambassador to Paris. He saw through the Austrian pretense that sending a mere minister was only an economic calculus. Francis II had balked at sending an ambassador in order to deny France the rank she had enjoyed under Louis XVI.[66] Subsequently, Napoleon suggested that the Directory should pass a decree declaring that "the independent peoples are equal in their rights, that France considers herself the equal of all the sovereigns whom she has vanquished and will not recognize any superiors." This procedure, he continued, would have the advantage of expediting the collapse of the old etiquette, would be "more worthy of us, and especially would be more in conformity with our interests."[67] Not surprisingly, this French insistence on rank continued under the Empire.[68] Another republic, that of the United States, had also contended with the issue of precedence. Madison lamented in a letter that "I blush to have to put so much trash on paper." Jefferson, who found the subject "distasteful," advocated pell-mell.[69] Jefferson wished to change the practices of his predecessors, "especially those which savored of anti-republicanism … I presume the courts of these agents will have too much good sense to attempt to force on us their allotment of society into ranks and orders, as we have never pretended to force on them our equality. Our ministers with them submit to the laws of their society; theirs with us must submit to ours."[70] "In this country," Madison told Merry, the British representative, "people were left to seat themselves at table with as little rule as around a fire."[71] At the dinner held to celebrate the acquisition of Louisiana, the United States adroitly sidestepped the issue by refusing to invite any foreign representatives.[72] That option was not generally available to the French who intended to assert the preeminence of revolutionary France.

Nonetheless, the revolutionaries rejected the "subtle games of ceremonial" that undergirded what Bély dubs the "*société des princes.*"[73] The revolutionaries tore asunder that "collective construction" in which ceremony served not only as a "political instrument in the relations between European states, but also as a mark of solidarity in the society of princes."[74] The sovereigns, in Bély's words, made up a rather "singular" family whose relations were ritualized to such an extent that even war did not hamper or impede "*une politesse internationale.*"[75] "*La société polie,*" that very strict code of manners, both underscored and reinforced the prestige of the upper classes. The revolutionaries refused to play that game, to enter into that "universe of usage."[76] They rejected the trappings of the aristocratic code that had created the impression among Voltaire and others that the French were "both the most polite and the most social" nation.[77] The aristocratic code mandated what the age called "honest dissimulation," which meant "that whatever you felt or thought, you must behave according to the rules of politeness" and you must do so seemingly without effort, with what Baldassare Castiglione, the quintessential courtier, called grace or "*sprezzatura* [nonchalance.]"[78] This theme of repression (and suppression) of emotions was epitomized at Versailles. The taste of courtly France had been partly forged by the cynical but brilliant maxims of François, duc de La Rochefoucauld (1613–1680), published in 1665. For La Rochefoucauld civility was "a desire to be repaid with civility, and also to be considered well bred."[79]

Aristocratic society harshly judged those both inside and outside the courtly circle. Those on the inside had to meet certain criteria. The courtier who wished to be thought gallant must be able to "say flattering things in an agreeable manner." Moreover, he should unequivocally reject any move toward nature: "Most young people think they are being natural when really they are just ill-mannered and crude."[80] His maxims reflected the hierarchical, absolutist, and aristocratic culture that the revolutionaries jettisoned. They also rejected the implicit foundation of this cult of manners that divided society. La Rochefoucauld's emphasis on artificiality and appearance instead of sincerity and transparency made him anathema to the revolutionaries.[81]

The revolutionaries could not but reject what Blanning has dubbed "the culture of power" and what Shakespeare dubbed "dissembling courtesy."[82] For Blanning, Louis XIV's authority was "as much a cultural as a military or diplomatic construct."[83] To accept that courtly etiquette with its reinforcement of that society and all its implicit assumptions would undermine the revolutionary system. Condorcet understood that issue all too well. In 1792 he was concerned that the ceremonial enacted by the king would keep men enslaved, even though they had a free constitution. He applauded the National Assembly's decision to have the chairs of the president and the king exactly the same, and to use "King of the French," not "Sire" and not "Majesty." For by such means "all sign of idolatry disappears."[84] As early as 9 September 1789 the radical *Révolutions de Paris* noted that "for those who cannot read, it will be as though these names and ceremonies had never existed. We should speak to the people of their glory by means of a public monument, for we must not forget in this revolution the powerful language of symbols."[85]

The revolutionaries emphasized the importance of ritual and gesture, not just as assertions or reflections of ideology, but as tools in the reconstruction of their world and the diplomatic system, as part of the creation of a revolutionary country and a revolutionary man. A contemporary noted that the new government will require "new manners." It was "unthinkable" that the citizens of a free state would conduct themselves like the slaves of despots.[86] A British observer noted as early as 1790 that "the inhabitants of Paris are so changed that you would scarcely" know them. He saw a "revolution in their manners as well as in their government."[87] Nor was he alone in that observation. In that same year what struck another British observer, admittedly "perplexed by the number and variety of ridiculous and absurd things," was the "contempt for all former regulations." Nothing, he noted, was more changed, "than the whole of their manners."[88] Nor was this view only voiced by the British. Christian Wilhelm von Bohm, the Prussian legation councilor since 23 November 1795, wrote home that the "manner of living and the usages of Parisians" were no longer recognizable. He noted in particular that that "fine and obliging" politeness has disappeared.[89]

The instructions to French diplomats reflected this change and explicitly addressed questions of etiquette. These injunctions emphasized the importance of the initial reception. The revolutionaries understood only too well what Cohen has pointed out, that the "threshold moments" of greeting and parting "define the nature of the social relationship."[90] French representatives were to forego the custom of three genuflections before foreign monarchs when presenting *lettres de créance* as a gesture unworthy of the representative of a free people.[91] In Spain the initial reception set the tone. The normally imperturbable Auguste Marquet de Montbreton d'Urtubise sent to Spain, found himself engaged in a war of etiquette. In crossing the frontier, he could not but notice the cordon of Spanish troops deployed, he thought, to limit the revolutionary contagion. He could even compare it to "a second expulsion of the Moors."[92] Montmorin advised him to ignore the search of his baggage at the frontier and the petty affronts at his official presentation, but he must have wondered how he could have ignored the Spanish warning that they intended to "take precautions" against him.[93] Early in the Revolution a number of French representatives tried to defuse the hostility by following the old usage. The prudent François Barthélemy had appealed to the Swiss by arriving at Soleure incognito, but following the former usage. Even after the overthrow of the king on 10 August the revolutionary government had sent him new credentials, but in the old form.[94] After Thermidor when the revolutionary winds had shifted against the Terror, Dominique Catherine, marquis de Perignon (1754–1818), the French representative (1796–1797), had an audience "in the usual manner" at the Spanish court, noted for its scrupulous adherence to etiquette. The British representative John Stewart, earl of Bute, thought it important to note that Perignon was "a well behaved, civilized man without that pretension affecting entirely the military."[95]

French representatives faced the difficulty of reconciling the conflicting demands of reflecting revolutionary values and of asserting France's power. Often official entrances, paraded as a defense of French honor, brought to mind the *ancien régime*. When General Jean-Baptiste Hannibal Aubert-Dubayet (1759–1797), a man known for his moderation as well as his arrogance, was sent to the Ottoman Porte in September 1796, he was accompanied by a large entourage. When he demanded that his formal entry resemble that of the ambassador of Russia, who had been hailed with great pomp, including a salute from the cannons, the Porte refused, but perhaps because of historic ties, accorded him other privileges. Still the Porte delayed his formal audience for four months and did not receive him until January 1797.[96] Another revolutionary Antoine-Bernard Caillard (1737–1807), who had served as secretary of the legation at Parma in 1769 and later appointed as Minister of Foreign Affairs, tried to combine the etiquette of the *ancien régime* with that of revolutionary France. After a number of missions, he represented France in Berlin (1795–1798).[97] Conscious of the "formalities that my admission demands," he underscored that men on foot received him when he left his carriage and that Karl Wilhelm Finck von Finckenstein, minister of foreign affairs, clad in grand attire, greeted him in the salon. They then proceeded to the king's apartments, where he presented his letters of credence. Throughout he noted a decided "penchant for France," which the Revolution had not altered. He was, nonetheless, careful to note that he went "with the simplicity coupled with the propriety and the regard owing to a great prince and to the etiquette of the court." He underscored that "it is possible to be well received without carrying the magnificence of the old regime."[98] Still Caillard thought that "nothing is more difficult than my position." "A republican minister was an entirely novel thing at Berlin." It was extremely important to avoid "a faux pas at the beginning" … "If I had attacked the *émigrés* before having establishing my personal reputation I would indubitably have had the entire world against me; the struggle would have been unequal and the republic would have been compromised." Instead he ignored the *émigrés* and adopted "a policy of integrity, decency, frankness, and simplicity."[99] In this case and many others the personality of the individual could lead to success or failure.

The republican representatives were inundated with continuing injunctions to break with the past. As Jean Debry argued in 1792, "the austerity of the forms of the republican regime ought to exclude the obsequious forms of the despotic regime."[100] Or, as one popular society insisted, "Our ambassadors" should no longer be "slaves in their style as in their opinions and their conduct."[101] Even minor concessions could plunge one onto the slippery slope where revolutionary principles would be compromised. Brissot argued that a representative of the people "should only respect liberty, truth. If under the pretext of treating with caution the emperor or the king of Spain one managed to keep us silent, it would soon be necessary for us to bow before the turban of the dey of Algiers" and "the mitre of the bishop of Liège."[102] The revolutionary diplomats could not but understand that "purity of intentions was not enough."[103]

Many of the diplomats of the new order deliberately and impudently broke the former rules of diplomatic conduct. This rejection of the conventions of politeness often shocked contemporaries, such as the British in the case of the French representative, Bernard François de Chauvelin. At the initial interview Grenville offered Chauvelin a small chair, but the envoy seized the largest armchair to avoid what he saw as a slight to the republic.[104] In informal meetings, Chauvelin with too great a sense of his own importance (as the British saw it) then "got into the habit of snatching up the largest chair available and sinking down into it in an abandoned surge of republican virtue."[105] Ignorance or truculence? Or something else? In private the English consciously insulted Chauvelin by calling him "that boy."[106] Republican zeal tended to erode their credibility. At Madrid, Michel Ange Bernard Mangourit (1752–1829), who voiced his belief that the present king would be the last, vilified the queen. He intended to but was dissuaded from planting a tree of liberty in the courtyard of the French representative's house.[107] That same Mangourit refused to participate in the traditional fêtes held at the court and insisted on wearing a special costume of red, white, and blue.[108] Dispatched in 1795 after Thermidor, he only lasted seven months. Complete ignorance of or disdain for the usages of the courtly world also undermined the mission of several other representatives. The repeated *faux pas* of Ferdinand Guillemardet, French ambassador to Spain (1798–1800), caused him to lose influence at the court of Madrid, one of the most punctilious courts in Europe.[109]

Diplomatic protocol and ceremony became a symbolic battleground on which the struggle with the old and the new order was enacted. What Brissot saw as "small diplomatic chicaneries, miserable quarrels of etiquette" that occurred with the French mission in Britain was part of that larger struggle.[110] The old ceremonial had reinforced certain expectations of behavior. In overturning those conventions, the French dismayed their hosts and challenged the assumptions of the international order. The hostility these actions generated led some like James Harris to argue that it was his duty to oppose "the herd of barbarians that are endeavouring to overrun us."[111] On the other hand, the French representatives, often floundering in the quicksand of ceremony, found it hard, if not impossible, to work within that system without being compromised by it.

At Rastatt the French diplomats were dismissive of the etiquette and impatient with the procedures of the congress. After 17 months Jean de Bry remarked that if he did not die of boredom, he would return on crutches and with eye glasses.[112] One of the revolutionary envoys, Jean Baptiste Treilhard (1742–1810), a lawyer of both finesse and energy, was also anxious to get the work done quickly and found himself increasingly impatient with all the "small chicaneries."[113] Talleyrand advised him: do not regard as a waste of time "these fastidious preliminaries, this exchange of notes, these uninteresting discussions, these secret intrigues," which will only place us in a position to "march to the denouement."[114] The French representatives regarded the Austrians and the Prussians as perfidious and insolently arrogant.[115] Still, the French were confident that "the simplicity and energy of a republican *politique* will prevail against the delays of the old diplomacy."[116]

The problems that surfaced at Rastatt were not unique as seen in Sieyès' mission to Berlin in 1798. Sieyès was determined to exemplify the revolutionary diplomat on his mission to Berlin in 1798. He accomplished that only too well and earned the sobriquet "*le démon de la Révolution.*"[117] At his first audience he announced that his instructions conformed to his political opinions and that his ministry would be "open, loyal, friendly, suitable in everything to the morality of my character."[118] One cannot but wonder how this self-righteous and solipsistic pronouncement was viewed in Berlin. His mission, he underscored, would be one of "great simplicity."[119] Nor did he intend to act like an ordinary minister. Instead he loved "moral and social order" and would "not countenance all the projects of the Directory and would even oppose them on occasion"[120]—a statement that would have baffled, if not appalled, the Prussians. The king found this regicide, notorious revolutionary, and defrocked priest objectionable and protested his appointment. The Frenchman intended to reject what disgusted him, what "revolted his republican soul."[121] This ideological rigidity did not endear him to his hosts. Nor was he gracious; his written communications, always using the republican calendar, lacked any tact or circumspection. "As soon as one begins to reason the Germans think one is retreating," he wrote back to Paris.[122] Not surprisingly, the Prussians soon passed from "suspicion, to irritation and from irritation to hatred and contempt."[123] Sieyès, who spoke no German, found himself blocked at every turn by Christian August Heinrich Kurt, Graf von Haugwitz, the Minister of Foreign Affairs, who had been dubbed by Mirabeau, the minister of adjournments. The sentinel was placed at Haugwitz's door, he concluded, "to stop affairs from entering." Sieyès dubbed Haugwitz the "minister of inaction" or the "minister for the obstruction of foreign affairs."[124] It was not possible, he finally concluded, to "drag anything from him." Sieyès reacted by ignoring or overriding all usages and diplomatic forms and threatening that "the Directory will make peace with you, without you, or against you."[125] Finckenstein suspected that Sieyès was not as ignorant of diplomatic forms as he claimed but Haugwitz, whom Sieyès had attempted to circumvent, thought his proceedings very "strange."[126] Sieyès' purported ignorance served to make French *démarches* even more incalculable. The Prussians viewed his actions as both cunning and suspicious and thought that the French overrode the rules of formality in order to obtain their way "*tout par la force.*"[127] Sieyès' insistence that proper respect be accorded to the representative of a great nation coupled with his behavior soon meant that he was shunned and isolated.[128] This revolutionary diplomat was conscious enough of the constraints of etiquette to fear that a "precipitous and clandestine [departure] without taking leave" would have been construed as a step ordered by the government and "a tacit declaration of war." He decided to return to Berlin to satisfy "all the formalities of usage."[129] Ultimately, the king allowed him to take leave at a ball without the usual ceremonial. Not all set aside their personal feelings or their revolutionary inclinations. Nor had Sieyès most of the time.

Other French representatives also disregarded those "punctiliously staged sociodramas," those ceremonies which reinforced the "calibrated cohesion in the upper class."[130] The problems that surfaced at Berlin were not unique as seen in the negotiations of James Harris in 1796 and 1797. When Harris set out on his mission, Burke quipped that it was hardly surprisingly his journey was a slow one for he "went all the way on his knees."[131] This veteran diplomat certainly went with a number of reservations. "I feel I have done right in accepting the mission," he confided to his wife. "I shall not shrink from it tho it certainly takes me from a bed of roses and lays me on a bed of thorns."[132] Still the mission began well enough. He assured Grenville that the officials at Calais who welcomed him were "all equally civil, none of them using any of the new modes of address."[133] He confided to his wife that it was "impossible to have been received with more civility."[134] He admitted that he was received with "more [ceremony] than we usually required or afforded."[135]

Although the Jacobins were scandalized by the magnificence of Harris's entrée,[136] Harris had followed his instructions (and not incidentally his own inclinations) in insisting that the French accord him all the rights and prerogatives of a public minister and treat him according to "the established laws and customs."[137] These demands set the tone for the French who saw him as inflexible and rigid on insignificant details. The 50-year-old Harris did not hesitate to lecture the French Foreign Minister Delacroix about the differences between limited and full powers and between instructions and powers. Not surprisingly, Delacroix was not disposed to listen to Harris' hectoring criticism of what Delacroix referred to as the "simplicity of republican forms." Delacroix only remarked that "such secondary difficulties" would not impede the negotiations.[138] Harris, however, found no "deficiency on his part in point of civility or etiquette."[139] Delacroix, who regarded Harris' tenacious insistence on form and methods as either a ruse or bad faith, did not hesitate to point out that "[w]e are no longer in the decrepitude of monarchical France but in all the strength of an adolescent republic."[140] On one occasion, according to Harris, Delacroix broke out in a "republican rant."[141] Increasingly frustrated with the deadlock, Harris described Delacroix as "an unsteady head on the edge of a high precipice."[142]

Mutual suspicions dogged the negotiations: the French saw Harris as "a devil of a spy" but those more sympathetic to the British condemned Delacroix's "bizarre and brusque tone" as more befitting a bad secretary than a minister of foreign relations.[143] Interestingly enough, later some of the French representatives apologized for Delacroix's "brutal manners." Harris suspected that Delacroix had "boasted that he had treated him badly [to reaffirm his revolutionary credentials] since in reality he had always been very honest to me in his manner." He admitted that Delacroix had tried "terrification, by letting out some strong Jacobin phrases; but when he found this kind of declamation did not affect me, he left it off."[144]

Harris certainly missed some of the amusements and amenities of the former Paris. In the new revolutionary Paris, he could not find "lodging fit for a dog," although the French maintained their culinary reputation and he was "very well fed."[145] More importantly, what made his previous negotiation "boys' play in comparison" was the lack of society "or any means of meeting," except in cafés and public places.[146] Months later, he had the same complaint: "We live quite by ourselves partly from there being really no society here…. [There is] literally nothing to see & nothing to do."[147] In Harris' view, the first interview went "perfectly well." He thought it necessary to remark to his wife that "his home, his Attendants, his Manners in short every thing [sic] but his dress differed in nothing from old times except the feeling that I was in a new position."[148]

On a subsequent mission to the peace negotiations at Lille in 1797, Harris was equally pleased by the "attention in point of form."[149] At Lille he was received by a detachment of *chasseurs* and the firing of cannons. In return, he "observed all the possible Etiquette on this occasion" and underscored "how necessary & useful it is not to depart from them."[150] Indeed in 1797, Harris was cautioned to be "fully prepared" for the French to insist upon "extraordinary privileges." He was instructed to "adhere to forms observed in former negotiations … to regulate the different points of etiquette on a footing of equality."[151] Harris came to conclude that negotiations with "those devils" were impossible.[152] There were too many like Maret, "a rank jacobin—an unbridled Jacobin" whose goal was to "totally revolutionize at the blow of a canon [sic] without examining the why."[153] As the negotiations with France collapsed, the discordance between revolutionary France and an aristocratic representative of Britain was highlighted. Harris noted that he could not find any—and he underscored "rational"—motive for the French conduct. He thought that the Directors Barras and Reubell were both "daring and inconsistent" and did "not look forward beyond the circumstances of the Moment."[154] Still he got along well with the negotiators who "acted openly and fairly with me." In general, Harris found the plenipotentiaries "as civil in their manner as possible ... yet their conduct is more violent and absurd than was ever heard of." He found it "a very interesting curiosity to see the real Jacobin's manner and costume ... insolent, with an air and affectation of protecting civility."[155] The negotiations may have been doomed at the outset, but the replacement of the French plenipotentiaries after the fructidor coup by more intransigent ones hardly helped.[156] One of Harris' servants, a man of gigantic stature and girth, could not be persuaded that his master was safe in France and insisted on sleeping outside his door.[157]

Harris found Lille even more inhospitable than Paris. There he was "being stewed alive in a hot fortified town without a single human being to converse with."[158] Harris' travails in both Paris and Lille illustrate how revolutionary France had destroyed the informal contacts and the sociability that had expedited agreements in the *ancien régime*. Furthermore, their attention to form masked a larger issue, a major shift in the way revolutionaries conducted diplomacy. They were less accommodating, more intransigent and blunter than those of the *ancien régime*. Revolutionaries belligerently adhered to certain conditions and refused to participate in the give and take so integral to the old diplomacy. "The concessive world of eighteenth-century, conducted by ambassadors who were members of the same international society, had collapsed to be replaced by a much more confrontational and grasping approach."[159] Not a few of the British had no belief in the possibility of peace. Had peace been signed, the statesman Grenville wrote, "you would only have a truce with an enemy who will be always be happy to ferment a revolution in this country."[160] By 1800 Harris had concluded that no further talks should be arranged "because I am confident they will neither be honourable either to the country or to the negotiation."[161]

Francis James Jackson (1770–1814), a minister *ad interim* to France (1801–1802), shared that assessment. Jackson even argued that Britain should neither send nor receive a representative from revolutionary France because the French "in their new code of etiquette had broke through all the forms and ceremonials." A British ambassador would be forced "either to be in a perpetual state of dispute, or to submit to [affronts] no Ambassador ever suffered before."[162] Jackson linked his unpopularity to his contesting issues of precedence and to his refusal to become "servile and subservient."[163] The negotiations were again plagued by disputes over form which the British insisted upon and the French tended to ignore. The French saw such issues as mere technicalities or as stumbling blocks deliberately placed in the way of agreement; they tended to underestimate, perhaps deliberately, the importance of procedures which the British saw as intrinsic to the success or failure of the negotiations themselves.[164] For the British form was linked to substance. Jackson recounted to Harris that the French "attempts to deceive, their duplicity, their bad faith, insolence, and vanity, surpassed his utmost belief." He found Bonaparte "sarcastic, vulgar, and impertinent," but clever and witty and Talleyrand, then Minister of Foreign Affairs, "the most barefaced teller of untruths he ever met." No one but Barbé Marbois "had even a desire of passing for an honest man."[165]

The most frequent criticism leveled at the French was arrogance.[166] All too typical was Auckland's condemnation of a French note as "stupid, ill conceiv'd & insolent."[167] As late as 1797, Harris noted that the "once elegant manners" of Ange-Elisabeth-Louis-Antoine Bonnier d'Alco (1750–1799) had been succeeded by the "Jacobinical arrogance of his party." He blamed this transformation on the "Jacobinical violence of his principles" and on Bonnier's character, which was "as bad as possible." Not surprisingly, the frustrated Harris found Bonnier "haughty and impracticable in business."[168] In contrast, Harris praised Treilhard, formerly an *avocat* in the *parlement* of Paris, whose reputation had won him election to the Estates General as a representative of the Third Estate. A talented and eloquent man, he had served on the Committee of Public Safety after the fall of Robespierre, then in the Five Hundred, and subsequently as a member of the *cour de cassation*, the highest court of appeals in France.[169] Although a regicide and a fervent republican, Treilhard, nonetheless, "talked and talked well and like a man who knows the usage of the world." Harris praised his countenance "a good one" and his manners "easy and well bred."[170] That opinion was confirmed by Metternich, who thought that Treilhard was "in general very polite." That made the contrast all the more striking with his colleague, who was the "quintessential lout or boor."[171] Yet even Treilhard did not hesitate to shout and bang the table to underscore his arguments during meetings.[172] In Sicily he did not hesitate to use intimidation to make the Bourbons "fear for their lives."[173]

The revolutionaries disdained what the foreign minister Lebrun called "miserable quarrels of etiquette."[174] Nor was he the only revolutionary to do so. John Adams at the Court of St. James lamented that "[t]here are a train of ceremonies yet to go through ... It is thus the essence of things is lost in ceremony in every country of Europe. We must submit to what we cannot alter. Patience is the only remedy."[175] Jean Ternant (1740–1816), the minister plenipotentiary of France to the United States, 1791–1793, wrote the French foreign minister that he would not follow the practices of the British representative George Hammond. He refused to "receive or to make visits of pure ceremony." He disdained "this ridiculous affair of etiquette" and would not engage in a "puerility" so foreign "to the principles of our government." Nonetheless, he thought it important to underscore that the president's audience with Hammond was private as his had been and was as "little conspicuous or striking as that given me."[176]

The omission of certain conventional gestures can even be seen in the conduct of another French minister to the United States (1794–1795), Joseph Fauchet (1761–1834). Fauchet initially appeared to be a welcome alternative to Genet but he was appointed as US-French relations deteriorated. His opposition to John Jay's negotiations with Britain and the subsequent treaty led him to deliberately neglect diplomatic amenities; he boycotted the President's receptions and avoided the Secretary of State, Edmund Randolph. A contemporary thought that he was "badly viewed by good society and does not enjoy any credit."[177] To make matters worse, he narrowly avoided capture by the British on his way home and was only able to embark after a six-week wait.[178] His successor Adet also proved problematic as did his wife because of her incivilities.[179] Victor Du Pont, secretary at the legation, noted that he had "neither sangfroid nor moderation," and moreover, he "gesticulates and salutes like an Italian."[180] Many Americans, he noted, are discontented with Adet, who, he admitted, wrote a great deal and worked hard but "paints all in black." Adet, he noted, was not invited anywhere "in a country where the conventions and etiquette are more followed than any court in Europe." Du Pont himself found that "abominable." In a free country or a republican state, "republicans ought to be contemptuous of these usages and act with dignity of a free man." Still he deplored French functionaries, these "petit republican despots" who when sent abroad did not realize that they should serve the republic and not act against her by condemning everything and in "quarreling with those you ought to flatter." There were too many Jacobins.[181] The Americans found Victor with his civility and cultivated manners a welcome contrast to his successor, an extreme Jacobin with dissolute habits.[182]

The revolutionaries' disdain of diplomatic protocol was such that when it was observed, it occasioned comment. Florimond Claude, comte de Mercy-Argenteau, noted that a 1793 letter of the foreign minister Lebrun to Baron Grenville, the British foreign secretary, was remarkable because of its "style." For the first time Lebrun had "adopted diplomatic forms in the titles and in the measure of the style."[183] As early as May 1793 the Committee of Public Safety directed its agents to "accord all consideration and usages necessary to facilitate the conclusion [of a treaty between France and Sweden] and discard the difficulties that emerge from the etiquette of courts."[184] Such *Realpolitik* considerations were also seen in the Maghreb where the French consul kissed the hand of the bey as stipulated by the treaty of 1742, although that agreement had been repudiated by the Committee of Public Safety. The rationale that this was a mere courtesy did not disguise the submissive nature of the gesture which continued until 1836.[185] Interestingly enough the British faced the same problem in Tunis in 1796 when the bey refused to proceed without the ceremonial kiss. The British decided to withdraw the title of "ambassador" so that "His Majesty's Honor" would not suffer "by his compliance."[186]

When the Directory had deliberately dispatched military officers to Genoa, Venice, Rome, and Vienna, Napoleon instructed them to intimidate the ministers of foreign powers and to ignore the dictates of monarchical protocol.[187] In October 1798, Marie-Caroline, queen of Naples and of Sicily, deplored the arrival of the new French representative, the "republican Minotaur," General Lacombe Saint-Michel (1751–1812), an artillery officer, who had been elected to the Legislative Assembly and then to the Convention. After the death of the king, he had served in Corsica, where he was promoted to general. She noted rather caustically that he acted with the new "*gentilesse républicaine*."[188] This tendency to use military men only accelerated under the Consulate and the Empire. General Guillaume Marie Anne Brune (1763–1815), named ambassador to the Turks in 1802, a man of middle-class origins, was imbued with Jacobinism. The proud general acted inconsiderately, even brutally, and disdained all forms of etiquette, although his predecessors in the post for the last ten years had followed social conventions.[189] Five years later, the British ambassador in Russia noted rather patronizingly that the French representative Anne Jean René Savary, duc de Rovigo, had "quite the tone or manners of the garrison."[190] There were exceptions. Pierre marquis Riel de Beurnonville (1752–1821), who came from a modest family and who had served in the military since 1774, had risen through the ranks and become Minister of

War in 1793. When he was sent to Berlin (1800–1802), he remarked that "circumstances have changed" because of "our regeneration." He did not wish to follow the "prejudices" of anyone. He decided to practice "the most grand politeness towards all the world even toward our enemies."[191] He was the proverbial exception that proved the rule.

Most would agree with the verdict of Madame de Staël, who was speaking about the Napoleonic period (although it was just as true earlier) that these men, "these new debutants in politeness could not conceive that ease was in good taste. In truth, if they had been at their ease, they would have committed strange inconsistencies, and arrogant stiffness was much better suited to them in the new part they wished to play."[192] She might have been speaking of Napoleon, who excelled even the generals in his disregard of form. Napoleon's normal métier was to issue commands rather than make requests: he rarely compromised.[193] Napoleon's preference for soldiers as negotiators contrasts sharply with that of Metternich, a professional and experienced diplomat, who thought that soldiers were not suitable for diplomatic missions. Napoleon in contrast noted that we soldiers "understand one another better" and that diplomats "do not know how to get through an affair." When he urged the Emperor Francis to have Field Marshal Johann I Joseph, prince of Liechtenstein, deal with him instead of diplomats, the emperor unwisely agreed. Instead of parleying with experienced professionals at the Austrian foreign office, Napoleon negotiated at the Schönbrunn with an ingenuous general who was clearly outflanked.[194]

Bonaparte was not hesitant to use unconventional means to achieve his end. In 1797 the Austrian Cobenzl complained about Napoleon's bad faith. When Cobenzl rejected his demands, Napoleon did not hesitate to assert that "the empire was an old harlot which for some time all the world had violated." He went on that the "constitution of the empire is only a pretext to reject my demands." Nor did he hesitate to remind the Austrians that they negotiated in the midst of his grenadiers. In the face of Austrian calm, Napoleon "acted like a fool." He scrawled his name on the document, put on his hat, and, with brusque movements that broke a porcelain serving dish, asserted that the "truce is then broken and war declared; but remember that before the end of autumn I will have crushed your monarchy like this porcelain."[195] He then stalked out. He continued his shouting as he strode up the street. The Austrian complained to the foreign minister, Johann Amadeus Franz de Paula Baron Thugut, that Bonaparte had not followed the proper procedure when he signed the *procès-verbaux*. He attributed this "irregularity" to his "caprice of wishing to put oneself uppermost on all the forms [rather] than to a design to encroach on our sphere."[196] On another occasion Napoleon "rose with the utmost fury, vomited imprecations," scribbled his name in an illegible fashion, and put his hat on in the chamber of the conference and stormed out the door. Cobenzl, who thought his "clamoring" could only be attributed to inebriation, requested instructions in these "so difficult circumstances."[197] The personal display of anger was effective, according to Cohen, because it infringed "the diplomatic convention of imperturbability and good manners" and implied that the envoy was not willing to abide by existing rules. Second, it graphically conveyed the message more effectively than "carefully drafted speeches and diplomatic notes … [whose] form belies their substance."[198] These kind of histrionic and calculated gestures, for which Napoleon was so infamous, were certainly intended to intimidate and only reinforced Cobenzl's view that the French were "our insatiable enemies."[199]

In the face of a hostile Europe, the Directory tried to reconcile republican usages with existing usages. Questions of etiquette were to be resolved by referring to usage and reciprocity. The only exception was that republican states were to be given special consideration. Within the carapace of the international system, the Directory was forced to act within certain constraints. At the reception of the Ottoman ambassador some might have been astonished to see the former ceremonial reestablished in response to the formalistic spirit of the Porte.[200] The same considerations determined the actions of the French representative to the Porte. Raymond Verninac de Saint-Maur[201] made a spectacular entrée into Constantinople on 26 April 1795. A military band and a detachment of French troops with fixed bayonets announced his formal entrance. Fittingly enough, the grand vizir called him *citoyen* since there was no comparable word in Turkish. His successor, General Aubert du Bayet, the minister of war, was appointed to elevate the prestige of France. The 38-year-old general had been released from prison after Thermidor. He decided to enter Constantinople at night rather than compromise the reception he thought necessary. The ceremony he orchestrated mandated a salvo of artillery by two French frigates and great pomp with the horses bedecked as grandly as the participants. It began at 5 am with a guard of honor of janissaries, a company of light infantry, a group of artists, deputations of soldiers and sailors, his private guard, and so. Bayet appeared in full-dress uniform on a magnificent charger. He was conducted to the throne room by pages and eunuchs and received with "Oriental pomp." The dais was covered in silver and encrusted in diamonds. After the traditional ceremony, the return of the cortège took an hour and a half.[202]

The anomaly of that ceremony only underscored the reshaping of diplomatic procedures in the revolutionary mold and the gulf between France and the rest of Europe. The Convention had not employed any elaborate ceremonial. Upon arrival the foreign minister presented his *lettres de créance* to the president of the Convention, who made a speech and then gave the "republican accolade." This minimal ceremony had been used with the minister plenipotentiary of Tuscany, Comte Francesco Xaverio Carletti; the ministers plenipotentiary of the Batavian republic, Jacob Blaauw and Casparus Meyer; and the ambassador of Sweden, Baron Erik Magnus de Staël-Holstein. There was a change after Thermidor. The Thermidoreans provided a higher salary for the minister of foreign affairs in view of his role in representing the nation and with the expectation that his garb should be more elaborate than that of his colleagues.[203] The institution of a revolutionary regime did not mean that procedures were less entangled in etiquette as Monroe, who was sent as minister plenipotentiary to France in 1794, discovered. The commissar of foreign affairs had told him that "as soon as the form of my reception" was settled he would be informed. He underscored that there would be some delay because of the recent fall of Robespierre and his partisans and because of the "necessity of making some regulation ... it being the first instance in which a minister had been addressed to the Republic."[204] As such he was to be solemnly received by the National Convention. Monroe, a man attached to the cause of France and to the Revolution, waited for more than ten days with no progress in sight. News that the minister of Geneva had been there for six weeks awaiting his reception could not have cheered him.[205] When he was finally received, he was accorded an elaborate "fraternal" reception that was more formal than usual. The details were to be reported in the gazette in order to depress the enemies of the republic. The members of the Committee of Public Safety wanted the reception of James Monroe to underscore the friendship and fraternity of the two republics; moreover, they seized the opportunity to display the character and strength of a newly freed nation. "The fall of the throne of the tyrant has swept away in its debris the old diplomacy and the tradition of all these ridiculously ostentatious ceremonies which have fostered the pride of courtesans," the committee intoned. "Let the despots put all their glory and their grandeur in a vain representation. The proud republic hates the false display of monarchs; the majesty of the people is simple, open like liberty." Previously, a minister from abroad had confronted a corrupt court and its arrogant slaves. Now he would see a new spectacle, friendship, freedom, the people, and its representatives. When the US representative confirms "this fraternal alliance," "the soul of two republican peoples will meet and unite" and all vainglorious ceremony will disappear.[206] The president of the Convention, Merlin de Douai, would give Monroe the *accolade fraternelle* in token of the friendship of the two nations. Monroe did not disappoint. In his speech on 15 August 1794, Monroe spoke of himself as the representative of "their sister republic."[207] After Merlin de Douai welcomed him, Monroe ascended the steps and embraced the president amid enthusiastic applause. The assembly then resolved that the American and French flags should be intertwined and placed in the hall. Cheers resounded first for the French and then for the American republic. Even a contemporary, Louis Guillaume Otto, subsequently noted that never had diplomacy presented a more touching scene that triggered "tears of joy in the number of spectators."[208]

By the spring of 1795 the Committee of Public Safety drew up specific recommendations on the reception of foreign ambassadors. We can see the shifting of the revolutionary winds. Before 9 thermidor the spokesman, Merlin du Douai, noted that there was "no diplomacy except at the blow of the cannon," but the Convention has indicated its respect for the "institutions of diplomacy, which pertain to international law." Hitherto friendly states had not sent ambassadors, only ministers, residents, and envoys. No questions concerning etiquette were raised; "fraternity settled the questions and protocol was improvised." Still he pointed out that the difference between an ambassador and the others needed to be recognized. Ambassadors, he pointed out, "have a more elevated character." "In the past France had sent ambassadors, not ministers to Switzerland, Holland, and Venice." The distinctions accorded them may seem "minute," but they "express the mutual degree of confidence … it seems indispensable to maintain them at least until a general accord is reached … and other rules established." Following the practice of giving an armchair to the ambassador who sat directly in front of the sovereign, the Committee of Public Safety proposed that ambassadors be seated in an armchair in front of the president. The representatives were to be accorded the titles stipulated in the *lettres de créance*. Following the decree's adoption, the Swedish ambassador was introduced to the National Convention and placed in the armchair and invited to share "the joys of the most touching fraternity … [and to] receive the republican accolade."[209]

Still later the Venetian ambassador, representative of another republic, was more highly honored. On 31 July 1795 the Convention greeted Alvise Guerini, the Venetian representative, with cheers for the two republics. He then delivered a speech in which he boasted that Venice had enjoyed her liberty for 11 centuries.[210] It was a moment which, from the hindsight of the betrayal in 1797, when the Venetian republic was dissolved and partitioned, was not devoid of a certain irony. The French betrayed others as well, most notably the Swiss. In the context of later events the effusive reception of Etienne Salomon Reybaz, the Genevan minister, on 23 August 1794 was equally ironic. During that reception Merlin de Thionville, as president, spoke of the Genevese as descendants of William Tell. The assembly then resolved to hang the Genevese flag alongside the French and American colors. At his presentation to the *conseil exécutif provisoire*, Reybaz, the "citizen minister" from the republic of Geneva, had criticized the ostentation and vanity of the ceremonies of the *ancien régime*. "On the one hand," Reybaz proclaimed, "one saw men elevated as demi-gods.... On the other, servile worshippers intoxicated with the incense they poured at the feet of their idols." Undoubtedly he exaggerated, but he made his point. He, by contrast, was merely "a simple citizen" who reported to others "honored with the same title."[211] Some representatives were accorded a more informal reception. In 1796, Harris' coach was met by 300 individuals, mostly *poissardes*. When some tried to give him the fraternal embrace, the appalled aristocrat kept his head and avoided such proximity by throwing money to the receptive crowd.[212]

The Directory moved toward a partial restoration of diplomatic form and more solemnity. An *arrêt* of 28 brumaire, an IV established the procedure for the first reception of the diplomatic corps, all of whom had been previously recognized. In that light it stipulated a simple audience with presentation to the president. Nevertheless, the constitutional guard was to render military honors. The Directors were to appear in the ceremonial costume: blue facing and blue sleeves were lined with white and richly embroidered in gold on the outside as were the lapels, a long white vest, again embroidered in gold, pantaloons of white silk, a blue belt with gold fringe, and an orange red cloak. To top it, or rather them, off they wore round black hats with a tricolor plume and a sword borne on a red-orange belt. The Directors were surrounded by ministers in costume and by numerous military officers. Because the foreign ministers to be presented were not given instructions on their attire, their costume varied from the elaborate uniform of the baron de Staël to the simple black morning coat without sword of the Genevan minister, Reybaz. The bungling of the presentation that did not seem to conform to any pattern and the presence of some rather disreputable individuals in the crowd did not make a good impression. Following its democratic principles, the door of the Luxembourg was open to all. At least one spectator was astonished to see Reubell receiving petitions from a very mixed crowd including "rascals" and injured soldiers.[213]

It was true in revolutionary France as it had been in the *ancien régime* that "apparent trifles," in the words of Charles Cotesworth Pinckney (1746–1825), Monroe's successor, "often indicate matters of consequence."[214] Those "trifles" reflected, in the words of the American representative at The Hague, "the etiquette of European republics, ostentatious of guards and music – scarfs and plumes."[215] Under the Consulate, the etiquette became even more militaristic in tone. Robert Livingston, the American minister, reported from Paris that "[e]verything here has a military appearance." On the 15th of every month, he noted that 5000 troops were assembled before the Palace and reviewed by the first consul. Immediately after the awards were distributed, the ministers passed through a line of guards into the hall of ambassadors. Each apartment and hall they passed through had "guards under arms."[216] A new etiquette both more republican and more militaristic had replaced the old one. As in the *ancien régime*, ceremony served to legitimate the new and underscore the power of the Revolution.[217]

Notes

1. Norbert Elias, *The Court Society*, trans. Edmund Jephcott (New York: Pantheon, 1983), 117–118.
2. Patrice Higonnet, *Goodness Beyond Virtue, Jacobins during the French Revolution* (Cambridge, MA: Harvard University Press, 1998), 80.
3. Napoleon to the Minister for Foreign Affairs, Rastatt, 30 November 1797, quoted in Napoleon, *Napoleon Self-Revealed*, edited by J. M. Thompson (New York: Houghton Mifflin Company, 1934), 52–53.
4. Jeroen Duindam, *Vienna and Versailles: The Courts of Europe's Dynastic Rivals, 1550–1780* (Cambridge: University Press, 2003), 181. See also Ute Daniel, "Überlegungen zum höfischen Fest der Barockzeit," *Niedersächsisches Jahrbuch für Landesgeschichte* 72 (2000): 45–66; Benjamin Marschke, "'Von dem am Königl. Preussischen Hofe abgeschafften Ceremoniel': Monarchical Representation and Ceremony in Frederick William I's Prussia," in *Orthodoxies and Diversity in Early Modern Germany*, ed. Randolph C. Head and Daniel Christensen, 227–252

(Boston: Brill Publishers, 2007); Milos Vec, *Zeremonial-Wissenschaft im Fürstenstaat: Studien zur juristischen und politischen Theorie absolutischer Herrschaftsrepräsentation* (Frankfurt am Main: Vittorio Klostermann, 1998) and Barbara von Stollberg-Rilinger, "Zeremoniell, Ritual, Symbol: Neue Forschungen zur symbolischen Kommunikation im Spätmittelater und Früher Neuzeit," *Zeitschrift für historische Forschung* 27 (2000): 389–405.
5. Cannadine, "Introduction: Divine Rites of Kings," in *Rituals of Royalty: Power and Ceremonial in Traditional Societies*, ed. Cannadine and Price, 3.
6. Edmund Burke, "A Letter to a Member of the National Assembly in Answer to Some Objection to His Book on French Affairs," in *Works of Right Honourable Edmund Burke*, 1791 Reprint (London: Bohn, 1855), 2: 537.
7. Elias, *The Court Society*, 86–87.
8. Jean Jacques Rousseau, *The First and Second Discourses*, edited by Roger D. Masters (New York: St. Martin's Press, 1964), 36. Art, he fulminated, "molded our manner and taught our passions to speak an affected language." Ibid., 37.
9. Ibid., 39 and 37.
10. Jean Jacques Rousseau, *Discourse on the Origins and Foundations of Inequality among Men* (New York: Pocket Books, 1971), 180. Also see Bernard Mandeville, *The Fable of the Bees or Private Vices, Publick Benefits* (Oxford: Clarendon Press, 1957), 1: 349.
11. Quoted in Clark, *Compass of Society*, 297.
12. Darnton, "The French Revolution: Intellectuals and Literature."
13. Edmund Burke, *The Writings and Speeches of Edmund Burke*, vol. 9 edited by William B. Todd (Oxford: Clarendon Press, 1991), "Fourth Letter on a Regicide Peace," 14.
14. Muir, *Ritual in Early Modern Europe*, 125.
15. Norbert Elias, *The History of Manners, The Civilizing Process, State Formation and Civilization*, trans. Edmund Jephcott (Oxford: Basil Blackwell, 1982), 315.
16. A. A. E. C.P., État Unis, vol. 54, part 2, fol. 92, Pichon, Georgetown, 26 pluviôse, an 10.
17. Edmund Burke, "Letters on a Regicide Peace," in *The Works*, 5: 208.
18. Gerald W. Chapman, *Edmund Burke: The Practical Imagination* (Cambridge, MA: Harvard University Press, 1967), 202.
19. Edmund Burke, "A Letter to a Member of the National Assembly in Answer to Some Objection to His Book on French Affairs," in *The Works of Right Honourable Edmund Burke* (London: Bohn, 1855), 2: 537.
20. Edmund Burke, *Reflections on the Revolution in France* (Harmondsworth, England: Penguin Books, 1968), 172.

21. Burke, "A Letter to a Member of the National Assembly in Answer to Some Objection to His Book on French Affairs," in *The Works*, 2: 537.
22. Bertrand Barère, *Memoirs of Bertrand Barère Chairman of the Committee of Public Safety During the Revolution*, translated by De V. Payen-Payne (London: H.S. Nichols, 1796) 1: 309–310. Perhaps unconsciously he echoed Fénelon's warning that two things endanger "the government of peoples." The first, unjust authority could be checked even if by a coup but luxury "which corrupts manners" was "almost incurable." Kings could be corrupted by excess authority, but luxury "empoisons a whole people." (Quoted in Sonenscher, *Before the Deluge*, 106.
23. Quoted in Elias, *The Court Society*, 117–118. Also see Peter Burke, *The Fabrication of Louis XIV* (New Haven: Yale University Press, 1992).
24. Elias, *The Court Society*, 71, 207.
25. Ibid., 207–208.
26. Quoted in ibid., 231.
27. Quoted in Belissa, "La Diplomatie et les traités dans la pensées des lumières," 297.
28. François de Callières, *Letters (1694–1700) of Francois de Callières to the Marquise d'Huxelles*, edited by Laurence Pope (Lewiston: Edwin Mellen Press, 2004), 228.
29. In *Henry V*, act iv, scene 1, he asks: "And what have kings, that privates have not too? Save ceremony, save general ceremony?" Quoted in Cannadine, "Introduction: Divine Rites of Kings," in *Rituals of Royalty*, ed. Cannadine and Price, 1.
30. Belissa, "La Diplomatie et les traités dans la pensée des lumières," 306.
31. Comte F.-G. de Bray, *Memoires du comte de Bray* (Paris: Plon Nourrit et Cie., 1911), 103.
32. Ibid., 109, 111, 120.
33. The British minister to Russia, Alleyene Fitzherbert, confided to his sister that the time he spent with the empress at a country house as part of her private society, not as the British representative, was "so much more agreeable … we were not troubled with the smallest degree of ceremony and etiquette." Derbyshire Record Office, Papers of Alleyne Fitzherbert, D/239M/F12338 to his sister, St. Petersburgh [sic], 23 August 1785.
34. Robert Oresko, "The House of Savoy in Search for a Royal Crown in the Seventeenth Century." In *Royal and Republican Sovereignty in Early Modern Europe*, edited by Robert Oresko, G. C. Gibbs, and H. M. Scott, 273–350 (Cambridge: University Press, 1997), 274.
35. For a vivid discussion, see Lucien Bély, "Souveraineté et souverains: la question du cérémonial dans les relations internationales à l'époque moderne," *Annuaire-bulletin de la Société* de l'histoire de France 130 (1993): 27–43.

36. Hamish M. Scott, "Diplomatic Culture in Old Regime Europe, in *Cultures of Power in Europe During the Long Eighteenth Century*, edited by Hamish Scott and Brendan Simms (Cambridge: University Press, 2007), 59–60.
37. Jacques-Pierre dit Brissot de Warville, *Discours sur l'office de l'Empereur du 17 février 1792 et dénonciation contre M. Delessart, ministre des Affaires étrangères prononcé à l'Assemblée nationale le 10 Mars 1792 by J. P. Brissot, député du département de Paris* (Paris: Imprimerie. Nationale, n.d.), 28.
38. Barthélemy, *Papiers de Barthélemy*, 2: 417.
39. Arno Mayer, *The Persistence of the Old Regime: Europe to the Great War* (New York: Pantheon Books, 1981), 136.
40. Vattel, *The Law of Nations*, 149.
41. H. G. Koenigsberger, "Republicanism, Monarchism and Liberty." In *Royal and Republican Sovereignty in Early Modern Europe*, edited by Robert Oresko, G. C. Gibbs, and H. M. Scott, 43–74 (Cambridge: University Press, 1997), 57.
42. Oresko. "The House of Savoy in Search for a Royal Crown in the Seventeenth Century," in *Royal and Republican Sovereignty*, ed. Gibbs, Oresko, and Scott, 294.
43. Ibid., 342.
44. The jurist Georg Friedrich von Martens, whose treatise appeared in French in 1789, included an extensive section on precedence. George Friedrich Martens, *Summary of the Law of Nations* (Philadelphia: Thomas Bradford, 1795), 136–144.
45. Jeremy Black, *British Diplomats and Diplomacy, 1688–1800* (Exeter: University of Exeter Press, 2001), 97.
46. Duindam, *Vienna and Versailles*, 184.
47. Cited in Scott, *The Birth of a Great Power System 1740–1815*, 124.
48. Duindam, *Vienna and Versailles*, 187.
49. Jean Baptiste Colbert, *Journal inédit de Jean-Baptiste Colbert, marquis de Torcy*, edited by Frédéric Masson (Paris: Plon Nourrit, 1884), xiii–xiv.
50. Bély, "Souveraineté et souverain, 41.
51. Aulard, *Recueil des actes du comité de salut public*, 4: 476.
52. Barthélemy, *Papiers de Barthélemy*, 2: 290–294; François-Alphonse Aulard., ed. "Instructions générales des agents diplomatiques de la République française, 1er juin 1793," *La Révolution française* 13 (1887): 66–73.
53. *Moniteur* 24: 294, 26 April 1795, 4 floréal.
54. P.R.O., FO 5/4, fol. 101, Executive Council, at Paris, 4 January 1793. *The Correspondence between Citizen Genet, Minister of the French Republic, to the United States of North America and the Officers of the Federal Government; to which are prefixed the Instructions from the Constituted*

Authorities of France to the Said Minister. All from Authentic Documents (Philadelphia: Benjamin Franklin Bache, 1793).
55. N.A., General Records of the Department of State, RG59, Diplomatic Despatches, France (34), vol. 4, James Monroe to the Secretary of State (Paris, 6 December 1795).
56. Boccardi's dispatch of 20 November 1795 quoted in Guyot, *Le Directoire et la paix de l'Europe*, 92, fn 1.
57. Vattel, *The Law of Nations*, 149.
58. Guyot, *Le Directoire et la paix de l'Europe*, 89.
59. Hermann Hüffer, *Der Rastatter Congress und die zweite Coalition* (Bonn: Adolph Marcus, 1878), 1: 254.
60. Dry, *Soldats ambassadeurs*, 375–376 and Hüffer, *Der Rastatter Congress*, Chap. 9, esp. 254–55.
61. Pickering responded that private publications were not under government control and, moreover, that "it was not for his Government to determine questions of rank among foreign powers." Beckles Willson, *Friendly Relations: A Narrative of Britain's Ministers and Ambassadors to America* (1791–1930) (Boston: Little, Brown and Company, 1934), 20.
62. *Correspondance de Napoléon I* (Paris: Henri Plon, 1859), 2: 489, Napoleon to Directors, Leoben, 27 germinal, an V (16 April 1797).
63. Hüffer, ed., *Quellen zur Geschichte des Zeitalters der französischen Revolution*, 463, Cobenzl to Thugut, Udine, 18 October 1797.
64. R. B. Mowat, *The Diplomacy of Napoleon* (London: Edward Arnold & Co., 1924), 34.
65. Ibid., 35.
66. Guyot, *Le Directoire et la paix de l'Europe*, 688.
67. *Correspondance de Napoléon I*, 3: 73, Napoleon to Directors, 8 prairial, an V (27 May 1797).
68. As late as 1811 the French representative to Russia underscored that he had been given a seat on the same side as the tsar. Moreover, his audience of leave had followed the same ceremonial as his presentation. Like a diplomat of the *ancien régime*, he had been given the customary gift of a portrait in diamonds. Nicolas Mikhailowitch, *Les Relations diplomatiques de la Russie et de la France d'après les rapports des ambassadeurs d'Alexandre et de Napoléon*. (Petrograde: Manufacture des papiers de l'Etat, 1907), 5: 305, letter of 4 February 1811. As late as 1812 the government in Paris sanctioned the decision of the French representative in Naples to fight a duel with his Russian counterpart over precedence. Scott, *The Birth of a Great Power System, 1740–1815*, 124.
69. Dumas Malone, *Jefferson and His Time vol. 4: Jefferson the President: First Term, 1801–1805* (Boston: Little Brown and Company, 1970), 385.
70. Ibid., 386, Thomas Jefferson to William Short, 23 January 1804.

71. Ibid., 385.
72. Ibid., 386–387.
73. Lucien Bély, *La Société des princes: XVIe–XVIIIe siècle* (Paris: Fayard, 1999), 406 and 396.
74. Bély, "Souveraineté et souverains," 43 and 28.
75. Ibid., 28 and 35. See also Daniel "Überlegungen zum höfischen Fest der Barockzeit," 45–66 and Stollberg-Rilinger, "Zeremoniell, Ritual, Symbol," 389–405.
76. Bély, *La Société des princes*, 10.
77. David A. Bell, *The Cult of the Nation in France: Inventing Nationalism, 1680–1800* (Cambridge, MA: Harvard University Press, 2001), 148.
78. Muir, *Ritual in Early Modern Europe*, 120.
79. François, duc de La Rochefoucauld, *Maximes suivies des réflexions diverses* (Paris: Editions Garnier Frères, 1967), 68 #260.
80. Ibid., 67 #260; 93 #393; 29 #100; 89– #372. Also see François, duc de La Rochefoucauld, *Maxims* (Baltimore: Penguin Books, 1959), intro. and 68, 83, 47, 81.
81. "The practice of honest dissimulation," as Jon Snyder has argued, "was dialectically linked to the Old Regime culture of display and observation." Jon R. Snyder, *Dissimulation and the Culture of Secrecy in Early Modern Europe* (Berkeley: University of California Press, 2009), 47. Interestingly enough, Callières, who wrote the foundational text on *ancien régime* diplomacy, argued in 1696 that that very *bel esprit*, the manners and wit of the court, "makes people ill-suited to the conduct of public business." Callières, *Letters (1694–1700)*, 14. See Francois de Callières, *Du bel esprit* (Amsterdam: Pierre Brunel, 1695), 151.
82. Shakespeare, *Cymbelline*, I, I, 84, quoted in Snyder, *Dissimulation and the Culture of Secrecy in Early Modern Europe*, 33.
83. Blanning, *The Culture of Power and the Power of Culture*, 5.
84. Condorcet, *Oeuvres*, 10: 399–400.
85. Quoted in Stanley J. Idzerda, "Inconoclasm during the French Revolution," *American Historical Review* 60 (July 1955): 15.
86. Quoted in Leora Auslander, *Cultural Revolutions: Everyday Life and Politics in Britain, North America and France* (Berkeley, CA: University of California Press, 2009), 113.
87. Miles, *The Correspondence of William Augustus Miles*, 1: 159 Miles to Lord Rodney, Paris, 23 August 1790.
88. Great Britain, HMC, The Manuscripts of J. B. Fortescue, Esq., Preserved at Dropmore (London: By Eyre and Spottiswoode, 1894), 1: 608, 610. Also see BL Add. Mss. 58910 to Grenville, Paris, 27 Sept. 1790, fol. 142.
89. Bailleu, ed. *Preussen und Frankreich von 1795 bis 1807*, 1: 37, Paris, 10 December1795.

90. Raymond Cohen, *Theatre of Power: The Art of Diplomatic Signalling* (New York: Longman, 1987), 90–91.
91. Der Derian, *On Diplomacy*, 179.
92. Geoffrey de Grandmaison, *L'Ambassade française en Espagne*, 37, 50, 51.
93. Ibid., 39–43 and 53.
94. Henri Stroehlin, *La Mission de Barthélemy en Suisse (1792–1797)* (Geneva: Henry Kundig, 1900), 23 and 56.
95. B. L., Add. Mss. 36813, from Bute at Madrid, 30 April 1796 to Grenville.
96. Michaud, *Biographie universelle*, 2: 576–577.
97. *Dictionnaire de biographie française*, edited by J. Balteau, Michel Prévost, and Roman d'Amat (Paris: Libraire LeTouzey et Ané, 1933–) 6: 843.
98. Bailleu, ed. *Preussen und Frankreich von 1795 bis 1807*, 1: 429–430, Report of Caillard from Berlin, 1 Nov. 1795.
99. Report of Caillard from Berlin, 28 March 1797, in ibid., 1: 457.
100. *Archives parlementaires* 52: 314, 4 October 1792.
101. A. N., DXXIII, carton 2 dossier 34, Society of the Friends of the Constitution at Cherbourg to the Diplomatic Committee, 2 September 1792.
102. Brissot, *Discours de J. P. Brissot, député sur les dispostions des puissances étrangères*, 43.
103. Iiams, *Peacemaking from Vergennes to Napoleon*, 59. As late as 1801, Joseph Bonaparte told Charles Cornwallis (1738–1805), the British plenipotentiary at the congress of Amiens, that he was "a stranger to the arts of negotiation and would not attempt to carry any points by the cunning of chicanery." He thought that Cornwallis with his "line of life," presumably a reference to his military career, would welcome such an approach. P.R.O., FO 27/59 Cornwallis to Hawkesbury, Paris, 26 November 1801.
104. J. Holland Rose, *William Pitt and the Great War*, 1911 reprint (Westport, CT: Greenwood Press, 1971), 79.
105. Frank L. Kidner, Jr. *The Girondists and the "Propaganda War" of 1792: A Re-evaluation of French Revolutionary Foreign Policy from 1791 to 1793*, unpublished Ph.D. dissertation Princeton University, 1971, 396.
106. B. L., Add. Mss. 59051, fols. 34–37, to Dorset, Paris, 16 March 1792.
107. Ibid., 118–123.
108. Ibid., 116–123.
109. Grandmaison, *L'Ambassade française en Espagne*, 165.
110. Brissot, *Rapport fait au nom du comité de défense générale*, 3.
111. Malmesbury Papers, Merton College, Oxford F3.3 (3) 86, letter of August 16, 1794.
112. Guyot, *Le Directoire et la paix de l'Europe*, 670.
113. Raymond Koechlin, "La Politique française au congrès de Rastatt," *Annales de l'école libre des sciences politiques*, 1 (1886): 404.

114. Pallain, ed. *Le Ministère de Talleyrand sous le Directoire*, 211–212, Talleyrand to Treilhard, 27 February 1798.
115. Guyot, *Le Directoire et la paix de l'Europe*, 672–673.
116. Koechlin "La Politique française au congrès de Rastatt," 404, letter of 25 December 1797.
117. Brendan Simms, *The Impact of Napoleon: Prussian High Politics, Foreign Policy and the Crisis of the Executive 1797–1806* (Cambridge: University Press, 1997), 93.
118. Bailleu, ed. *Preussen und Frankreich von 1795 bis 1807*, 1: 214, fn. 1.
119. Armand François, comte de Allonville, *Mémoires tirés des papiers d'un homme d'état sur les causes secrètes qui ont déterminé la politique des cabinets dans les guerres de la révolution* (Paris: Michaud, 1832), 6: 179.
120. John Harold Clapham, *The Abbé Sièyes: An Essay in the Politics of the French Revolution.* (London: P. S. King and Son, 1912), 206–207.
121. Guyot, *Le Directoire et la paix de l'Europe*, 716–717.
122. Mann, *Secretary of Europe*, 45.
123. Clapham, *The Abbé Sièyes*, 210.
124. Guyot, *Le Directoire et la paix de l'Europe*, 717–719 and Mann, *Secretary of Europe*, 45.
125. Guyot, *Le Directoire et la paix de l'Europe*, 717–719.
126. Bailleu, ed. *Preussen und Frankreich von 1795 bis 1807*, 1: 234, Graf Haugwitz to Graf Finckenstein, Berlin, 25 August 1798.
127. Finkenstein quoted in Lothar Kittstein, *Politik im Zietalter der Revolution: Untersuchungen zur preussischen Staatlichkeit 1792–1807* (Wiesbaden: Franz Steiner Verlag, 2003), 142.
128. Clapham, *The Abbé Sièyes*, 208.
129. Bailleu, ed. *Preussen und Frankreich von 1795 bis 1807*, 1: 500–501, report of Sièyes to Talleyrand, Berlin, 24 May 1799.
130. Mayer, *The Persistence of the Old Regime*, 137.
131. Edmund Burke, "Four Letters on the Proposals for Peace with the Regicide Directory of France" in *Burke Select Works*, edited by E. J. Payne (Oxford: Clarendon Press, 1894), xxxviii.
132. Hampshire Record Office, 631/3/3, to his wife from Sir James Harris, husband October 16, 1796.
133. Harris, *Diaries and Correspondence*, 3: 266, Harris to Grenville, Paris, 23 October 1796.
134. Hampshire Record Office, 631/3/8, Harris to his wife, Calais, 18 October 1796.
135. Hampshire Record Office, 631/3/9, Harris to his wife, 21 October 1796.
136. Aulard, *Paris pendant la réaction thermidorienne et sous le Directoire*, 3: 542.
137. B. L., Add. Mss. 59130, fol. 6–10. Draft of instructions for Harris, 1796.

138. P.R.O., FO 27/46 fol. 231, Harris to Lord Grenville, 28 November 1796.
139. Harris, *Diaries and Correspondence*, 3: 266, Harris to Grenville, Paris, 23 October 1796.
140. Ibid., 3: 353, Harris to Grenville, Paris, 20 December 1796.
141. Ibid., 3: 269. Harris to Grenville, Paris, 27 October 1796.
142. Edmund B. d'Auvergne, *Envoys Extraordinary: the Remarkable careers of Some Remarkable British Representatives Abroad* (London: George G. Harrap & Co. Ltd., 1937), 73–74.
143. Bailleu ed. *Preussen und Frankreich von 1795 bis 1807*, 104, Sandoz-Rollin from Paris, 14 November 1796.
144. Harris, *Diaries and Correspondence*, 3: 484, 27 August 1797.
145. Hampshire Record Office, 631/3/11, Harris to his wife, Paris, 27 October 1796.
146. Ibid., 631/3/10, Harris to his wife, 25 October 1796.
147. Ibid., 631/3/12, to his wife from Sir James Harris, husband, Paris, 31 October 1796.
148. Malmesbury Papers, Merton College, Oxford F3.3 (3) 13, letter of 23 October 1796.
149. Ibid., F3.3 (1) 166, letter of 3 July 1797.
150. Ibid., F3.3 (1) 167, letter of 5 July 1797.
151. P.R.O., FO, 27/49 fol. 206, 29 June 1797.
152. Hampshire Record Office, 631/4/13 Harris to his wife, 20 September 1797.
153. Harris, *Diaries and Correspondence*, 3: 521, 31 August 1797.
154. P.R.O., FO 27/50, fol. 316–317, Harris, 19 September 1797.
155. Ibid., 3: 560, 17 September 1797.
156. Harris, *Diaries and Correspondence*, 3: 539, 3: 592, 11 and 29 September 1797.
157. Ibid., 3: 527, Lille 11 September 1797.
158. Malmesbury Papers, Merton College, Oxford F3.3 (3)29i, letter of [1797?].
159. Scott, "Diplomatic Culture in Old Regime Europe," 83.
160. Gower, *Private Correspondence*, 1: 174, Granville to Lady Stafford, 21 September 1797. Also see National Library of Ireland, letters from Bristol to Hamilton, 14 July 1797: "No one hopes anything from the Farsical congress at Lisle."
161. Hampshire Record Office, 631/5/5 Harris to his wife, 1800.
162. Harris, *Diaries and Correspondence*, 4: 75, 1802.
163. Ibid., 4: 75.
164. Much earlier that problem had surfaced with Chauvelin, who was sent to France as relations began to deteriorate. He wrote home that he did not want "any point of form" to stand in the way of "friendly communica-

tions" between France and Great Britain." P.R.O., FO 27/40, fols. 169–172, minutes of a conference with M. Chauvelin, 29 November 1792.
165. Harris, *Diaries and Correspondence*, 4: 73–74. As late as 1801 one British envoy could remark that he had dined with individuals who had "the dress of mountebanks and the manners of assassins." Cornwallis, *Correspondence*, 3: 410, Viscount Brome to Major-General Ross, Amiens, 12 December 1801.
166. See for example, B. L., Add. Mss. 36813, Bute to Grenville, 2 April 1797, fol. 220, private "arrogance of the French mission at Madrid."
167. Hampshire Record Office, Wickham Papers, 38M 49/1/1/15, Auckland to Wickham, 12 April 1796.
168. P.R.O., FO 27/50 Harris, Lille, 11 September 1797.
169. Jean François Eugène Robinet, ed. *Dictionnaire historique et biographique de la Révolution et de l'Empire 1789–1815* (Paris: Libraire historique de la Révolution et de l'Empire, 1899), 2: 791–792.
170. James Harris, *Diaries and Correpondence of James Harris, first Earl of Malmesbury.* (London: Richard Bentley, 1844), 3: 555, 13 September 1797.
171. Clemens Wenzel Nepomuk Lothar, Fürst von Metternich, *Mémoires, documents et écrits divers laissés par le Prince Metternich, chancelier de cour et d'état*, edited by Richard de Metternich. (Paris: E. Plon et Cie, 1881), 1: 354, 22 December 1797, to his wife.
172. Scott, *The Birth of a Great Power System, 1740–1815*, 279.
173. Iiams, *Peacemaking from Vergennes to Napoleon*, 159.
174. Black, "From Pillnitz to Valmy," 141.
175. Quoted in Norman A. Graebner, *Ideas and Diplomacy: Readings in the Intellectual Tradition of American Foreign Policy* (New York: Oxford University Press, 1964), 36.
176. Turner, ed., *Correspondence of the French Ministers to the United States*, 1: 68–69, Ternant to Montmorin, Philadelphia, 13 November 1791.
177. Hagley, W3-261, Victor Du Pont to the family, 28 June 1795.
178. Joseph Fauchet, *Mémoire sur les État unis d'Amérique*, 85–123.
179. Hagley, W3-275, Victor Du Pont to the family, Charleston, 10 November 1795.
180. Ibid., W3-261, Victor Du Pont to the family, 28 June 1795.
181. Ibid., W3-267, Victor Du Pont to the family, 2 August 1795.
182. Ibid., W3-275, Victor Du Pont to the family, Charleston, 10 November 1795.
183. Florimond Claude, comte de Mercy-Argenteau, *Briefe des Grafen Mercy-Argentau k.k. Bevollmächtigen Minister in den Österreichischen Niederlanden an den K. K. Ausserordentilichen Gesandten zu London Grafen Louis Starhemberg, von 26 December 1791 bis August 1794*, ed. A. Graf Thurheim

(Innsbruck: Wagnerschen Universitats-Buchhandlung, 1884), 84, Mercy, Brussels, 26 May 1793.
184. Aulard, ed. *Recueil des actes du comité de salut public*, 4: 185–186.
185. Scott, *The Birth of a Great Power System*, 278.
186. National Maritime Museum, WDG16/1, William Waldegrave 1796 Proceedings at Tunis, 2.
187. Guyot, *Le Directoire et la paix de l'Europe*, 688 and 720. On another occasion Napoleon voiced the belief that the old etiquette would collapse by its "old age." Napoleon, *Correspondance de Napoléon I*, 3: 73, Napoleon to Directory, 8 prairial an V (27 May 1797).
188. Marie Caroline, queen of Naples, *Correspondance inédite de Marie Caroline, reine de Naples et de Sicile*. (Paris: Emile-Paul, 1911), 1: 533, 1798, #290 and 534, 1798.
189. Allonville, *Mémoires*, 9: 360.
190. Lord Granville Leveson Gower (First Earl Granville), *Private Correspondence 1781 to 1821*, ed. Castalia Countess Granville (New York: E. P. Dutton and Company, 1916), 2: 279, 1807.
191. Bailleu, ed. *Preussen und Frankreich von 1795 bis 1807*, 1: 519, Beurnonville to Hauterive, Berlin, 1 Feb. 1800.
192. Anne Louise Germaine Necker, Baroness de Staël-Holstein, *Ten Years' Exile or Memoirs of that Interesting Period of the Life of the Baroness de Staël-Holstein* (Fontwell, Sussex: Centaur Press Ltd., 1968), 39.
193. Mowat, *The Diplomacy of Napoleon*, 96.
194. Ibid., 228–229.
195. François Pierre Guizot and Henriette Elizabeth Guizot de Witt, *The History of France from the Earliest Times to 1848* (Boston: Dana Estes & Company, 1885), 6: 443; Andrew Roberts, *Napoleon* (New York: Viking, 2014), 149.
196. Hüffer, ed. *Quellen zur Geschichte des Zeitalters der französischen Revolution*, 323, Gallo, Merveldt, Degelmann to Thugut, Udine 1 September 1797; also see Sorel, *L'Europe et le Révolution française*, 5: 245–248.
197. Ibid., 458, Cobenzl to Thugut, Udine, 14 October 1797.
198. Cohen, *Theatre of Power*, 109.
199. Hüffer, ed., *Quellen zur Geschichte des Zeitalters der französischen Revolution*, 445, Cobenzl to Thugut, 10 October 1797.
200. Guyot, *Le Directoire et la paix de l'Europe*, 91–92.
201. Michaud, *Biographie universelle*, 43: 223.
202. Frédéric Clément-Simon, *Le premier Ambassadeur de la République française à Constantinople: le Général Aubert du Bayet* (Paris: imp. De la "Renaissance latine," 1904), 6–10; A. A. E., C.P., États-Unis, vol. 47, part 1, fol. 111. Le Redacteur, no. 443, 13 ventôse an 5.

203. Lois du 30 fructidor an 3, art 2 and of 3 brumaire, an 4, art 16 in Guyot, *Le Directoire et la paix de l'Europe*, 190.
204. N.A., General Records of the Department of State, RG59, Diplomatic Despatches, France (34), vol. 4, James Monroe to the Secretary of State, Paris, 15 August 1794. See also A. A. E., États-Unis, C. P., vol. 41, part 4, fol. 276–289, commissar of foreign relations to Committee of Public Safety, 22 thermidor, an II.
205. Ibid., James Monroe to the Secretary of State, Paris, 25 August 1794.
206. *Moniteur*, 21: 496, #329, August 1794 See also A. A. E., États-Unis, C.P., vol. 41, part 4, fol. 280, commissar of foreign relations to Committee of Public Safety, 22 thermidor, an II.
207. Ibid.
208. A. A. E., C.P., États-Unis vol. 47, part 6, fol. 409, par M. Otto, Consideration sur la conduite du gouvernement des États Unis ... 1789–1797.
209. *Moniteur* vol. 24: 292–293, 23 April 1795, Meeting of 4 floréal, Merlin du Douai.
210. John Goldworth Alger, *Paris in 1789–1794: Farewell Letters of Victims of the Guillotine* (London: George Allen, 1902), 98–99.
211. Aulard, ed., *Recueil des actes du comité de salut public*, 1: 343, 19 December 1792.
212. Edmund Burke, *The Correspondence of Edmund Burke*, Volume 9, Part 1, May 1796–July 1797, ed. R. B. McDowell (Illinois: The University of Chicago Press, 1970), 101–102, Edmund Burke to Earl Fitzwilliam, 30 October 1796, fn. 7.
213. Guyot, *Le Directoire et la paix de l'Europe*, 91.
214. NA, General Records of the Department of State, RG59, Diplomatic Despatches, France (34), vol. 5, 17 November 1796.
215. NA, The Netherlands (M42), vol. 3, W.V. Murray, The Hague, 4 February 1798.
216. New York Historical Society, Robert Livingston Papers, Paris, Livingston, to Secretary of State, 10 Dec. 1801.
217. See Vec, *Zeremonial-Wissenschaft im Fürstenstaat*.

References

Alger, John Goldworth. *Paris in 1789–94: Farewell Letters of Victims of the Guillotine*. London: George Allen, 1902.

Allonville, Armand François, comte de. *Mémoires tirés des papiers d'un homme d'état sur les causes secrètes qui ont déterminé la politique des cabinets dans les guerres de la révolution*. 13 vols. Paris: Michaud, 1831–1838.

Archives Parlementaires de 1787 à 1860. Series 1: 1789–1800. Vol. 15: *Assemblée nationale constituante du 21 Avril au 30 Mai 1790*. Edited by M. J. Mavidal and M. E. Laurent. Paris: Paul Dupont, 1883.

Aulard, François-Alphonse, ed. "Instructions générales des agents diplomatiques de la République française, 1er juin 1793." *La Révolution française* 13 (1887): 66–73.

———, ed. *Paris pendant la réaction thermidorienne et sous le Directoire: Recueil de documents pour l'histoire de l'esprit public à Paris*. Vols. 2–3. Paris: Librairie Noblet, 1899.

———, ed., *Recueil des actes du Comité de salut public avec la correspondance officielle des représentants en mission et le registre du conseil exécutif provisoire*. 27 vols. Paris: Imprimerie nationale, 1889–1923.

Auslander, Leora. *Cultural Revolutions: Everyday Life and Politics in Britain, North America and France*. Berkeley, CA: University of California Press, 2009.

D'Auvergne, Edmund B. *Envoys Extraordinary: The Romantic Careers of Some Remarkable British Representatives Abroad*. London: G. G. Harrap & Co. Ltd, 1937.

Bailleu, Paul, ed. *Preusssen und Frankreich von 1795 bis 1807. Diplomatische Correspondenzen*. Osnabrück: Otto Zeller, 1965.

Barère de Vieuzac, Bertrand. *Memoirs of Bertrand Barère Chairman of the Committee of Public Safety During the Revolution*. 4 vols. Translated by De V. Payen-Payne. London: H. S. Nichols, 1896.

Barthélemy, François. *Papiers de Barthélemy, ambassadeur de France en Suisse, 1792–1797*. Edited by Jean Kaulek and Alexandre Tausserat-Radel. 6 vols. Paris: Alcan, 1886–1910.

Belissa, Marc. "La Diplomatie et les traités dans la pensée des lumières: 'negociation universelle' ou école du mensonge." *Revue d'histoire diplomatique* 3 (1999): 291–317.

Bell, David A. *The Cult of the Nation in France: Inventing Nationalism, 1680–1800*. Cambridge, MA: Harvard University Press, 2001.

Bély, Lucien. *La Société des princes: XVIe–XVIIIe siècle*. Paris: Fayard, 1999.

———. "Souveraineté et souverains: la question du cérémonial dans les relations internationales à l'époque moderne." *Annuaire-bulletin de la Société de l'histoire de France* 130 (1993): 27–43.

Black, Jeremy. *British Diplomats and Diplomacy, 1688–1800*. Exeter: University of Exeter Press, 2001.

———. "From Pillnitz to Valmy: British Foreign Policy and Revolutionary France 1791–1792." *Francia: Forschungen zur westeuropäischen Geschichte* 21 (1994): 129–146.

Blanning, T. C. W. *The Culture of Power and the Power of Culture: Old Regime Europe, 1660–1789*. Oxford: Oxford University Press, 2002.

Bray, F.-G., comte de. *Mémoires du comte de Bray*. Paris: Plon Nourrit et Cie., 1911.

Brissot de Warville, Jacques-Pierre. *Discours de J. P. Brissot, député sur les dispositions des puissances étrangères, relativement à la France, et sur les préparatifs de guerre ordonné par le Roi*. Paris: Imprimerie nationale, 1791.
———. *Discours sur l'office de l'Empereur du 17 février 1792 de dénonciation contre M. Delessart, ministre des affaires étrangères prononcé à l'Assemblée nationale le 10 mars 1792*. Paris: Imprimerie nationale, n.d.-a.
———. *Rapport fait au nom du Comité de défense générale sur les dispositions du gouvernement britannique envers la France, et sur les mesures à prendre*. Paris: Imprimérie nationale, s.d.
Burke, Edmund. *The Correspondence of Edmund Burke*. 10 vols. Chicago: University Press, 1958–1978.
———. "Four Letters on the Proposals for Peace with the Regicide Directory of France." In *Burke Select Works*, ed. E.J. Payne. Oxford: Clarendon Press, 1894.
———. *Reflections on the Revolution in France*. Harmondsworth: Penguin Books, 1968.
———. *The Writings and Speeches of Edmund Burke*. 9 vols. Oxford: Clarendon Press, 1980–1991.
———. *The Works of The Right Honourable Edmund Burke: Charge Against Warren Hastings*. London: Henry G. Bohn, 1855.
Burke, Peter. *Fabrication of Louis XIV*. New Haven: Yale University Press. 1992.
Callières, François de. *Du bel esprit ou sont examinez les sentimens qu'on en a d'ordinaire dans le monde*. Amsterdam: Pierre Brunel, 1695.
———. *Letters (1694–1700) of François de Callières to the Marquise d'Huxelles*. Edited by Lawrence Pope and William Brooks. Queenston: The Edwin Mellen Press, 2004.
Cannadine, David. "Introduction: Divine Rites of Kings." In *Rituals of Royalty: Power and Ceremonial in Traditional Societies*, edited by David Cannadine and Simon Price, 1–19. Cambridge: University Press, 1987.
Chapman, Gerald W. *Edmund Burke: The Practical Imagination*. Cambridge, MA: Harvard University Press, 1967.
Clapham, John Harold. *The Abbé Sieyès: An Essay in the Politics of the French Revolution*. London: P. S. King and Son, 1912.
Clark, Henry C. *Compass of Society: Commerce and Absolutism in Old-Regime France*. Lanham: Lexington Books, 2007.
Clément-Simon, Frédéric. *Le premier ambassadeur de la République française à Constantinople: Le Général Aubert du Bayet*. Paris: Imprimerie de la "Renaissance latine," 1904.
Cohen, Raymond. *Theatre of Power: The Art of Diplomatic Signaling*. London: Longman, 1987.
Colbert, Jean Baptiste. *Journal inédit de Jean-Baptiste Colbert, marquis de Torcy*. Edited by Frédéric Masson. Paris: E. Plon, Nourrit et cie, 1884.
Condorcet, Marie Jean Antoine Nicolas Caritat, marquis de. *Oeuvres de Condorcet*. Paris: Firmin Didot frères, 1847–1849.

———. *Correspondence of Charles, First Marquis Cornwallis*. Edited by Charles Ross. 3 vols. London: John Murray, 1859.

Daniel, Ute. "Überlegungen zum höfischen Fest der Barockzeit." *Niedersächisches Jahrbuch für Landesgeschichte* 72 (2000): 45–66.

Darnton, Robert Choate. "The French Revolution: Intellectuals and Literature." Lecture, University of Montana, June 1, 1989.

Der Derian, James. *On Diplomacy: A Genealogy of Western Estrangement*. Oxford: Basil Blackwell, 1987.

Dictionnaire de biographie française. Edited by J. Balteau, Michel Prevost and Roman d'Amat. 123 vols. Paris: Librairie Letouzey et Ané, 1933–2013.

Dry, Adrien Fleury. *Soldats ambassadeurs sous le Directoire, an IV-an VIII*. Paris: Plon, 1906.

Duindam, Jeroen. *Vienna and Versailles: The Courts of Europe's Dynastic Rivals, 1550–1780*. Cambridge: Cambridge University Press, 2003.

Elias, Norbert. *The History of Manners, The Civilizing Process, State Formation and Civilization*. Translated by Edmund Jephcott. Vol. 1. New York: Urizen Books, 1978.

———. *The Court Society*. New York: Random House, 1983.

Fauchet, Joseph. "Mémoire sur les États Unis d'Amérique." Edited by Carl Ludwig Lokke. *Annual Report of the American Historical Association* 1 (1936): 83–123.

Gower, Lord Earl Granville Leveson. *Lord Granville Leveson Gower (First Earl Granville): Private Correspondence 1781 to 1821*. Edited by Castalia Countess Granville. Vols. 1–2. New York: E.P. Dutton and Company, 1916.

Graebner, Norman A., ed. *Ideas and Diplomacy: Readings in the Intellectual Tradition of American Foreign Policy*. New York: Oxford, 1964.

Grandmaison, Charles-Alexandre Geoffroy, de. *L'Ambassade française en Espagne pendant la Révolution (1789–1804)*. Paris: Plon, 1892.

Great Britain, Historical Manuscripts Commission. *The Manuscripts of J. B. Fortescue, esq., Preserved at Dropmore*. 4 vols. London: Eyre and Spottiswoode, 1892–1905.

Guizot, François Pierre, and Guizot de Witt, Henriette Elizabeth. *The History of France from the Earliest Times to 1848*. 8 vols. Boston: Dana Estes and Company, 1869–1878.

Guyot, Raymond. *Le Directoire et la paix de l'Europe: Des traités de Bâle à la deuxième coalition, 1795–1799*. Paris: Félix Alcan, 1911.

Harris, James. *Diaries and Correspondence of James Harris, First Earl of Malmesbury*. 4 vols. 1844. Reprint. New York: AMS Press, 1970.

Higonnet, Patrice L.-R. *Goodness Beyond Virtue: Jacobins during the French Revolution*. Cambridge, MA: Harvard University Press, 1998.

Hüffer, Hermann, ed. *Quellen zur Geschichte des Zeitalters der französischen Revolution. Teil 2: Quellen zur Geschichte der diplomatischen Verhandlungen. Erster Band: Der Frieden von Campoformio*. Innsbruck: Wagner, 1907.

———. *Der Rastatter Congress und die zweite Coalition*. 2 vols. Bonn: Adolph Marcus, 1878–1879.

Iiams, Thomas M. *Peacemaking from Vergennes to Napoleon: French Foreign Relations in the Revolutionary Era, 1774–1814*. Huntington, NY: Robert E. Krieger Publishing Company, 1979.

Idzerda, Stanley J. "Iconoclasm during the French Revolution." *American Historical Review* 60 (1955): 13–26.

Kidner, Frank L., Jr. "The Girondists and the 'Propaganda War' of 1792: A Reevaluation of French Revolutionary Foreign Policy from 1791 to 1793." Unpublished Ph.D. diss., Princeton University, 1971.

Kittstein, Lothar. 2003. *Politik im Zeitalter der Revolution: Untersuchungen zur preussischen Staatlichkeit 1792–1807*. Wiesbaden: Franz Steiner Verlag.

Koechlin, Raymond. "La Politique française au congrès de Rastadt (1797–1799)." *Annales de l'école libre des sciences politiques* 1 (1886): 394–425.

Koenigsberger, H. G. "Republicanism, Monarchism and Liberty." In *Royal and Republican Sovereignty in Early Modern Europe*, edited by Robert Oresko, G. C. Gibbs, and H. M. Scott, 43–74. Cambridge: University Press, 1997.

La Rochefoucauld, François, duc de. *Maximes suivies des réflexions diverses*. Paris: Editions Garnier Frères, 1967.

Malone, Dumas. *Jefferson and His Times*. Vol. 4: *Jefferson the President: First Term, 1801–1805*. Boston: Little, Brown, and Company, 1970.

Mandeville, Bernard. *The Fable of the Bees: or, Private Vices, Public Benefits*. Vol. 1. Oxford: Clarendon Press, 1957.

Mann, Golo. *Secretary of Europe: The Life of Friedrich Gentz, Enemy of Napoleon*. Translated by William H. Woglom. London: Oxford University Press, 1946.

Marie-Caroline, Queen of Naples. *Correspondance inédite de Marie-Caroline, Reine de Naples et de Sicile avec le marquis de Gallo*. Edited by M.-H. Weil and Marquis C. Di Somma Circello. 2 vols. Paris: Émile-Paul Éditeur, 1911.

Marschke, Benjamin. "'Von dem am Königl. Preußischen Hofe abgeschafften Ceremoniel': Monarchical Representation and Ceremony in Frederick William I's Prussia." In *Orthodoxies and Diversity in Early Modern Germany*, edited by Randolph C. Head and Daniel Christensen, 227–252. Boston: Brill Publishers, 2007.

Martens, Georg Friedrich von. *Summary of the Law of Nations*. Philadelphia: Thomas Bradford, 1795.

Mayer, Arno J. *The Persistence of the Old Regime: Europe to the Great War*. New York: Pantheon Books, 1981.

comte de Mercy-Argenteau, Florimond Claude Charles. *Briefe des Grafen Mercy-Argentau K. K. Bevollmächtigen Minister in den Österreichischen Niederlanden an den K. K. Ausserordentilichen Gesandten zu London Grafen Louis Starhemberg, von 26 December 1791 bis August 1794*. Edited by Graf Andreas Thürheim. Innsbruck: Wagner, 1884.

Metternich-Winneburg, Clemens Wenzel Neopomuk Lothar Fürst von. *Mémoires: Documents et écrits divers laissés par le Prince de Metternich, chancelier de cour et d'état.* 2 vols. Paris: E. Plon et Cie., 1881.

Mikhailowitch, Nicolas. *Les Relations diplomatiques de la Russie et de la France d'après les rapports des ambassadeurs d'Alexandre et de Napoléon.* Vols. 1–7. Petrograd: Manufacture des papiers de l'État, 1905–1914.

Miles, William Augustus. *The Correspondence of William Augustus Miles on the French. Revolution, 1789–1817.* Edited by Charles Miles Popham. 2 vols. London: Longmans, Green, and Company, 1890.

Moniteur, seule histoire authentique et inaltérée de la Révolution française. 32 vols. Paris: Plon Frères, 1847–1863.

Mowat, R. B. *The Diplomacy of Napoleon.* London: Edward Arnold & Co., 1924.

Muir, Edward. *Ritual in Early Modern Europe.* Cambridge: University Press, 1997.

Napoléon I. *Correspondance de Napoléon I.* 32 vols. Paris: Imprimerie Impériale, 1858–1869.

Napoleon. *Napoleon: Self-Revealed.* Translated and edited by J. M. Thompson. Boston: Houghton Mifflin Company, 1934.

Oresko, Robert. "The House of Savoy in Search for a Royal Crown in the Seventeenth Century." In *Royal and Republican Sovereignty in Early Modern Europe,* edited by G. C. Gibbs, Robert Oresko, and H. M. Scott, 223–250. Cambridge: University Press, 1997.

Pallain, G., ed. *Le Ministère de Talleyrand sous le Directoire.* Paris: Plon, Nourrit et cie., 1891.

Roberts, Andrew. *Napoleon.* New York: Viking, 2014.

Robinet, Jean-François-Eugène, ed. *Dictionnaire historique et biographique de la Révolution et de l'Empire 1789–1815.* Paris: Libraire historique de la Révolution et de l'Empire, 1899.

Rose, J. Holland. *William Pitt and The Great War.* 1911. Reprint. Westport, CT: Greenwood Press, 1971.

Rousseau, Jean-Jacques. *Discourse on the Origins and Foundations of Inequality among Men.* New York: Pocket Books, 1971.

———. *The First and Second Discourses.* Edited by Roger D. Masters. New York: St. Martin's Press, 1964.

Scott, Hamish M. *The Birth of a Great Power System, 1740–1815.* London: Longman, 2006.

———. "Diplomatic Culture in Old Regime Europe. In *Cultures of Power in Europe During the Long Eighteenth Century,* edited by Hamish Scott and Brendan Simms, 58–85. Cambridge: University Press, 2007.

Simms, Brendan. *The Impact of Napoleon: Prussian High Politics, Foreign Policy and the Crisis of the Executive, 1797–1806.* Cambridge: University Press, 1997.

Snyder, Jon R. *Dissimulation and the Culture of Secrecy in Early Modern Europe.* Berkeley: University of California Press, 2009.

Sonenscher, Michael. *Before the Deluge: Public Debt, Inequality, and the Intellectual Origins of the French Revolution.* Princeton: Princeton University Press, 2007.

Sorel, Albert. *L'Europe and la Révolution française.* 8 vols. Paris: E. Plon Nourrit et cie, 1897–1904.

Baron de Staël-Holstein, Anne Louise Germaine Necker. *Ten Years Exile: Or Memoirs of that Interesting Period of the Life of Baroness De Staël-Holstein written by Herself During the Years 1810, 1811, 1812, and 1813.* Fontwell, Sussex: Centaur Press Ltd, 1968.

von Stollberg-Rilinger, Barbara. "Zeremoniell, Ritual, Symbol: Neue Forschungen zur symbolischen Kommunikation im Spätmittelater und Früher Neuzeit." *Zeitschrift für historische Forschung* 27 (2000): 389–405.

Stroehlin, Henri. *La Mission de Barthélemy en Suisse (1792–1797).* Geneva: Henry Kundig, 1900.

Turner, Frederick Jackson, ed. *Correspondence of the French Ministers to the United States, 1791–1797.* 2 vols. 1903. Reprint. New York: Da Capo Press, 1972.

Vattel, Emerich De. *The Law of Nations: Or, Principles of the Law of Nature Applied to the Conduct and Affairs of Nations and Sovereigns.* New York: AMS Press, 1982.

Vec, Miloš. *Zeremonial-Wissenschaft im Fürstenstaat: Studien zur juristischen und politischen Theorie absolutistischer Herrschaftsrepräsentation.* Frankfurt am Main:Vittorio Klostermann, 1998.

Willson, Beckles. *Friendly Relations: A Narrative of Britain's Ministers and Ambassadors to America (1791–1930).* Boston: Little, Brown, and Company, 1934.

CHAPTER 5

Instruments of the Revolution: Language and Dress

Man lives immured within the Bastille of a word. — Thomas Paine[1]

I never saw such ill-conditioned animals. — Metternich[2]

This transformation in manners ran in tandem with a change in language and dress; in both, revolutionaries consciously broke with the traditions of the *ancien régime*. They jettisoned the elaborate court dress, which reflected and reinforced the aristocratic society and the hierarchical code. The self-consciousness of the revolutionaries about dress and its politicization was grounded in what Daniel Roche has termed the *ancien régime*'s elaborate "culture of appearances" that "had provided an established set of assumptions about the legibility of identity and status through varieties of dress" and that mandated displays of magnificence.[3] The revolutionaries rejected the elaborate hierarchical coding of status but accepted the assumption that dress reflected identity as did language. Grégoire was speaking for many revolutionaries when he underscored "the reciprocal influence of manners on language and language on manners."[4] Just as etiquette took on a republican dimension, language assumed a republican inflection. The parlement of Paris understood this shift as early as 1781: "The partisans of the new philosophy have a special idiom of their own. The same word does not have the same implication, … in short the same meaning in the mouth of modern writers as in the language of the rest of humanity, or at least those who have not been initiated into their enigmatic formulations."[5] The creation of the new world and the projection of the Revolution's image abroad required a new lexicon, grounded in linguistic strategies and rhetorical tropes.[6] This linguistic preoccupation echoed an earlier revolution in the ancient world. According to Thucydides, "[w]ords had to change their ordinary meaning and to take that which was now given them.... The advocate of extreme measures was always trustworthy; his opponent a man to be suspected."[7] Saint-Just phrased it a bit differently: "What language shall I speak to you? How can I depict for you errors of which you have no idea, how can I make you feel the evil that a word reveals, that a word rectifies?"[8] The Swiss Frédéric César de la Harpe (1754–1838), a man sympathetic to the Revolution, thought that language has been the Revolution's "first instrument and the most surprising instrument of them all."[9] The men sent to foreign courts were instructed in how to wield that tool.

The revolutionaries, who understood only too well how language buttressed the court society, inherited its obsession. As Baker has argued, although "the French Revolution assumed its meaning as a radical rupture with the past ... it was far from being an immaculate conception."[10] It was not accidental that the diplomat François de Callières (1645–1717), who wrote the seminal tract *On the Manner of Negotiating with Princes*, also composed two works on civility: *Des mots à la mode et des nouvelles façons de parler* (1692) and *De la Science du monde et des connaissances utiles à la conduite de la vie* (1717). In the first essay this quintessential insider describes the court vocabulary as a "strange jargon"[11] and in another as "a certain kind of singular language which one uses at certain times and among certain persons."[12] Diplomats who operated in an international arena were more steeped in that usage than most. To a man like Talleyrand, who straddled both worlds, the language of the court suffered from an "excess of words which impoverished it." The "polite" language of monarchical France, he complained, was pauperized by its vices. Its "ancient obsequious forms" reflected the "ruinous luxury" of the court. "In this paradoxical logic, abundance became misery, the multiplication of periphrases, the circumlocution, and other superfluities added to the destitution."[13] This language reinforced the hierarchical aristocratic order by excluding those who had not mastered it. As Barère explained, it was a language that "one had to spew out ... in a special way to appear well bred."[14]

It is hardly surprising that Barère among others cautioned that it was necessary to "destroy this aristocracy of language" that would "establish a polite nation" in our midst. "We have revolutionized the government, the laws, the customs ... revolutionize then the language which is their daily instrument."[15] Rousseau's injunction that it was impossible for a people to remain free and speak a "slavish tongue" was echoed, lest they forget, by the journalist Elysée Loustalot, who warned patriots: "the abuse of words has always been one of the principal means employed to enslave the people."[16] Revolutionary man must free himself of the linguistic manipulation of the *ancien régime*, a regime in which man "lives immured within the Bastille of a word."[17] The language of liberty ought to be "clear, pure, invariable," one revolutionary intoned, "because the change of words brings about the change and alteration of ideas."[18]

The revolutionaries used language as a weapon to turn the courtly world upside down. For Burke this was a kind of "linguistic terror" ... "a radical new violence that tears man from his word and world."[19] Burke predictably aligns with other counter-revolutionaries who think that "the classical and vernacular languages should not change: arbitrary linguistic change interrupts this dialogue across the centuries and radically changes the meaning of the 'inherited' world."[20] To the revolutionary, a linguistic revolution was needed to eliminate the aristocratic usages of the past, to strip away the mask that concealed and perpetuated the oppression beneath. "Revolutionary political culture, however, was grounded," as Gordon points out, "in the substantive ideal of *civisme*, not the formal ideal of *civilité*. Virtuous deeds, not polite manners, were important.... The purpose of speech was not to create truth but to prove to others that one identified with it.... With the truth defined in advance, politeness could be nothing but a superfluous ornament to language, and language itself could only be a tool of didacticism and denunciation."[21] Diplomats, understanding the importance of this semiotic transformation, sought to ensure that their language would reflect, in Grégoire's words, a "spirit of truth" and "laconic pride."[22] Language was then not only an instrument of representation, but also a battleground on which the struggle for a new world was fought. What strikes the unprepared reader is the linguistic self-consciousness or what Guilhaumou calls the "linguistic conscience" of the revolutionaries.[23] We do not have to adopt linguistic reductionism to understand that words for the revolutionaries both mirrored and created reality. The French revolutionaries fought over words and the world they reflected or created, both at home and abroad.[24] Speaking French itself was a political act that liberated people from the linguistic oppression of the past. Revolutionary diplomats shared this belief in a "politics of language"[25] or what Loustalot in November 1789 called "the magical power of a word."[26] In 1791, Talleyrand acknowledged that the National Assembly knows how much effect "signs have on ideas and through them on the habits which it wishes to create or to consolidate."[27] He argued that the ancient obsequious forms, the linguistic distinctions grounded in class distinctions, had to be eliminated.[28]

Those sent abroad were instructed to distance themselves from the usages of the *ancien régime*, to proscribe forever that jargon, the "last vestiges of feudalism."[29] They should avoid this "deluge of words that only serves to entangle ideas."[30] The representative at The Hague certainly did that. He omitted any salutation, merely beginning the text of the letter and, according to a British commentator, exceeded the French representative in London, Chauvelin, in "original simplicity."[31] We can assume that he did not intend this remark to be a compliment. In breaking with the usage of the past, the revolutionaries were to speak what Robespierre called "the language of truth,"[32] or what Grégoire called "the idiom of liberty."[33] In 1792, Maure, later a member of the Committee of Public Safety, could argue that "[t]hose who elected us have not sent us here to unfurl grand phrases and to parade ornate wit," a sign of the *ancien régime*.[34] Interestingly, the French representatives were instructed to assert the primacy of French in treaties, for French had displaced Latin as the international language and had acquired "a privileged position."[35] Still it had to be purged of the usages of the past. During the Terror, on 20 prairial, an II (8 June 1794), one speaker pointed out that "[u]nder despotism, language bore the marks of baseness; it was the jargon of ... the scum of humanity." By contrast, the "language of Republicans must stand out by frankness, and with a dignity that is mid-way between abjectness and roughness."[36] Some found it difficult to strike that balance. Miot de Melito noted of Fabre d'Eglantine, a Dantonist, embezzler, and not incidentally a poet and dramatist, that "his manner of talking was graceful, but affected. Notwithstanding his efforts to conform to the Revolutionary style of speech, it was evidently antipathetic to him, and the ring of a refined education was heard through a coarse exterior."[37] Miot de Melito and others understood that language was an important gauge of ideological purity. After fructidor 1797 the Minister of Foreign Affairs, asked to identify disguised aristocrats who would be purged, reported that no one used the word *Monsieur* and no one displayed in either language or dress the frivolity bordering on aristocracy.[38]

The diplomatic corps was not exempted from the attempt to refashion language in the revolutionary image. Their battleground was more challenging because the diplomatic language of the *ancien régime* and of the international stage was the antithesis of transparent or, as the French representative to Russia, Armand Augustin Louis de Caulaincourt, argued in 1810, "sterile" and "useless in many instances."[39] Guillaume de Bonne-Carrère (1754–1825), head of the political section in the Ministry of Foreign Affairs, who was promoted to director general of foreign affairs, noted that with the change in the political system, "the idiom of liberty" replaced "the style grovelling with slavery."[40] It was not, moreover, merely the words, but also the tone that was to be banished. The aristocratic politeness so characteristic of the French was to be removed from the language.[41] That language that had been a "slave," that had "flattered kings, corrupted courts, subdued peoples" had for too long a time been "deceitful in the books of public education, crafty in the tribunals, fanatical in the temples." Now it was "purified" and "ennobled" [an odd word to use]. Its "puerile distinctions have disappeared with the grimaces of ridiculous courtesans and the baubles of a perverse court." Now could be heard "the vigorous accent of liberty and equality"[42] or what one called "the pure and simple language of nature."[43]

In the place of the vocabulary and tone of the court, the diplomats were to adopt the revolutionary idiom. The French revolutionaries forbade the use of certain words: king, prince, highness, *pair, duc, marquis, comte, baron, banneret, vidames, chevalier, écuyers,* among others.[44] For Loustalot, the first editor of the *Révolutions de Paris*, "[i]t is necessary ... to abandon not only the former words but the ancient ideas to which they were attached."[45] Grégoire's call to revolutionize the language was to be answered by a new dictionary and purportedly even a new grammar.[46] The publication of the *Dictionnaire néologique des hommes et des choses* (an VIII) soon followed. [And not incidentally polemical counter-revolutionary dictionaries].[47] That dictionary was particularly needed because as François-Urbain Domergue, the "linguistic conscience of the revolution," "the patriot grammarian," and not coincidentally the editor of the *Journal de la langue française*, contended: it was necessary "to elevate our language to the height of our constitution" and to "define new words which the new ideas have rendered necessary."[48] Callières' jargon had been displaced or replaced by a plethora of new words.[49] Those who consulted the 1798 edition of the *Dictionnaire de l'académie* would have found 418 new words and in that of 1801, 2800.[50] This language, purified "in the fire of liberty," appeared to the royalists a corruption, a "monstrous solecism," or, in the words of Louis Gabriel Ambroise Bonald (1754–1840), a "barbarous and ridiculous nomenclature."[51] The British representative had an even stronger reaction: he was shocked by the language in the Assembly, dubbing it "le langage des Halles."[52] Even a man as sympathetic to the Revolution as La Harpe noted that an intolerable jargon, a veritable mockery had replaced the French language.[53]

Those sent abroad were to use, in Mercier's words, "the virile expressions" of the republican language, which will "make monarchical language turn pale forever."[54] They should speak, in the words of Brissot, a language "worthy of Romans" or "the noble brevity of the Spartans."[55] Accordingly, the Minister of Foreign Affairs advised the French agent in Stuttgart to adopt an energetic and frank tone. "It is," he continued, "the only tone that all French negotiators ought to have henceforth, because it is the only one which is suitable to a great nation proud and free."[56]

One of the litmus tests for ideological purity for the revolutionary diplomat was the use of *tu* instead of *vous*, the best known attempt to change social customs and to found democracy "on fraternity."[57] Many eighteenth-century stylists had argued that *tu* was more sincere and more natural than *vous*. For Voltaire, "*tu* was the language of truth and *vous* that of compliment."[58] In the words of Condillac, in the beginning of the world undoubtedly one said *tu* to all, but later "*vous* became the language of the slave before his master."[59] *Vous* smacked of the subservience of the *ancien régime*. As early as 1791 a writer argued that *toi* was the only expression fitting for liberty and denounced the absurdity of *vous*. At that time the editor could still make the case for conserving the use of *vous*.[60] The publicist Antoine Tournon, editor of the *Mercure universel* and author of *Grammaire des sans-culottes: Elements de la langue nationale*, attacked the use of *vous* as "servile and feudal."[61] For the revolutionaries *tu* reflected that transparence, so important to Rousseau.[62] The *Chronique de Paris* of 3 October 1792 could contend that "Si *vous* convient à Monsieur, *toi* convient à Citoyen."[63]

According to Tocqueville the revolutionaries harbored a "fanatical faith in their vocation—that of transforming the social system root and branch" or what Furet dubbed a "lay eschatology."[64] In that spirit on 21 brumaire, an II (11 November 1793), Claude Basire (1761–1794) demanded a decree that one should *tutoyer* to all. He was opposed by his colleague Thuriot in the name of liberty: "one knows well that le *vous* is absurd … but is it not contrary to liberty to prescribe to citizens the manner in which they should express themselves? It is not a crime to speak French badly."[65] Many disagreed. After 10 brumaire an 11 (31 October 1793), the Committee of Public Safety used *tu* in its official correspondence and this usage spread into the public parlance of the revolutionary government.

A simple egalitarian style would now predominate, as *vous* with its hierarchical baggage was replaced by *tu* with its leveling propensities. Still later, when Charles-François Delacroix, Minister of Foreign Affairs from November 1795 to July 1797, announced to the president of the *Conseil des Anciens* that he had been chosen as Minister of Foreign Relations by the Directors, he said, "Je te prie, citoyen président." Delacroix was one of the last men in power to use it in his official letters.[66] We also see it in the diplomatic corps. An official in the foreign ministry used *tu* to address Jean-Antoine-Joseph Fauchet (1761–1834), the minister to the United States.[67] Fauchet mixed his revolutionary metaphors in signing a letter to Edmund Randolph, the American Secretary of State, "je *vous* salue fraternellement."[68] By contrast, Russian revolutionaries, who grappled with the same issue, decreed that all people should address each other with the formal "you" *vy* instead of the intimate *ty*.[69] The adoption of *tu* and the larger debate over language casts light on Furet's contention that as part of that "network of signs" that so dominated the Revolution language must "reflect values as in a mirror."[70]

Diplomats were not isolated from what Mercier called the "new politeness of equality."[71] The Committee of Public Safety instructed these "true republicans" to assume no other title except that of citizen and minister of the republic.[72] Throughout their correspondence diplomats addressed each other as citizen colleague, or citizen followed by the proper name. Interestingly, there were some among the general population who objected. A committee on 11 January 1791 argued that the abolition of *Monsieur* would not in itself create greater fraternity because fraternity did not depend on an expression, but on a sentiment of the heart that should be free. They objected to a law that tended "to substitute the appearance of fraternity for fraternity itself." Moreover, it was "impolitic, immoral and contrary to the constitution to force one to affect ... a sentiment that he could not have." They wanted the liberty to address anyone as they pleased for "this liberty is the only safeguard of real fraternity."[73] These, of course, were voices speaking in the proverbial and linguistic wilderness. The publicist Antoine Tournon, the linguistic militant, emphasized the importance of the word "citizen,"[74] as did the *Mercure universel* of 5 October 1792. The latter cautioned that the word "citizen" was not "synonymous with the word *monsieur*." Nor was it merely "a change of fashion.... This error should be rectified, the word *monsieur* is a diminutive of monseigneur; it derives from feudal antiquity; the word citizen comes in contrast from the social pact of equality."[75] The Directory decreed in 15 August 1796 that employees should not use the "homicidal word" *monsieur*.[76] In that same year Carnot discovered what he called "a real scandal." Some representatives were substituting the word *monsieur* for that of *citoyen*. Those who wished to "*Monsieuriser* can return to coteries who accept this language but these messieurs ought to resign." "We know the influence of words on things," he warned. He enjoined all government employees to ensure that this directive was observed. When this letter did not achieve the desired result, it was followed by a decree of 18 fructidor (4 September), which stipulated that ambassadors, envoys, consuls, and any others employed outside France were not to give or receive any other appellation except that of *citoyen*.[77] Problems still occurred. Dominique Catherine de Perignon, who served in Spain from 1796 to 1797, was instructed to return to the former *sans-culotte* style and to accept only the title of citizen in his formal relations. This revolutionary style was not very well received at the formal Spanish court. The Prince of Peace mocked such usage and asked if he should *tutoyer fraternellement* "his excellency," an appelation banned by Delacroix in a circular of 22 thermidor, an IV (9 August 1796).[78] The French representative to the United States, Pierre Auguste Adet, reassured him that French agents in the United States were too aware of the "dignity of the title of citizen" to substitute that of "excellence."[79] Such ideas were by no means unique to France. Another republic, the United States of America, consistently refused for over a hundred years to send ambassadors, who ill befitted the simple democracy of America. Thomas Jefferson instructed the American consul in Morocco to inform the sultan that "we never send an ambassador to any nation. Let him understand that this may be a custom of the Old World, but it is not ours."[80] At least initially republican France followed the same policy, although expediency soon triumphed.

Diplomats could turn to a repertoire of revolutionary injunctions that provided a common thread or warp throughout the Revolution. Within the fabric of revolutionary usage, the weft, which is inserted under and over the warp, could vary. Those variations could trap the unwary. Nor could these injunctions provide for every contingency. Diplomats often found the style in flux. A change of ministers could mean a change in the prescribed and proscribed parlance. Claude-Antoine de Valdec de Lessart (1742–1792), who served as Comptroller-General (1790), as Minister of the Interior (1791), and later as Minister of Foreign Affairs (1791–1792), complained "about the variety and unsuitability of some of the terms of address and signature used." The king, he reported, had decided on "a simple style, freed from all ceremonial and perfectly analogous to the spirit and to the principles of the Constitution."[81] In 1791, Emmanuel Marie Louis, marquis de Noailles, the French ambassador in Vienna since 1783, changed his language to accommodate the new regime. An observer noted that his stock phrase, "the King my master," was seldom now on his lips. That phrase was replaced by nation, decree, constitution. His language had changed as had his table, now bedecked with tricolored ribbons.[82] In response to questions from others, the government instituted a formulary. Employees of the state were only to use republican language, to use *citoyen* instead of *monsieur*, to use the republican calendar, and to treat the people with civility and respect.[83] The language of accreditation also changed. Baptiste-Dorothée-Villars (1742–) was sent to Mainz in May 1792 "in the name of a free nation and of a constitutional king."[84] After the overthrow of the king, one club advocated the elimination of obsolete expressions such as "the king, my master."[85] Those attuned to revolutionary sensibilities used the salutation "*Salut et fraternité aux amis de la république*" and closed with "*salut et fraternité.*"[86]

As the revolutionary tides shifted, so did the language. As the British representative Sir Robert Liston, who was stationed at Constantinople, cynically noted: "Each of those gentlemen adopted the system of the day. Descorches affected the cynical manners of the Jacobins because Robespierre was in power. Verninac wears powder and assumes a varnish of aristocracy because the moderates are at the head of affairs for the moment." After Thermidor, Raymond Verninac preferred to use M. or Madame rather than citizen. The words may have changed but that did not dispel Liston's suspicions or his hostility. "Neither, I believe, is at bottom good for anything. Descorches was more smooth and dangerous and had made very considerable progress tainting the minds of the Turks and the Greeks with the fantastick [sic] theory of liberty and equality.... Verninac has arrived with the idea of building upon this foundation."[87] Others also tacked to the revolutionary gales. Joseph Philippe Letombe, the French consul general in the United States, sent a circular to all consuls notifying them that all French officials of whatever rank outside of France should give and receive only the denomination of citizen.[88] Some were critical. In 1797, in the midst of the Directory, Otto of the Foreign Office was drawing up a report on France's relations with the United States. In that report he emphasized that he would "speak the cold language of reason, persuaded that those who would read it would prefer this language to that misleading eloquence which since the beginning of the revolution has parodied and disfigured the most palpable truths."[89]

Revolutionary dictates often did not mesh with the sensibilities of foreign governments. Early in the Revolution, the king's minister to the United States (1788–1789), Éléonore François Élie, comte de Moustier, had objected to the appointment of Brissot as the king's envoy on the grounds that his tone was too assertive. His enthusiasm for liberty and hatred of tyranny would be unacceptable even to another republic.[90] Chauvelin, the French representative in London, hardly endeared himself to his hosts when he adopted the Jacobin jargon of the time.[91] If we can believe the British representative, another republic, the United Provinces, was alienated by the behavior of the French representative, Emmanuel de Maulde Hosdan (1792–1793), whose decision to adopt the new phraseology made him "a source of amusement and anecdote."[92] When William Eden, 1st Baron Auckland, noted the *naïveté* of the French minister, we can hear the disdain in his voice. According to Auckland, Maulde asked the Dutch statesman Fagel if they could meet in his garden, since it would be good to "distance oneself occasionally from the vapors of diplomacy in order to chat with lovely nature, so simple, so true, so moving."[93]

Maulde's *à la républicaine* behavior may have made him the butt of various jokes, but those actions also had a seditious side.[94] The Dutch interception of his correspondence and his own activities created a more dangerous picture. The British representative called him "a very nasty character," who colluded with printers and "malcontents."[95] "A dangerous fellow," Auckland concluded, "notwithstanding his ridiculous patelinage and indiscretion."[96] Two of Maulde's secretaries were involved in spreading propaganda that was regarded as seditious. Maulde may represent an isolated case of the "colossal egotism of a petty noble" combined with a "pathological" case of "a confirmed liar" and "mild paranoic," but his behavior was not atypical of those sent abroad.[97] Even Auckland could concede that "the facility of assertion" among the new French ministers "gives them much advantage in all verbal communications, especially with our extreme delicacy in not disclosing (with whatever provocation) things which we have engaged to keep secret."[98] The downside was that Maulde also illustrates how certain behavior engendered a mutually reinforcing hostility. A much more experienced practitioner on the linguistic tightrope, Talleyrand, late in the Directory in 1799, defended his conduct and attempted to rebut the argument that he had alienated the United States by underscoring that his language had been deferential, moderate, and dignified.[99]

The use of certain words or phrases often triggered disputes between France and her neighbors. In its declaration of war against Spain in 1793 the National Convention tried to claim the moral high ground and justified its conduct as "conciliatory, sincere and loyal." The French representative, they emphasized, had spoken with "the firm tone" befitting the representative of the republic.[100] The Spanish objected to the French use of the term "Spanish nation," which they found "incompatible with the sovereignty of the king of Spain." To this sally, the French representative replied that the French government can only employ a language "that conforms with its principles."[101] Later, in 1797, as relations with Venice deteriorated, an aide to Bonaparte impertinently addressed the doge as "*signor doge*" instead of "*Serennissimo Principe.*"[102] Nor could the free language of a revolutionary be used by others, even had they been inclined to do so. Dominique-Joseph Garat (1749–1833), Minister of Justice in 1792, emphasized that it was "imprudent" for despots to attempt to use "the clear and simple language of reason and the tone of free peoples."[103]

The revolutionary government, nonetheless, found it necessary to caution some of its agents about giving offense in trifles. For example, the representatives were to follow the forms and usages adopted by the allied and neutral powers when communicating with foreign governments. As early as 16 May 1793 the Committee of Public Safety in the ongoing negotiations with Sweden empowered its agents "to employ the ordinary titles of the king of Sweden, the denomination of Swedish majesty."[104] "Any reasonable Frenchman does not want to take offense," the revolutionary council argued in the spring of 1795 in the midst of the Thermidorean reaction, if foreigners did not want to adopt "our revolutionary style," that is "*tu*," the familiar form of "you." They should not infer from this refusal that foreigners were hostile to the revolution.[105] In this case as in others *Realpolitik* overrode ideological dictates.

The men who were sent to negotiate with France often found the way littered with linguistic landmines. Revolutionaries took offense when the American representative Gouverneur Morris, American minister plenipotentiary (1792–1794), used the phrase "my court," which they thought "unrepublican." Morris' description of the French in 1792 as "cattle driven before a thunderstorm" and of France "standing on a vast volcano" reflected his hostility to events in France.[106] Some, at least, thought that Morris deliberately flaunted his aristocratic predilections and royalist sympathies. These thoughtless gestures led one Frenchman to conclude that it proved his "ill will" and that he betrayed his own countrymen "as well as us."[107] In this instance, as in so many others, French revolutionaries saw "themselves as engaged in a high-stakes linguistic power struggle."[108] Not surprisingly, the French government objected to Morris, whose "sentiments and principles [were] diametrically opposed to the revolution" and asked for someone to be appointed who was "more agreeable to the republic."[109] Some Francophilic Americans shared those reservations. Monroe voiced his unease over Morris' "known attachment" to monarchy and his contempt for the Republic. That sentiment, he felt, made Morris "unfit to represent us." Moreover, Morris' "general brutality of manner and indiscretion" gave him "a wonderful facility in making enemies and losing friends."[110]

In contrast, James Monroe enjoyed the reputation within the French Foreign Office of being "a man of probity … [who] loves France and the revolution."[111] Monroe was so attuned to the new language that he dated his letter to the Minister of Foreign Affairs 8 December 1795, 10 frimaire l'an 4 and the 20th year of the American republic.[112] Monroe continued that practice in 1796, dating his letter 2 September 1796, or 17 fructidor, 21st year of the independence of the United States, and addressed his correspondent as citizen minister.[113] These actions could not but leave a positive impression among the Directors who only received foreign ministers who bore the title of "citizen."[114] In 1795, Peter Ochs, a Swiss revolutionary, maintained that the man who was to be employed in France had to be a "master of the spoken word … as well as of the new terminology [who] always takes care to seize the diverse nuances of language."[115] Others were not as sensitive. The British negotiator Harris who went to France in 1797 purportedly did not understand the French objection to his use of the title of "King of France" in discussing prior treaties. To him this was "cavilling for a mere word."[116] One might think this was part of the jockeying for position on the linguistic background in the negotiations, but this remark was more likely a snipe at the French obsession with discarding "royalist" references.

Diplomats sent to France also found the revolutionary enthusiasm that precluded humor difficult to handle. Puns, witticisms, and epigrams were disdained. Not surprisingly, the revolutionaries deprecated wit and humor, for words were too important to be treated as a joke. A Lyons shopkeeper is rumored to have contended that those "who have wit" must be mistrusted. A "time when words were fraught with peril," as Richard Cobb notes, "was not a time to make jokes."[117] Brissot with his "inflexible republican spirit" was appalled at the use of humor. He denounced ridicule, epigrams, sarcasm, and the well-turned witty phrase. Virtue and republicanism increased, he claimed, in inverse proportion to the use of puns and epigrams. He would have agreed with the denunciation of a contemporary who was immediately identifiable because he spoke with the "witty, elegant, rational, irreligious and immoral voice of the establishment."[118] That lack of humor is the counterpoint to "their sincerity, their conformity, or their desire to excel one another in revolutionary zeal."[119]

Like language, dress was part of the emphasis placed on transparency and was modified to conform to the revolutionary agenda: dress was to be simple like manners.[120] The knee breeches of the aristocracy were replaced with the trousers of the workers. It was, in Balzac's formulation, a debate between silk and cloth.[121] The concern with those signs surfaced early in the Revolution. On 15 October 1789 many members of the Constituent Assembly refused to wear the dress mandated by the king for the various orders of the Estates General because the prescribed dress indicated one's status in the hierarchical order. Decrees soon followed. The revolutionary assemblies formally abolished the obligation to wear religious habit (October 24, 1789), any decoration belonging to the knights and to corporations (30 July 1791), and the costume for judges (1793).[122] In 1790 an observer from abroad noticed that even the hairstyles were different. The curls, toupees, and plaits of hair worn down the back were gone and replaced with what was called *têtes à la Romaine*, either cropped hair with no powder or little black wigs.[123] Military costume, especially that of the national guard, became fashionable.[124] It was no accident that a visitor to Paris in the summer of 1792 could report that he saw "no face that was painted except on stage."[125] The unmistakable appearance of the revolutionaries left them open to mockery.[126] For most though the revolutionary attire was not a fit subject for ridicule. When François-Nicolas Vincent, the Secretary General of War, at the end of a banquet mocked the representatives of the people (*mannequins habillés*), the prosecutor Fouquier-Tinville, a dangerous man to offend, took note of the quip that "vilified the national representation."[127]

Dress was not to be mocked, for it "was an important aspect of the definition of revolutionary practice." It was, in Devocelle's words, a way "to transcribe visually certain principles and ideological values."[128] The debate that swirled around the national attire indicates the importance revolutionaries attached to what Grégoire called the "language of signs"; for him "distinctive costumes are part of this idiom."[129] As an indication of his sympathies, the artist Anne Louis Girodet (1767–1824), then in Rome, executed a self-portrait in which he portrayed himself wearing a bonnet rouge, which he could never have worn in public. In private he could flaunt his republican sympathies.[130] Others were not so hesitant. David could vaunt that the pensioners of the *Académie de France* in Rome wore large cockades in their hats as a deliberate insult to the duchesse de Polignac.[131] Roland's decision to go to the Tuileries clad in a simple black suit with a round hat and shoes tied with strings created a furor because it was a deliberate rejection of court dress.[132] Foreign courts saw it in those very terms. Paul I, tsar of Russia (1796–1801), forbade even what he thought of as the appearance of Jacobinism; he prohibited the wearing of round hats, tail coats, vests, large collars, and big ties,—all clothing identified with revolutionary France.[133] When Paul was told that the French officers wore large whiskers, he ordered every man at court to shave.[134]

Some revolutionaries were aware of the problematic nature of dress and understood that it could be easily manipulated. In 1794, Claude Payan condemned the emphasis on appearances as part of a "system which wanted everywhere to substitute the exterior of patriotism for patriotism itself, and words for things."[135] This cautionary note was not heeded. The dictates of the new fashion were just as inflexible as that of the old. Although the Assembly had voted to establish liberty of dress in 1793, the decree mandating the wearing of cockade (29 May 1790) was not annulled. The cockade became important because it was part of that symbolic deployment so integral to the revolutionary faith. As late as 1796 Harris found it a "general usage, prescribed by popular custom." Although the French government did not insist on his staff wearing it, "[t]he wearing of the national cockade is so universal in the streets, and so unpleasantly enforced by the populace, that it is impossible to appear in them without it." Although he refused to allow his staff to wear it when they were acting "in an official capacity," the British official, no supporter of the Revolution, had no alternative but to have his staff don it when they went out.[136] Grenville (1759–1834) wrote to reassure him that the cockade, "like every other part" of his and his suite's dress, was "without consequence," except when acting in an official capacity. He advised him not to attach "to them an importance which they have not."[137] Still the emotive power of the cockade was felt outside France. As late as the Directory Barthélemy informed the Swiss that all French citizens in that area should wear the cockade, as did the French representative in Turin, Ginguené.[138] This mandate posed some difficulties for those who traveled abroad. Léonard Bourdon, a Jacobin and terrorist, was identifiable and vulnerable because of his attire. When Bourdon alighted at an inn, a quarrel broke out with the Prussians there and one of them tore the cockade from his hat and ripped it apart. When he complained, the commandant replied that his dress and his frequenting of an ale house "might suit their notions of equality," but it did not befit his station. The Prussian added that his distinctive badges, that is, the tricolor, were not particularly appreciated.[139] As late as 1808 Napoleon insisted on the recall of Maximilian Graf von Merveldt, the Austrian ambassador to Russia, because of his "outrageous conduct." Merveldt had invited the French representative to a dinner attended by an individual who donned the fleur de lys, even after the Austrians had forbidden wearing the cross of St. Louis and the white cockade in Vienna.[140]

Clothing served not only as a representation of the new order, but also as an agent of regeneration. In December 1793 *La Société populaire et républicaine des arts* even suggested that citizens should wear the same dress in order to obliterate all distinctions. The government never adopted that proposal. The issue surfaced again on 14 floréal, an VII (3 May 1799), when the head of 5th division of the Ministry of the Interior reported on the ideal dress that would be "political, moral, commercial, hygienic, picturesque and artistic." Clothes should be uniform to ensure equality and simple, not ostentatious, to avoid the corrupting luxury of previous times.[141]

Within the larger framework of dress the question arose of how to identify the representatives of the nation. As Richard Wrigley argues, "The need for authority to be represented—and to be consolidated by such representation—was rendered urgent by resistance to, or competition with the 'constituted authorities,'" both at home and abroad.[142] This issue plagued another republic, that of the United States. Franklin consciously calibrated his image and dressed plainly in a brown suit with unpowdered hair. Other US diplomats did not fare as well. George Erving with his dirty boots was mistaken for a courier and later with a uniform trimmed with braid galloons for a footman in livery. Such gaffes led the Secretary of State James Monroe to introduce an official garb for US diplomats.[143] As early as April 1792 French public functionaries had been enjoined to wear some indication of their authority. Many resorted to "the quasi-emblematic form of sashes, badges, medals, and ribbons."[144] These symbols served to identify the official and to signal his allegiance to the new revolutionary order. Barras made a point of emphasizing that he did "not think that the respect for a republican authority should lie in the elaboration and richness of its costume." On the contrary, he believed "that the day has come when officials' simplicity should be their first distinction."[145] As the Committee of Public Safety argued in 1794 the costume should be adapted "to republican mores and to the character of the revolution."[146] On 14 May 1794 the Committee of Public Safety asked David to present his ideas on improving the actual costume. His designs should be guided by certain principles: hygiene—the costume should not impede circulation; liberty—the costume should not be influenced by the frivolity of despots; and distinctive—so the French would not be confused with other servile peoples. Completed within ten days, the series of eight water colors prescribed costumes that were never worn.[147] Despite a prolonged and extensive debate, the only costume adopted before the Directory was that of the "représentant du peuple aux armées." It mandated a tricolor waist sash and a hat with three feathers with a gold-striped braid covering part of the cockade.[148] A report of 29 fructidor, an III (15 September 1795), emphasized the importance of an official costume: the dignity of the costume should elicit the respect of the citizens for the magistrate and lead the magistrate to respect himself. The author discussed the appropriate attire for the legislative corps, the executive, the administrative, and the judicial. Although he omitted the diplomatic corps, the author underscored that "it was essential to give to all foreign nations a grand idea of the republic. Not long ago at Constantinople all eyes were struck by the imposing march and the cortège of the French minister." He posited that "a special costume for the diplomatic agent had perhaps added to the brilliance of the ceremony."[149]

During the Directory, an official costume evolved that reflected the project of Grégoire of 3 brumaire, an IV (25 October 1795). The costume included ankle boots, vests, and tight pantaloons that echoed the designs of David.[150] This outfit did not fail to astonish foreigners. An outside observer such as Metternich "could not believe his eyes." He found everything "extraordinary" and the costume "very ugly." He noted that François de Neufchâteau (1750–1828) always wore the ministerial costume: a black coat with an enormous round collar in red-orange linen, a vest of the same material and color, embroidered in black, culottes of the same, small ankle boots, a large sabre, and a hat à la Henri IV with enormous plumes.[151] This garb was fortunately not extended to the diplomatic corps.

There were disjointed attempts to address the omission of diplomatic attire. The selection of diplomatic garb was part of the larger search for an appropriate revolutionary costume, which would "identify the voice of the nation" and which would also "prevent the French from being confused with people of other nations still branded by the shackles of servitude."[152] Wearing French colors may have accomplished that goal. Most of the representatives abroad, as exemplified by Adet in the United States, understood "the sacred obligation" to wear the tricolor.[153] In many cases the French representatives whether Miot de Melito in Rome and Sémonville in Piedmont with the tricolor festooning their hats or Mackau in Naples with his "grand and visible tricolor plumes" may have been too easily identifiable.[154] Another Frenchman in Rome, Hugou de Bassville, who bedecked himself, his family, and his suite with the tricolor, generated even more antipathy—and with tragic consequences. Respect was hardly the emotion evoked.

Apart from the tricolor, for most of the Revolution there was no official uniform for those who represented France abroad, although there were isolated attempts to stipulate the appropriate costume. That debate included consuls, who also fell under the preview of the Department of Foreign Affairs after the Republic transferred them from the Department of the Navy. In 1794, a decree stipulated that consuls should wear a white broadcloth vest and pants and a blue broadcloth coat, faced with red serge, with red broadcloth collars and cuffs with facings of scarlet. Gilded metal buttons stamped with the seal of the republic and intertwined olive and laurel branches on the collar and the cuffs were embroidered in gold and proclaimed the man a citizen of republican France.[155] Victor du Pont, consul in Charleston, was informed that he should think of himself as "not only an agent of commerce and of the marine but also a political agent."[156] We can only get inadvertent glimpses of what they wore from contemporaries but can assume that the official dictates would be followed given the surveillance these men underwent. Apparently one vice consul offended sensibilities in a fellow republic, that of United States. In his dismissal it was noted, and not favorably, that he kept the habits and military style in his dress and that had made him appear ridiculous. He had worn a very short waistcoat, a large sabre, and two epaulettes.[157] At a time when it was problematic to choose the right garb, many diplomats selected the default, some kind of military attire, but even that choice entailed difficulties.

For diplomats, the revolutionaries at one time envisaged a simple working uniform with a gold medallion of olive branches on the breast of the tunic. They rejected a more military design because it conflicted with the image of a minister of peace and friendship.[158] Until 1796, French diplomats wore the outfit they preferred, often that of the national guard, as

Miot de Melito did at his audience with the pope.[159] On 14 germinal, an IV (24 March 1796), the Directors advised the diplomats that they would not have a specific costume, but should wear a medal, analogous to that worn by judges, suspended by a gold chain which would by its elegance and beauty "enrich in a dignified manner the simple clothes of a minister."[160] A decree subsequently stipulated that French representatives should adopt the same uniform worn by the commissioners to the armies: blue coat, vest, and pants, a red-and-white sash with tricolor fringes, and a red hat with a tricolored plume.[161] This distinctive dress would ensure that the French representatives would incarnate "the dignity of the Republic."[162] In July 1796 the Minister of Foreign Relations sent French representatives a letter describing the authorized dress. When Jean Baptiste Lallement, the French representative at Venice, went to the Opera, the prescribed dress was so "novel" that it attracted the attention of the spectators.[163] Adet, the representative to the United States, replied that he had understood that agents could choose between this costume and that of the locale. He argued that the "simplicity" of clothing in the United States accorded with republican principles and furthermore that ordinary clothing would be preferable to garb that would be too new and too striking to the Americans.[164] Because there was no official costume, some adopted the costume of a representative on mission. Goya portrayed Ferdinand Pierre Marie Dorothée Guillemardet, who was in Spain from 1798 to 1800, wearing a sash and a tricolored plume.[165] His colleague in Prussia, Sièyes, had initially appeared in unpowdered hair in an austere habit, except for the large tricolored sash on his chest. At the insistence of the Prussian minister, Christian August Heinrich Haugwitz (1752–1832), he had initially strapped on a sabre. For the rest of his tenure he refused to appear with the traditional *épée* and decided to dress simply or, as he argued, as a minister of peace. He then appeared with unpowdered hair, clad in a dark blue coat, with a collar embroidered in green silk depicting olive branches. A huge tricolor scarf lay across the coat.[166] A contemporary, Friedrich August von der Marwitz, remarked in 1798 that Sieyès' appearance clad in a red, white, and blue toga at a court function in Berlin was "a terrible omen of the time"[167] and also an indication of the penchant for classical illusions. One wonders whether he was more surprised by the classical garb or the revolutionary colors. This garb only reinforced the hostility of the court, which regarded him as a regicide and a dangerous reformer. The revolutionary legacy continued into the Third Republic. As late as 15 April 1882 that republic stipulated that ambassadors and ministers plenipotentiaries should wear a specific costume.[168] Another republic, that of the United States, also took care to underline its republican cast. In 1853 the Secretary of State noted that representatives should show "their devotion to republican institutions" by appearing at official functions in "the simple dress of an American citizen."[169]

Those stationed abroad set out to distinguish themselves by their dress partly in order to create the correct impression at home. In 1792, Maulde, the French representative stationed at The Hague, was invited to a large ball attended by over 300 individuals. Everyone appeared in court attire except Maulde, who wore what the British representative deprecatingly described as a "strange dress between a frock and a full dress coat." Maulde made his excuses and awkwardly contended that his trunks had not yet arrived, but the British minister suspected that "these singularities" were to enable him to introduce "impertinent paragraphs into his correspondence with the Jacobins."[170] Further south and four years later, in Madrid in May 1796 Mangourit requested a special costume: a tricolor sash and band and silver buttons emblazoned with the image of the republic.[171] During the negotiations at Lille, Harris noted that Ange-Élisabeth-Antoine Bonnier d'Alco, who came from a wealthy and prominent family, had assumed a revolutionary appearance: "His countenance vile, his dress and address affectedly Jacobin and his whole accoutrement in the same character; he looked like a proselyte to those principles, and rather ashamed to be in good company, to which he had once belonged." His secretary, Derché, also had "a Jacobin appearance."[172] At the Congress of Rastatt in 1797 the French diplomats wore blue frock coats with yellow buttons emblazoned with the inscription "*Liberté, Egalité*" and the figure of Liberty.[173] Metternich was clearly surprised that they wore neither cockades nor scarves[174] but was shocked by the change from the inimitable elegance of the *ancien régime* to the "slovenliness" of the Revolution: "I declare that in all my life I never saw such ill-conditioned animals. They see no one, are sealed up in their apartments, and are more savage than white bears. Good God! how this nation is changed." For him the change was not positive:

> the most perfect amiability is replaced by a dull sinister air, which I can only fully describe by calling it Revolutionary! ... What a pack of wretches they are here. All these fellows have coarse muddy shoes, great blue pantaloons, a vest of blue or of all colours, peasants' handkerchiefs, either silk or cotton

round the neck, the hair long, black, and dirty, and the hideous head crowned by an enormous hat with a great red feather. One would die of fright, I believe, if one met the best clothed of them in a wood. They have a sullen air, and seem more discontented with themselves than with anyone else.[175]

The aristocratic disdain echoes down to us. Napoleon, richly dressed in the garb of a "warrior sovereign," had also made an impression at Rastatt, arriving in a berlin drawn by eight horses and with a military escort.[176]

To Metternich their attire was but another indication of their presumptuous conduct.[177] He was appalled and enraged when he witnessed the revolutionaries' rejection of the eighteenth-century European conventions regarding diplomatic attire. There was no doubt that these men were not crafted in the mold of diplomats of the *ancien régime*, whom Napoleon had derisively dubbed "the brilliant butterflies of the panniers age."[178] "Agreement on manners [and dress]," according to a twentieth-century commentator, "went hand-in-hand with—indeed was a metaphor for—agreement on ideology." Sartorial conformity implied a shared "commitment to the preservation of the existing structure of international society and the assumptions upon which it rested."[179] If a diplomat chose to flout such conventions, the article of clothing must have some widely known significance or the gesture would be lost, thus the tricolor which bedecked most revolutionaries. Defying sartorial conventions meant rejecting the international system as then constituted. It was no accident that Thomas Jefferson once greeted the British minister in an old bathrobe and slippers. Dress was particularly critical because at the outset it foreshadowed the difficulties to come.

This lexicon of words, gestures, symbols, and garb was consciously adopted as an affirmation and confirmation of the revolutionary faith. The utterance of specific phrases coupled with certain intonations and the wearing of a distinctive dress were important on at least two levels: one to understand the dynamic of what has been called revolutionary culture, the second to gauge the possibility of accommodating a revolutionary power within an international system. The revolutionaries challenged the Europeans' assumption of a common diplomatic culture and even the possibility of an international order. They were challenging the very concept of Europe as it had been formulated up until that time: "a commonwealth … virtually one great state," in which, in the words of Burke, "no citizen of Europe could be altogether an exile in any part of it." For him "correspondence in laws, customs, manners, and habits of life" had more force than treaties. "They are obligations written in the heart."[180]

NOTES

1. Quoted in Blakemore, *Burke and the Fall of Language*, 84.
2. Clemens Wenzel Neopomuk Lothar, Fürst von Metternich-Winneburg, *Memoirs of Prince Metternich, 1773–1815*, ed. Richard Metternich (New York: Charles Scribner's Sons, 1880), 9 December 1797 to his wife, 1: 350–351 and 1: 353.
3. Richard Wrigley, *The Politics of Appearances: Representations of Dress in Revolutionary France* (Oxford: Berg, 2002), 232.
4. Quoted in Sophia Rosenfeld, *A Revolution in Language: The Problem of Signs in Late Eighteenth-Century France* (Stanford, CA: Stanford University Press, 2001), 164.
5. Quoted in Daniel Gordon, *Citizens without Sovereignty: Equality and Sociability in French Thought, 1670–1789* (Princeton: University Press, 1994), 43.
6. As Rosenfeld has argued "political thought and semiotic or epistemological theory bolstered one another in a very particular way." This "distinctive fusion," she argued, "was in good part responsible ... for the singular character of the revolutionary transformation that began in that nation in 1789." Rosenfeld, *A Revolution in Language*, 245.
7. Thucydides, *History of the Peloponnesian War*, trans. Richard Crawley (London: Everyman, 1993), 164.
8. Saint-Just, *Oeuvres complètes*, 2: 478, 27 July 1794.
9. Philippe Roger, "The French Revolution as 'Logomachy'" in *Language and Rhetoric of the Revolution*, ed. John Renwick (Edinburgh: University Press, 1990), 6.
10. Keith Michael Baker, *Inventing the French Revolution: Essays on French Political Culture in the Eighteenth Century* (Cambridge: University Press, 1990), 10.
11. "Des Mots à la mode et des nouvelles façons de parler," 1696 edition as quoted in Gordon, *Citizens without Sovereignty*, 105.
12. See Callières, *Du bel esprit*, 16. Later Beaumarchais was criticized for the worldliness of his style, his epigrams, and puns. Mercier noted that this style, which "always revolts against nature itself," "injects wit at every occasion" and "always aims for the epigram." Quoted in Sarah Maza, *Private Lives and Public Affairs: The Causes Célèbres of Prerevolutionary France* (Berkeley: University of California Press, 1993), 295.
13. Philippe Roger, "Le Débat sur la 'langue révolutionnaire'," in *La Carmagnole des muses: l'homme de lettres et l'artiste dans la Révolution* (Paris: Armand Colin, 1988), 177–178.
14. Steven Blakemore, "Revolution in Language: Burke's Representation of Linguistic Terror," in James A. W. Heffernan, ed., *Representing the French*

Revolution: Literature, Historiography, and Art, 3–23 (Hanover: University Press of New England, 1992), 5.
15. Bertrand Barère de Vieuzac, *Rapport et projet de décret ... sur les idioimes étrangers et l'enseignement de la language française ... séance du 4 vendémiaire (an II)* (Paris: Imp Nat. (an II)), 7, 11.
16. Jean-Jacques Rousseau, *On the Origin of Languages* (New York: Frederick Ungar, 1966), 72–73; Loustalot quoted in Barny, "Les Mots et les choses chez les hommes de la Révolution française," 105.
17. Paine, quoted in Blakemore, *Burke and the Fall of Language* (Hanover, University Press of New England, 1988), 84.
18. *L'Orateur du peuple*, 7 no. 50, 395–396.
19. Blakemore, *Burke and the Fall of Language*, 90. See also Blakemore, "Revolution in Language: Burke's Representation of Linguistic Terror," in *Representing the French Revolution*, ed. Heffernan, 12.
20. Blakemore, *Burke and the Fall of Language*, 80.
21. Gordon, *Citizens without Sovereignty*, 233 and 235.
22. Grégoire, "Rapport sur la nécessité et les moyens d'anéantir les patois," quoted in Rosenfeld, *A Revolution in Language*, 172. In Paine's view, one that is "free, bold, and manly." Paine, quoted in Blakemore, *Burke and the Fall of Language*, 83.
23. Guilhaumou, *La Langue politique et la Révolution française*, 30.
24. According to Gumbrecht, the revolutionaries used language to build political consensus, to develop group identity, and to secure institutional unanimity. Hans Ulrich Gumbrecht, *Funktionen parlamentarischer Rhetorik in der Französischen Revolution: Vorstudien zur Entwicklung einer historischen Textpragmatik* (Munich: Wilhelm Fink Verlag, 1978).
25. Guilhaumou, *La Langue politique et la Révolution française*, 9.
26. Barny, "Les Mots et les choses chez les hommes de la Révolution française," 96–106.
27. Quoted in Roger, "The French Revolution as 'Logomachy'," in *Language and Rhetoric of the Revolution*, edited by Renwick, 9.
28. Blakemore, *Burke and the Fall of Language*, 80.
29. Grégoire in Michel de Certeau, Dominique Julia, and Jacques Revel. *Une Politique de la langue: La Révolution française et les patois: l'Enquête de Grégoire* (Paris: Gallimard, 1975), 313.
30. Brissot, *Discours sur l'office de l'Empéreur du 17 février 1792*, 17.
31. Gower, *Private Correspondence*, 1: 43, to his mother, 19 June 1791.
32. *Révolutions de Paris* of 7 December 1789 in Jacques Guilhaumou, *La Langue politique et la Révolution française: De l'Evènement à la raison linguistique* (Paris: Meridiens Klincksieck, 1989), 137; Jacques Guilhaumou. "Discourse and Revolution: The Foundation of Political Language (1789–1792)," in *Culture and Revolution: Cultural Ramifications of the French Revolution*, ed. Levitine, 130.

33. Henri-Baptiste Grégoire, *Rapport sur la nécessité et les moyens d'anéantir les patois et d' universaliser l'usage de la langue française* (Paris: Imp. Nat., n.d.), 22.
34. Quoted in Peter France, "Speakers and Audience: The First Days of the Convention," in *Language and Rhetoric of the Revolution*, ed. Renwick, 60.
35. A. A. E., États-Unis, CP, vol., 52, part 6, fol. 337, Paris 8 vendémiaire 1800, note the demand that the treaty be written only in French. A. A. E., États-Unis, CP, vol. 52, part 7 fol. 346, Paris, 9 vendémiaire, year 9 (20 September 1800). Note discussion after the treaty was signed in both English and French on the question of whether French was to be recognized as the original language of the treaty.
36. Quoted in France, "Speakers and Audience," in *Language and Rhetoric of the Revolution*, edited by Renwick, 54.
37. Miot de Melito, *Memoirs*, 25.
38. Guyot, p. 549 quoted in Linda and Marsha Frey, "'The Reign of the Charlatans is Over'," 726.
39. Mikhailowitch, *Les Relations diplomatiques de la Russie et de la France* 5: 35, letter of 10 June 1810.
40. France, *Recueil*, vol. 28: *États allemands*, tome 1: *L'Electorat de Mayence*, 282.
41. An article in the *Mercure* quoted in Bell, *The Cult of the Nation in France*, 172.
42. Barère in name of Committee of Public Safety, Rapport du comité de Salut Public sur les idiomes," 8 pluviose, an II, quoted in *Une Politique de la langue*, ed. Certeau, Julia, and Revel, 291.
43. An article in the *Mercure national* of 14 December 1790 entitled "On the Influence of Words and the Power of Usage," quoted in Guilhaumou, *La Langue politique et la Révolution française*, 51–52.
44. F. A. Aulard, *La Société des Jacobins*, 2: 456, 25 May 1791, pamphlet.
45. Barny, "Les Mots et les choses chez les hommes de la Révolution française," 96–105.
46. Grégoire, *Rapport sur la nécessité et les moyens d'anéantir les patois et d' universaliser l'usage de la langue française*, 28.
47. Roger, "Le Débat sur la 'langue révolutionnaire," in *La Carmagnole des muses*, 168 and 175. Doumergue wanted a dictionary that would be "vraiment politique." Quoted in Guilhaumou, "La Language politique: Des Notions-concepts en usage," in *La Révolution à l'oeuvre: Perspectives actuelles dans l'histoire de la Révolution française*, ed. Jean-Clément Martin (Rennes: Presses Universitaires de Rennes, 2005), 131.
48. Guilhaumou, *La Langue politique et la Révolution française*, 196, 70–72, 78.
49. Annie Geffroy, "Les Dictionnaires socio-politiques 1770–1815: Une Bibliographie," in *Dictionnaire des usages socio-politiques (1770–1815)*

(Paris: INALF, 1988), 13. See also Sonia Branca-Rosoff, "Les Mots de parti pris: Citoyen, Aristocrate et insurrection dans quelques dictionnaires (1762–1798)," in *Dictionnaire des usages socio-politiques (1770–1815)* (Paris: INALF, 1988), 47–73.
50. Roger, "Le Débat sur la 'langue révolutionnaire'," 157 and 179.
51. Ibid., 180; Gerard Gengembre, *La Contre-Révolution ou l'histoire désesperante* (Paris: Imago, 1989), 259 and 260.
52. P.R.O., FO 27/36 Paris, January 28, 1791, Earl Gower.
53. Roger, "Le Débat sur la 'langue révolutionnaire'," 58.
54. Quoted in Roger, "The French Revolution as 'Logomachy," 7.
55. Brissot, *Discours de J. P. Brissot, député sur les dispositions des puissances étrangères*, 41; Brissot, *Discours sur l'office d l'Empéreur*, 17. In the steps of his patron Brissot, Lebrun (1763–1793), foreign minister (1792–1793), told the National Convention that one of his duties was to ensure that through its agents at the courts a language "always imposing, always free, always worthy of a great people" would be heard. Pierre-Henri-Marie Lebrun-Tondu, *Compte rendu à la convention nationale par le ministre des affaires étrangères, dans la séance du 26 Septembre 1792, l'an premier de la république française* (Paris: De l'Imprimerie nationale, 1792), 7.
56. Bélin, *La Logique d'une idée-force*, 2: 114.
57. Aulard, *Études et leçons sur la Révolution française*, 25.
58. Francois Marie Arouet de Voltaire, *Correspondence*, edited by Theodore Besterman (Geneva: Institut et Musés Voltaire, 1953), 3: 138, Voltaire to Jacob Vernet, 14 September 1733. See also Voltaire, *Oeuvres complètes* (Paris, 1825), 2: 71–74, for his famous missive on "*vous*" and "*tu*." Montesquieu argued more forcefully that "our *vous* is a defect of modern languages," "contrary to nature." Quoted in Brunot, *Histoire de la langue française*, 9, 2: 689.
59. Etienne Bonnot de Condillac, *Oeuvres complètes* (Paris: Lecointe et Durey, 1821), 6: 480.
60. *Journal de la langue françoise*, 1 janvier 1791, 16–22.
61. Guilhaumou, *La Langue politique et la Révolution française*, 131 and 134.
62. That transparence, as Derrida tells us, had "tested the concealment within speech itself, in the mirage of its immediacy." Speech was to be "transparent and innocent." Jacques Derrida, *Of Grammatology*, trans by Gayatri Chakravorty Spivak (Baltimore: Johns Hopkins University Press, 1974), 138, 140, and 141.
63. Philippe Wolff, "Le Tu révolutionnaire." *Annales historiques de la Révolution française*, 279 (Janvier–Mars 1990): 89. In a petition to the Convention of 10 brumaire, an II (13 October 1793), a revolutionary maintained that "the principles of our language ought to be as important to us as the laws of our republic." Specifically, he then argued that "the

spirit of fanaticism, of pride, of feudalism, has led us to adopt the habit of using the second person plural when we speak to one person. Many evils still result from this abuse ... which under the pretext of respect banishes the principles of fraternal virtue." The adoption of *tu* would entail less arrogance, less distinction, less hostility, and would encourage more familiarity, and consequently, here the definitive argument, more equality. Quoted in John Hardman, ed., *French Revolution Documents* (New York: Barnes and Noble, 1973), 2: 132–133. See also Linda S. Frey and Marsha L. Frey, "Et *tu*: Language and the French Revolution," *History of European Ideas* 20 (1995): 505–510.

64. Tocqueville, *The Old Regime and the French Revolution*, 156; Furet, *Interpreting the French Revolution*, 53.
65. Wolff, "Le Tu révolutionnaire," 89.
66. Dry, *Soldats, ambassadeurs sous le Directoire*, 1: 33.
67. A. A. E., CP, États-Unis, vol. 44, fol. 184, Lequoy to Fauchet in 1795.
68. A. A. E., CP, États-Unis, vol. 40, fol. 139, Fauchet to Randolph.
69. Stites, "Russian Revolutionary Culture," 138.
70. Furet, *Interpreting the French Revolution*, 48.
71. Louis Sébastien Mercier, *Le Nouveau Paris* (Paris: Mercure de France, 1994), 194.
72. Aulard, *Recueil des actes du Comité de salut public*, 4: 185–186, the Committee of Public Safety meeting of 16 May 1793, morning.
73. Aulard, *Études et leçons sur la Révolution française*, 30 fn.
74. Guilhaumou, *La Langue politique et la Révolution française*, 196 and 135.
75. Ibid., 136.
76. Alphonse Aulard, *Paris pendant la réaction thermidorienne et sous le Directoire: Recueil de documents pour l'histoire de l'esprit public à Paris* (Paris: Librairie Noblet, 1899), 3: 394. This usage spread beyond the confines of France to its armies abroad. Miot de Melito, *Memoirs*, 104.
77. Masson, *Le Département des affaires étrangères pendant la Révolution, 1787–1804*, 379.
78. Grandmaison, *L'Ambassade française en Espagne pendant la Révolution (1789–1804)*, 134; Dry, *Soldats, ambassadeurs sous le Directoire*, 1: 33.
79. Turner, ed. *Correspondence of the French Ministers to the United States 1791–1797*, 2: 965–956, Adet to Minister of Foreign Relations, 29 October 1796.
80. Montell Ogdon, *Juridical Bases of Diplomatic Immunity: A Study in the Origin, Growth and Purpose of the Law* (Washington, DC: J Byrne and Co., 1936), 144–145. Also see Francis Deak, "Classification, Immunities, and Privileges of Diplomatic Agents," *Southern California Law Review* 1 (March–May 1928): 217–218.
81. Church, *Revolution and Red Tape*, 59.

82. Jacques Rambaud, *Memoirs of the Comte Roger De Damas (1787–1806)* (London: Chapman and Hall, 1913), 145.
83. Church, *Revolution and Red Tape*, 94, 97, 119.
84. France, *Recueil*, vol. 28, États Allemands. Tome 1: L'Electorat de Mayence, 283.
85. A. N., D XIII, carton 2, dossier 34, Society of the Friends of the Constitution at Cherbourg to the Diplomatic Committee, 6 September 1792.
86. Merlin de Thionville, in Allonville, *Mémoires* 3: 214; A. A. E., Correspondance politique, États-Unis, vol. 46 Deforgues was careful to show his attachment to the Revolution and always signed his letters "salut et fraternité." A. N., Police générale, Comité de sûreté générale, 5 Commission des 24, documents diplomatiques et historiques, F7/4390/2.
87. National Library of Scotland, Papers of Sir Robert Liston, 5572, fol. 196–197, Constantinople, Liston to Whitworth, 12 May 1795.
88. Hagley, Letombe to Victor Du Pont, circular of 26 ventôse, an 6, citing the decree of 18 fructidor.
89. A. A. E., CP, États-Unis, vol. 47, part 6, fol. 401, M. Otto, Considération sur la conduite du gouvernement des États-Unis ... 1789–1797.
90. J.-P. Brissot de Warville, *J. P. Brissot, Correspondance et papiers* (Paris: Librarie Alphonse Picard et Fils., 1911), 177.
91. Rose, *William Pitt and The Great War*, 59.
92. Murley, "The Origins and Outbreak of the Anglo-French War of 1793," 223.
93. B. L., Add. Mss. 58920, fol. 129 Auckland to Grenville, The Hague, 3 July 1792; Lord Auckland to Lord Grenville, private, 1792 July, The Hague, HMC, *The Manuscripts of J. B. Fortescue*, 2: 287.
94. Kidner, "The Girondists and the "Propaganda War" of 1792," 396.
95. B. L., Add. Mss. 58920, fol. 118, Auckland to Grenville, 22 June 1792.
96. B. L., Add. Mss. 58920, fol. 129 Auckland to Grenville, 6 July 1792.
97. After rumors circulated that he was profiteering at the republic's expense, he was recalled and told to present his accounts. Murley, "The Origins and Outbreak of the Anglo-French War of 1793," 224–230 and 242.
98. Great Britain, HMC, *The Manuscripts of J. B. Fortescue*, 2: 377 Lord Auckland to Lord Grenville, private, 3 February 1793, The Hague.
99. NA., General Records of the Department of State, RG59, Diplomatic Despatches, Great Britain (M30), vol. 8, Rufus King, 30 July 1799.
100. France, Convention nationale, *Décret de la Convention nationale, qui déclare que la république française est en guerre avec l'Espagne, du 7 mars 1793, l'an 2e de la république française*, No 549 (Moulins: De l'Imprimerie nationale de G. Boutonnet, 1793), 6 and 8.
101. Ibid., 9 and 10.

102. Lincolnshire Record Office, Papers of Sir Richard Worsley, 14, fol. 169, Sir Richard Worsley to Grenville, Venice, 19 April 1797.
103. Comte Dominique-Joseph Garat, *Considérations sur la Révolution française, et sur la conjuration des puissances de l'Europe, contre la liberté et les droits des hommes*. France: n.p., an quatrième de la liberté [1792], 2.
104. Aulard, ed., *Recueil des actes du Comité de salut public*, 4: 185–186.
105. "*Tutoiement*," Paris, 14 germinal, an III, La Commission des relations extérieures à la Commission des Administrations civile, police et tribunaux, in Hardman, ed., *French Revolution Documents*, 2: 406–407.
106. De Conde, *Entangling Alliance*, 332.
107. Theodore Roosevelt, *Gouverneur Morris* (Boston: Houghton Mifflin Co, 1888), 254–255 and De Conde, *Entangling Alliance*, 322–323.
108. Rosenfeld, *A Revolution in Language*, 4.
109. A. A. E., CP, États-Unis, vol. 39, fol. 297, to Fauchet, brumaire, year 2? Also see A. A. E., CP, États-Unis, vol. 37, fol. 100 Paris, 3 février 1793.
110. University of Virginia, Alderman Library, James Monroe Collection, James Monroe to St. George Tucker, 24 January 1792.
111. A. A. E., CP, États-Unis, vol. 44, part 4, fol. 415, internal memoire of a Doutre of the 6th section [1795?].
112. Ibid., fol. 440.
113. Ibid., vol. 46, part 2, fol. 167, Monroe to Minister of Foreign Affairs, 2 September 1796.
114. Masson, *Le Département des affaires étrangères*, 389.
115. Peter Ochs, *Korrespondenz des Peter Ochs (1752–1821)*, edited by Gustav Steiner (Basel: Verlag von Henning Oppermann, 1927), 1: 438 Ochs to Haugwitz, Bale, 8 February 1795.
116. Great Britain, *The Official Correspondence relative to the negotiation for peace, between Great Britain and the French Republic, as laid before both Houses of Parliament* (London: J. Wright, 1797), Harris, Lille, 11 July 1797, 22–23: P.R.O., FO, 27/49, fol. 206, 29 June 1797.
117. Richard Cobb, "Some Aspects of the Revolutionary Mentality," in *New Perspectives on the French Revolution: Readings in Historical Sociology*, edited by J. Kaplow, 305–337 (New York: John Wiley and Sons, 1965), 309–310.
118. Robert Choate Darnton. "Trends in Radical Propaganda on the Eve of the French Revolution (1782–1788)," Unpublished dissertation, Oxford, 1964, 86.
119. Cobb, "Some Aspects of the Revolutionary Mentality," 310.
120. *Le Patriote François*, 1789, no. 10, 7 août, 3.
121. Quoted in Philip Mansel, *Dressed to Rule: Royal and Court Costume from Louis XIV to Elizabeth II* (New Haven, CT: Yale University Press, 2005), 84.

122. Devocelle, "D'un Costume politique à une politique du costume," 85.
123. Great Britain, HMC, *The Manuscripts of J. B. Fortescue*, 1: 608.
124. Daniel Roche, *La Culture des apparences: Une Histoire du vêtement (XVIIe–XVIIIe siècle)* (Paris: Fayard, 1989), 147.
125. *A Trip to Paris in July and August 1792* (London: Minerva Press, 1793), 66 and 88.
126. A counter-revolutionary song satirized the revolutionaries' appearance: "God what a sight!/It fills you with pity in faith/God what a sight!/ you'd take them for jockeys/They've got just the look/the rig and the hair cut/God what a sight!" "Comme ils sont faits!/Cela fait pite, je vous jure/Comme ils sont faits!/On les predrait pur des jokais/Ils en ont la tournure/L'accoutrement et la coiffure/Comme ils sont faits!" Quoted in France, "Speakers and Audience," 67.
127. Cobb, "Some Aspects of the Revolutionary Mentality," 309.
128. Devocelle, "D'un Costume politique à une politique du costume," 83.
129. Grégoire, *Rapport sur le projet de décret*, 2.
130. Wrigley, *The Politics of Appearances*, 130, fn 79.
131. Ibid., 112 and 130 fn. 105.
132. Gita May, *Madame Roland and the Age of Revolution* (New York: Columbia University Press, 1970), 206–207.
133. Godechot, *La Grande Nation*, 2: 689.
134. Prince Adam Czartoryski, *Memoirs of Prince Adam Czartoryski and his Correspondence with Alexander I*, edited by Adam Gielgud (London: Remington and Co., 1888), 1: 195.
135. Quoted in Wrigley, *The Politics of Appearances*, 233, 17 mess, an II/5 July 1794.
136. James Harris, *Diaries and Correspondence of James Harris, First Earl of Malmesbury*, 1844 Reprint (New York: AMS Press, 1970), 3: 260, Harris to Grenville, Paris, 23 October 1796.
137. Great Britain, HMC, *The Manuscripts of J. B. Fortescue*, 3: 276, Grenville to Harris, Private, 22 November 1796.
138. André Michel, ed., *Correspondance inedite de Mallet du Pan avec la Cour de Vienna (1794–1795)* (Paris: E. Plon, Nourriet et Cie., 1884), 2: 103, 1796; Wrigley, *The Politics of Appearances*, 130 fn 11.
139. P.R.O., FO 38/3, Leer, 22 May 1798.
140. Mikhailowitch, *Les Relations diplomatiques de la Russie et de la France*, 7: 30, 2 April 1808 from Minister of Foreign Affairs.
141. Devocelle, "D'un Costume politique à une politique du costume," 89 and 96–97; Daniel Roche, "Apparences révolutionnaires ou révolution des apparences," *Les Vêtements de la liberté*, edited by Nicole Pellegrin, 193–201 (Aix en Provence: Alinea, 1989), 200.
142. Wrigley, *The Politics of Appearances*, 60.

143. David Paul Nickles, "US Diplomatic Etiquette during the Nineteenth Century," in *The Diplomats Word: A Cultural History of Diplomacy, 1815–1914*, edited by Markus Mösslung and Torsten Riotte (Oxford: University Press, 2008), 296–297. The attire was changed several times but when ordinary evening dress was mandated, US diplomats were often mistaken for waiters (ibid., p. 298 fn 40). At other times they were asked why they dressed as undertakers. The US minister replied that "[w]e could not be more appropriately dressed then we are, at European courts, where what we represent is the burial of monarchy" (ibid., 300). At least one American came to the conclusion that this was "no time for indulging oddities of any kind." If "gold lace and silk stockings" enabled to have any influence, he would wear them (ibid., 303).
144. Wrigley, *The Politics of Appearances*, 61.
145. Quoted in Mansel, *Dressed to Rule*, 76.
146. Decree of 25 floréal, an II (14 mai 1794), in Devocelle, "D'un Costume politique à une politique du costume," 89.
147. Pierre Arizzoli-Clementel, "Les Arts du décor," in *Aux Armes and Aux Arts! Les Arts de la Révolution, 1789–1799*, edited by Philippe Bordes and Régis Michel, 280–311 (Paris: Adam Biron, 1988), 306. Also see Charlotte Hould, "La Propagande d'état par l'estampe," in *Les Images de la Révolution française*, edited by Michel Vovelle, 29–37 (Paris: Publications de la Sorbonne, 1988), 30–32; Madeleine Delpierre, "A Propos d'un manteau de représentant du peuple de 1798 recemment offert au musée du costume," *Bulletin du musée carnavalet*, 25 (1972): 13–23.
148. Wrigley, *The Politics of Appearances*, 79.
149. Edmond Launay, *Costumes, insignes, cartes, médailles, des députés, 1789–1898* (Paris: Mottteroz, n.d.), 46–48.
150. Jean-Marc Devocelle, "D'un Costume politique à une politique du costume: Approches théoriques et idéologiques du costume pendant la Révolution française," in *Modes et révolutions, 1780–1804* (Paris: Musée de la mode et du costume, Palais Galliéra, 1989), 93.
151. Metternich, *Mémoires*, 1: 371, 3 June 1798, to his wife.
152. Hunt, *Politics, Culture and Class in the French Revolution*, 85; Roche, *Le Culture des Apparences*, 147. Reference to a new national costume quoted in Jennifer Harris, "The Red cap of Liberty," *Eighteenth-Century Studies*, 14 (spring 1981): 306.
153. Turner, ed., *Correspondence of the French Ministers to the United States, 1791–1797*, 2: 967, Adet to Minister of Foreign Relations, 2 November 1796.
154. Miot de Melito, *Memoirs*, 64; Allonville, *Mémoires*, 1: 350; and Attilio Simioni, *Le origini del risorgimento politico dell'italia meridionale* (Rome: Casa Editrice Giuseppe Principato, 1925), 1: 441.

155. Decree of 11 frimaire, an III (1 December 1794), in Masson, *Le Département des affaires étrangères*, 346, fn. 3. Also see Paris, Musée de la mode et du costume, *Uniformes civils français, cérémonial, circonstances, 1750–1980* (Paris: Musée de la mode et du costume, 1982), 31.
156. Hagley, W3-3881, Adet to Victor Du Pont, instructions, 20 Mess. III [8 July 1795], instructions of 6 nivôse.
157. A. A. E., CP, États-Unis, vol. 44, fol. 184, Lequoy to Fauchet in 1795.
158. Der Derian, *On Diplomacy*, 179. Moreau le Jeune also provided an illustration of a projected costume for diplomats. Devocelle, "D'un Costume politique à une politique du costume," 93, cites Moreau le Jeune, illustration of project for ambassador's costume and Biblothèque historique de la Ville de Paris, cat. 220.
159. Miot de Melito, *Memoires*, 66.
160. Dry, *Soldats, ambassadeurs sous le Directoire*, 1: 31–32, 4 messidor an IV (22 June 1796).
161. Masson, *Le Département des affaires étrangères pendant la Révolution, 1787–1804*, 388.
162. Guyot, *Le Directoire et la paix de L'Europe*, 92. For example, Perignon received outside of his salary of 150,000 *francs*, a sum of 75,000 *livres*.
163. Lincolnshire Record Office, Papers of Sir Richard Worsley, 14, fol. 113–114, Worsley to Grenville, Venice, 14 December 1796.
164. Turner, ed. *Correspondence of the French Ministers to the United States, 1791–1797*, 2: 965, letter of 8 brumaire, an 5 (29 October 1796).
165. Paris, Musée de la mode et du costume, *Uniformes civils français, cérémonial, circonstances, 1750–1980*, 31.
166. Conrad Engelbert Oelsner, *Des Opinions politiques du Citoyen Sieyès* (Paris: Goujon fils, 1800), 265 and Sorel, *L'Europe et le Révolution française*, 5: 333.
167. Quoted in Simms, *The Impact of Napoleon*, 90.
168. Paris, Musée de la mode et du costume, *Uniformes civils français, cérémonial, circonstances, 1750–1980*, 31.
169. Quoted in Mansel, *Dressed to Rule*, 138.
170. B. L., Add. Mss. 58920, fol. 104 Auckland to Grenville, 5 June 1792 and Colenbrander ed., *Gedenkstukken der Algemeene Geschiedenis van Nederland van 1795 tot 1840*, 1: 282, Auckland to Grenville, 5 June 1792.
171. Grandmaison, *L'Ambassade française en Espagne pendant la Révolution (1789–1804)*, 120.
172. Harris, *Diaries and Correspondence*, 3: 555, 13 September 1797.
173. Metternich, *Memoirs*, 1: 353, 12 December 1797 to his wife.
174. Ibid., 1: 367, 6 December 1797 to his wife.
175. Ibid., 1: 350–351 and 1: 353, 9 December 1797 and 12 December 1797 to his wife.

176. Sorel, *L'Europe et le Révolution française*, 5: 266 and 268.
177. Joseph Alex, Freiherr von Helfert, *Der Rastadter Gesandtenmord* (Vienna: Wilhelm Braumüller, 1874), 24.
178. Napoleon, *Napoleon's Letters to Marie Louise*, edited by Charles De La Roncière (New York: Farrar & Rinehart Inc., 1935), 169, 15 July 1813.
179. Cohen, *Theatre of Power*, 61.
180. Burke quoted in Chapman, *Edmund Burke: The Practical Imagination*, 185–186.

References

Allonville, Armand François, comte de. *Mémoires tirés des papiers d'un homme d'état sur les causes secrètes qui ont déterminé la politique des cabinets dans les guerres de la révolution*. 13 vols. Paris: Michaud, 1831–1838.
Arizzoli-Clementel, Pierre. "Les Arts du décor": *Aux Armes and Aux Arts! Les Arts de la Revolution, 1789–1799*. Edited by Philippe Bordes and Régis Michel, 280–311. Paris: Adam Biro, 1988.
Aulard, François-Alphonse, ed. *La Société des Jacobins: Recueil de documents pour l'histoire du club des Jacobins de Paris*. 6 vols. Paris: Librairie Jouast, 1887–1897.
———, ed. *Paris pendant la réaction thermidorienne et sous le Directoire: Recueil de documents pour l'histoire de l'esprit public à Paris*. Vols. 2–3. Paris: Librairie Noblet, 1899.
———, ed. *Recueil des actes du Comité de salut public avec la correspondance officielle des représentants en mission et le registre du conseil exécutif provisoire*. 27 vols. Paris: Imprimerie nationale, 1889–1923.
———. *Études et leçons sur la révolution française*. Paris: F. Alcan, 1902.
Baker, Keith Michael. *Inventing the French Revolution: Essays on French Political Culture in the Eighteenth Century*. Cambridge: Cambridge University Press, 1990.
Barère de Vieuzac, Bertrand. *Rapport et projet de décret ... sur les idioimes étrangers et l'enseignement de la language française ... séance du 4 vend (an II)*. Paris: Imprimerie Nationale (an II).
Barny, Roger. "Les Mots et les choses chez les hommes de la Révolution française." *Pensée* 202 (1978): 96–115.
Bélin, Jean. *La Logique d'une idée-force: l'Idée d'utilité sociale et la révolution française*. Paris: Hermann et Cie., 1939.
Bell, David A. *The Cult of the Nation in France: Inventing Nationalism, 1680–1800*. Cambridge, MA: Harvard University Press, 2001.
Blakemore, Steven. *Burke and the Fall of Language: The French Revolution as Linguistic Event*. Hanover, NH: Published for Brown University Press by University Press of New England, 1988.

———. "Revolution in Language: Burke's Representation of Linguistic Terror." In *Representing the French Revolution: Literature, Historiography, and Art*, edited by James A. W. Heffernan, 3–23. Hanover: University Press of New England, 1992.

Branca-Rosoff, Sonia. "Les Mots de parti pris. Citoyen, aristocrate et insurrection dans quelques dictionnaires (1762–1798)." In *Dictionnaire des usages sociopolitiques (1770–1815)*, 47–73. Paris: INALF, 1988.

Brissot de Warville, Jacques-Pierre. *Discours de J. P. Brissot, député sur les dispositions des Puissances étrangères, relativement à la France, et sur les préparatifs de guerre ordonné par le Roi*. Paris: Imprimerie nationale, 1791.

———. *J. P. Brissot, Correspondance et papiers*. Paris: Librarie Alphonse Picard et Fils., 1912.

Brunot, Ferdinand. *Histoire de la langue française des origines à 1900*. 14 vols. Paris: Armand Colin, 1905–1927.

Callières, François de. *Du bel esprit ou sont examinez les sentimens qu'on en a d'ordinaire dans le monde*. Amsterdam: Pierre Brunel, 1695.

Certeau, Michel de, Dominique Julia, and Jacques Revel. *Une Politique de la langue: La Révolution française et les patois: L'enquête de Grégoire*. Paris: Gallimard, 1975.

Chapman, Gerald W. *Edmund Burke: The Practical Imagination*. Cambridge, MA: Harvard University Press, 1967.

Church, Clive H. *Revolution and Red Tape: The French Ministerial Bureaucracy 1770–1850*. Oxford: Clarendon Press, 1981.

Cobb, R. C. "Some Aspects of the Revolutionary Mentality." In *New Perspectives on the French Revolution: Readings in Historical Sociology*, edited by J. Kaplow, 305–337. New York: Wiley, 1965.

Cohen, Raymond. *Theatre of Power: The Art of Diplomatic Signaling*. London: Longman, 1987.

Condillac, Étienne Bonnot de. *Oeuvres complètes*. Paris, Lecointe et Durey, 1821–1822.

Czartoryski, Adam Jerzy, Prince. *Memoirs of Prince Adam Czartoryski and His Correspondence with Alexander I*. Edited by Adam Gielgud. 2 vols. London: Remington and Co., 1888.

Darnton, Robert Choate. "Trends in Radical Propaganda on the Eve of the French Revolution, 1782–1788." Master's Thesis, Oxford University, 1964.

De Conde, Alexander. *Entangling Alliance: Politics and Diplomacy Under George Washington*. Durham, NC: Duke University Press, 1958.

Deak, Francis. "Classification, Immunities, and Privileges of Diplomatic Agents." *Southern California Law Review* 1 (March–May, 1928): 209–252, 332–354.

Delpierre, Madeleine. "A Propos d'un manteau de représentant du peuple de 1798 récemment offert au Musée du costume." *Bulletin du Musée carnavalet* 25 (1972): 13–23.

Der Derian, James. *On Diplomacy: A Genealogy of Western Estrangement*. Oxford: Basil Blackwell, 1987.
Derrida, Jacques. *Of Grammatology*. Translated by Gayatri Chakravorty Spivak. Baltimore: Johns Hopkins University Press, 1974.
Devocelle, Jean-Marc. "D'un Costume politique à une politique du costume: Approches théoriques et idélogioques du costume pendant la Révolution française." In *Modes et révolutions, 1780–1804*, 83–103. Paris: Musée de la mode et du costume, Palais Galliera, 1989.
Dry, Adrien Fleury. *Soldats ambassadeurs sous le Directoire, an IV–an VIII*. Paris: Plon, 1906.
France. Convention nationale. *Décret de la Convention nationale, qui déclare que la république française est en guerre avec l'Espagne, du 7 mars 1793 l'an 2 de la république française*. Moulins: Imprimerie nationale de G. Boutonnet, 1793.
———. Commission des Archives diplomatiques au ministère des affaires étrangères. *Recueil des instructions données au ambassadeurs et ministres de France depuis les traités de Westphalie jusqu'à la Révolution française*. Vol. 28. *États Allemands*, part 1. *L'Electorat de Mayence*. Edited by Georges Livet. Paris: Centre National de la recherche scientifique, 1962.
France, Peter. "Speakers and Audience: The First Days of the Convention." In *Language and Rhetoric of the Revolution*, edited by John Renwick, 50–67. Edinburgh: Edinburgh University Press, 1990.
Frey, Linda, and Frey, Marsha. "Et tu: Language and the French Revolution." *History of European Ideas* 20 (1995): 505–510.
Furet, François. *Interpreting the French Revolution*. Cambridge: Cambridge University Press, 1981.
Garat, Comte Dominique-Joseph. *Considérations sur la Révolution francoise, et sur la conjuration des puissances de l'Europe, contre la liberté et les droits des hommes*. [France: s.n., an quatrieme de la liberte, 1792].
Geffroy, Annie. "Les Dictionnaires socio-politiques 1770–1815: Une Bibliographie." In *Dictionnaire des usages socio-politiques (1770–1815)*, 7–46. Paris: INALF, 1988.
Gengembre, Gérard. *La Contre-Révolution ou l'histoire désespérante*. Paris: Imago, 1989.
Godechot, Jacques. *La Grande nation: L'Expansion révolutionnaire de la France dans le monde de 1789 à 1799*. Paris: Aubier, 1956.
Gordon, Daniel. *Citizens Without Sovereignty: Equality and Sociability in French Thought, 1670–1789*. Princeton: University Press, 1994.
Gower, Lord Earl Granville Leveson. *Lord Granville Leveson Gower (First Earl Granville): Private Correspondence 1781 to 1821*. Edited by Castalia Countess Granville. Vols. 1–2. New York: E. P. Dutton and Company, 1916.
Grandmaison, Charles-Alexandre Geoffroy de. *L'Ambassade française en Espagne pendant la Révolution (1789–1804)*. Paris: Plon, 1892.

Great Britain. *The Official Correspondence Relative to the Negotiation for Peace, Between Great Britain and the French Republick, as Laid Before Both Houses of Parliament.* London: J. Wright, 1797.

Great Britain, Historical Manuscripts Commission. *The Manuscripts of J. B. Fortescue, esq., Preserved at Dropmore.* 4 vols. London: Eyre and Spottiswoode, 1892–1905.

Grégoire, Henri. *Rapport sur la nécessité et les moyens d'anéantir les patois et d'universaliser l'usage de la langue française.* Paris: Impimerie Nationale., n.d.

———. *Rapport et project de décret présenté au nom du Comité d'instruction publique, sur les costumes des législateurs et des autres fonctionnaires publics.* [Paris]: De l'Imprimerie nationale, an 3 [1795].

Guilhaumou, Jacques. "Discourse and Revolution: The Foundation of Political Language, 1789–1792." In *Culture and Revolution: Cultural Ramifications of the French Revolution*, edited by George Levitine, 118–133. College Park, MD: Department of Art History, 1989a.

———. *La Langue politique et la Révolution française: De l'Evènement à la raison linguistique.* Paris: Méridiens Klincksieck, 1989b.

———. "La langue politique des notions-concepts en usage." In *La Révolution à l'oeuvre: Perspectives actuelles dans l'histoire de la Révolution française*, edited by Jean-Clément Martin, 125–138. Rennes: Presses Universitaires de Rennes, 2005.

Gumbrecht, Hans Ulrich. *Funktionen parlementarischer Rhetorik in der französischen Revolution: Vorstudien zur Entwicklung einer historischen Textpragmatik.* Munich: Wilhelm Fink Verlag, 1978.

Guyot, Raymond. *Le Directoire et la paix de l'Europe: Des traités de Bâle à la deuxième coalition, 1795–1799.* Paris: Félix Alcan, 1911.

Hardman, John, ed. *French Revolution Documents.* 2 vols. New York: Barnes and Noble, 1973.

Harris, James. *Diaries and Correspondence of James Harris, First Earl of Malmesbury.* 4 vols. 1844. Reprint. New York: AMS Press, 1970.

Harris, Jennifer. "The Red Cap of Liberty: A Study of Dress Worn by French Parisans 1789–1794." *Eighteenth-Century Studies* 14 (1981): 283–312.

Helfert, Joseph Alexander, Freiherr von. *Der Rastadter Gesandtenmord.* Vienna: Wilhelm Braumüller, 1874.

Hould, Claudette. "La Propagande d'état par l'estampe." In *Les Images de la Révolution française*, edited by Michel Vovelle, 29–37. Paris: Publications de la Sorbonne, 1988.

Hunt, Lynn. *Politics, Culture and Class in the French Revolution.* Los Angeles: University of California Press, 1984.

Journal de la langue françoise. Paris, 1791.

Kidner Jr., Frank L. "The Girondists and the "Propaganda War" of 1792: A Reevaluation of French Revolutionary Foreign Policy from 1791 to 1793." Unpublished Ph.D. Diss., Princeton University, 1971.

Launay, Edmond. *Costumes: Insignes, cartes, médailles des députés, 1789–1898.* Paris: Motteroz, 1981.
Lebrun-Tondu, Pierre Henri Hélène Marie. *Compte rendu à la convention nationale par le ministre des affaires étrangères, dans la séance du 26 Septembre 1792, l'an premier de la république française.* Paris: De l'Imprimerie nationale, 1792.
Mansel, Philip. *Dressed to Rule: Royal and Court Costume from Louis XIV to Elizabeth II.* New Haven, CT: Yale University Press, 2005.
Masson, Frédéric. *Le Département des affaires étrangères pendant la Révolution, 1787–1804.* Paris: E. Plon, 1877.
May, Gita. *Madame Roland and the Age of Revolution.* New York: Columbia University Press, 1970.
Maza, Sarah. *Private Lives and Public Affairs: The Causes Célèbres of Prerevolutionary France.* Berkeley: University of California Press, 1993.
Mercier, Louis Sébastien. *Le Nouveau Paris.* Paris: Mercure de France, 1994.
Metternich-Winneburg, Clemens Wenzel Neopomuk Lothar, Fürst von. *Memoirs of Prince Metternich.* Edited by Prince Richard Metternich. 5 vols. New York: C. Scribner's Sons, 1880–1882.
———. *Mémoires: Documents et écrits divers laissés par le Prince de Metternich, chancelier de cour et d'état.* 2 vols. Paris: E. Plon et Cie., 1881.
Michel, André, ed. *Correspondance inédite de Mallet Du Pan avec la cour de Vienne, 1794–1798.* Vol. 2. Paris: Librairie Plon, 1884.
Mikhailowitch, Nicolas. *Les Relations diplomatiques de la Russie et de la France d'après les rapports des ambassadeurs d'Alexandre et de Napoléon.* Vols. 1–7. Petrograd: Manufacture des papiers de l'État, 1905–1914.
Miot de Melito, André F. *Memoirs of Count Miot de Melito, Minister, Ambassador, Councillor of State.* Edited by Wilhelm August Fleischmann. New York: Charles Scribner's Sons, 1881.
Murley, J. T. "The Origin and Outbreak of the Anglo-French War of 1793." Unpublished Ph.D. Diss., Oxford, 1959.
Napoleon. *Napoleon's Letters to Marie Louise.* Translated and edited by Charles de La Roncière. New York: Farrar & Rinehart, 1935.
Nickles, David Paul. "US Diplomatic Etiquette During the Nineteenth Century." In *The Diplomats World: A Cultural History of Diplomacy, 1815–1914,* edited by Markus Mösslung and Torsten Riotte, 287–316. Oxford: University Press, 2008.
Ochs, Peter. *Korrespondenz des Peter Ochs (1752–1821).* Edited by Gustav Steiner. 3 vols. Vol. 1: Basel: Hermann Opperann. Vols. 2 and 3: Basel: Emil Birkhauser & cie., 1927–1937.
Oelsner, Conrad Engelbert. *Des Opinions politiques du citoyen Sieyès.* Paris: Goujon fils, 1800.
Ogdon, Montell. *Juridical Bases of Diplomatic Immunity: A Study in the Origin, Growth and Purpose of the Law.* Washington, DC: J. Byrne & Co., 1936.
L'Orateur du peuple, 7 no. 50.

Paris. *Musée de la mode et des costume: Uniformes civils français cérémonial circonstances, 1750–1980*. Paris: Musée de la mode et du costume, 1983.

Le Patriote françois. Paris, 1789–1793.

Rambaud, Jacques. *Memoirs of the Comte Roger de Damas, 1787–1806*. London: Chapman and Hall Ltd, 1913.

Roche, Daniel. *La Culture des apparences: une histoire du vêtement*. Paris: Fayard, 1989.

Roger, Philippe. "Le Débat su la 'langue révolutionnaire'." In *La Carmagnole des muses: l'homme de lettres et l'artiste dans la Révolution*, 157–184. Paris: Armand Colin, 1988.

———. "The French Revolution as 'Logomachy'." In *Language and Rhetoric of the Revolution*, edited by John Renwick, 4–17. Edinburgh: University Press, 1990.

Roosevelt, Theodore. *Gouverneur Morris*. Boston: Houghton Mifflin Co., 1888.

Rose, J. Holland. *William Pitt and the Great War*. 1911. Reprint. Westport, CT: Greenwood Press, 1971.

Rosenfeld, Sophia. *A Revolution in Language: The Problem of Signs in Late Eighteenth-Century France*. Stanford, CA: Stanford University Press, 2001.

Rousseau, Jean-Jacques. "Essay On The Origin of Languages." In *Milestones on Thought: On the Origin of Language*, edited by John H. Moran and Alexander Gode. New York: Frederick Ungar Publishing Co., 1966.

Saint-Just, Louis de. *Oeuvres complètes de Saint-Just*. Edited by Charles Vellay. 2 vols. Paris: Librairie Charpentier et Fasquelle, 1908.

Simioni, Attilio. *Le origini del risorgimento politico dell'Iitalia meridionale*. 2 vols. Rome: Giuseppe Principato, 1925–1930.

Sorel, Albert. *L'Europe and la Révolution française*. 8 vols. Paris: E. Plon Nourrit et cie, 1897–1904.

Stites, Richard. "Russian Revolutionary Culture: Its Place in the History of Cultural Revolutions." In *Culture and Revolution*, edited by Paul Dukes and John Dunkley, 132–141. London: Pintner, 1990.

Thucydides. *History of the Peloponnesian War*. Translated by Richard Crawley. London: Everyman, 1993.

Tocqueville, Alexis de. *The Old Regime and the French Revolution*. Translated by Stuart Gilbert. Garden City, NY: Doubleday, 1955.

A Trip to Paris in July and August 1792. London: Minerva Press, 1793.

Turner, Frederick Jackson, ed. *Correspondence of the French Ministers to the United States, 1791–1797*. 2 vols. 1903. Reprint. New York: Da Capo Press, 1972.

Voltaire, François Marie Arouet de. *Oeuvres complètes*. Paris: E. A. Leguier, 1820–1826.

———. *Correspondence*. Edited by Theodore Besterman. 23 vols. Geneva: Institut et Musée de Voltaire, 1953–1958.

Wolff, Philippe. "Le Tu revolutionnaire." *Annales historiques de la Revolution française* 279 (janvier–mars, 1990): 89–94.

Wrigley, Richard. *The Politics of Appearances: Representations of Dress in Revolutionary France*. Oxford: Berg, 2002.

CHAPTER 6

"Empire of Images": The Deployment of Symbols

The French appalled the Austrian minister Metternich when they commissioned a tricolor flag in sugar which they placed on top of a pyramid of biscuits. "I swear to you," Metternich confided to his wife, "that I entirely lost my appetite at the sight of those execrable colors."[1]

The republicans displayed (their enemies would say "brandished") the colors of the republic, a symbol of revolution and, in some instances, an incitement to riot. Such men were as ideologically driven as their counterparts on the various revolutionary committees. Mercy d'Argentau, the former Austrian ambassador to France, was not alone in regarding these representatives as "missionaries."[2] In a world in which symbolism was the very substance of discourse, they alienated *ancien régime* governments at the outset. They vaunted the new order and flaunted its symbols. Were these gestures and words, bonnets and flags ultimately without significance? A meaningless taunting of aristocratic Europe? The new diplomatic style reflected the republican code and reinforced the republican ideology. The revolutionaries realized that the *ancien régime*'s "system of power was embedded in the language, the social codes, and the behavior patterns of every life" and that "political systems are held together, are made to stick by the force of culture."[3] Their actions were part of an attempt to forge a

---

Fabre quoted in Simon Schama, *Citizens: A Chronicle of the French Revolution* (New York: Alfred A. Knopf, 1989), 771.

© The Author(s) 2018
L. Frey, M. Frey, *The Culture of French Revolutionary Diplomacy*, Studies in Diplomacy and International Relations,
https://doi.org/10.1007/978-3-319-71709-8_6

new community, which, as Durkheim argued, "is not made up merely of the mass of individuals who compose it, the ground which they occupy, the things which they use, and the movements which they perform, but above all is the idea which it forms of itself."[4] This emphasis on self-definition fits in with the revolutionary idea of a new man and a new society.

Nor were these men, whether Bernadotte in Vienna or Bassville in Rome, atypical of the revolutionaries who defied diplomatic conventions and challenged established procedures. The new diplomatic style reflected what Fabre d'Eglantine called "the empire of images," or Mirabeau the "language of signs."[5] They not only draped their embassies with tricolor flags and painted escutcheons depicting the image of liberty (what one German secret agent called "that terrible standard of revolt") but also commissioned culinary masterpieces with political messages and none too subtle ones at that.[6] The actions of the French representative to Geneva, Louis-Pierre Resnier, who had urged the syndics to hang the French flag in the city hall, were not atypical of those sent abroad. The Genevans had refused that request but allowed the flag to be carried in a solemn *cortège* that would go through the hall.[7] These celebrations stretched to Constantinople. There, Descorches, perhaps because of ever-present suspicions about his noble birth, celebrated the revolutionary *fêtes* with a particular ardor. He set the scene when he destroyed most of the emblems of royalty in the ambassadorial residence (though not a statue of Louis XV, removed later). To celebrate July 14, he declared that all Frenchmen would come together at noon to hear the reading of the "Declaration of the Rights of Man and the Citizen" and to swear an oath. A banquet, toasts, and a ball followed. To illustrate the international flavor of the event, those with cosmopolitan sentiments were invited, notably a Milanese, a Pole, and a Hungarian. The participants sang the *Marseillaise* and *la carmagnole* and danced around a liberty tree. After the six-hour celebration, the crowd shouted: the republic or death.[8] Through their actions men like Resnier and Descorches attempted to discredit the *ancien régime* and validate the new revolutionary government. The behavior of the French diplomats ranged from the innocuous to the seditious, from violating formerly accepted rules of etiquette to instigating riots.

Perhaps one of the most obvious examples in the diplomatic sphere of the centrality of the symbolic system was the killing of the French secretary, Nicolas Jean Hugou de Bassville (1753–1793), at Rome in January 1793. Before this assignment Bassville had earned a reputation as a radical journalist.[9] In a pamphlet published in 1789, he had argued that "priests were ... a state within the state, an additional burden supported by the civil body." Priests, he continued, were "degraded by the vow of obedience, corrupted by a barbarous and coarse education." Enduring a "spiritual slavery," the celibate are "a useless weight on the earth." He called on the nation to reform the clergy, to "make your priests citizens and spouses."[10] Such views were hardly a harbinger of success in the papal city. This Freemason, and like so many, a shameless self-promoter, had been serving as secretary of the embassy at Naples since 12 August 1792. After news of the fall of the monarchy reached Naples, Bassville and the rest of the embassy found themselves isolated: "They avoid and fear us like lepers carrying the most revolting disease."[11] Bassville was bored and had little or nothing to do. A dispatch from the minister of foreign affairs, Lebrun, with the new seal of the republic on its letterhead inspired him; he hired a painter, possibly Wicar, to reproduce the image that he placed over the *fleur de lys* on the embassy's coat of arms. That evening he caused a sensation at the opera by wearing the uniform of a member of the National Guard, festooned with the blue, white, and red cockade.

A mere one week later, his superior sent him to Rome to intercede for two artists who had been imprisoned and to act as a personal observer. French relations with Rome were strained. The French assembly had confiscated church property and invaded and annexed the papal territories of Avignon and Venaissin. Hostility to the French had only increased after the fall of the monarchy. The massacre of the Swiss Guard enraged the Vatican soldiers, who were countrymen of the victims. The actions of revolutionaries in Marseilles, who had burnt an effigy of the pope, defaced the papal coat of arms, and broken into the papal consulate, had understandably not improved relations. The slaughter of the Swiss Guard and of the priests during the September Massacres had made the supporters of the Revolution in Rome "detested and even loathed," in the words of Girodet-Trioson, a French artist studying in Rome.[12] Some of the artists in Rome had fled. Rumors spread that Swiss guards were intending to avenge their compatriots by burning down the academy and massacring the students.[13] On 22 September 1792 the papal authorities arrested Joseph Chinard for having a cockade in his room and for creating a statue which depicted Apollo or reason trampling a woman in a nun's garb, an allegorical figure of superstition who clutched a chalice and a crucifix.[14] He had also sculpted another statue, Jupiter striking down the aristocracy. Provocation enough. The other man from Lyons, an architect, Ildephonse Ratter, who had shared an apartment with the sculptor, was adjudged guilty by association. Alarmist and inaccurate accounts, coupled with the pleas of the relatives of the two artists, led the executive council to send a letter of protest to the pope.[15] Lebrun promised retribution if French demands were not met. He then demanded that the Academy in Rome be suppressed, the director deprived of official standing, and responsibility for the property and the students turned over to the agent of the Republic in Rome.

By the time Bassville reached Rome, the French fleet had drawn near and the men had been freed—perhaps not coincidentally. Bassville began to scheme to be appointed minister. To further French ambitions and his own, Bassville was to assess the strength of the fortifications and the military capability of the papal states, which had broken off relations with France in 1792. Rome provided Bassville an even larger and more challenging forum. He found the people of Rome "still today what they had been." It was not "impossible to change them," he noted, "but it would require time, great care and strong precautions."[16] As a self-proclaimed delegate of the Revolution, he did all he could to promote revolutionary ideals and to incite popular unrest. He terrorized the French *émigrés* who had settled in Rome; he had a number of them expelled and their domestics assaulted. According to one of his supporters, for the first time "the style of a true Republican" was heard.[17] He encouraged the radical elements, spread revolutionary propaganda, and turned the French Academy in the Mancini Palace in Rome into a revolutionary club.[18] He distributed the tricolor cockade to those guileless or committed enough to wear it and paraded throughout the city wearing the revolutionary colors.

Meanwhile, the Convention had adopted David's suggestion to "eradicate all monuments to feudalism and to idolatry" at the Academy. The artists should, he advised, "knock down all these monuments to arrogance and slavery and grind them into dust with all the emblems of priestly oppression."[19] David recklessly overrode the concern for the students' welfare voiced by one deputy who wanted to wait until the French army arrived. Bassville was not exactly unarmed for he wielded the threat of the French fleet stationed nearby. Unfortunately, during the fateful period the navy was disabled by storms. Following the Assembly's injunction, Bassville applauded and encouraged the antics of a 27-year-old reckless naval officer, Jean Charles de Flotte, who persuaded the students at the French Academy to tear down the statue of the founder, Louis XIV, by Domenico Guidi, while chanting the revolutionary anthem, the *Marseillaise*. Louis was either trundled off to a coal cellar or broken to pieces. The students then installed a bust of Brutus and a tableau depicting the Rights of Man in the dining room.[20] The portraits of popes and cardinals were removed from the walls of the Academy and those of revolutionaries hung in their place.[21] Bassville also reclothed the guards in the new uniform and outfitted them with a cockade. These events were certainly, in his words, "a spectacle" for the Romans. Meanwhile, far from complimentary ditties began to circulate throughout Rome about Bassville and his clumsy attempts to spark an insurrection.

Bassville's fatal *coup de grâce* (actually it was a *coup de razor*) proved to be his decision to take down the traditional *fleur de lys* on the French Academy and the consulate and replace it with a tableau representing the republic.[22] No matter how the commentators differ in detail or in interpretation, none dispute that he lost his life for that attempt. When informed that the *fleur de lys* was to be replaced by a symbol of the republic, the pope declared that he would sooner die than consent to the republic's escutcheon being displayed in his city and under his eyes.[23] In order to contest that decision Bassville and Flotte met with Cardinal Zelada, the papal secretary of state. Flotte, not accidentally in a national uniform with a cockade in his hat and a Phyrgian cap dangling from his button hole, threatened that France would declare war and send in 500,000 troops if the arms of the republic were not placed over the academy and the consul's house.[24] Flotte presented an ultimatum: if the republican escutcheons were not in place within 48 hours, Rome would be destroyed. The Frenchmen declared that they had their orders and would put up the arms of the republic whether the pope forbade it or not. Zelada warned them that they courted danger by erecting the emblem and by wearing the revolutionary livery.[25] There is some evidence that Bassville realized the danger. Although he had urged his wife and son in Naples to join him for Christmas, Bassville cautioned the students to leave the city. At the same time he assured Lebrun that he would remain "to protect and defend the other Frenchmen ... to die with them, if the scoundrels wish to arm against us."[26] The painter Girodet assured his correspondent on 9 January 1793 that "there was not yet any danger but that the moment would not be long delayed."[27]

Despite the papal ban, Bassville proceeded. Four artists, including Girodet, had undertaken to paint the emblem which they had only seen on official stationery. They finished it in one day and one night.[28] Although this work was subsequently destroyed, Wicar designed one modeled after it for the portal of the French legation in Florence. The goddess, wearing the Grecian tunic and a Phyrgian cap, holds the fasces in one hand and a spear in another. Bassville's prediction that for the Romans this would be "a day of their exaltation, *un jour de fête*,"[29] turned out to be rather optimistic. Still he had the acuity to urge officials to take the necessary precautions to ensure that the "priestly rabble respect the sacred sign of our regeneration."[30] Rumors of plots to burn down the Academy and the Frenchmen in it had reached him.[31]

Nonetheless, the French had the royal escutcheons taken down during the night of either 1 or 2 January 1793. Bassville acknowledged that that had caused "a great deal of fermentation" among an "agitated and superstitious people." Still he was resolved to remain at his post.[32] After a heated argument with Bassville and Flotte, Digne, the French consul in Rome, refused to allow the republic's escutcheon to be placed on the consulate unless the Holy See consented.[33] Although he stuck to that decision, he was concerned that his opposition not be construed as unpatriotic.[34] In his view, Bassville and Flotte had needlessly infuriated the Romans by their arrogance.[35] His words turned out to be prophetic. Although the government multiplied the number of patrols, such precautions could neither prevent nor control the riot that occurred on 13 January.[36] On that day Flotte, Bassville, and Bassville's wife and infant son had gone by carriage to the Corso. All was quiet until they reached the Piazza Colonna, where the crowd instantly recognized them. They would have been impossible to miss, for the inhabitants of the coach, the servants, and the coachmen wore the national cockade. Flotte was seen waving a small national flag out the window as they drove. According to one version, Bassville's 20-month-old son was holding his mother's tricolor handkerchief. Romans surrounded the carriage, shouting, "You are the French scoundrels." When the crowd started throwing stones, the carriage raced through the narrow streets to a private palazzo. The party, as yet uninjured, took refuge in the house of the banker Moutte, where the Bassvilles had been living. When the crowd pursued them, breaking windows and attempting to force the doors, Moutte hid Bassville's family and servants in the attic. Flotte abandoned his colleagues, who were unsuccessfully attempting to wedge furniture against the door, fled through a window, and hid in a courtyard for seven hours before escaping. The crowd succeeded in forcing their way in and mortally stabbing Bassville before the patrols could arrive. France, in the words of a French citizen in Rome, had "lost a true patriot."[37] Bassville's wife and child, along with the banker, had escaped. The house was pillaged and burned. Bassville received both medical support, the attendance of two surgeons, and spiritual sustenance, the sacrament of Extreme Unction. It is questionable how much this avowed revolutionary benefitted from the latter in particular. The 49-year-old Bassville died the following day about 7 p.m.—the only victim in the wave of Francophobia which swept through Rome. He had succeeded in causing an uprising, but not the one he had envisaged.

A crowd had also gathered in front of the Academy. Armed with sticks and stones, they broke windows and forced the doors. The Romans burst into the Academy and surprised the students, who, in Girodet's words, "still had the brushes in our hands." They fled before the mob and were saved, again in Girodet's words, by the "tortuous streets and [their] cool heads."[38] Shortly after the rioters gained entry and milled about inside, a patrol arrived and dispersed them, but not before they had pillaged the Academy.[39] Girdodet reported that "the furious rabble ... instantly reduced the doors, windows, and glass to dust, as well as all the statues on the stairways and in the apartments."[40] On both the 13th and the 14th January 1793 crowds assembled chanting "Vive le pope!" "Vive la Religion!" Some houses, notably that of the banker Moutte and some merchants, known for their pro-revolutionary stances, were also ransacked. The Romans placed a plaque on the Corso to commemorate the triumph of popular justice and to thank the Madonna for her intervention. Vincenzo Monti published an emotional anti-French poem on the theme, which went through several editions and carried the memory of Bassville's death into the nineteenth century.[41] Many Frenchmen fled the city. The pope meanwhile increased the number of patrols and tried to calm the populace.

Back in Paris, Lebrun had penned a letter of rebuke to Bassville in which he condemned his actions: "You have not foreseen that which it should have been easy to see, namely that the pope, not yet having recognized the French Republic, could not easily consent to the erection of a new escutcheon.... Prudence and decency should counsel you to reach an understanding with the secretary of state." He warned him not to "compromise the dignity of the Republic and the tranquility of the French who remained in Rome." He then ordered him to return to Naples. The warning and the order came too late.[42] Lebrun also sent a chargé, Cacault, from Paris to treat with the papacy. He was to tell Bassville that he had exceeded his orders. His representations on the raising of the escutcheon were "irregular, inconvenient, formally disavowed and considered as not having been made."[43] The chargé was told to protect his fellow citizens and to follow etiquette and the accepted customs.[44]

Lebrun changed his stance when word arrived of the secretary's demise. In life an incompetent bungler, Bassville in death became a great patriot. The executive council in a memo to the Convention falsely alleged that Bassville had been invested with a public character. The subsequent decree of the National Convention underscored "the manifest violation of the *droit des gens*.[45] The executive council demanded "a signal vengeance" for an outrage to the national sovereignty, "evidently provoked" by the government of Rome.[46] The papal version took a different tone, emphasizing the lack of ministerial authority of Bassville, Flotte, or Mackau and underscoring the provocation of the French and the accidental killing of Bassville in the *mêlée*.[47]

The revolutionary government exploited the incident to attack the "hypocritical insolence of Rome" and to launch violent diatribes against the clergy.[48] Typical of revolutionary propaganda was Prudhomme's highly colored account of the incident with the subtitle "Always the Priests" in his *Révolutions de Paris*.[49] For Prudhomme, the pope had caused the "liberticide"; superstition had poisoned the people of Rome; fanaticism still reigns and exercises all its horrors.[50] In light of the "hypocritical insolence of Rome," the executive council chose to see Bassville as a "victim of his patriotism." The council strove to "avenge" the injury to the French and that of "mankind."[51] The government demanded reparation from Rome, expulsion of the French *émigrés*, punishment of the instigators of the revolt, and repair of the French Academy. And the other principals? The government later appointed Flotte commander of a naval vessel. At least one French citizen had thought that he had acted "with prudence and courage."[52] The French recalled Mackau from Naples because the court refused to receive him.[53] Marie Caroline, queen of Naples, thought Mackau "a fop, a Pulcinella acting the part of Scipio Africanus, a man without character who has nothing to be proud of but who wants to play an important role, but above all to keep his position."[54] The French artists who had been in Rome at the time acquired not only an irrefutable and possibly undeserved reputation for patriotism, but also lucratic government appointments, as did Bassville's servants. The Convention formally adopted Bassville's son and pensioned his widow, who received part of the eventual settlement from Rome.[55] Years after Bassville's death, the incident lived on in popular folklore. French generals stationed in Italy referred to the Romans as being "fouled" by the assassination of Bassville. In 1796, when Napoleon invaded the papal states, he insisted on reparations for the damage done to the French republic by the assassination of Bassville.[56] The Treaty of Tolentino of 1797 stipulated that the pope should indemnify the victims and send certain masterpieces to France to compensate for those destroyed.[57] The dispute over one cultural icon had triggered the pillage of others.

The incident surrounding General Jean-Baptiste-Jules Bernadotte also revolved around symbols and illustrates the more prominent role of the military.[58] He had only been at his post in Vienna for a few months when mobs stormed the embassy. On 13 April 1798, a crowd, variously estimated at between 300 and 3000, invaded the French embassy, seized the tricolor, and looted the premises. Although neither the French ambassador nor his staff were killed, let alone injured, Bernadotte labeled the rioters "assassins."[59] Many accused the French of deliberately provoking the local populace, for in the short time Bernadotte had been in the capital he had managed to generate a great deal of ill will.

Even his appointment had been controversial, not only reflecting the intransigent attitude of the French toward their persistent foe, but also underscoring the dearth of qualified French diplomats during the Revolution and the importance of the military. During the Directory, seven generals and one admiral served in the diplomatic corps.[60] For the Viennese, Bernadotte personified the French army and the regicide government of France. The appointment of men like Bernadotte also reflected Napoleon's calculated use of intimidation in dealing with other states. Neither the appointment nor the arrival of the envoy was propitious. The Directory had ordered Bernadotte to travel directly to his post, without observing the customary formalities of notifying the host country of the appointment. The Directors used this ploy to bypass the certain protests that would and did follow.[61] Bernadotte had proceeded immediately to Vienna without waiting for his secretaries, his instructions, his credentials, or his passports. The failure to observe customary courtesies alienated the Austrians at the outset, as did Bernadotte himself. Arriving at the border without the necessary credentials, Bernadotte bluntly informed the guards who tried to turn him away that such an action would be regarded as an act of war. These and other actions fueled the suspicions of many that the shrewd and knowledgeable Bernadotte was deliberately trying to provoke the Austrians.

Bernadotte, who had only accepted the mission out of a sense of duty and who would have preferred another military assignment, had reservations about this posting. In that regard at least Bernadotte proved astute. Not only Bernadotte but also his staff were remarkably ill-suited to the challenge. His entourage included military men, personally selected by Bernadotte, and relatively young and inexperienced neophytes, chosen by the Directory. The mission then had all the ingredients of a disaster. The stark uniform adopted by Bernadotte and his entourage made them stand out as did Bernadotte's stature and good looks. Bernadotte, who was also noted for his charm, could have capitalized on both and won over the Austrians. Unfortunately, he did not.

Bernadotte's initial view of the populace as "fanatical" and the court as despicable did not change during his short tenure. He deplored distinctions of rank, which he deemed degrading, and insisted on being addressed as "citizen." Yet at the same time he had to follow the orders of the Directory to maintain "all the prerogatives of monarchical France,"[62] such as insisting on his right of precedence before all other secular states. These demands proved unpopular, as did Bernadotte's rigorous adherence to the practices of the old regime, some of which were outdated. In so doing he alienated not only the Austrians, but also his fellow representatives. At court, Bernadotte did little better. He found Baron Franz Maria von Thugut (1736–1818), the Austrian foreign minister, "contemptible." Thugut, in turn, regarded him as "frightening" and his demands "revolting" and avoided contact whenever possible.[63]

For Thugut, Bernadotte symbolized the Directory's plan to pursue with "an unheard of enthusiasm … the consummation of projects to destroy Europe." Bernadotte and his entourage, he warned, "reckon on the coming explosion in all corners of Europe."[64] Nonetheless, the Austrians were remarkably tolerant of Bernadotte's peccadilloes because they needed and wanted peace. After military setbacks in Italy, the Austrians had signed the peace of Campo Formio on 18 October 1797. That agreement recognized the French reorganization of Italy including the French satellites, the Ligurian and the Cisalpine republics. France subsequently created the Roman and Helvetic republics in March 1798. Bernadotte's actions did little to ease a potentially volatile situation. Bernadotte complained incessantly about the smallest affront. He launched violent diatribes against the French *émigrés* in Vienna and complained when they wore or displayed the emblems of the old regime such as the cross of St. Louis or the white cockade, the color of the house of Bourbon. When a court almanac described Louis XVIII as king of France, Thugut heard from Bernadotte. The locals also heard from his staff. When his men attended a play they hissed and caused an uproar when the players shouted, "*Vive le roi!*" Some of his entourage also insulted a cross and blasphemed—and this in Vienna, noted for its staunch Catholicism.[65] On a more serious level, Bernadotte also engaged in seditious plots; he used the ambassadorial residence as a gathering point for French Jacobins, partisans of the Revolution, and dissident Poles. Fortunately or not, the government was well informed of the Frenchman's "secret maneuvers."[66] The government also resented Bernadotte's other provocations, most notably his ordering his entourage to wear the national cockade and the revolutionary hat. The populace and the government saw both as symbols of a revolution they despised and a regicidal regime they abhorred. Still worse was to follow.

Bernadotte decided to display a large tricolor, four yards long and emblazoned with "*République française. Ambassade de Vienne. Liberté. Égalité*" on the outside of the embassy. Because in monarchical countries a flag without an escutcheon was viewed as a call to revolution, this gesture was particularly ill-considered.[67] Bernadotte chose to first display the flag on 13 April 1798, a national holiday that commemorated those who had voluntarily enlisted to defend the city against Napoleon. This was scarcely a conciliatory gesture. A curious crowd soon gathered on Wallnerstrasse. The onlookers did not know what to make of the flag; some interpreted it as a warning and others as a sign that the French would treat Vienna as a conquered state, still others as the despised tree of liberty. Whatever the individual view, the Austrians generally saw the flag as a symbol of a despised conqueror. The initially passive crowd started to shout and throw stones at the flag. Bernadotte appeared and ordered the Viennese to disperse with what he later described as "republican energy" and to warn them that all those who insulted the representative of "a generous nation" would be severely punished. When the police, now on the scene, urged Bernadotte to take down the flag to avoid a possible disturbance, he refused. Putting his hand on his sword, Bernadotte threatened to "cleave the head of any person that should touch the flag."[68] As the crowd grew more aggressive, one energetic individual vaulted the balcony and seized the flag, hurling it to the spectators who carried it to the Schotzen Platz and burned it, all the while shouting patriotic slogans, such as "long live the emperor." Back at the embassy, the throng started to break the windows and knock down the doors. They gained entry to the ground floor and were starting to pillage the apartments when troops arrived about 10 or 11 p.m. approximately five hours after the crowd had initially gathered. The police, greatly outnumbered, had waited for reinforcements. Bernadotte and his suite who had taken refuge on the first floor were uninjured, as were the majority of the crowd. A few in the crowd were wounded when one of Bernadotte's servants panicked and fired.

Throughout the *mêlée*, Bernadotte had dispatched three notes in which he complained to the Austrian foreign minister about the "scandalous scene." The tone predictably was blunt and threatening. He demanded, unavailingly, an immediate and unequivocal response. He wanted the government to condemn this offense, to replace the flag, to station officers at the embassy, and to punish the malefactors promptly. He could not remain, he said, in such an inhospitable country, where the *droit des gens*, "consecrated by the respect of all civilized peoples," was violated in "so frightful" a manner.[69] When Thugut's emissary, Baron von Degelmann, the plenipotentiary designate to France, arrived, expressing regrets and attempting to justify the delay, Bernadotte refused to listen and demanded his passports. He sent a predictably colored version of the events to some of his fellow ambassadors and wrote the head of the army in Italy, urging his countrymen to exploit the situation and commence hostilities against the old foe.[70] Even after the emperor issued a proclamation expressing his great displeasure over the incident and promising to punish the guilty, Bernadotte was not appeased. He demanded immediate reparation, the prompt arrest of the rioters, the dismissal of the foreign minister, the head of the military, and the chief of police, and insisted that he could not stay in Vienna after the flag had been so outraged.[71] Undoubtedly, Bernadotte had seized the opportunity to leave a post and a court he despised. Even before this incident he had requested a recall and prepared for his departure.

Bernadotte refused to leave early in the morning in order to avoid possible trouble, but insisted on leaving very publicly at high noon on 15 April. He had been at his post only a little over a month and half. For Bernadotte, it was "a great day," as it was for many Austrians. One of the Austrian ministers candidly confessed that he was delighted by the departure.[72] Bernadotte left Vienna in seven coaches escorted by a regiment. Detachments of cavalry, posted along the route, ensured his safety and dispersed the crowds. One observer thought his behavior "ridiculous" and his designs "perfidious." "The French," he noted, "carry peace in their mouth and perfidy in their soul."[73] That very day the Austrian ministers wrote the Directory, expressing their regret over the unfortunate incident. The "excess of public effervescence" had been both regrettable and unavoidable. Lastly, they underscored their desire that Bernadotte continue to represent France.[74] How sincere the Austrians were in that regard is certainly questionable. What is unquestionable, however, is the Austrians' desire to avoid war.[75] Bernadotte meanwhile had preempted the Austrian government and dispatched a special courier with his version of the incident.

Although the Directory was divided, the pacific faction prevailed. Talleyrand thought the insult real because "it is impossible to suppose in a government as strong, as absolute as that of Vienna such disorder had taken place without being able to prevent or stop it."[76] Still wars would be too frequent if each time an ambassador was insulted, the nation resorted to war.[77] Both Talleyrand and Napoleon thought that Bernadotte had been at fault. Talleyrand characterized the ambassador as both "frivolous and imprudent."[78] In Napoleon's view Bernadotte had allowed "his temper to master his judgment, and committed serious errors."[79] Still the Directory protested this "violent infraction of the *droit des gens.*"[80] Talleyrand expressed his confidence that those who had "outraged in the person of the French ambassador the republic itself" would be severely punished.[81] Bernadotte did not get the justice he sought, at least not immediately. And Bernadotte? He was subsequently offered another diplomatic post, which he sensibly declined. Bernadotte's "folly," as some termed it, created a sensation at Paris and the ongoing peace conference at Rastatt and increased diplomatic tensions.[82] The incident is still commemorated today. At the centennial of the event in 1898 Wallnerstrasse was renamed Fahnengasse or Flag street. Bernadotte had achieved a type of immortality after all—a living memorial to his folly.

Such actions were not limited to Vienna or Rome, for in the train of the French representatives went the symbols of the Revolution. The Spanish ambassador Simón de las Casas left Venice in 1795 after the Republic had given the French chargé permission to place the French arms over his residence.[83] When those sympathetic to France began to wear tricolor cockades, they were seized by the police (although released at the insistence of the French minister).[84] As sentiment turned against the French, many Venetian citizens began to wear the Venetian cockades of blue and orange,[85] and later to tear down the French arms. Tilly, the French representative to another republic, Genoa, had made an even more public statement. At a masked ball, he and a number of other Jacobins, clad in hats festooned with the tricolor, sprightly entered and insisted that the more courtly *contredanses*, not incidentally associated with England, such as the *alexandrines* and the *allemandes*, be replaced by the *carmagnole* and the traditional French dance, the *périgordine*. These dances were accompanied by a great deal of yelling, whistling, and whooping. During the *carmagnole* he threw an enormous hat in the air more than 50 times.[86] To lend additional spirit to the occasion the French also sang the *ça ira*. Alas, someone stole the hat, perhaps as a souvenir of a memorable evening, which ended when soldiers were summoned. Tilly, in the British view, a villain, also arranged for the planting of a liberty tree in the faubourg of the city, confirming for many the aptness of his nickname "the scourge of Italy."[87]

The flaunting of republican symbols—wearing liberty bonnets, planting liberty trees, festooning embassies with tricolor flags, creating culinary tricolor flags in sugar—was not unconnected with the commitment to a more open system. Many revolutionaries rejected the culture of secrecy, so embedded in the *ancien régime*.[88] Still the ensuing debate underscores the gulf between rhetoric and reality, between ideology and *Realpolitik*. The dignity and power of a free nation mandated that the former secret policy be cast aside in favor of open diplomacy. "Secrecy only furthers injustice; it only produces mistakes," Pétion argued. "One can hide from peoples the interests of kings when the kings are all and the people are nothing.... All our evils must be attributed to such shady procedures, to the clandestine operations of the ministers" and to diplomats who had been only "titled spies."[89] The conclusion that the old diplomacy had brought France ruin was seemingly inescapable, but the analysis was erroneous and simplistic. If French diplomacy had failed, it was not because it was either aristocratic or secret. Secrecy, what Pétion called "*le mystère*," can produce only errors and injustice. Such men "betray their contemporaries, they sacrifice their descendants."[90] Pétion's view reflected the cacophony of contempt echoed by other revolutionaries from different factions. Secrecy meant that treaties "would be turned over to intrigues, to the passions of ministers and ambassadors."[91] Armand-Désiré, duc d'Aiguillon, one of the first nobles who had joined the Third Estate, thought the new system would end the intrigues of courts as well as the vicious practice of distributing pensions to foreign officials.[92] During a debate in 1792, one deputy and *avocat*, a Jacobin and later a Girondin, Jean Baptiste Michel Saladin, voiced the sentiments of many when he argued that a nation that has renounced conquest, a nation that wishes only to defend itself, a nation that wishes only to conserve its rights, does not need secrecy in its political relations. Even at that time others, such as Guillaume Mouysset, the former judge, argued that the French should not deceive themselves. Such fine phrases about banishing secret diplomacy were excellent when liberty has been well established, but it was not prudent "when we have to combat a throng of tyrants who hide themselves in the dark, who secretly undermine our liberty."[93]

Those doubts were not voiced by Pierre Henri Hélène Marie Lebrun-Tondu, minister of foreign affairs (1792–1793), who enjoined the French representatives abroad to proclaim by their words and by their actions that "all dissimulation, all intrigue, all frivolous actions will be banished from the negotiations of a people distinguished from other nations by its candor, its rectitude, and its courage." In all your negotiations "the glitter of your probity should be the only magnificence surrounding you. Be proud and simple like a republican."[94] Robespierre shared this faith in open diplomacy. In his report on the political situation of the republic of 17 November 1793, he contended that the advantage of a powerful republic lies in its diplomacy that "is one of good faith.... Just as an honest man can open his heart and his home with impunity to his fellow citizen so a free people can reveal to nations all the foundations of its policy."[95]

The new rules of conduct that were to guide the agents of France were revealed by the representative Descorches, ironically sent incognito to the Porte, but stopped en route in Venice. "Frankness," he intoned, would replace "the adulterous and insolent language, almost always insignificant and often perfidious, of the former ministry.... Truth, sincerity, fidelity in its engagements" would be the new policy of France.[96] As late as January 1795 during the Thermidorean regime, François Antoine Boissy d'Anglas (1756–1828), the courageous centrist deputy who served on the Committee of Public Safety in 1795 and was proscribed in fructidor 1797, delivered a speech later adopted as a Declaration of Principles of the French People. In that speech he praised the "principles of justice and candor upon which the government of France now rests." The French, emerging from the "sleep of slavery," had "resumed their place among nations." They were, accordingly, "ready to negotiate with frankness."[97] "Speak," he continued, "with that noble candor which befits the majesty of the French people and you will soon see the diplomatic subtleties of your enemies confounded by the wisdom of your advice as you have seen their temerity punished by the courage of our warriors."[98] This comparison of diplomats with soldiers who served on another front and one that would be equally victorious became a common trope in the rhetoric of the time.

The policy of transparent diplomacy had interesting ramifications. In August 1790, the foreign minister Montmorin had scandalized European ministers accredited to France when he had read the dispatches of the French ambassador in Madrid to the deputies.[99] As a riposte, Fernán Nuñez, the Spanish ambassador to France, resorted to publishing his notes to Montmorin and Montmorin's response.[100] This system may not have functioned as intended. The US' *chargé* William Short noted that he did not write to the minister of foreign affairs, Montmorin, because whenever something "is not communicated to the assembly a minister is regarded with so evil and jealous an eye as does more harm than good." The minsters in this situation, he noted, also try to avoid putting anything in writing.[101] The new policy had the unintended consequence of not promoting, but inhibiting public discourse. The decree of 2 January 1792 stipulated that the minister of foreign affairs should send foreign intelligence to the diplomatic committee within three days.[102] Suspicion still lingered. The minister could select certain documents and extracts and deceive by omission. So a subsequent decree in February sought to remedy this problem by providing the committee with copies of official correspondence and of instructions. In February 1792, Delessart communicated then not just extracts but the original dispatches to the committee.[103] Dumouriez, who became the minister of foreign affairs the following month in March 1792, ironically enough had served as a secret diplomatic agent under Étienne François, duc de Choiseul, minister of foreign affairs (1758–1770). He advocated, and at least temporarily practiced, an open diplomacy, communicating the entire diplomatic correspondence to the Diplomatic Committee.[104] Dumouriez then went one step further and revealed the instructions he sent to the French representatives to other foreign ministers. He took these steps, as he explained to the French agent in Berlin, because "the system I have adopted … is open, loyal and constitutional."[105]

The publication of dispatches opened another front in the contest of revolutionary France with other powers. The letter from Louis XVI to George III was published in Paris and in French journals in London before Chauvelin, the French representative in London, sent it to the British monarch.[106] Grenville, the British Foreign Secretary, found the French habit of bypassing (and undercutting) the British Foreign Office and appealing either to Parliament or the people offensive. In a letter to Chauvelin, Grenville presumed that such acts sprang from ignorance of the correct usage rather than a deliberate intention to set aside "the rules and forms established." Chauvelin should, he underscored, address any correspondence to the secretary of state, not to the two houses of Parliament.[107] Note here the presumption of ignorance of form—an accusation often hurled at the revolutionaries. Still Grenville took the precaution in April 1792 of drawing up his dispatch "with a view to public discussion," noting that "that can hardly be avoided however desireable [sic] it would have been." Even Chauvelin agreed that public access compromised negotiations and narrowed the room for maneuver.[108] Still, more than one power could play that game. At least one revolutionary diplomat found that this tactic boomeranged. When Chauvelin published his note of 28 December

1792 in the *Morning Chronicle* of 7 January, Grenville riposted by publishing his response in the *True Briton* and the *Sun* of 16 January.[109] One British commentator thought Chauvelin's policy of publishing his official correspondence with Grenville "wonderful"—for Grenville, he exulted, enjoyed an evident "superiority, in both style and matter"[110]—an outcome the French no doubt did not anticipate. Nor were the British alone in turning this weapon against the French. Jean-Jacques O'Kelly Farrel, the French minister plenipotentiary at Mainz, found himself in an awkward position and complained in June 1792 about the publication of his dispatches and "the travesties in the journals and public papers."[111]

Even French representatives to friendly powers printed their dispatches. Genet informed Jefferson that he intended to publish his correspondence and his instructions on the grounds that "the politics of regenerated France" was based on "candor, frankness and publicity," not "the mysterious secrecy of court." Genet asked Jefferson to distribute his translated instructions to Congress in order to counter the "odious and vile machinations that have been plotted against me."[112] In response and probably as a preemptive maneuver, Jefferson had his correspondence with both Genet and Hammond, the British representative, not only communicated to Congress, but also printed.[113] At this time every French minister accredited to the United States was either initially disaffected with the government or soon became so. With the exception of Jean Baptiste Ternant, minister 1790–1793, and the consul general Philippe Joseph de Letombe, all issued printed appeals to the people in an attempt to overturn the policy of the administration.[114] In 1796, Pierre-Auguste Adet, the French representative to the United States, did not hesitate to condemn the Federalists for ruining Franco-American relations and to call on those sympathetic to France to wear the tricolor. George Cabot, a retired Federalist senator from Massachusetts, denounced the manifesto, but thought that "[i]f the devil is in company, it is always best to see his cloven hoof." Washington thought Adet's behavior worse than Genet's—quite an achievement—and Madison thought that the crisis could be "perverted into a perpetual alienation" of France and the United States. Some editorials even demanded Adet's recall.[115] In light of the deteriorating relations, France suspended the functions of Adet, noting that it was not "a sign of rupture but a mark of legitimate discontent."[116] At least one Napoleonic representative to the United States (1804–1811), Louis Marie Turreau, orchestrated the publication of some documents, but he sent them to France to be translated so that their publication would not be linked to him. Interestingly enough, he viewed their publication as "inconsistent with his public functions."[117] Such scruples were not shared by Napoleon, who did not hesitate to use any weapon that came to hand and continued the policy of diplomacy by the press. In 1800, he ordered the publication in the *Moniteur* of the proclamations of the US president and various letters.[118] By contrast, Sir Arthur Paget, the British representative to Vienna (1801–1806), resigned when his dispatch on the capitulation of Ulm was published. He thought that his discussion of confidential material and of specific individuals had irreparably undermined his ability to negotiate.[119]

French debates on foreign policy were also to be public. As early as 1790, the principled archbishop of Aix, Jean-de-Dieu Raymond de Cucé de Boisgelin, argued that publicity would only strengthen negotiations concerning war and peace.[120] Louis XVI as well as others objected. In the note he left after the abortive flight to Varennes, Louis XVI queried whether negotiations that were supposed to be secret could be entrusted to an Assembly that deliberated in public.[121] In an attack of April 1794 carefully leveled against the ministry of foreign affairs, Saint Just called for the publication of the correspondence of the ministers with the courts of Sweden, Denmark, Genoa, Switzerland, and Venice (with the notable and pragmatic exception of the Turks) and the elimination of all expenses dubbed secret.[122] Despite the obvious drawbacks, the Assembly concluded that negotiations for peace were to be public. Of course such tactics could enable the French to seize the initiative in negotiations.

The ramifications of this policy redounded with a vengeance. In 1795, we can glimpse the revolutionaries grappling with its practical difficulties. The Committee of Public Safety, the lawyer and diplomat Cambacérès noted, was authorized to negotiate and to draft treaties. But how could the assembly ratify treaties or articles of treaties that should not be public? "Premature publicity" could undermine the position of a power who allied with the republic or one who had received a sum of money either as an indemnity for the past or as a subsidy for the future. Nor were these the only times when publication of the provisions would undermine the republic's foreign policy. France needed to "show some indulgence for the diplomacy of Europe, accustomed to the false day of cabinets" for "its sick eyes dread the sun." Only by degrees could it be rejuvenated and turned over to "the day of publicity." Moreover, a time of war demanded "more rapid and more powerful measures." Cambacérès suggested a decree empowering the Committee of Public Safety to negotiate in the name of the republic. Treaties could be signed either by the committee or by plenipotentiaries chosen by the committee. The treaties would not be validated until ratified by the National Convention. In the case of secret agreements or secret articles, a commission of 12 members would determine if they should remain secret and if they conformed to "the principles and interests of the republic."[123]

There were at least two major issues raised in this discussion: was a republic compatible with secret diplomacy and what if anything was the role of a committee, should a policy of secrecy be adopted? The objections ranged from the ideological to the practical. For some the inseparability of the interests of the government and the people would dictate that the Committee of Public Safety could not negotiate secret treaties.[124] Such decisions belonged to the representatives of the people. For Cambacérès secrecy was incompatible with a government "where those who exercise the power of the people love to take the universe as witness of their actions and of their resolutions." Yet, "il ne faut pas diplomatiser sur la place publique." Still the moral high ground was not abandoned. Alexandre Edmé Pierre Villetard, a wine merchant, contended that treating in secret was not "worthy of the grandeur of the French people," whose "great diplomacy is founded on justice." The French should, he argued, "treat like the Roman Senate."[125] What exactly were these "great diplomatic secrets," another queried, for which the "principles of wisdom" should be sacrificed?[126] On a more practical note, Pierre Joseph Duhem, a physician and a Jacobin known for appearing in military dress with a sabre, argued that there should "absolutely not" be secret articles in diplomacy for the simple reasons that "almost all secrets are badly guarded."[127] Another argued that no secret articles should be allowed when ratifying a treaty, because representatives would be ratifying something they had not seen.[128] In certain circumstances secrecy was "necessary," Jean François Boursault, a former actor and theater manager, admitted, but given that assumption, the question then became "how secrecy would be maintained and not jeopardize liberty."[129] Other points were raised. How could an enemy coalition be broken without secret pacts?[130] If the commission differed from the committee, there was no way to resolve the impasse. Because of the composition of the commission and the committee, a majority of the commission could trump a unanimous committee. "You would then have a government with two heads."[131]

Some thought that the republic must resort to secrecy to deal with its many enemies and that the committee should be authorized not to communicate certain articles and should not "quibble about the responsibility."[132]

Still the specter of the power of the Committee of Public Safety who had ruled during the Terror must have been haunted many. Antoine Claire Thibadeau, a one-time member of the Mountain, queried whether it was safe to entrust such decisions to the Committee of Public Safety, which would have governed well, had they not usurped the authority of the Convention. The creation of a commission would weaken the Committee of Public Safety which should have the same power as the executive of foreign governments. Nor could the commission effectively check the power of the committee because the commission would come to share the opinion of the committee simply because all their information would come from them.[133] Jean Pelet, a Protestant *avocat* who had spoken against Robespierre and for freedom of the press, pointed out the opposite problem: there would be no viable way to break a stalemate if the Committee of Public Safety came to one conclusion and the commission another. Another, Jean Pierre Chazal, a former *avocat* and an implacable enemy of the Jacobins, did not hesitate to underscore the "great danger" of not examining the work of the Committee of Public Safety. Couthon, Saint-Just, and Robespierre, members of the Committee of Public Safety, "had betrayed the Convention and liberty." Moreover, the Convention wisely rejected proposals "that come out of the laboratories of your committees." A commission should be created for each treaty. Its members would guarantee that the treaty "conforms to the principles and interests of the republic."[134]

Legitimate concerns were raised not just about the advisability, but also about legality; could the representatives delegate to an intermediary body, a commission, power bestowed on them by the people? Another member contended that in the case of secret treaties, it would be the Committee of Public Safety that concluded the peace, not the Convention, which according to the constitution was to exercise that power.[135] The Committee of Public Safety as currently constituted enjoyed their confidence, but the future could not be guaranteed.[136] These sentiments were echoed by Jean Frédéric Hermann, a professor of law, who argued that the right to make secret articles would vest too much power in the Committee of Public Safety which "could perhaps march one day against you." Moreover, certain concessions should be forbidden including any that would jeopardize the natural boundaries.[137]

Cambacérès made the definitive argument by relying on the widely accepted analogy of France with the Roman republic. He called on representatives to distinguish between the current crisis and the future. There was a difference between "the circumstances in which we find ourselves and that of a constitutional government, which will be based on principles and which will reign in peace. Perhaps then we will have no other diplomacy than that of Popilius [A Roman noted for his inflexible defense of Rome] and that it is the diplomacy I believe worthy of a free people but we are not yet at that time. The new born democracy is surrounded by enemies." The "multitude of theoretical abstractions raised" should not override practical considerations. If the discussions were extended, the debate would only delay the current negotiations, which would not, he assured them, "compromise the honor of the republic."[138] He held out the possibility of peace, which was "as necessary to Europe as to our republic."[139] Louis-Marie de La Révellière-Lépeaux, the lawyer who had been proscribed along with the Girondins and who later advocated the cult of theophilanthropy, noted that the most vigorous republics have "perished under the weight of their own victories … inconstant fortune has often cheated courage and betrayed the most sacred cause." Given the state of Europe, "if you refuse the proposition made by the committee, you will distance the peace to an epoch" far off. Secrets were necessary in order to achieve "a prompt and honorable peace…. It is always impossible in the eyes of all thinking beings to establish liberty by tyranny, justice by injustice, and morality by immorality."[140]

Oddly enough, that argument led to the conclusion that "all reasonable means" should be seized, even "extra-constitutional measures."[141] In the end the Convention voted to enact the law of 27 ventôse, an III (17 March 1795), that allowed secret articles to be drawn up, provided that they did not contradict public ones. They would be executed "as though they had been ratified." The interests of the republic overrode any qualms about the legality or advisability of secret engagements. As soon as circumstances permitted, any secret provisions were to be made public. The committee was charged with the responsibility of negotiating treaties. They could sign treaties or delegate that right to designated plenipotentiaries.[142] The radical Antoine Christophe Merlin de Thionville made the interesting argument that only the enemies of peace opposed secret articles.[143]

As late as 1796 the British representative Harris, sent to negotiate with the Directory, bemoaned the publication in a paper under French government control of his *mémoire*, the government's response, his powers, and an account of the first conference. Although such measures were "extraordinary," he thought that "so unexpected" "a mode of proceeding" should have been foreseen. His response was to observe a strict silence. Delacroix justified the publication as a preemptive move because so many in Paris were disposed to "censure and find fault" that the Directory felt obliged to publicly state what had occurred.[144] William Grenville, the foreign secretary, thought that "so many obvious difficulties" would be "thrown in the way" that it would "render the negotiation difficult" and inevitably "make every demand on either part more peremptory and every concession more reluctant."[145] Grenville attributed "the unprecedented conduct" of the Directory "rather to their ignorance of the usual mode of carrying on such negotiations and to the uncertainty and difficulties under which they act, on account of their own precarious situation, than to any settled system of policy."[146] This charitable view underscores the gulf between the dictates of revolutionary policy and the traditions of the British foreign office and perhaps an ever-widening misunderstanding. The tactic of publishing certain memoranda had the advantage of being aligned with revolutionary assumptions and at the same time of giving plenipotentiaries some protection against suspicions leveled against their conduct. From London Grenville demanded an explanation for the French conduct and deplored publication of documents during a negotiation; it "changes so entirely the course" of the discussion.[147] That opinion was seconded by the lawyer Guillaume Alexandre Tronson du Coudray, a member of the Council of Ancients, who thought such publications violated both the rules of hospitality and the *droit des gens*.[148]

Harris then changed tack. He outlined to Charles Delacroix, minister of foreign affairs, the difficulties created by publication of the proceedings and the impossibility of conferring freely on any issue when what was said would be published.[149] Harris was ordered to find out whether the details of the negotiations were to be made public before proceeding. He told Delacroix that if the public were aware of the initial conditions, it would make any alterations or modifications very difficult. Delacroix finally agreed that the negotiations would be kept secret until the preliminaries were signed and that any projected treaty submitted by Harris would not be printed without his consent and would be marked confidential.[150] By 1797 the British changed tack yet again and decided to beat the French at their own game by selecting and publishing extracts from Harris' correspondence.[151] Jeremy Black underscores the costs of this "open" policy. "It was all too easy in a spirit of Enlightenment optimism or Revolutionary enthusiasm to call for a new international order based on true interests, rational alliances of open diplomacy: and to suggest that anything that opposed this process was reactionary, redundant and repellent … Such an analysis was, however, both naive and dangerous for it underrated the complexities of the situations and dangerous because it suggested that those with contrary views were obscurantist and unnecessary, if not worse."[152] Predictably, these negotiations failed.

The Directory also dealt with the issue of secret articles. A 1796 law provided that the secret articles of various treaties should be turned over to the Directors.[153] Secret articles were soon concluded. For example, secret articles were included in the articles drawn up near Leoben, 29 germinal, an V (18 April 1797).[154] The representative of Francis II tellingly noted that the Leoben preliminaries looked like the treaties of partition and exchange concluded by monarchs over the centuries. General Henri Jacques Guillaume Clarke edited his report to the Directory that urged ratification, noting contradictions in the text and advising that perhaps the secret articles could be amended when the treaty was definitive.[155] In that same year on 2 November 1797, Talleyrand, in his instructions to the French representatives at Rastatt, cited article seven of the secret treaty that if one of the contracting parties acquired some portion of land in German territory, an equal portion should be accorded the other.[156] As he cautioned Treilhard, "the communication of secret articles of a treaty is never only a premeditated indiscretion but a proof of incomplete confidence and often a trap."[157] Other secret articles followed and not infrequently and unsurprisingly contradicted the public ones.

Some of the same questions surfaced in July 1799, when Talleyrand, with his well-known verbal and moral dexterity, argued that the constitution did not adequately define the power of the Directors concerning external relations. He noted that if the legislature wanted to know about the dispatches from or the instructions to its agents, other than what was voluntarily provided by the executive, or even provide additional instructions, it would trigger "confusion, [and] embarrassment," discredit the government's actions abroad, and exacerbate the situation. The new law, he advised, should accord the Directors the right to include secret articles, to conclude secret conventions, and to allow a fixed sum for secret expenses. Looking back on the ideas he had espoused in November 1792 on the relations of France and other states, he admitted that "later events have rendered them superannuated." Others he repudiated.[158] The Directory also restored the exclusive right of competence over foreign affairs to the minister. On 22 messidor, an VII (10 July 1799), the Directory forbade foreign diplomatic agents from reporting to anyone except the minister of foreign relations. They could not communicate with other ministers except through his intermediaries. In 1810, Napoleon reinforced that decision by forbidding ministerial departments from communicating with foreign diplomatic representatives and mandating that all communications had to go through the foreign office.[159] Ironically enough, a voice from much earlier in 1792, that of Brissot, had cautioned that "diplomacy cannot be popular, that is to say, open, simple." The republic that professed to base its policy on truth and sincerity could not operate within the international system. But a republic, he urged, could wage war.[160]

These moves merely ratified decisions previously taken that had also violated the dictates of revolutionary ideology—secret deliberations,[161] secret additions to instructions,[162] secret funds,[163] and secret agents. Those issues had surfaced early.[164] Secret correspondence continued. As early as June 1793 the minister of foreign affairs directed that some letters from London be kept in a separate file that was to be placed in a carton of secret correspondence.[165] Sometimes such measures backfired. In thermidor, an II, Philibert Buchot, the Commissar of Foreign Relations from April to November 1794, known for both for his stupidity and his drinking, had the unenviable task of reporting to the Committee of Public Safety that the secretary general of the Commission of Foreign Relations had told him that a letter addressed directly to Deforgues, then minister of foreign affairs, by Joseph Fauchet, then minister plenipotentiary in the United States, had been placed with three others in a bureau only accessed by the commissar. Buchot had read it to Robespierre but saved it to give to Barère, who would pass it on to the Committee of Public Safety. Buchot regretted that he could not produce it. The letter was now lost "perhaps because of all the precautions I took to conserve it. It is an accident which is not unheard of."[166] As the secret correspondence increased, one could only hope that the cataloguing improved.

The revolutionary governments were not very successful in jettisoning other aspects of what Barère called "the deceitful forms of the diplomacy of despots."[167] Virtually the same arguments that revolved around secret articles surfaced in the debate over allocating money to the foreign office for clandestine negotiations.[168] Some questioned whether a secret fund that was not subject to public scrutiny should exist. This "brigandage of finances" would endanger liberty and foster ministerial corruption. Although some argued that such an appropriation would set an iniquitous, as well as a dangerous, precedent and would mean the return of the despicable old diplomacy under the pretext of public utility, others pointed out that the money would expedite the peace and avoid human bloodshed. The latter argument swayed the majority of the assembly and expediency trumped principle in the spring of 1792.[169] The secret funds lingered on. Still, in 1792, Lebrun was careful to give an account of the expenses of the bureau, including the secret funds.[170] Shortly thereafter, in October 1792 the Convention provisionally suspended the payment of pensions from the secret funds of the foreign office.[171] At that time 2 million *livres* had been allocated to secret expenses and 400,000 livres used without any accountability. Pierre Joseph Cambon, who was known for his financial acuity and his independence and who served on the Committee of Finance, wanted the ministers to justify the sums spent.[172] Like a duck, the issue kept resurfacing. In 1793 the minister of foreign affairs Dumouriez was given control over a 6-million-livre fund set aside for secret outlays.[173] In April 1794, Saint Just leveled an attack against the administration of foreign affairs, in which he urged that all monies distributed to neutral powers, the so-called secret expenses, should be abolished.[174] Still "secret" funds continued. Nor was this all.

Very early in the Revolution spies were hired. As early as 1792 secret agents were sent to England.[175] Chauvelin, the minister plenipotentiary (1792–1793) in London, had attempted to communicate a confidential despatch through a private agent but the British, in Grenville's words, "disliked the mode of intercourse, and have stopped it for the future."[176] Jean-Louis Soulavie in Geneva from 1793 to 1794 could list five secret agents in that city alone.[177] While on a mission to the Upper Rhine in 1793, Hérault de Séchelles, a member of the Committee of Public Safety, had reorganized the secret agents.[178] During the next year, 1794, the Committee of Public Safety authorized Barthélemy in Switzerland to send secret agents to the coalition countries.[179] In that year they sent Antoine-Bernard Caillard to Amsterdam and Prandier to Poland[180]—only two among many. Certainly some of the secret negotiations were begun and secret agents dispatched because of the momentum of the Revolution in which at least some "sought in private to moderate uncompromising attitudes which they were forced to maintain in public."[181] That decision accounts for the secret missions to London and to The Hague. The combination of public bluster and private hesitancy made for a dangerous situation but such missions allowed the government to negotiate in "secret without making concessions in public."[182]

The Directory followed where the Committee of Public Safety had not feared to tread. The Directors who had no diplomatic relations with most of Europe turned to secret agents, especially in Berlin, Basel, Geneva, and Venice.[183] Pierre-Claude, marquis de Poterat, was dispatched to Vienna in 1795 and Basel in 1796. In 1797 a secretary of the Madrid embassy suggested sending a secret agent, disguised as a goldsmith selling jewels, to influence the queen.[184] When Talleyrand initially proposed his scheme of "double diplomacy," he infuriated Barras, a man not given to quibbling over moral issues. Nor was Barras mollified when Talleyrand argued that this policy would "place the diplomacy of the Republic on a level with that of the kings." One would hardly think that was a compelling argument. In this case Talleyrand certainly misjudged his audience. In Barras' view Talleyrand had flaunted a "luxury of perfidy" by even suggesting corrupting further "an institution not highly moral in its practice." As late as 1798 we see the revolutionaries' hostility to diplomacy, a system impelled by "the privilege of hypocrisy." Barras' deliberate choice of such value-laden terms as "luxury" and "privilege" damned Talleyrand by associating him with the *ancien régime*. Nonetheless, Talleyrand's schemes were implemented.[185] Such practices during the Directory led some to complain about the existence of a secret bureau and to question its constitutionality.[186] Under the consulate and Empire, Napoleon did not hesitate to resort to such tactics. He even advised Talleyrand that he should have ten spies, not one, in a town like Hamburg.[187]

Nor was that the only compromise. The revolutionaries used ciphers in their correspondence and did not hesitate to intercept and decode the correspondence of others. As early as 1792, St. Croset proposed writing secret dispatches on taffeta to disguise the composition. Practical considerations alone deterred him and he turned back to an ordinary cipher.[188] After discussing the secret clauses of Campo Formio, Talleyrand advised Sieyès, who had been sent to Berlin, to send his correspondence in code, "an indispensable precaution."[189] Under the Consulate, Talleyrand regularly had couriers intercepted in order to read confidential dispatches.[190] Under Napoleon there was a secret organization of 44 employees who intercepted mail going outside France. They stole ciphers from embassies and intercepted and copied dispatches. Outside France, elite gendarmes robbed couriers.[191]

Nor did the revolutionaries disdain to use "gifts," so notorious under the *ancien régime*. As early as May 1793 the Committee of Public Safety recognized the necessity of giving gifts to the Barbary chiefs and to the *deys* of Egypt.[192] Again the Directory followed with "gifts of usage" for those who negotiated treaties and conventions.[193] The Directors had not been the first to tread on revolutionary principles. Nor were they the last. Under the Consulate, Talleyrand advised General Antoine François, comte d' Andréossy, when he was appointed ambassador in London in 1802 to temporize: the lack of instructions or the necessity of consulting the government, he advised, are always good excuses. Never give a direct response.[194] Napoleon echoed that when he advised: "If you ever find yourself speaking unnecessarily, and from the heart, say to yourself, 'I have made a mistake' and don't do it again."[195] Later in 1807, Napoleon complained to the minister of foreign affairs that a French representative had been "extremely imprudent" in showing his dispatches. "This conduct is insane," he continued. "Even if you had only said 'bon jour' in your letter, it should not be shown or even read before a stranger."[196] Napoleon similarly advised Talleyrand in drafting his public report not to compromise the secrecy necessary to such operations.[197] Napoleon's stance stood in sharp contrast to Dumouriez's policy on public disclosure. The Revolution had come full circle. By 1800 it had changed and so had the revolutionaries: the idealists of 1792–1794 had been replaced by pragmatists, the dreamers with conquerors.

Notes

1. Metternich, *Memoirs*, 1: 368, letter of 7 April 1798.
2. Heinrich Ritter von Zeissberg, *Quellen zur Geschichte der Politik Österreichs während der französischen Revoutionskriege (1793–1797)* (Vienna: Wilhelm Braumüller, 1885–1890), 2: 129, Mercy to the Emperor, Brussels, 9 March 1794. Auckland at The Hague noted the "ardour of the French missionaries." B. L., Add. Mss. 59139, fol. 89, 19 November 1792.
3. Darnton, "The French Revolution: Intellectuals and Literature."
4. Durkheim quoted in Gordon, *Citizens without Sovereignty*, 242.
5. Quoted in Schama, *Citizens*, 771 and 537.
6. Guyot, *Le Directoire et le paix de l'Europe* (Paris: Félix Alcan, 1912), 683, 692, and 673.
7. Chapuisat, *De la Terreur à l'annexion*, 93.
8. Marcère, *Une Ambassade à Constantinople*, 2: 5–14.
9. Jean Alexis Borrelli, *À l'Assemblée nationale, sur les moyens de former la constitution et les loix, sans tumulte, sans confusion, & avec toute la décence qui doit caracteriser des législateurs* (Paris: Chez Barrois le jeune, 1789).
10. Nicolas Jean Hugou de Bassville, *Le Cri de la nation à ses pairs, ou Rendons les pretres citoyens* (Paris: l'Imprimerie de Monsieur, 1789), 2, 5, 6, 11, 12.
11. Quoted in Jane Van Nimmen," The Death of Bassville: A Riot in Rome and Its Repercussion on the Arts in France," in *Culture and Revolution*, ed. Levitine, 299 fn 7.

12. Anne Louis Girodet-Trioson, *Oeuvres posthumes de Girodet-Trioson*, edited by P. A. Coupin (Paris: Renouard, 1829), 2: 418, letter of 3 October 1792.
13. Thomas Crow, *Emulation: Making Artists for Revolutionary France* (New Haven: Yale University Press, 1995), 148.
14. *Les Muses de Messidor: Peintres et sculpteurs de la Révolution à l'Empire* (Lyon: Musée des Beaux-Arts, 1989), 76.
15. France, "too just to have anything to hide, even in diplomacy, too powerful to resort to threats but too proud to conceal an outrage, is ready to exact punishment if peaceful complaints receive no response." Quoted in Crow, *Emulation: Making Artists for Revolutionary France*, 148.
16. Anatole de Montaiglon and Jules-Joseph Guiffrey, eds., *Correspondance des directeurs de l'Académie de France à Rome* (Paris: Charavay, 1908), 17: 206, Bassville to Lebrun, 2 January 1793.
17. René Trinquet, "L'Assassinat de Hugou de Bassville, (13 Janvier 1793)," *Annales révolutionnaires*, 7 (1914): 350.
18. Montaiglon and Guiffrey, ed., *Correspondance des directeurs de l'Académie de France à Rome*, 16: 513–533.
19. Crow, *Emulation: Making Artists for Revolutionary France*, 149–150.
20. Frédéric Masson, *Les Diplomates de la Révolution: Hugou de Bassville à Rome, Bernadotte à Vienne* (Paris: Charavay Frères Editeurs, 1882), 64.
21. Maurice Andrieux, *Daily Life in Papal Rome*, translated by Mary Fitton (London: George Allen and Unwin, 1968), 202.
22. Simioni, *Le Origini del risorgimento politico dell'Italia meridionale*, 2: 1–4.
23. Girodet-Tiroson, *Oeuvres posthumes*, 2: 422, letter of 9 January 1793.
24. George III, *The Later Correspondence of George III*, edited by A. Aspinall (Cambridge: University Press, 1962), 1: 643–644.
25. Montaiglon and Guiffrey, eds., *Correspondance des directeurs de l'Académie de France à Rome*, 16: 209–210, *mémoire* to Bassville, dated 8 January 1793.
26. Henry Lapauze, *Histoire de l'Académie de France à Rome* (Paris: Plon-Nourrit, 1924), 1: 449.
27. Girodet-Trioson, *Oeuvres posthumes*, 2: 422, letter of 9 January 1793.
28. Ibid., 1: viii.
29. Lapauze, *Histoire de l'Académie de France à Rome*, 1: 447.
30. Masson, *Les Diplomates de la Révolution*, 64.
31. Trinquet, "L'Assassinat de Hugou de Bassville (13 Janvier 1793)," 353.
32. Montaiglon and Guiffrey, eds., *Correspondance des directeurs de l'Académie de France à Rome*, 16: 207–208, Bassville to Lebrun, 8 January 1793.
33. Leone Vicchi, *Les Français à Rome pendant la Convention (1792–1795)* (Paris: H. Le Soudier, 1893), cxxii. Vicchi reprints most of the relevant primary materials.
34. Ibid., 21, letter to Mackau, 12 January 1793.

35. Ibid., xcciv.
36. Crow contends that it was an "officially santioned riot" against the French. *Emulation: Making Artists for Revolutionary France*, 153.
37. A. N., Police générale, Comité de Sureté Générale, Comité diplomatique, F7/4398, André Clavaison? 1793?
38. Girodet-Tiroson, *Oeuvres posthumes*, 424–425.
39. For an inventory of the Academy, see Lapauze, *Histoire de l'Académie de France à Rome*, 1: 379–380.
40. Quoted in Crow, *Emulation: Making Artists for Revolutionary France*, 155.
41. Vincenzo Monti, *La Bassvilliana e la mascheroniana poemetti* (Rome: G. B. Paravia e comp., 1889). See also Georges Bourgin, "L'Assasinat de Bassville et l'opinion romaine en 1793," *Mélanges d'archéologie et d'histoire*, 13 (1913): 365–373.
42. Vicchi, *Les Français à Rome pendant la Convention (1792–1795)*, cxxii, letter of 25 January.
43. Ibid., cxxxiii.
44. Ibid., cxxxiv.
45. Montaiglon and Guiffrey, eds., *Correspondance des directeurs de l'Académie de France à Rome*, 16: 252–253, conseil exécutif to the Convention, 1 February 1793 and 253–254, Decree of National Convention, 2 February 1793.
46. France, Convention nationale, *Décret de la Convention nationale, du 2 février 1793, l'an second de la république française, relatif à l'attentat commis sur la personne du citoyen Bassville, secrétaire de legation, chargé des affaires de la république française à Rome* (Toulon: De l'Imprimerie de Surre, fils, [1793?]), 1.
47. Montaiglon and Guiffrey, eds., *Correspondance des directeurs de l'Académie de France à Rome*, 16: 220–226, relation published on 16 January 1793. At least one British correspondent thought the "unlucky event was evidently accompanied by French insolence and impudence." B. L. Add. Mss. 41199, fol. 108, from? 29 January 1793 to Grenville.
48. Aulard, ed., *Recueil des actes du Comité de salut public* 2: 37–38, 1 February 1793. See also pp. 39–40.
49. French papers resounded with calls for a "just vengeance." Girodet-Trioson, *Oeuvres posthumes de Girodet-Trioson*, 428.
50. Prudhomme, *Révolutions de Paris*, 2–9 February 1793, #187: 290–295. The French government wanted "to take all measures to secure a memorable vengeance." Aulard, ed., *Recueil des actes du Comité de salut public*, 2: 37, 22 janvier 1793.
51. Aulard, ed., *Recueil des actes du Comité de salut public*, 2: 39, 1 fevrier 1793.
52. A. N., Police générale, Comité de Sûrété Générale, Comité diplomatique, F7/4398, André Clavaison?
53. Marie-Caroline, *Correspondance*, 1: 90.

54. Marie Caroline, queen of Naples, remarked that the murder of Bassville "fait vomir feu et flammes aux français." Ibid., 1: 93.
55. France, Convention Nationale, *Décret de la Convention nationale, du 2 février 1793*, 1. Also see Vicchi, *Les Français à Rome pendant la Convention (1792–1795)*, meeting of 2 February 1793, 55. For another account of the incident see George III, *Later Correspondence*, 1: 643–644.
56. Vicchi, *Les Français à Rome pendant la Convention (1792–1795)*, 157, Bonaparte to Directory, 3 messidor, an IV.
57. For a note on the state of the Academy, see Beaucamp, *Le Peintre lillois Jean-Baptiste Wicar*, 2: 340–341.
58. Sorel, *L'Europe et le Révolution française*, 5: 306–307; Guyot, *Le Directoire et la paix de l'Europe*, 688–689; Bailleu, ed., *Preussen und Frankreich von 1795 bis 1807*, 1: 186 ff.
59. Karl A. Roider, *Baron Thugut and Austria's Response to the French Revolution* (Princeton: Princeton University Press, 1987), 275–276.
60. Linda and Marsha Frey, *"Proven Patriots": The French Diplomatic Corps, 1789–1799*, Appendix C.
61. Alfred Ritter von Vivenot, *Zur Geschichte des Rastadter Congresses* (Vienna: Wilhelm Braumüller, 1871), no. XXX: 155–159, 176.
62. Dry, *Soldats, ambassadeurs sous le Directoire*, 375.
63. Roider, *Baron Thugut and Austria's Response to the French Revolution*, 268; Vivenot, *Zur Geschichte des rastadter Congresses*, no. XXX: 155–156.
64. Roider, *Baron Thugut and Austria's Response to the French Revolution*, 269.
65. Masson, *Les Diplomates de la Révolution*, 182–183.
66. Vivenot, *Zur Geschichte des rastadter Congresses*, no. XXX: 156.
67. Guyot, *Le Directoire et la paix de l'Europe*, 693 and Masson, *Les Diplomates de la Révolution*, 186.
68. Masson, *Les Diplomates de la Révolution*, 190. See also William Auckland, *The Journal and Correspondence of William, Lord Auckland*, 4 vols. (London: Richard Bentley, 1862) 3: 406–408, Sir Morton Eden to Lord Auckland, Vienna, 16 April 1798; 3: 405, Sir Morton Eden to Lord Auckland, Vienna.
69. Masson, *Les Diplomates de la Révolution*, 193–195.
70. Ibid., 200.
71. Ibid., 203.
72. Great Britain, HMC, *The Manuscripts of J. B. Fortescue*, 3: 182, Starhemberg to Grenville, April 1798.
73. Maurice-Henri Weil, *Un Agent inconnu de la coalition, Le Général de Stamford d'après sa correspondance inédite (1793–1806)* (Paris: Payot and

Cie., 1923), Stamford to the prince of Orange, Berlin, 12 May 1798, 117–119.
74. Masson, *Les Diplomates de la Révolution*, 207–208.
75. The War of the Second Coalition would break out in December 1798, although Austria did not join until March 1799.
76. Pallain, ed. *Le Ministère de Talleyrand sous le Directoire*, 231, Talleyrand to Treilhard, 26 April 1798.
77. Ibid., 231.
78. Roider, *Baron Thugut and Austria's Response to the French Revolution*, 277.
79. Napoleon, *Napoleon Bonaparte: Memoirs, Dictated by the Emperor at St. Helena to the Generals Who Shared His Captivity*, edited by Somerset De Chair (London: Soho Book Co., 1936), 273.
80. Guyot, *Le Directoire et la paix de l'Europe*, 695.
81. Vivenot, *Zur Geschichte des rastadter Congresses*, 156–159, 25 April 1798.
82. Ibid., 176. Masson, *Les Diplomates de la Révolution*, 149 ff; Guyot, *Le Directoire et la paix de l'Europe*, 688–704; Roider, *Baron Thugut and Austria's Response to the French Revolution*, 269–284; Dry, *Soldats, ambassadeurs sous le Directoire*, 357–468.
83. Lincolnshire Archives, Papers of Sir Richard Worsley, 14, fol. 15, Worsley to Grenville, Venice, 30 June 1795.
84. Ibid., 14, fol. 61, Worsley to Grenville, Venice, 10 June 1796.
85. Ibid., 14, fol. 161, Worsley to Grenville, Venice 29 March 1797.
86. Ibid., 15, fol. 38, 8 February 1794 and fol. 40, 15 February 1794, fol. 44; B. L. Add. Mss. 59154, fol. 34, Drake to Lord Grenville, private 20 February 1794. Also see earlier letter in B. L., Add. Mss. 46823, fols. 71–72, John Trevor to Francis Drake, 5 August 1793 and B. L., Add. Mss. 46827, fols. 152–153? to Drake, Genoa, 2 February 1794.
87. B. L., Add. Mss. 46827, fols. 156, To Drake, Genoa, 22 February 1794. These actions were viewed as seditious and, coupled with his arrogance, led to demands for his recall. See B. L., Add. Mss. 46827, fols 163? to Drake, Genoa, 8 March 1794; B. L., Add. Mss. 46827, fol. 165? to Drake, Genoa, 18 March 1794; and B. L. Add. Mss. 46827, fol. 166? To Drake, 29 March 1794; Devon Record Office, CP 243, 3 September 1790, Genoa, Joseph Brane to Francis Drake.
88. See Snyder, *Dissimulation and the Culture of Secrecy in Early Modern Europe*. This concern about transparency is also illustrated by Pierre Manuel's publication of excerpts from Bastille records in 1789 and the government's of the material found in November 1792 in the iron cabinet in the Tuileries Palace. The discovery of the king's secret correspondence and the duplicity of many of his correspondents had made his trial inevitable. Thanks to David Bell for underscoring these incidents.

89. Pétion de Villeneuve in Buchez and Roux, ed., *Histoire parlementaire*, 6: 63, 27 May 1790.
90. *Moniteur* 4 (1790): 389–391.
91. Ibid., 4 (1790): 411, Menou on 20 May 1790.
92. Armand, duc d'Aiguillon in ibid., 6: 52, 16 May 1790. Candor and loyalty would replace "the guile of cabinets" and the "diplomatic mysteries." Ibid., 7: 396, 28 July 1790.
93. Guillaume Mouysset in *Archives parlementaires*, 35: 585 and 587, 17 February 1792.
94. Barthélemy, *Papiers*, 1: 327–328.
95. Maximilien Robespierre, *Oeuvres de Maximilien Robespierre*, ed. Albert Laponneraye (Paris: l'Éditeur, 1840), 10: 175–176.
96. Marcère, *Une Ambassade à Constantinople*, 1: 19, 18 February 1793.
97. *Annual Register*, 1795, 188–195.
98. *Moniteur*, 23: 340 and 341–343, 11 pluviôse, 1795, 341–343.
99. Fugier, *Histoire des relations internationales*, 4: 22.
100. Carlos Jose Gutierrez de los Rios y Sarmiento, duque de Fernán Núñez, *Note remise à M. le comte de Montmorin par M. l'Ambassadeur d'Espagne* (France: n.p., 1790?).
101. N. A., General Records of the Department of State, RG59, Diplomatic Despatches, France (34), vol. 1, William Short, Paris, 3 October 1790.
102. Martin, "Le Comité diplomatique," 31, fn 57.
103. Ibid., 19.
104. A. N., D XXIII, carton 1, dossier 1, Dumouriez to Koch, 30 April 1792.
105. Bélin, *La Logique d'une idée-force*, 2: 114–115.
106. Sorel, *L'Europe et la Révolution française*, 2: 440.
107. P.R.O, FO 95/100, Grenville to Chauvelin, 45, 25 May 1792.
108. Quoted in Black, *British Foreign Policy in an Age of Revolutions, 1783–1793*, 462.
109. Murley, "The Origins and Outbreak of the Anglo-French War of 1793," 413.
110. Auckland, *Journal and Correspondence*, 2: 423, Mr. Burges to Lord Auckland, Whitehall, 31 July 1792.
111. France, *Recueil, Vol. 28: États Allemands*, Tome 1: *L'Electorat de Mayence*, 278.
112. P.R.O., FO 5/4, fol. 101, *The Correspondence between Citizen Genet, Minister of the French Republic, to the United States of North America and the Officers of the Federal Government; to which are prefixed the Instructions from the Constituted Authorities of France to the Said Minister. All from Authentic Documents* (Philadelphia: Benjamin Franklin Bache, 1793).

113. University of Virginia, Alderman Library, Special Collections Thomas Jefferson papers, Thomas Jefferson to Martha Randolph, Philadelphia, 22 December 1793.
114. Turner, ed. *Correspondence of the French Ministers to the United States 1791–1797*, 2 vols. (New York: Da Capo Press, 1972), 1: 12. For Adet's publication, see AAE, CP États-Unis, vol. 46, part 3, fols. 239–240.
115. Matthew Q. Dawson, "'Stop the Wheels of Government:' America's French Party during the Directory Government and the Rise of Bonaparte, 1796–1798," unpublished MA thesis, Florida State University, 1996: 60–61.
116. A. A. E., CP États-Unis, vol, 46, part 2, 6 fructidor, an IV, fol. 133–139.
117. A. A. E., CP États-Unis vol. 62 fol. 119; also see B. L., Add. Mss. 59100, fol. 31, 15 May 1798, Grenville to?, on the publication in 1798 of the dispatches of the American commissioners at Paris.
118. Napoleon, *Correspondance* (Paris: Henri Plon, 1867), 21: 316–317, to Champagny, duc de Cadore, Paris, 13 December 1800. As part of a larger propaganda campaign in 1809 he ordered that the information on the government's negotiations with Algiers be published in order to underscore the "disgusting and horrible" nature of the Algerian deeds. Napoleon, *Correspondance*, 18: 171, to the comte de Champagny, Minister of Foreign Relations, Benavente, 4 January 1809.
119. Sir Robert Adair, *Historical Memoir of a Mission to the Court of Vienna in 1806* (London: Longman, Brown, and Longmans, 1844), 11.
120. Jean de Dieu-Raymond de Boisgelin de Cuce, *Opinion de M. l'Archévêque d'Aix sur le droit de faire la paix & la guerre, prononcée le 21 mai dans l'Assemblee nationale.* (France: s.n., 1790?), 28.
121. Paul H. Beik, ed. *The French Revolution* (New York: Walker and Co., 1970), 163, 20 June 1791, Louis XVI.
122. Saint-Just, *Oeuvres complètes*, 2: 350.
123. *Moniteur*, 23: 598–599, Cambacérès, 13 ventôse, an III (1795).
124. Ibid., 23: 679, Cambacères on 23 ventôse.
125. Ibid., 23: 682, Villetard.
126. Ibid., 23: 681, Chazal, 26 ventôse, an III (16 March 1795).
127. Ibid., 23: 681–682, Duhem.
128. Ibid., 23: 682, Duboy.
129. Ibid., 682.
130. Ibid., 683.
131. Ibid., 677.
132. Ibid., 23: 674 séance of 22 ventôse, an III (1795). Discussion on the projected decree is continued on 676–677.
133. Ibid.
134. Ibid., 681, Chazal, 26 ventôse, an III (16 March 1795).

135. Ibid., Albitte, 682–683.
136. Ibid.
137. Ibid., 23: 684.
138. Ibid., 683–684.
139. Ibid., 690.
140. Ibid., 23: 711.
141. Ibid., 23: 712.
142. Ibid., 23: 714–718. France, *Bulletin des lois de la République, an III, 1794–1795*, no. 705. Also see Bourgoing, *Histoire diplomatique de l'Europe pendant la Révolution française*, 4: 142–144.
143. Pierre Rain, *La Diplomatie française de Mirabeau à Bonaparte* (Paris: Plon, 1950), 110.
144. B. L., Add. Mss. 59131, Harris to Grenville, private, Paris, 12 November 1796.
145. B. L., Add. Mss. 59132, fols. 52–53, Grenville to Harris, 7 November 1796.
146. P.R.O., FO 27/46 fol. 195–196, Grenville to Harris 2 November 1796; B, Add. Mss. 59132, fol. 54, Grenville to Harris, 23 November 1796.
147. P.R.O., FO 27/46 fol. 136–139, Grenville to Harris, 7 November 1796.
148. P.R.O., FO 27/46 fol. 122, Tronson de Coudray to Council of Ancients and to Harris, 8 brumaire, an V.
149. P.R.O., FO 27/46 fol. 146–147, Harris to Grenville, Paris, 12 November 1796.
150. P.R.O., FO 27/46 fol. 227–228, Harris to Grenville, 28 November 1796.
151. Harris, *Diaries and Correpondence*, 3: 591, 27 September 1797.
152. Black, "From Pillnitz to Valmy: British Foreign Policy and Revolutionary France 1791–1792," 135–136.
153. France, *Bulletin des lois de la République, an* 4, no. 444.
154. Napoleon, *Correspondance*, 2: 498. Also see Prince Charles Maurice de Talleyrand-Périgord, prince Bénévent, *Lettres inédites de Talleyrand à Napoléon, 1800–1809*, edited by Pierre Bertrand (Paris: Perrin et cie., n.d.), 138 Talleyrand to Napoleon, 12 vendémiaire, an XIV (4 October 1805).
155. Rain, *La Diplomatie française*, 147.
156. Pallain, ed. *Le Ministère de Talleyrand sous le Directoire*, 167–169.
157. Ibid., 190, Talleyrand to Treilhard, 6 January 1798.
158. Ibid., 439–447, Talleyrand to Jean Gérard Lacuée (1752–1841), of the Council of 500, 2 July 1799. In year VIII (December 1799) the constitution of the Consulate provided in article 51 that secret articles of a treaty could not contradict the articles patent. France, *Bulletin des lois de la République*, an VIII, Bulletin #333, article 51 and secret committee, article 50.
159. Amédée Outry, "Histoire et principes de l'administration française des Affaires Étrangères," *Revue française de science politique*, 3 (1953): 495.

160. Brissot, *Discours de J. P. Brissot deputé de Paris sur la necessité d'exiger uns satisfation de l'Empéreur*, 8–9.
161. Antonin Debidour, ed., *Recueil des actes du Directoire exécutif (procès-verbaux, arrétés, instructions, lettre et actes divers)* (Paris: Imprimerie nationale, 1910), 1: 545, Délibération secrète du pluviôse an IV, (1 février 1796).
162. Ibid., 1: 549, for example to citizen Cacault at Geneva, 4 février 1796.
163. Arthur Chuquet, *Dumouriez* (Paris: Librairie Hachette, 1914), 71 Dumouriez received six million in secret funds to use in foreign lands. This was the same Dumouriez who had written Biron, 13 April 1792, that he would not "ruin the nation with secret expenses." Prince Charles Maurice de Talleyrand-Périgord, prince Bénévent, *La Mission de Talleyrand à Londres, en 1792: Correspondance inédite de Talleyrand avec le Departement des affaires étrangères le Général Biron*, etc. *Ses lettres d'Amérique à Lord Lansdowne*, edited by G. Pallain (Paris: Librairie Plon, 1889), 202, Dumouriez to Biron, 13 April 1792.
164. On 30 messidor, an II (18 July 1794), a memo to the commissars of the republic in the United States underscored the importance of not "compromising the secrecy of our operations." A. A. E., États-Unis, CP, vol. 41, part 3, fol. 235 Paris, 30 messidor, an II.
165. Aulard, ed. *Recueil des actes du Comité de salut public*, 5: 45.
166. A. A. E., États-Unis, CP vol. 41, part 5, fols. 291–292.
167. *Adresse des députés du peuple à la Convention nationale avec la réponse du président* (Angers: Imp. Nat., n.d.), 11.
168. A. N., Police générale, comité de Sûreté générale, comité diplomatique, F7/4397, the expenses of the foreign service for the first nine months of 1791 included a section on the secret service of over 2 million *livres*. The secret expenses were larger than the public.
169. *Archives parlementaires*, 42: 431–435, Rouyer, Danthon and Vergniaud, 26 April 1792. See also AN, DXXIII, carton 1, dossier I, Dumouriez to Koch, 23 April 1792. Also see A. Debidour, ed. *Recueil des actes du Directoire exécutif*, 1: 142, 7 frimaire, an IV. The Directory also authorized sums that would be encumbered "Comme dépenses sècretes du Département des relations extérieures et que le détail n'en sera jamais rendu public."
170. Lebrun, *Compte-rendu*, 8.
171. A. N., F/7 Police Générale, 4395, Comité de sûreté générale, fol. 256, 21 October 1792.
172. Danton, *Discours*, 212.
173. Aulard, *Recueil des actes du Comité de salut public*, 5: 537, 13 août 1793.
174. Saint-Just, *Oeuvres complètes*, 2: 350.
175. Aulard, ed., *Recueil des actes du Comité du salut salut public*, 1: 30. Also see, 5: 114, 28 June 1793 and 5: 98, 27 June 1793.

176. Great Britain, HMC, *Manuscript of J. B. Fortescue*, 2: 366, Grenville to Auckland, 15 January 1793.
177. Albin Mazon, *Histoire de Soulavie* (Paris, 1893), 179, 251. In a meeting of 1 frimaire, an III (21 November 1794), the Committee of Public Safety authorized the French representative in Switzerland, Barthélemy, to send into coalition countries secret agents "sans mandat et sans caractère." Aulard, ed., *Recueil des actes du Comité de salut public*, 18: 273–274.
178. Emile Dard, *Un Épicurien sous la Terreur: Hérault de Séchelles (1759–1794)* (Paris: Perrin et cie., 1907), 316.
179. Aulard, ed. *Recueil des actes du Comité de salut public*, 18: 273, 21 November 1794.
180. Godechot, *La Grande Nation*, 1: 86; Julien Grossbart, "La Politique polonaise de la Révolution française jusqu'aux traités de Bâle," *Annales historiques de la Révolution française*, 7 (1930): 143.
181. Murley, "The Origins and Outbreak of the Anglo-French War of 1793," 405.
182. Ibid., 480.
183. Guyot, *Le Directoire et la paix de l'Europe*, 84–85. Also see Bernard Nabonne, *La Diplomatie du Directoire et Bonaparte d'après les papier inédits de Reubell* (Paris: La Nouvelle Edition, 1951), 112–114.
184. Grandmaison, *L'Ambassade francaise en Espagne pendant la Révolution (1789–1804)*, 116.
185. Barras, *Memoirs*, 3: 301–302, 10 fructidor to 2ième complémentaire an VI (August–September 1798).
186. François, comte Barbé de Marbois in Masson, *Département des affaires étrangères*, 385.
187. André Palluel, ed. *Dictionnaire de l'Empereur* (Paris: Plon, 1969), 428.
188. A. N., D XXIII, comité diplomatique, part 1, 28 April 1792.
189. Pallain, ed. *Le Ministère de Talleyrand*, 350, Talleyrand to Sieyès, 24 September 1798. Also see 381, Talleyrand to Sieyès, 9 September 1798.
190. Georges Lacour-Gayet, *Talleyrand 1754–1838*, 4 vols. (Paris: Payot, 1933), 2: 46.
191. Léonce Pingaud, *Un Agent secret sous la Révolution et l'Empire: Le comte d'Antraigues* (Paris: Plon, Nourriet et cie., 1894), 261.
192. Aulard, ed., *Recueil des actes du Comité de salut public*, 4: 163, 14 May 1793.
193. Guyot, *Le Directoire et la paix de l'Europe*, 92.
194. Lacour-Gayet, *Talleyrand*, 2: 46.
195. Thompson, ed., *Napoleon Self-Revealed*, 120, Napoleon to Prince Eugene, Viceroy of Italy, Milan, 5 June 1805.
196. Napoleon, *Correspondance*, 16: 78, Napoleon to Champagny, 6 October 1807.
197. Ibid., 6: 612–613, 26 October 1800.

References

Adair, Sir Robert. *Historical Memoir of a Mission to the Court of Vienna in 1806.* London: Longman, Brown, Green, and Longmans, 1844.

Adresse des députés du peuple à la Convention nationale avec la réponse du président. Angers: Imprimerie Nationale, n.d.

Andrieux, Maurice. *Daily Life in Papal Rome in the Eighteenth Century.* Translated [from the French] by Mary Fitton. London: Allen and Unwin, 1968.

Auckland, William Eden, first baron. *The Journal and Correspondence of William, Lord Auckland.* 2 vols. London: Richard Bentley, 1861–1862.

Aulard, François-Alphonse, ed. *Recueil des actes du Comité de salut public avec la correspondance officielle des représentants en mission et le registre du conseil exécutif provisoire.* 27 vols. Paris: Imprimerie nationale, 1889–1923.

Bailleu, Paul, ed. *Preusssen und Frankreich von 1795 bis 1807. Diplomatische Correspondenzen.* Osnabrück: Otto Zeller, 1965.

Barras, Paul, vicomte de. *Memoirs of Barras, Member of the Directorate.* New York: Harper and Brothers, 1895.

Barthélemy, François. *Papiers de Barthélemy, ambassadeur de France en Suisse, 1792–1797.* Edited by Jean Kaulek and Alexandre Tausserat-Radel. 6 vols. Paris: Alcan, 1886–1910.

Bassville, Nicolas Jean Hugou de. *Le Cri de la nation à ses pairs, ou Rendons les pretres citoyens.* Paris: l'Imprimerie de Monsieur, 1789.

Beaucamp, Fernand. *Le Peintre lillois: Jane-Baptiste Wicar (1762–1834), Son Oeuvre et son temps.* 2 vols. Lille: E. Raoust, 1939.

Beik, Paul H., ed. *The French Revolution.* New York: Walker and Co., 1971.

Bélin, Jean. *La Logique d'une idée-force: l'Idée d'utilité sociale et la révolution française.* Paris: Hermann et Cie., 1939.

Black, Jeremy. *British Foreign Policy in an Age of Revolutions, 1783–1793.* Cambridge: Cambridge University Press, 1994a.

———. "From Pillnitz to Valmy: British Foreign Policy and Revolutionary France 1791–1792." *Francia: Forschungen zur westeuropäischen Geschichte* 21 (1994b): 129–146.

Borrelli, Jean Alexis. *À l'Assemblée nationale, sur les moyens de former la constitution et les loix, sans tumulte, sans confusion, & avec toute la decence qui doit caracteriser des législateurs.* Paris: Chez Barrois le jeune, chez le marchands de nouveautés du Palais-Royal, 1789.

Bourgin, Georges, "L'Assassinat de Bassville et l'opinion romaine en 1798." *Mélanges d'archéologie et d'histoire* 13 (1913): 365–373.

Brissot de Warville, Jacques-Pierre. *Discours de J. P. Brissot, député de Paris sur la necessité d'exiger une satisfaction de l'Empereur.* Paris: Imprimerie nationale, 1792.

Buchez, Philippe-Joseph-Benjamin, and Prosper-Charles Roux-Lavergne, eds. *Histoire parlementaire de la Révolution française.* 40 vols. Paris: Paulin, 1834–1838.

Chapuisat, Édouard. *De la Terreur de l'annexation: Génève et la république française, 1793–1798.* Geneva: Edition ATAR, 1912.

Chuquet, Arthur Maxime. *Dumouriez.* Paris: Librairie Hachette & Cie, 1914.

Crow, Thomas. *Emulation: Making Artists for Revolutionary France.* New Haven: Yale University Press, 1995.

Danton, Georges Jacques. *Discours de Danton.* Edited by André Fribourg. Paris: Société de l'histoire de la Révolution française, 1910.

Dard, Émile. *Un Épicurien sous la Terreur: Hérault de Sechelles (1759–1794).* Paris: Perrin et cie., 1907.

Darnton, Robert Choate. "The French Revolution: Intellectuals and Literature." Lecture, University of Montana, June 1, 1989.

Dawson, Matthew Q. "'Stop the Wheels of Government': America's French Party During the Directory Government and the Rise of Bonaparte, 1796 to 1798." Unpublished Master's Thesis, Florida State University, 1996.

Debidour, Antonin, ed. *Recueil des actes du Directoire Exécutif (procès-verbaux, arrêtés, instructions, lettres et actes divers).* Paris: Imprimerie nationale, 1910.

Dieu-Raymond de Boisgelin de Cuce, Jean de. *Opinion de M. l'Archévêque d'Aix sur le droit de faire la paix & la guerre, prononcee le 21 mai dans l'Assemblée nationale.* France: s.n., 1790.

Dry, Adrien Fleury. *Soldats ambassadeurs sous le Directoire, an IV–an VIII.* Paris: Plon, 1906.

Fernán Núñez, Carlos Jose Gutierrez de los Rios y Sarmiento, duque de. *Note remise a M. le comte de Montmorin/par M. l'Ambassadeur d'Espagne.* France: s.n., 1790.

France. *Bulletin des lois de la République, an III, 1794–1795,* no. 705.

France. Commission des Archives diplomatiques au ministère des affaires étrangères. *Recueil des instructions données au ambassadeurs et ministres de France depuis les traités de Westphalie jusqu'à la Révolution française. Vol. 28. États Allemands, part 1: L'Electorat de Mayence.* Edited by Georges Livet. Paris: Centre National de la recherche scientifique, 1962.

———. Convention nationale. *Décret de la Convention nationale, du 2 février 1793, l'an second de la république française, relatif à l'attentat commis sur la personne du citoyen Bassville, secrétaire de legation, chargé des affaires de la république française à Rome.* Toulon: De l'Imprimerie de Surre, fils, [1793?].

Frey, Linda, and Marsha Frey. *"Proven Patriots": The French Diplomatic Corps, 1789–1799.* St. Andrews, Scotland: St. Andrew Studies in French History and Culture, 2011. http://research-repository.st-andrews.ac.uk/handle/10023/1881.

Fugier, André. *Histoire des relations internationales. Vol. 4: La Revolution française et l'empire napoléonien.* Paris: Hachette, 1954.

George III. *The Later Correspondence of George III.* Vols. 1–3. Edited by A. Aspinall. Cambridge: University Press, 1962–1967.

Girodet-Trioson, Anne Louis. *Oeuvres posthumes de Girodet-Trioson.* Edited by P. A. Coupin. 2 vols. Paris: Renouard, 1829.

Godechot, Jacques. *La Grande nation: L'Expansion révolutionnaire de la France dans le monde de 1789 à 1799.* Paris: Aubier, 1956.

Gordon, Daniel. *Citizens Without Sovereignty: Equality and Sociability in French Thought, 1670–1789.* Princeton: University Press, 1994.

Grandmaison, Charles-Alexandre Geoffroy de. *L'Ambassade française en Espagne pendant la Révolution (1789–1804).* Paris: Plon, 1892.

Great Britain, Historical Manuscripts Commission. *The Manuscripts of J. B. Fortescue, esq., Preserved at Dropmore.* 4 vols. London: Eyre and Spottiswoode, 1892–1905.

Grossbart, Julien. "La Politique polonaise de la Révolution française jusqù aux traités de Bâle." *Annales historiques de la Révolution française* 6 (1929): 476–485; 7 (1930): 129–151.

Guyot, Raymond. *Le Directoire et la paix de l'Europe: Des traités de Bâle à la deuxième coalition, 1795–1799.* Paris: Félix Alcan, 1911.

Harris, James. *Diaries and Correspondence of James Harris, First Earl of Malmesbury.* 4 vols. 1844. Reprint. New York: AMS Press, 1970.

Lacour-Gayet, Georges. *Talleyrand, 1754–1838.* 4 vols. Paris: Payot, 1928–1934.

Lapauze, Henri. *Histoire de l'Académie de France à Rome. Vol. 1: 1666–1801.* Paris: Plon-Nourrit et cie, 1924.

Lebrun-Tondu, Pierre Henri Hélène Marie. *Compte rendu à la convention nationale par le ministre des affaires étrangères, dans la séance du 26 Septembre 1792, l'an premier de la république française.* Paris: De l'Imprimerie nationale, 1792.

Marcère, Édouard de. *Une Ambassade à Constantinople: La Politique orientale de la Révolution française.* 2 vols. Paris: Felix Alcan, 1927.

Marie-Caroline, Queen of Naples. *Correspondance inédite de Marie-Caroline, Reine de Naples et de Sicile avec le marquis de Gallo.* Edited by M.-H. Weil and Marquis C. Di Somma Circello. 2 vols. Paris: Émile-Paul Éditeur, 1911.

Martin, Virginie. "Le Comité diplomatique: homicide par décret de la diplomatie (1790–1793)?" *La Révolution française: Cahiers de l'Istitute d'histoire de la Révolution française* 3 (2012): 1–33.

Masson, Frédéric. *Les Diplomates de la Révolution: Hugou de Bassville à Rome, Bernadotte à Vienne.* Paris: Charavay frères, 1882.

Mazon, Albin. *Histoire de Soulavie.* Paris: Fischbacher, 1893.

Metternich-Winneburg, Clemens Wenzel Neopomuk Lothar, Fürst von. *Memoirs of Prince Metternich.* Edited by Prince Richard Metternich. 5 vols. New York: C. Scribner's Sons, 1880–1882.

Moniteur, seule histoire authentique et inaltérée de la Révolution française. 32 vols. Paris: Plon Frères, 1847–1863.

Montaiglon, Anatole de, and Guiffrey, Jules-Joseph, eds. *Correspondance des directeurs de l'Académie de France à Rome.* 17 vols. Paris: Charavay, 1887–1908.

Monti, Vincenzo. *La Bassvilliana e la mascheroniona poemetti.* Edited by Giuseppe Finzi. Rome: Paravia, 1889.

Murley, J. T. "The Origin and Outbreak of the Anglo-French War of 1793." Unpublished Ph.D. Diss., Oxford, 1959.

Les Muses de Messidor: Peintres et sculpteurs de la Révolution à l'Empire. Lyon: Musée des Beaux-Arts, 1989.

Nabonne, Bernard. *La Diplomatie du Directoire et Bonaparte d'après les papiers inédits de Reubell.* Paris: La Nouvelle edition, 1951.

Napoleon. *Napoleon: Self-Revealed.* Translated and Edited by J. M. Thompson. Boston: Houghton Mifflin Company, 1934.

———. *Napoleon Bonaparte: Memoirs, Dictated by the Emperor at St. Helena to the Generals Who Shared His Captivity.* Edited by Somerset De Chair. London: Soho, 1936.

Napoléon I. *Correspondance de Napoléon I.* 32 vols. Paris: Imprimerie Impériale, 1858–1869.

Outry, Amédée. "Histoire et principes de l'administration française des affaires étrangéres." *Revue française de science politique* 3, nos. 2, 3 (1953): 298–318, 491–510.

Pallain, G., ed. *Le Ministère de Talleyrand sous le Directoire.* Paris: Plon, Nourrit et cie., 1891.

Palluel, André. *Dictionnaire de l'Empereur.* Paris: Plon, 1969.

Pingaud, Léonce. *Un Agent secret sous la Révolution et l'Empire, Le Comte d'Antraigues.* Paris: E. Plon Nourrit et cie., 1894.

Prudhomme, Louis-Marie. *Révolutions de Paris.* Paris: n.p., 1789–1794.

Rain, Pierre. *La Diplomatie française.* 2 vols. Paris: Plon, 1943, 1950.

Robespierre, Maximilien. *Oeuvres complètes.* Edited by Marc Bouloiseau and Albert Soboul. 10 vols. Paris: Presses universitaires de France, 1950–1967.

———. *Oeuvres de Maximilien Robespierre.* Edited by Albert Laponneraye. 3 vols. Paris: l'Éditeur, 1840.

Roider, Karl A. *Baron Thugut and Austria's Response to the French Revolution.* Princeton: Princeton University Press, 1987.

Saint-Just, Louis de. *Oeuvres complètes de Saint-Just.* Edited by Charles Vellay. 2 vols. Paris: Librairie Charpentier et Fasquelle, 1908.

Schama, Simon. *Citizens: A Chronicle of the French Revolution.* New York: Alfred A. Knopf, 1989.

Simioni, Attilio. *Le origini del risorgimento politico dell'Iitalia meridionale.* 2 vols. Rome: Giuseppe Principato, 1925–1930.

Snyder, Jon R. *Dissimulation and the Culture of Secrecy in Early Modern Europe.* Berkeley: University of California Press, 2009.

Sorel, Albert. *L'Europe and la Révolution française.* 8 vols. Paris: E. Plon Nourrit et cie, 1897–1904.

Talleyrand-Périgord, Charles Maurice de, prince de Bénévent. *Lettres inédites de Talleyrand à Napoleon 1800–1809.* Edited by Pierre Bertrand. Paris: Perrin et Cie., 1889a.

———. *La Mission de Talleyrand à Londres, en 1792: Correspondance inédite de Talleyrand avec le Département des affaires étrangères, le Général Biron, etc.; ses lettres d'Amérique à Lord Lansdowne.* Edited by G. Pallain. Paris: E. Plon Nourrit et Cie., 1889b.

Trinquet, René. "L'Assassinat de Hugou de Bassville." *Annales révolutionnaires* 7 (1914): 338–368.

Turner, Frederick Jackson, ed. *Correspondence of the French Ministers to the United States, 1791–1797.* 2 vols. 1903. Reprint. New York: Da Capo Press, 1972.

Van Nimmen, Jane. "The Death of Bassville: A Riot in Rome and Its Repercussions on the Arts in France." In *Culture and Revolution, Cultural Ramifications of the French Revolution,* edited by George Levitine, 282–302. College Park, MD: Department of Art History, University of Maryland, 1989.

Vicchi, Leone. *Les Français à Rome pendant la Convention (1792–1795).* Paris: H. Le Soudier, 1892.

Vivenot, Alfred Ritter von. *Zur Geschichte des Rastadter Congresses.* Vienna: Wilhelm Braumüller, 1871.

Weil, Maurice-Henri. *Un Agent inconnu de la coalition, Le Général de Stamford d'après sa correspondance inédite (1793–1806).* Paris: Payot and Cie., 1923.

Zeissberg, Henrich Ritter von. *Quellen zur Geschichte der Politik Oesterreichs während der französischen Revolutionskriege (1793–1797).* 4 vols. Vienna: Wilhelm Braumüller, 1885–1890.

CHAPTER 7

"Quite in the Clouds": French Emissaries Abroad

The diplomats, often chosen for their revolutionary ardor, flouted established manners and customs and vaunted their republican credentials. The receiving government often found them difficult if not impossible to deal with. The truculence of the republican envoys often doomed negotiations at the outset. The revolutionary creed influenced the tenor and pace of and sometimes undermined negotiations. Inherent in revolutionary diplomacy was a tacit, but more often overt, subversion of the established order, even in so-called fellow republics. These actions limited what Menning has dubbed the "bounds of the possible." "In diplomacy, language and style are the building blocks of compromise or confrontation, the ingredients on which the outcome of many a negotiation or maneuver may hinge, the essence of a perpetual game of defining and redefining the bounds of the possible."[1] A couple of examples from that "perpetual game" may illumine what happened when the two systems collided. In 1797 Bonaparte and Cobenzl strained the patience of the other. Bonaparte complained that Cobenzl (1753–1809) was too used "to having his own way" [and this from Bonaparte] and was not accustomed to negotiating. Cobenzl was too "intractable." He would resort to "talking loudly" and using "imperious gestures" while being intentionally imprecise.[2] In his letters Cobenzl returned the compliment—and with a vengeance. Bonaparte acted "like a man from a hovel."

Miot de Melito, *Memoirs*, 119.

He complained not just about his unpredictable moods and his theatrics, but about his ill manners.[3] Such complaints could be attributed to the stresses inherent in the negotiations for peace in 1797, but they also represent the hydra-like problems raised when a diplomat schooled in the customs of the *ancien régime* confronted a representative who followed the dictates of the revolutionary agenda. Admittedly, Napoleon may represent the extreme case with his aggressive personality. These differences may not have made peace impossible but they did make it more unlikely.

Baron Thugut, the Austrian minister of foreign affairs, found himself in a similar situation when he was forced to deal with Jean-Baptiste Bernadotte, the first French revolutionary ambassador to Austria. In Roider's words, "the arrogance, aggressiveness and bumptiousness that characterized the revolution came right to the foreign minister's doorstep."[4] In Thugut's words, Bernadotte, "plucked ... from the raw, wild, arrogant French officer corps," had neither "the necessary education [nor] the experience for his post."[5] These "deficiencies" impelled him to antagonize others. On his part, Bernadotte interpreted Thugut's refusal to "argue vigorously and forthrightly on all major points ... as a sign of weakness and dissipation."[6] In these and countless other instances the revolutionaries were attempting to construct, a "theatre of power."[7] French diplomats were very aware of how appearances and settings could be manipulated to convey a certain message. Diplomats schooled in the *ancien régime* often found themselves puzzled by the behavior of the revolutionaries stationed abroad because the revolutionaries were seeking to transform the system, to project their symbolic universe on the international order.

Nor were these differences without consequence. The issue of perception has been addressed by Fisher, a former foreign service officer, who underscored that the greater the cultural differences, the greater the "potential for misunderstanding."[8] Before negotiations even begin, different values and mannerisms and various verbal and nonverbal behaviors can weaken confidence. Culture, he found, affects negotiations in four ways: first it conditions "one's perception of reality"; second, it blocks out "information inconsistent ... with culturally grounded assumptions"; third, it enables one party to project "meaning on to the other party's words and actions"; and fourth, it can lead one individual to attribute incorrect motives to the other.[9] In the revolutionary era a member of the *ancien régime* and a French diplomat found themselves operating under different assumptions and from different frames of reference. Nowhere is this more clearly revealed than in Metternich's candid letters to his wife from Rastatt. "All their servants look like porters," he complained, "and the masters themselves are dressed in a vulgar way, dress coats and pantaloons."[10] These letters revealed his shock about the behavior of the revolutionaries, "that pack of wretches." He certainly understood that they were challenging the implicit rules which had undergirded the international system. These encounters confirmed the conviction among the allied elites that "[w]e are at war with armed opinions."[11]

The turnover in the French diplomatic corps and the loss of so many veteran diplomats of the *ancien régime* severed the ties that bound that corps to a larger international elite."[12] Those individuals, often bound by familial alliances, shared norms and values, and a code manifested in forms and gestures. The rules that guided that society can be seen in an incident that threatened to break off the negotiations at Baden in 1714. The representatives there celebrated the feast day of the king, that of Saint Louis, with Mass and a gala, sponsored by the French delegation. The deliberate absence of the Austrian delegation caused great resentment among the French. A member of the French delegation, Charles-François, comte Vintimille du Luc, confided to Villars that the Austrians had subjected themselves to ridicule and were "unable to hide their shame" and their fear that their actions would be disavowed by Vienna.[13] He thought the code of civility should override hostilities generated by the war and the resentments fostered by the negotiations. As Antoine Pecquet (d. 1762), who served as *premier commis* of foreign affairs from 1723 to 1740, explained, they were part of "a kind of independent society."[14] That common outlook transcended state boundaries and was fostered by attendance at various institutions, including the diplomatic school at Strasbourg. In the early years of the Revolution those ties could still be exploited. For example, Hugh Elliot, a classmate of Mirabeau, had been sent to Paris to stop the French from aiding Madrid during the Nootka Sound controversy in 1791.[15] Even at that time Elliot witnessed the changes in revolutionary France. He described the French scene to Pitt as "a theatre where the present is little connected to the past, and where the denouement cannot be foreseen by any stretch of human capacity ... [a] confused and unexplored Labyrinth of Political embarrassments."[16]

As the members of the French diplomatic corps resigned or were purged, new actors emerged, but few were veterans of old. There were exceptions. Barthélemy (1747–1830) had served as legation secretary at Vienna and could exploit those memories with the veteran diplomat Thugut. Louis-Guillaume Otto (1754–1817) had studied with Metternich at Strasbourg. Otto had begun his diplomatic career as the secretary to Chevalier de la Luzerne, the minister to Bavaria and subsequently to the United States. Barthélemy and Otto had moved from the so-called second *couche* of diplomacy up the revolutionary ranks. Still, most were members of a new revolutionary generation who rejected the aristocratic code; they were not *de la famille* in the words of the duc de Broglie.[17] They had shattered, according to Burke, the linguistic community of Europe and replaced the traditional vocabulary with the "gypsy jargon" of the Revolution, that "antagonistic world of madness, discord, vice, confusion, and unavailing sorrow."[18] As Blakemore has argued, "When Burke alludes to a Europe that speaks 'the same language,' he means the language of ideas rather than language per se."[19] In some cases then diplomats could not hear the other. The revolutionaries who understood the language of the *ancien régime* rejected it. To prove their revolutionary credentials to those both at home and abroad, they did so publicly. Saint-Just argued that developments rendered the war the republic waged an "inevitable war, a universal war, a cosmopolitan war." No state in Europe was governed by our principles: "The purity of those principles will not admit any pact with error, any pact with any sort of tyranny."[20] What he saw was a general degradation of Europe. Interestingly, Grenville writing later saw the struggle with revolutionary France in the same Manichaean terms as an "unexampled struggle" between good and evil. He thought the Directory could neither wish for peace nor "venture to make it." He indeed expected "that the greatest part of the next century will be as much distracted by wars of Constitution and government ... as former centuries have been by Wars of Religion, or territorial aggrandizement."[21]

We can glimpse how the British grappled with the best way to deal with the French representatives in June of 1792 when peace was still possible and nine months before the French declaration of war against Britain (February 1793). William Eden, first baron Auckland, who served as envoy to France (1786–1788), ambassador to Spain (1788–1789), and then to the United Provinces (1790–1794), discussed with Grenville what strategy should be adopted *vis à vis* the French representatives. Auckland thought Grenville, the British Foreign Secretary, was "too tolerant of the ignorance and absurdity of the French Mission" in London and hinted that Grenville should request Chauvelin's recall. Auckland confided that he did not want to allow the French representative Maulde to visit his home at The Hague. Grenville wanted, however, to avoid any "*éclat*": A quarrel with France, he thought, would only encourage the partisans of

France. "Showing pique and ill humor ... without meaning to go further, would certainly be undignified and hazardous."[22] Auckland riposted that it was in the French interest to send men whose conduct was "inoffensive." Chauvelin's "wrong-headedness" was so notorious that he could be removed without any scandal and without giving undue importance to the French doctrines. In his private and in his public life he avoided "dealing with wrong-headed men even for right purposes and [resolved] not to temporize with them under the idea that the forbearance may for the moment be unimportant."[23] This discussion occurred before neutrality slid into hostility and when peace still seemed possible.

Mutual antipathy also undermined the possibility of negotiation as did revulsion at the fate of the king and the violence of the terror. The Prussian Kutzleben thought the French "regicides and savages."[24] In Turin, John Trevor, for example, complained about the "madness of Jacobin perfidy and Insolence."[25] Perkins Magra, the consul at Tunis, called them "those scoundrel assassins."[26] George Baldwin, stationed in Alexandria, in talking about the "iniquitous crimes" of August 10, "that day of infamous memory," called them "monsters of hell."[27] This hostility made negotiations more difficult as illustrated in the Franco-Austrian talks in 1795–1796. The interactions reinforced the negative impressions on both sides. The foreign minister Thugut complained to the French about the "irregularity with which you conduct your political affairs and of the indiscreet, indecent and venal conduct of your agents," but most especially their chicanery.[28] Thugut commended Sigmund Ignaz, Freiherr von Degelmann, for his "circumspection" in his interview with the French representative Pierre Claude, marquis de Poterat. Although Poterat was "personally less ill intentioned than the others," Degelmann should be "on his guard." He must always take precautionary measures "with any agent of a government like that of France which only seeks to sow dissensions among the allies and disregards all the rules of good faith and of probity." "Such men have no scruples" and will employ "the most wicked and odious maneuvers" to achieve their ends. Guard against "the snares of black faith," but maintain a tone and appearance of confidence.[29] Thugut's perceptions, whether correct or not, prejudiced the negotiations from the onset. Nor were such suspicions exclusive to the allied coalition. On their part the French spoke of the "pride and avidity" of the Austrians. Delacroix, the minister of foreign affairs, cautioned Poterat to take care not to "prostitute the dignity of the French republic."[30] To Barthélemy, Delacroix confided: "I do not hardly know what advantage they [The Austrians] hope to gain. It appears that the cabinet of Vienna is as unacquainted with republican diplomacy as its armies are astonished with our revolutionary tactics."[31]

The public face of republican France thus projected onto the diplomatic parquet was hardly an amenable one. The British tended to see the French as "stupid, ill concern'd & insolent."[32] And that was a fairly positive assessment. Worsley in Venice, who witnessed French depredations, thought that peace could not be concluded "with the French whore."[33] He later noted that the French were moving south "in imitation of the Goths and Vandals whom they appear proud of rivaling in cruelty and injustice."[34] Not a few of the British, such as George Canning, the under secretary of state for foreign affairs 1795–1799, distrusted even the possibility of negotiations: "We have not arrived at the wild and unshackled freedom of thought, which rejects all habit, all wisdom of former times, all restraints of ancient usage … and Judges upon each subject … without reference to recognized principle or established practice."[35] Negotiations tended to reinforce Burke's earlier impression that it was necessary to put "an end to this Common Evil."[36] Burke was hardly alone. Thugut thought that the French menaced Europe "with a complete subversion."[37]

During the negotiations at Udine that would culminate in the treaty of Campo Formio, Thugut advised Maximilian Graf von Merveldt, the emperor's plenipotentiary, that he might think it "merely a trifle to invoke reason, justice and the faith of treaties," or in other words, that an invocation of principles would be wasted on such men. Still it was essential to demonstrate that we have only ever demanded "the execution of engagements undertaken between the two powers" so that any delays in the reestablishment of peace "will not be imputed to us."[38]

Still another Austrian negotiator, Cobenzl, found dealing with a purportedly drunk Bonaparte a difficult task in 1797. He complained that the French advanced new pretensions at each conference (a recurring issue) that delayed the conclusion of the negotiations. He found himself subject to "barbarous" phrases and "indecent" scenes. He forced himself, he confided, in one "disagreeable scene" to remain calm and to adopt a tone of dignity and of reserve in contrast "to the impetuosity of Bonaparte's ardor and to the iniquity of the Directory's pretensions." Although Bonaparte subsequently excused his behavior on the grounds of the "ardor of his youth" and his background in the military (which he contrasted with Cobenzl's experience and diplomatic career) and on the necessity of both parties' defending their countries' interests, it is clear that such scenes were deliberately staged to disorient and intimidate.[39]

The clash of viewpoints was particularly obvious when the two sides met, for each regarded the other as defenders of an absurd and dangerous political system. Even on seemingly trivial issues they were confrontational. The negotiations at Rastatt that lasted from November 1797 to April 1799 only underscored the gulf between the parties and deepened their mutual antipathy.[40] As one ally noted, "there can be no reliance on a Power decidedly bent on the subversion of every part of Europe." "Resistance to that Power," he concluded, "affords the only means of safety."[41] The contrast between the revolutionary diplomats and that of the other delegates could not have been more obvious. The ten plenipotentiaries of the Empire appeared in elaborately brocaded uniforms or ecclesiastical vestments.[42] In contrast the French refused to bend to traditional etiquette; they wore coats and trousers instead of the customary attire.[43] The dress was merely an opening salvo in the struggle to come.

Worse followed. Bonaparte took pains to insult the delegates: he offended the princes of the Church with citations from the Gospels, denigrated the Empire as a "metaphysical body," and flew into a rage when he saw the Swedish representative Axel Fersen, the alleged lover of Marie Antoinette. The French republic, he asserted, would not allow such men to "come and outface the ministers of the greatest people on earth. The French nation puts its self-respect even before its political interests."[44] Such scenes shocked and alienated the more traditional diplomats. In general the attitude of the French representative was "singular," "brutal," and "offensive." Cobenzl, writing home to Vienna, saw a "deliberate and studied impertinence. They affect a lack of respect, a rudeness in complete contradiction with the usages of European diplomacy." The infuriated Austrian underscored that the French "do not cease to mock the German plenipotentiaries and their attitude becomes in the same proportion more intolerable, proud and arrogant as the deputation of the Empire offers more advances and concessions."[45] Cobenzl bitterly concluded that he "would not wish my cruelest enemy to be condemned to treat with" such men "without the power to show them the baton."[46] Zinzendorf summed up the Austrian view: "The negotiations contrasted so entirely with all previous negotiations ... the violation of all principles, all usages accepted by civilized nations."[47] That remark underscores his perception that France was outside of civilized Europe.

Even when the conventions of a polite society were observed, the delegates of the Holy Roman Empire were suspicious. The 24-year-old Metternich confided to his wife that he dined with Treilhard and

Ange-Élisabeth-Louis-Antoine Bonnier d'Alco (1750–1799), who were "very polite, giving all the titles, etc." They were, he admitted, "good company." Still he was revolted: "I believe that I see a cell of the *septembriseurs* of the guillotiners in all that."[48] Such polite encounters seem to have been rare. On most occasions, Treilhard, although both courteous and polished in his social relations, deliberately ignored the restraint so characteristic of the diplomacy of the old school. "I have never seen," one diplomat wrote, "such conduct among civilized men and even less among men of affairs."[49] Unlike the more cultivated Treilhard, Bonnier generally had the manners of a boor.[50] The Duke of Brunswick categorized them as "men of blood who dictate the law at Rastatt with a revolting impudence." Their tone did not conform to diplomatic usage: it was ignoble and increasingly rude. He advised against treating with them in secret because their "hypocrisy toward the strong and their insolence towards the weak opens an immense battle and leads to all kinds of intrigues." Such negotiations can only lead to a "painful" situation.[51] Metternich, hardly an impartial observer, confided to his wife on Christmas day that their religion was limited to "good wine and good cheer." "They know no other God than their stomach and no enjoyment but that of their senses."[52] When Metternich hung a portrait of Francis I and even arranged the chairs so that a visitor when seated could not turn his back on the emperor, the French representative Debry in turn displayed a portrait of the conqueror of Italy. He opposed an idol with an idol.[53] A member of the Danish legation, Christian Ulrich Detlev von Eggers, noting their "severe and abrupt manner," conjectured that the "republicans believe it is not useful to try to give themselves an amiable air. It is perhaps also the sentiment of their irresistible power which chases from their spirit all idea of conciliation."[54] What the Austrians thought an "arbitrary bluntness," unprecedented in the diplomatic tradition, was designed "to check and to stop the operations of the congress."[55] The seeming arbitrariness of French actions led another to see "a real state of anarchy."[56] There are no means, he argued, to judge political probabilities in this unique situation. The proceedings at Rastatt were unlike any "in the annals of the world," "making political calculations even more complicated than those we have up to now."[57] The meetings of 1798 only "confirmed Thugut's perception of revolutionary France as an insatiable power with which there could be no peace."[58] Not incidentally Thugut called Bonaparte the "new Charlemagne" or the "new Tamerlane"—the latter perhaps a more accurate assessment of his viewpoint.[59] The resumption of war ended the proceedings at Rastatt.

Tragically, two of the three French deputies were killed and a third was injured on the way home.

Hostile perceptions were not limited to Rastatt. What is striking is that even though governments and personnel in France changed, the perceptions of the French revolutionaries by allied powers tended to remain the same. Frederick Augustus Hervey, 4th earl of Bristol, did not mince words: he foresaw the "downfall of that Gang of Thieves, Pickpockets, highwaymen, cut-throats and cut-purses ... the crowing Cocks."[60] His enmity may have been partially fueled by his imprisonment by the French for espionage for 18 months in 1798, the year before. In allied eyes French violations of traditional norms of conduct were intended to intimidate. In 1803, Whitworth viewed Talleyrand with suspicion and assumed that his tone was "nothing more than a trick, in the hope of intimidating me." He looked at the exchange as a "trial" in which "honesty and plain dealing [triumphed over] duplicity and low cunning."[61] He was even more appalled at the behavior of Napoleon, who treated José Maria de Souza Botelho, the Portuguese representative, "with the utmost indignity, and more than once gave him almost reason to fear that he would not confine himself to words." Charles Whitworth found it painful to report "such indecencies" when Napoleon was "so violent as to exceed all bounds."[62]

Certainly perceptions differed radically as can be seen in the descriptions of a reception held by the Directory which admittedly had taken a more conciliatory stance. In 1796 Peter Ochs, who called on the French to overthrow the Swiss government, reported favorably on his reception. He was struck by the brilliance and the dignity of the ceremony: the grand staircase, the sumptuousness of the armchairs, the marbled salon, the large table covered with rich green cloth. It was gay, friendly, and fraternal. Moreover, it was a "TYPE OF DIPLOMACY TOTALLY NEW WHICH WAS WORTH AS MUCH AS THE OLD DIPLOMACY" [his capitalization].[63] Another Swiss patriot, Frédéric-César de La Harpe, who had gone to Paris to solicit French aid to secure the rights of the French-speaking Vaudois, agreed. He wrote to his closest friend in November 1796 that the French minister was "in grand costume ... a very pleasing physiognomy and a very affable exterior. Nothing was more polite," but he concluded that "Oh, everything has changed."[64]

We have another witness, Sandoz-Rollin, the Prussian minster in Paris, who cast a more critical eye on developments in France. His unciphered report, again in 1796, underscored the compliments of usage, the presence of four ushers dressed like ancient heralds of arms and of six ministers clad in black velour with red-fire satin. This superficial assessment may have been written knowing that it would be intercepted. The portion of the same report in cipher is more critical. "Nothing," he notes, "was more ill-ordered … no order, no decency, no etiquette." "Delacroix did not know when or to whom to present him." Sandoz-Rollin was not told when to speak. He found some of the proceedings "astonishing" and others "embarrassing." There was, however, "more decency and more propriety" in the antechamber of the audience room,[65] where, he noted, the force and impetuosity of Reubell and the superior amiability and understanding of Carnot, whose "demeanour revealed nothing of the jacobinism which one knows is in his soul." Four months later he did not know "any foreign envoy who does not complain about the variability of thinking and of acting of those employed as ministers and who does not complain especially about the harshness of forms … in the smallest affairs."[66] He concluded that France "has no system" to guide its negotiations and its relations with the European powers.[67] This assessment was echoed by Paolo Guerini, the secretary and brother of the Venetian minister. He was recalled after his letter which discussed "the anarchy and confusion" of the French government in disrespectful terms was intercepted by the French.[68]

The gulf between France and the more traditional diplomatic corps could not but be widened by the injunctions of the French government. "Make no mistake," Fouché instructed, "to be genuinely republican, every citizen must experience and effect within himself a revolution equal to that which has changed the face of France. There is nothing, absolutely nothing, in common between the slave of a tyrant and the inhabitant of a free State; the manners and customs of the latter, his principles, his sentiments, his actions, must be of an entirely new kind.… The republic has no use for any but free men; it has made up its minds to exterminate all the others."[69] A few of those sent abroad found themselves unequal to that task but others embraced the cause of revolutionary republicanism and sought to export the revolution abroad, or, as the British saw it, "disseminate the poison."[70] An experienced diplomat and, later in his life, a member of the *Institut*, André François Miot de Melito (1762–1841) found himself caught in the crossfires of revolutionary expectations and the dictates of diplomacy. After his appointment as minister plenipotentiary to the Grand Duke of Tuscany in February 1795, Miot noted that he was careful not to violate the established rules of etiquette and intended to "conform to all the customs of the country." His arrival in Florence caused "a sensation and excited malevolent curiosity"; people "expected to see a sort of savage, clothed in an extraordinary manner, using the coarsest language, having no idea of the rules of society, and ready ostentatiously to violate them." He strove to counter these expectations: "My habits, my mode of life, the deference to the customs of the country I—was scrupulous to show, and the care with which I respected even its prejudices soon dispelled these first impressions." Perhaps this difference between expectation and reality accounted for the favorable reception he received.[71] Miot followed the same policy at Turin. He "conformed at once to the customs of the country and of the Court ... [and] carefully avoided any affectation of republican austerity in my manners or mode of life." Moreover, he demonstrated his intention to respect treaties and refused to countenance agitators. Miot was in an unenviable position, for he "could not know the real intentions of the Executive Directory, divided, as it was, into two factions, nor could [he] guess which of those factions would triumph."[72] Moreover, he found himself trying to counter secret machinations directed from Paris and the reports of a secret agent, who was trying to undermine him.[73] His fears that he would be regarded at home as a "lukewarm republican" were not ill-founded and he was ultimately dismissed.[74] He had become, in his words, "a stranger to our diplomacy."[75] Although the revolutionary government appointed some men of "real merit and incorruptible honesty," he found that they all shared the government's "dogmatic and proselytizing spirit."[76]

Miot de Melito has left an account of his encounter with two of his colleagues in 1798 in the wake of the shift to the left after the coup of fructidor. In this encounter the actions of French revolutionary diplomats are seen through the eyes of an experienced and at least initially sympathetic Frenchman. These voices from a distant and now muffled past permit a glimpse of one diplomat in particular as he attempted to reshape his world and as he manipulated the symbols so important to the revolutionary faith. In his retrospective remembrance, Miot, then 36 years old, recalled his surprise at his countrymen's "language" and intentions. Both the *littérateur* Pierre Louis Ginguené (1748–1816), who arrived at Turin on 23 March 1798, and the historian and writer Dominique Joseph Garat (1749–1833), who was sent to Naples, were well-educated mature men, aged 50 and 49 respectively.[77] Miot noted that they were "very clever men," but were, nonetheless, "quite in the clouds." "As they had never had any experience of the difficulties which the habits and prejudices of peoples opposed to innovators, they seemed unaware that only time wears out errors ... and that to attack prejudices in the front is to give them new strength. But such were the means which these gentlemen proposed to employ." They also entertained very "strange ideas" about the functions of a diplomat. Thinking of themselves as "preceptors of kings," not as representatives, they were determined "to respect neither public nor private manners or custom, to conform to no usages, and above all, to withstand the etiquette of courts." They would be "as inflexible in outward forms as in principles." Miot quickly saw that they "brought [a certain] philosophical intolerance" to their tasks, whereas they "perceived that I could not attain to their height ... [and] pitied my simplicity and the timid course I had observed."[78]

Miot soon had a practical demonstration of their commitment. Ginguené's wife refused to wear the "ridiculous" dress of the Turin court and decided instead to appear in a white gown, white bonnet, and white cotton stockings to underscore Ginguené's republicanism and to defy the sartorial codes of the *ancien régime*. Ginguené, Miot tells us, "was delighted with and proud of his triumph." Miot, an experienced ambassador, had decided, on the contrary, that his wife would follow the customs of the country. He told Ginguené that he would never challenge "established usage, especially in such trifles as the shape of a gown, or a head-dress."[79] Against Miot's advice, Ginguené had also delivered a speech to the ruler at his first private audience. This interview foreshadowed the difficulties to come. Ginguené did not attempt to conceal his enmity toward the court. His arrogance, his violent and threatening language, and his "singular disregard of diplomatic customs" hardly endeared him to the court. The Sardinian government was so offended by the "tone of his communication" that they tried to bypass him and conduct the negotiations in Paris.[80] When the French occupied Turin, an allied capital during a time of peace, hostile crowds gathered. Ginguené insisted that the Sardinians end the demonstrations, requested the dismissal of a number of officials, and asked the archbishop to write a letter advising his flock to "live on good terms with the French." An exasperated Miot wondered: "How was it that a man of good sense did not see the absurdity of such a proceeding?" Miot noted that the Directory "would have preferred more suavity and dissimulation on the part of Ginguené" and gradually lost confidence in him.[81] He was recalled in less than seven months.

Garat fared little better and requested his own recall from Naples. He lasted little more than a month (7 May–28 June 1798). The court at

Naples and the queen, Marie Antoinette's sister, in particular regarded this notorious regicide with contempt. Garat had notified Louis XVI of his death sentence and later supervised his execution. Nicknamed Garat September for his justification of the September Massacres, he symbolized for many the worst excesses of the revolution. The Directory's ineptitude and insensitivity in sending him to that court did not preclude further errors—this time on his part. Garat, Talleyrand later complained, had become the laughingstock of Europe.[82] The disregard of diplomatic conventions, which seemed so "singular" to Miot, will strike anyone who has read the diplomatic history of the Revolution as indicative of a general pattern of behavior that was repeated in countless courts where revolutionary diplomats were stationed. Nor should these actions be attributed to ignorance, dim-wittedness, or truculence.

The career of a number of diplomats reflects how the dictates of revolutionary ideology molded both the private and the public face of republican France. Like all crusaders, they were not content to stay at home. These French representatives and many others proselytized for the revolutionary creed; they carried what Pitt deemed "opinions in arms."[83] Burke condemned these ministers as "emissaries of sedition," who come under the guise of ambassadors.[84] "There is no doubt," Burke warned, "that they will do as much mischief as they can…. Their houses will become places of rendezvous here, as everywhere else, and center of cabal for whatever is mischievous and malignant."[85] The Swiss journalist and moralist Jacques Mallet du Pan (1749–1800) voiced the suspicion of many that the Republic intended "to disseminate in Europe, in all the countries where the unfortunate ones had relations with France" Jacobins who, under "the cover of public character or envoys or consuls, made their residence a club and a center of conspiracy."[86] French representatives did little to assuage their fears that the French were intent on suborning their governments.

Not surprisingly, some governments refused to receive French representatives. In August 1792 the government of Liège refused to receive a minister plenipotentiary from France because of an irregularity in his *lettres de créance* or in the French view "*sous le pretexte d'une faute de forme.*"[87] Victor Amadeus III of Savoy declined to recognize the newly appointed *chargé d'affaires*, Charles Louis Huguet, marquis de Sémonville, who had a reputation as a dangerous agitator, and had him expelled from the territory.[88] Turin objected that they had not received any prior notification of the appointment of Sémonville as had "always been the usage."

He had neither requested passports as was usual nor announced his appointment.[89] Dumouriez saw this ploy as a "futile pretext" and asked if the people's interest should be subordinated to the "frivolous etiquette of the court." He called their refusal a "scandal," "an outrage," and a "violation of the *droit des gens.*" One cannot, he inveighed, "offend with impunity a free and just people." He demanded that a passport be issued to Sémonville and asked for a prompt and categorical response within 24 hours. When satisfaction for this insult was not forthcoming, he seized the pretext to occupy Savoy.[90]

For similar reasons, the Sublime Porte would not receive him. Lebrun's suspicions that the Porte's refusal could be blamed on the intrigues of various diplomats were not entirely unfounded.[91] The envoys of Austria, Prussia, and Naples had sent letters to discredit Sémonville.[92] In his note the Prussian envoy dubbed Sémonville a Jacobin, a member of that "vile sect composed of frightful fanatics dominated by democratic rage."[93] The Russian chargé argued that Sémonville, the advocate of a "false and dangerous system" … "will not be agreeable to his imperial majesty." Moreover, Sémonville had been rejected by several courts. It would be "a real mark of good intentions" to refuse to accept him.[94] The grand vizir found "reasons to fear that the conduct of the aforesaid Sémonville, given the cast of his character, would not be more fitting."[95] The assessment of Sémonville as "very dangerous" was widely shared. Christian Moritz, Freiherr von Kutzleben, who heard the rumor that Sémonville was going to be sent to London, voiced his concern to Grenville. Nor did Kutzleben want Morque, "a most violent democrat and a Jacobin," who hoped to "bring about a revolution here similar to that in France." Morque had also been unwise enough to reveal that he carried a knife and would not hesitate to use it on French aristocrats, even his own family.[96] Another option often employed was to delay the reception. Verninac, named envoy extraordinary to the Turks in 1795, was not received until 26 April 1796. His tenure was fairly short since his last audience was held on 22 October 1796.[97]

Such refusals or delays were understandable. France's representatives carried the new ideology abroad; their envoys distributed seditious propaganda, mobilized malcontents, meddled in local affairs, or engaged in what one disgruntled diplomatic official termed "contemptuous intrigues."[98] Others offended religious sensibilities by blaspheming or insulting the cross.[99] Their actions ranged from the innocuous to the seditious. In London in the spring of 1792, Miles objected to "the almost unpardonable imprudence" of Chauvelin, who had entertained the editors of opposition newspapers and dined at their homes. He went on to belabor "the departure from long-established usages and a palpable deviation from that dignified conduct which ought always to characterise the diplomacy of all nations." He thought it improper for Chauvelin to "mix familiarly with those who wished to subvert" the government. He concluded that since Chauvelin was invested "with a public character, the conduct which he had pursued was an affront to this Government."[100]

Jean Louis Girard Soulavie's initial behavior turned many of the Swiss against him. A letter to Deforgues of 7 July 1793 reveals his attitude: "I found this country [Lausanne] ... infested with *émigrés* and refractory priests.... We have proudly carried the tri-color cockade and maintained ... this tone of assurance and superiority which belongs to the French people."[101] That tone alienated many. The behavior of Soulavie, a historian, naturalist, notorious Jacobin, and *sans-culotte* and, not incidentally, a former priest and supporter of Robespierre, did not reassure the uneasy. Berne saw him as a dangerous man and warned the police to keep him under surveillance. The French foreign minister even rebuked Soulavie for the tone of superiority he had adopted. "It was a great error," Deforgues told him, "to think that this tone ever belongs to any people."[102] Soulavie even complained that at his reception the Genevans had offered him an armchair with cushions—a comfort contrary to equality.[103] One of the syndics of Geneva, complaining about "Le terrible Soulavie," asked, "How the great, the loyal French nation could entrust a position to a man who provokes its neighbors and allies?"[104] Interminable quarrels led, in the words of a French commentator, to a "personal war" between Soulavie, the French resident from 1793 to 1794, and the Genevan authorities.[105] Geneva officially protested in October 1793. His notes, they contended, were "absurd, insidious or offensive." His repeated demands for ammunition, wagons, and cannons and his refusal to countersign passports delivered by the government led the Genevan authorities to complain that he was treating them as enemies.[106] A secret agent sent by the Committee of Public Safety, Payan urged his recall, noting that Soulavie was "odious and contemptible."[107] Barthélemy, the French representative at Solothurn, complained that Soulavie had acted shamefully; he "has dishonored the republic."[108] He had certainly been promoting the French annexation of Geneva. In response to these complaints and in the wake of Thermidor, the Committee of Public Safety recalled him in September 1794. Soulavie had generated such animosity that he could hardly be called "a minister of peace," the misnomer commonly used, without ironic intent, by the revolutionaries.

Nor was he the exception. As late as 1798, the Austrians complained about the "secret maneuvers" of the French ambassador Bernadotte, who ordered his staff to don Phrygian caps and who encouraged dissident Poles to revolt against both Austria and Russia.[109]

The presence of these men posed a particular problem for the host governments. There were few physical attacks on French representatives with the significant exception of Baville, Bernadotte, and those sent to Rastatt, but there was often a marked antagonism. Many spoke of the danger from France as an "epidemic, a pestilence, a contagion."[110] In August 1791 and in the wake of the abortive flight of the royal family to Varennes and their virtual imprisonment, official representatives of France were isolated or coldly received, or even injured: Noailles at Vienna, Ségur at Berlin, Sémonville at Turin, Cacault at Naples, Bernard at Rome, Bourgoing at Madrid, Bigot de Saint-Croix at Trier, Villars at Mainz. Those same courts welcomed the secret agents of the king and the emissaries of the princes.[111] Barthélemy, sent in 1791, was not warmly received in Solothurn, where the news of the constitutional monarchy was not welcomed. Barthélemy was unable to occupy a building, belonging to the state, which the French had historically rented. He had to seek new quarters and was finally forced to turn to an inn. The king on news of the "indecent reception" ordered Barthélémy to leave Solothurn and move to another canton.[112]

Mackau, *chargé* in Naples from August 1792 to September 1793, was treated as a leper.[113] He had presented his credentials, clad in very large tricolor plumes. Given the queen's affection for her sister Marie Antoinette, it is not surprising that the government received him very coolly and the other foreign representatives refused to acknowledge this "violent democrat" formally or to visit him publicly.[114] Although he was driven by a spirit of proselytism, Mackau was certainly insecure and increasingly reluctant to act without specific authorization. His presentation had been delayed and he suspected his files burgled. His position could hardly have been improved by the French decision to stage a show of force by sending 14 warships to the Naples harbor.[115] The revolution of 10 August 1792 made his position insupportable. The queen scorned this intruder, the courtiers mocked him, and the court demanded his recall. His papers were stolen and he was invited to leave the realm within eight days.[116] Baptiste-Dorothée Villars at Mainz would have sympathized. On 4 June 1792, Villars complained about "his nullity" and the hostile measures and "perfidious courtesies" of the elector. The elector's soul, he contended, was "gangrened" by aristocracy.[117] In 1796, Miot de Melito, hardly the most radical of the revolutionaries, found the same hostile atmosphere in Rome; the people's minds filled with a "gloomy fanaticism," the populace "exclusively absorbed in religious practices," and "men's imaginations excited." Miot thought that "there would be no safety either for my countrymen or myself if the terror inspired by our victories and the near neighborhood of our armies were dispelled for even a single day, or if the fortune of war ceased for one instant to be favourable to us." A chilling premonition of the fate of Bassville.[118]

The French representative in Munich from September 1798 to March 1799, the able and charming Charles Jean Marie Alquier (1752–1826), was isolated and shunned.[119] When he was stationed at another post from 1801 to 1806, Marie Caroline, queen of Naples and of Sicily, and the sister of Marie Antoinette, noted that although he complained constantly about his isolation, he had not entertained and not had met anyone. Alquier was, she noted, an angry and dangerous man, "neither amiable, [nor] young, nor sociable." Moreover, he behaved like "an *enragé*."[120] Nor did he improve on further acquaintance. She continued to see him as a consummate villain, an accomplished liar, a foolish man, and an opportunistic agitator, who sought to assure his future by any means. She certainly wished for his recall but feared that in his stead the French would send a swashbuckler who would bring about their ruin.[121]

An equally talented Edmond-Charles Genet (1763–1834) found himself in a similar situation much earlier when he was sent to Russia. Genet had been raised in the traditions of the foreign office; he succeeded his father at the age of 18 as head of the translation bureau. He spoke Latin, Greek, Italian, Swedish, German, and English. He had served at embassies in Berlin and Vienna before the French sent him to St. Petersburg as *chargé d'affaires* in 1789. Catherine's initial favor soon changed to outright hostility. Genet alienated the Russian court by his tactless advocacy of revolution, what Dumouriez had praised as "proofs of [his] zeal and exactitude."[122] After the abortive flight of the king to Varennes in 1791, the Russian government ordered Genet not to appear at the court and placed him under surveillance. He soon discovered that the Russian police were dogging his footsteps, his secretaries ignored, his notes refused. Finally, in 1792, he was denounced as a "fool" and as a "Jacobin fanatic" and given eight days to leave.[123] Genet, whom Catherine of Russia dubbed that "demagogue *enragé*,"[124] was subsequently dispatched to the United States.

Genet certainly had higher hopes of success in another republic. In the instructions to Genet, Lebrun underscored the necessity of rendering "nugatory in the United States those scandalous insinuations so clandestinely spread through Europe by the enemies of the republic." Genet, who was "to adhere to the forms established for official communications," was not to "take any step, or make any overture which can give umbrage to the Americans in regard to the constitution which they have chosen and which differs in many points from the principles established in France." Lebrun warned him that George III's representatives and the *émigrés* would be watching him and would place "the most malicious construction" on his actions. Only "an open and patriotic conduct" could "put him beyond the reach of calumny and misconstruction." In closing, Lebrun claimed that the French government relied upon his "prudence and known moderation." There was a disjunction between these instructions and the attachments which were to follow, namely, blank letters of marque and officers' commissions.[125] The French were correct that the British representative was instructed to undermine Genet in the United States and intercept his correspondence.[126] As it turned out, Genet actually undermined himself. His official conduct, as the British representative Hammond noted, "furnishes additional irrefragable evidence … that in every country … in which the agents of the present-ruling party of France are permitted to reside, they invariably endeavor to foment discontents."[127]

When Genet arrived, he was welcomed by a significant number of Francophiles, including Jefferson, and he certainly began his mission with a great deal of enthusiasm. At a formal dinner in Philadelphia, Genet decorated his table with liberty trees. The guests took turns donning a Phyrgian liberty cap. Genet sang the *Marseillaise*. Everyone then joined in republican songs. Since the repertoire of republican songs was at that time limited and those who knew them even more so, Genet devised the expedient of replacing certain phrases with more republican ones in well-known songs. In one of these *contrafactum*, "God save the king" was replaced with "God save the rights of man." It is not recorded how he dealt with the extra syllables. These songs reflected the revolutionaries' belief that "a new consciousness would be catalyzed by the people's hearing music with a strong beat, based on popular tunes and simple enough so that the whole community could be swept up."[128] The toasts included "liberty to all the human race." To lend solemnity to the occasion, an artillery battery fired three rounds after each toast to the republic.[129] Indeed, toasts followed by the firing of cannon played an important part in the *fêtes* Genet attended.

Those evenings may make us smile, but Jefferson was not amused when Genet launched flagrant attacks on US neutrality: he equipped French privateers in US ports, dubbed appropriately *Républicain, Anti-George, Sans-Culotte, la Carmagnole, le Vainquer de la Bastille, Industrie*, and best of all—*Citizen Genet*—to capture British ships; issued French military commissions to American citizens; captured vessels within the jurisdiction of the United States; and tried to use American freebooters to invade Spanish Florida. When Jefferson pointed out that the arming of vessels violated the US policy of neutrality, Genet argued that "[l]et us explain ourselves as republicans. Let us not lower ourselves to the level of ancient politics by diplomatic subtleties."[130] Such conduct prompted John Quincy Adams to remark with some asperity that Genet had "publicly damned ... all the known rules and customs established in the intercourse of nations."[131] Even Jefferson finally had to concede that "[n]ever in my opinion was so calamitous an appointment made."[132] Jefferson has left us a rather amusing account of one of his encounters with Genet, noting that Genet "took up the subject instantly in a very high tone and went into an immense field of declamation and complaint ... the few efforts I made to take some part in the conversation were quite ineffectual."[133]

Predictably, Hammond, the British representative to the United States, objected to the secretary of state about Genet's rearming of two corsairs in Charleston with French commissions, his purchase of arms for France in New York, and the seizure of three English ships in Charleston and Philadelphia as violations of US neutrality.[134] Hammond noted that Genet had soon made himself an object of "public notoriety" and that at the very beginning of his mission he was "involved in a most serious misunderstanding with this government." Genet, he thought, had "created a distrust which can never be surmounted" by treating "with the most marked and wanton disrespect the members of the government" and by couching his notes to the government "in language the most offensive and intemperate."[135] Hammond found Genet's performance "singular" and his behavior "arrogant and contemptuous." Genet treated "with the most marked and wanton disrespect" anyone "distinguished either by their station or fortune," assumed a tone of "authority" in his communications with the government, and supported a club affiliated with the Jacobins in Paris.[136]

Genet, who treated the US government's remonstrances about the privateers with "contemptuous disregard," even commissioned another which he christened *Le Petit democrat*. He defied the executive authority and, according to Hammond, intended to "overawe" if not to "subvert" the government. Genet's "exceptionable" conduct provided "inescapable evidence" to Hammond that the French agents in every country, even in one as democratic as the United States, would invariably try to "foment discontent and to promote disunion between the people and the government."[137] When the United States told Genet to grant no new commissions, the arrogant Genet "treated its remonstrances with contemptuous disregard" and openly defied the executive authority.[138] Nor did Hammond lose the opportunity to underscore to the United States "the unparalleled insolence and presumption" of the French agents.[139] When Genet tried to bypass the secretary of state and sent a note to the president, Washington told Jefferson to inform him about the current usage and to note that it was beneath his "dignity" and his "character" to refute the declaration.[140] Genet then raised the stakes and published his correspondence with the US government, his instructions from France, and various memorials.[141] He even threatened the executive with an appeal to the people.[142]

Many Americans did not appreciate such tactics. John Quincy Adams sarcastically lauded Genet as "the original inventor of the science of typographical negotiation." "The glory of this discovery," he observed, "was reserved for Genet alone."[143] Still Genet persisted in Jefferson's words in throwing "down the gauntlet to the president."[144] And he continued to defend his conduct. Genet sent a long diatribe to Jefferson about his treatment.[145] In a public letter to Jefferson, he argued that "the politics of regenerated France" dictated that "the only art of her public agents [would be] that of having none."[146] And that did seem to be the case. Madison thought that Genet had acted like "a madman."[147] Even the French consul Hauterive found Genet's "accusations and denunciations … hostile acts."[148] The 39-year-old Hauterive, older and certainly more circumspect than the 30-year-old Genet, thought the conquest of Florida "a chimera."[149] The French consul foresaw Genet's fall. Genet, he thought, was "unwise enough to go down into the arena in person; the wild beasts will devour him." Hauterive himself thought Americans cold. Somewhat disillusioned, Hauterive thought that "[i]f God wants Liberty to win all the peoples of the earth, He has sown the first seeds on very damp ground."[150] Jefferson feared "an open rupture … between the French minister and us." Genet was, he deplored, "so evidently in the wrong."[151] In spite of his pro-French inclinations, Jefferson had to conclude that Genet's appointment was "calamitous." "Finding at length that the man was absolutely incorrigible," he observed, "I saw the necessity of quitting a wreck which could not but sink all who should cling to it."[152] Washington could only conclude that Genet was "entirely unfit for the mission on which he is employed."[153] Jefferson could not but acknowledge the failure of Genet, whom he dubbed "the missionary of a foreign nation."[154]

The frustration of the US government led to Genet's recall less than three months after his arrival in Philadelphia.[155] His short tenure justified Hamilton's labeling Genet "that burned-out comet."[156] With his fall, so went his plans. Hauterive noted that "[a]ll the scaffolding of an elaborate project has collapsed like a house of cards; Canada, St. Pierre, Newfoundland, Acadia, have gone up in smoke."[157] Perhaps symbolic of the mission as a whole, the privateer *le Citoyen Genet* was ordered to leave Philadelphia but was in such poor condition that she could not return to sea, and was allowed to enter the port only on condition that she be dismantled.[158] The *Sans-culotte* was captured by the British.

Back in Paris, the French republic quickly disavowed the "punishable conduct" of Genet. "Far from having authorized these procedures and criminal maneuvers," the French insisted that they had sought to maintain "the most perfect harmony" between the two countries.[159] In a report to the National Convention Robespierre attacked Genet on the grounds that he had put forth propositions contrary to the interests of both states.[160] "By a bizarre fatality the republic finds itself still represented" by the agent "of traitors," the disavowed Girondins. The indictment continued with the ultimate condemnation: "Genet has faithfully represented the views and instructions of the factions that chose him."[161] Genet's conduct did not go uncriticized by other French representatives, who admittedly may have been currying favor with the Jacobins. His successor, a man of less energy and less talent, as even Hammond admitted, undertook to "efface the unfavorable impression which Mr. Genet's extravagant and intemperate conduct has created."[162] Pierre Auguste Adet, minister to the United States from 1795 to 1797, complained to the Committee of Public Safety that the noisy processions and scandalous feasts sponsored by the French had not endeared them to the citizenry. In that light he decided not to celebrate 10 August, in order not to give a weapon to the English party, who would exploit it to render France "odious."[163] Other French envoys echoed that refrain. François Noël, the representative to another republic, Venice, remarked that Genet "went to a country well disposed, he has revolted the spirits and has lost us a neutrality, which was almost equivalent to an alliance."[164] Although the British representative Hammond deplored the conduct of Genet, he pointed out that "however intemperate, reprehensible and unwarranted his conduct may have been, he has not especially exceeded the spirit of his instructions."[165] Set within the larger context of the French Revolution and of France's view of international relations, Genet's debacle in the United States is more explicable.

The Committee of Public Safety sent a four-man commission to the United States to draft a report and arrest Genet: Jean Antoine, later Baron Fauchet, minister plenipotentiary; Le Blanc, secretary of the legation; La Foret, consul general; and Petry, a consul. In their first dispatch they noted that Genet had acted "very imprudently in provoking the resentment of the American government." The commission itself was soon split by the intrigues of those who wished to make use of the French influence to change the government and the constitution. The Jacobin Fauchet, a young lawyer of 33 and a friend of Robespierre, spoke no English. Fauchet and the legation secretary Le Blanc began a separate correspondence in which they complained that the American government was "sold to England," Genet was "unjustly persecuted," and their colleagues were "royalists and counter-revolutionaries." According to a report later drafted by Otto, a man who had served in the United States as *chargé*, they leveled "absurd reproaches" against Washington and "most absurd" calumnies about the American government.[166] Despite the divisions, Genet, a member of a discredited faction, would have been apprehended and executed in Paris had it not been for the intervention of Washington, who offered him asylum. Nor did Genet's recall end the problems. The French commission also found that Genet's accounts were in such disorder that it would be a "long and painful" exercise to try to balance them.[167] There had been prior indication of financial irregularities. The French consul complained that he was always short of money, while Genet spent "with the ease, prodigality and lack of consideration of kings"—certainly a damning indictment.[168] The repercussions of Genet's mission continued. In 1796 the Directory was approached by individuals recruited for the invasion of Florida who were seeking compensation.[169]

Louis-Guillaume Otto of the foreign office wrote a retrospective analysis of Franco-US relations that indicted French policy. He brought to that report a great deal of experience; Otto had served as secretary to the ambassador and then to the French embassy in the United States (1779–1784), as *chargé* (1785 and 1789–1791), and then as chief of the foreign ministry's premier bureau from 1792. After the fall of the Girondins, he had been dismissed. Only the delay of his arrest allowed him to escape execution during the Terror. In his report Otto deplored Genet's "astonishing" conduct. His actions, draping the tricolor in public places and arming corsairs, were soon eclipsed by his conduct in the two Carolinas, Virginia, and Maryland. Genet did not hesitate to remark on the "strange and tyrannical" nature of the US government. Anything that did not resemble the National Convention seemed to Genet despotic and contrary to the public good. He "conceived the absurd idea that the government was in opposition to the people" and that in order to ensure the triumph of the French cause, he should trigger a revolution by appealing the US government's decisions to the people. Moreover, his tone with the government was arrogant, contemptuous, reproachful, and insulting. When Jefferson demanded his recall, the French government could not refuse "so just" a demand. The French government, he concluded, "constantly betrayed the Americans."[170] This assessment was echoed by Victor Du Pont, French consul in Charleston, when his father asked him about the *"refroidissement"* of relations between the United States and France. Victor noted that the revolutionary government but especially the minister and consuls were sans-culottes and most of them were "without faith, without honor, without a sense of shame, without integrity." Moreover, the popular societies who wish to "govern in America as in France and who preach the equality of Robespierre" have also damaged relations.[171]

There were similar difficulties with another republic, that of Genoa. In 1791, Sémonville printed inflammatory pamphlets on a secret press and mobilized malcontents.[172] From Genoa he launched a series of propaganda attacks against Victor Amadeus, king of Sardinia. Those actions set the stage that his successor, Jean Tilly, the *chargé d'affaires* (May 1793–October 1794), followed. France had assured Genoa that Tilly had been instructed to cultivate good relations between the two republics, to conform to the law and regulations of that state, and to respect its neutrality. Despite these assurances, the officials there found his sentiments "extreme and menacing." He scorned the members of the government, acted disrespectfully toward Genoese officials, and used offensive expressions in his notes and letters. Even worse, he published manifestos designed to incite citizens to revolt and sponsored clandestine assemblies. In a short time, he had made himself "odious to the nation."[173] The Genoese government accused Tilly of issuing letters of marque to exiled brigands and of commissioning corsairs. On his part, Tilly demanded the arrest of a number of individuals who had sought asylum there. The Genoese, with no proof of their guilt, refused. They demanded his recall on the grounds that he was disturbing the public peace and encouraging malcontents.[174]

The Committee of Public Safety disavowed Tilly, whom Saint Just dubbed "a coward and a knave," condemned the irregularity of his conduct, and annulled the patents he had issued.[175] Tilly's protestations were ineffectual; he was denounced, possibly by Napoleon, recalled, and arrested by the Thermidoreans. His recall did not settle the disputes between the two republics. Nor was the tenure of his successor, Dorothée Villars, who arrived in October of 1794 and remained until March 1796, successful.[176] It was but a short step to Genoa's conquest, the establishment of the Ligurian Republic under Napoleon in 1797, and its eventual amalgamation into the French Empire in 1805.

Other representatives became involved in various schemes to promote international republicanism and to undermine the governments to which they were accredited. Michel-Ange-Bernard de Mangourit, a former noble, became a roving representative as he was shuttled from one post to another because of his notable failures in all. Mangourit, a committed republican, had been sent in 1792 as consul to Charlestown, where he became entangled in Genet's dubious schemes and was recalled after two years. As first secretary of the embassy in Spain, his intrigues angered Charles IV and he was again recalled. In the futile hope that his earlier mission would have been forgotten (and forgiven) he was appointed *chargé* to the United States, who refused to receive him. Still the revolutionary government had not lost faith in this energetic, but maladroit representative. This time he was sent to the Valais, where he followed his usual pattern of threats and conspiracies. After numerous complaints, he was recalled yet again in 1798, and sent to Naples and Ancona.[177]

Nor was this an isolated case of a representative fomenting conspiracy. Nicolas Michel Jolivet, *chargé* (May 1791–July 1792) in Liège, and Félix Desportes, minister plenipotentiary (June 1792–December 1792) in Zweibrücken, attempted to undermine the regimes to which they were accredited,[178] as did the secretary to the French legation in Brussels, François Deshacquets. His dismissal in April 1792 was engineered so that he could continue his activities underground.[179] In Rome, General Léonard Duphot, a man devoted to the Revolution and, according to Napoleon, "a general of the most promising talents," was serving as an aide to Joseph Bonaparte, the French representative in Rome.[180] He had been ordered to provoke an insurrection and succeeded only too well. He was caught up in the throng. Whether he urged the rioters onward or whether he had only been innocently swept along is still a matter of debate. What is certain is that he was killed in the *mêlée* between the soldiers and the crowd in December 1797.[181]

Many regarded these men as permanent conspirators against the European social order.[182] Others regarded them in a still more sinister light. In the view of William Wyndham, a member of the British Parliament, "Satan is surely got loose and there is rebellion again in Heaven!"[183] These "nobodies," as Burke called them, represented the revolutionary creed of the 1790s.[184] Their very presence and their articulation of an alternate world view challenged the old order. They were not content, however, simply to let the old order collapse on its own, as it inevitably would in their view. Instead, they expedited its collapse by fomenting sedition. Burke and others condemned the French revolutionary ministers, who came under the guise of ambassadors.[185] These "spies and incendiaries," these "active emissaries of democracy,"[186] and the French revolutionaries as a whole had, in Burke's view, brought about a "violent breach of the community of Europe."[187] Bourbon France had been bound by those bonds, but revolutionary France had broken them and cast them aside. "The changes made by that Revolution," according to this outspoken critic, "were not the better to accommodate her to the old and usual relations, but to produce new ones."[188] Pitt echoed these sentiments in his address to the House of Commons in February 1793, when he argued that the French "mean to carry their principles into every nation, without exception, subvert and destroy every government, and to plant on their ruins their sacred tree of liberty."[189] Both Burke and Pitt realized that the French upheaval posed an unprecedented challenge to the stability of the *ancien régime* and meant nothing less than the subversion of the international order. Nor were they alone. A contemporary historian at the University of Göttingen, Heeren, wrote that while he was "elaborating the history of the European states-system, he himself saw it overthrown in its most essential parts. Its history was in fact written upon its ruins."[190] For him it was the "final catastrophe."[191] Opposite the title page he quoted Schiller with telling effect: "The bond of the nations was broken, and the ancient edifice overthrown." Ironically, even the notorious regicide and terrorist Fouché would ask in 1815, "Are there no more bonds among peoples?"[192] The Austrian foreign minister, Baron Thugut, would later reach much the same conclusion. If "prompt remedies" were not immediately adopted, a "deplorable catastrophe would indubitably envelop all thrones." The actions and plans of this "arrogant republic" meant that there was not an instant to lose. If the various European powers did not conclude "a sincere accord ... for the conservation of their respective governments," all Europe would perish.[193]

Notes

1. Ralph R. Menning, *The Art of the Possible: Documents on Great Power Diplomacy, 1814–1914* (New York: McGraw Hill, 1996), xix.
2. Roider, *Baron Thugut and Austria's Response to the French Revolution*, 258 quotes Bonaparte to Talleyrand, 28 September 1797.
3. Ibid., 258 quotes L. Cobenzl to Thugut, 14 October 1797.
4. Ibid., 266.
5. Ibid., 277, Thugut to Reuss, Starhemberg, and Dietrichstein, 15 April 1798.
6. Ibid., 276.
7. Cohen used the term "theater" as a metaphor "for the repertoire of visual and symbolic tools used by statesmen and diplomats when they communicate on international issues." Cohen, *Theatre of Power*, i.
8. Quoted in Cohen, *Negotiating Across Cultures*, 14.
9. Fisher quoted in ibid.
10. Metternich, *Memoirs of Prince Metternich*, 1: 349, 3 December 1797, to his wife.
11. William Pitt quoted in John W. Derry, *William Pitt* (London: B. T. Batsford Ltd., 1982), 117.
12. François de Callières, *On the Manner of Negotiating with Princes*, trans. By A. F. Whyte (Washington, DC: University Press of America, 1963), 113.
13. Henri Mercier, "La Suisse et le Congrès de Bade," *Anzeiger für Schweizerische Geschichte* 15 (1971): 14.
14. Antoine Pecquet, *De l'Art de négocier avec les souverains* (The Hague: Jean Van Duren, 1738), 104.
15. National Library of Scotland, Papers of Hugh Elliott, Ms. 13000, fol. 182, Paris, 3 April 1791, death notice of Mirabeau, and on his mission NLS, 13022, fol. 294–341.
16. National Library of Scotland, Ms. 13022, fol. 294, Paris, 22 October 1790.
17. Quoted in Jacques Henri-Robert, *Dictionnaire des diplomates de Napoléon, histoire et dictionnarie du corps consulaire et impérial* (Paris: Henri Veyrier, 1990), 13.
18. Quoted in Heffernan, ed., *Representing the French Revolution*, 9 and 19.
19. Blakemore, *Burke and the Fall of Language*, 84.
20. Saint-Just, *Oeuvres complètes*, 2: 336.
21. B. L., Add. Mss. 59011, fols. 114–115, Grenville to Wickham, Cleveland Row, 27 January 1797.
22. B. L., Add. Mss. 58920, fol. 104, Grenville to Auckland, 19 June 1792.
23. B. L., Add. Mss. 58920, fol. 118, Auckland to Grenville, 22 June 1792.
24. B. L., Add. Mss. 59038, fol. 34, Kutzleben to Grenville, 5 August 1793.
25. B. L., Add. Mss. 46823, fol. 106, John Trevor to Francis Drake, 15 January 1794.

26. Duke University, Perkins Library, Special Collections, Papers of Perkins Magra, Perkins Magra to Lady Hamilton, undated.
27. Lincolnshire Record Office, Papers of Sir Richard Worsley, 13, fol. 200, George Baldwin to Richard Worsley, Alexandria, 27 August 1794.
28. Hüffer, ed. *Quellen zur Geschichte des Zeitalters der französischen Revolution.* 4, Poterat to Boissy d'Anglas, Vienna, 14 vendémiaire, an IV (5 October 1795).
29. Ibid., 25, Thugut to Degelmann, Vienna, 22 February 1796.
30. Ibid., 24, Delacroix to Poterat, Paris, le 30 pluviôse, an IV [19 February 1796].
31. Ibid., 62, Delacroix to Barthélémy, Paris, 28 messidor, an IV [16 July 1796].
32. Hampshire Record Office, Wickham papers 38M49/1/1/5, Auckland to Wickham, 12 April 1796.
33. Ibid., Papers of Sir Richard Worsley, 14, fol. 309, Worsley to Commander Tyler, Venice, 22 October 1796.
34. Ibid.,14, fol. 328, Worsley to Wyndham, 4 February 1797.
35. *The Anti-Jacobin* quoted in Dorothy Marshall, *The Rise of George Canning* (London: Longmans, Green and Co., 1938), 176–177.
36. Centre for Kentish Studies, Maidstone, U269 Sackville MSS C 186 Burke to Dorset, 11 September 1791.
37. B. L., Add. Mss. 59040, fol. 192, Thugut to Starhemberg, Vienna, 16 September 1796.
38. Ibid., 248–249, Thugut to Maximilian, Graf von Merveldt, Vienna, 7 July 1797.
39. Ibid., 462–477, Cobenzl to Thugut, Udine, 18 October 1797.
40. For the ill-fated negotiations and the tragic aftermath at Rastatt, see Frey and Frey, *The History of Diplomatic Immunity*, 311–312; Graf Hans von Schlitz, *Denkwürdigkeiten des Grafen Hans von Schlitz*, ed. by Albert Rolf (Hamburg: Rudolph's Verlags-Buchhandlugn, 1898) #18, 62–69; Friedrich von Gentz, *Staatschriften und Briefe*, edited by Hans von Eckardt (Munich: Drei Masken Verlag, 1921) 1: 16–29; Giuseppe Colucci, ed. *La Repubblica di Genova e la rivoluzione francese. Corrispondenze inedite degli ambasciatiori genovese a Paregi e pressso il congresso di Rastadt* (Rome: Tip della Mantellate, 1902), vol. 4: 159–175, especially the report of 2 maggio 1799; Oscar Criste, *Rastatt: L'Assassinat des ministres française. le 28 avril 1799* (Paris: Libraire Militaire R. Chapelot et Cie, 1900).
41. B. L., Add. Mss. 59041, fols. 151–152, minutes of Conference of Grenville with Stahremberg, 1798.
42. Guyot, *Le Directoire et la paix de l'Europe*, 569; Thompson, ed., *Napoleon Self-Revealed*, 52–53.
43. Metternich, *Memoirs*, 1: 350–351, 9 December 1797.

44. Guyot, *Le Directoire et la paix de l'Europe*, 568.
45. Criste, *Rastatt*, 10.
46. Franz Maria, Freiherr von Thugut, *Vertrauliche Briefe des Freiherrn von Thugut*, edited by Alfred Ritter von Vivenot, 2 vols. (Vienna: Wilhelm Braumuller, 1872) 2: 81, Cobenzl to Colloredo, Rastadt, 14 January 1798.
47. Kittstein, *Politik im Zietaler der Revolution*, 136 quotes report of Zinzendorf of 2 March 1798.
48. Metternich, *Mémoires*, 1: 346, 6 December 1797, to his wife.
49. Pingaud, *Jean de Bry*, 87.
50. Rain, *La Diplomatie française*, 176.
51. Weil, *Un Agent inconnu de la coalition*, 186–189, Duke of Brunswick to Comte Panin, 7 December 1798.
52. Metternich, *Memoirs*, 1: 359.
53. Pingaud, *Jean de Bry*, 91.
54. Criste, *Rastatt*, 10.
55. Ibid., 38.
56. Kittstein, *Politik im Zeitalter der Revolution*, 136, quotes Jacobi to Sandoz, 6 November 1798.
57. Ibid., 137, quotes Jacobi to Sandoz, 3 September 1798, and 137 quotes Jacobi to Sandoz, 22 September 1798.
58. Roider, *Baron Thugut and Austria's Response to the French Revolution*, 283.
59. Ibid., 372.
60. National Library of Ireland, Mss. 2262, Bristol to Sir William Hamilton, Trieste, 24 April 1799.
61. Oscar Browning, ed., *England and Napoleon in 1803: Being the Despatches of Lord Whitworth and Others* (London: Longmans, Green and Co., 1887), 102–103, Paris, 5 March 1803.
62. Ibid., 103–104, Paris, 7 March 1803.
63. Ochs, *Korrespondenz*. 2: 25, Ochs to Burckhardt, Paris, 9 June 1796.
64. Frédéric-César de La Harpe, *Correspondance de Frédéric-César de La Harpe sous le République Helvétique*, edited by Jean Charles Viaudet et Marie Claude Jequier (Neuchatel: Baconnière, 1982), 1: 99, La Harpe to Henri Monod, Paris, 5 November 1796.
65. Bailleu ed., *Preussen und Frankreich*, 1: 42, 3 January 1796.
66. Ibid., 1: 66, Sandoz-Rollin from Paris, 29 April 1796.
67. Ibid., 1: 83.
68. Lincolnshire Record Office, Papers of Sir Richard Worsley, 14, fol. 33, Sir Richard Worsley to Grenville, 15 January 1796. In all these instances the behavior of the French revolutionaries was not unlike those of the Chinese diplomats during the Cultural Revolution. The Chinese avoided "traditional diplomatic parlance," resorted to "spectacular" often "provocative" gestures, and in general evinced "an obvious unwillingness to

bend to the rules of diplomatic life that have been refined by international practice." Chinese diplomacy was thus "an instrument in the service of world revolution." The actions of these "red fighters on the diplomatic front" were to "contribute to opening a path to the kind of world they dream of and toward which they labor." See Philippe Ardant, "Chinese Diplomatic Practice during the Cultural Revolution," in *China's Practice of International Law*, edited by Jerome Alan Cohen, 86–128 (Cambridge, MA: Harvard University Press, 1972).

69. Stefan Zweig, *Joseph Fouché: The Portrait of a Politician*, translated by Eden and Cedar Paul (New York: Blue Ribbon Books, 1930), 35.
70. B. L., Add. Mss. 59370, Lyle Carmichael to Grenville, 22 December 1796.
71. Miot de Melito, *Memoirs*, 38, 42, and 43.
72. Ibid., 98.
73. Ibid., 99.
74. Ibid. 111 and 116.
75. Ibid., 117.
76. Ibid.
77. Both had been imprisoned during the Terror. Ginguené had written a comic opera, edited a weekly paper, and defended Rousseau in a work of 1791. He was appointed to the *Institut* of France and to the commission to reorganize public education. Born in the Basque country, Garat became an *advocat* at Bordeaux before coming to Paris where he contributed to the *Mercure de France* and the *Encyclopédie méthodique*. He also served as professor of history at the *lycée* before his election to the Estates General. Danton secured his appointment as Minister of Justice where he presided over the trial of the king. The next year he became Minister of the Interior. Appalled at the excesses he could not prevent, he resigned. Known for his integrity if not his resolution, this defender of Basque autonomy was hardly a radical. His friendship with Robespierre saved him when he was arrested as a Girondin. Nonetheless, he turned against Robespierre in Thermidor.
78. Ibid., 119.
79. Ibid., 119–120, and 125.
80. Ibid., 127.
81. Ibid., 128.
82. Bailleu, *Preussen und Frankreich von 1795 bis 1807*, 1: 211.
83. Tocqueville, *The Old Regime and the French Revolution*, 3.
84. Burke, *Burke's Politics*, 422–423.
85. Ibid., 424–425.
86. Jacques Mallet du Pan, *Correspondance inédite de Mallet du Pan avec la cour de Vienna (1794–1795)*, edited by André Michel (Paris: E. Plon, Nourrit et Cie., 1884), 2: 288.

87. Aulard, ed., *Recueil des actes du Comité de salut public*, 1: 17.
88. Goetz-Bernstein, *La Diplomatie de la Gironde*, 204–205.
89. A. N., D XXIII, comité diplomatique, part 1, Extract of order of king to government of Alexandria re: Sémonville, 20 April 1792.
90. *Archives parlementaires*, ser 1, 42: 426–430, session of 26 April 1792; A. N., D XXIII, Comité diplomatique, part 1, Dumouriez to M. Bourgoing at Madrid, Paris, 27 April 1792.
91. *Archives parlementaires*, 52: 613.
92. A. N., Police Générale, Comité de sûreté générale, 5 commission des 24, documents diplomatiques et historiques, F7 4390/2, report in the name of the comité diplomatique et de sûreté générale to Herault, deputy.
93. Ibid.
94. Ibid.
95. *Archives parlementaires*, 52: 613.
96. Great Britain, HMC, *The Manuscripts of J. B. Fortescue*, 2: 355, Baron Kutzleben to Lord Grenville, 11 December 1792.
97. Winter, *Repertorium*, 142.
98. Mazon, *Histoire de Soulavie*. 209–215 and 251.
99. Masson, *Les Diplomates de la Révolution*, 182–183.
100. Miles, *The Correspondence*, 1: 439–440.
101. Soulavie to Deforgues, 8 July 1793, *Papiers de Barthélemy*, 2: 284–285, #784, attached piece "a," as quoted in Silverman, "Informal Diplomacy: The Foreign Policy of the Robespierrist Committee of Public Safety," 60–61.
102. Peter Marc, *Genève et la Révolution* (Geneva: Kundig, 1921), 156–157, 159: Chapuisat, *La Suisse et la Révolution française*, 49.
103. Chapuisat, *La Suisse et la Révolution française*, 54.
104. Mazon, *Soulavie*, 252.
105. Ibid., 253–254.
106. Marc, *Genève et la Révolution*, 545–547.
107. Chapuisat, *De la Terreur à l'annexation*, 23.
108. Ibid., 81.
109. Baron Thugut quoted in Vivenot, *Zur Geschichte des Rastadter Congresses*, 155–156.
110. Fugier, *Histoire des relations internationales*, 27.
111. France, *Recueil, vol. 9: Russie*, part 2, 509.
112. François Barthélemy, *Mémoires de Barthélemy, 1768–1819* (Paris: Plon-Nourrit et cie., 1914), 74.
113. Simioni, *Le origini del risorgimento politico dell' Italia meridionale*, 1: 434–443.
114. B. L., Add. Mss. 41199, fol. 99, Naples, to Grenville, 24 January 1793; Add. Mss. 59150, fol. 76, Hamilton to Grenville, 21 January 1793.
115. Iiams, *Peacemaking from Vergennes to Napoleon*, 179.

116. Jules Basdevant, *La Révolution française et le droit de la guerre continentale* (Paris: L. Larose and Forcel, 1901), 66, also see Sorel, *L'Europe et le Révolution française* (Paris: E. Plon, Nourrit et Cie), 3: 401–433.
117. *France, Recueil, Vol. 28: États Allemands, part 1: L'Electorat de Mayence*, 486.
118. Miot de Melito, *Memoirs*, 64–65.
119. Quoted in Léonce Pingaud, *Jean de Bry, 1760–1835* (Paris: Plon, 1909), 87.
120. Marie-Caroline, *Correspondance*, 2: 538, Naples, 29 décembre 1804, and 560, Naples, 15 février 1805.
121. Ibid., *Correspondance*, 2: 593, 8 April 1805, Naples.
122. A. N., D XXIII, Comité diplomatique, part 1, Dumouriez to Genet, Paris, 4 June 1792.
123. William L. Blackwell, "Citizen Genet and the Revolution in Russia, 1789–1792," *French Historical Studies*, 3 (spring, 1963): 78, 79, 81.
124. Harry Ammon, *The Genet Mission* (New York: W. W. Norton & Company, 1973), 7.
125. P.R.O., FO 5/4 letter of Hammond, Philadelphia, 29 December 1793 enclosed fol. 105 Genet's publication—*The Correspondence between Citizen Genet, Minister of the French Republic, to the United States of North America and the Officers of the Federal Government; to which are prefixed the Instructions from the Constituted Authorities of France to the Said Minister. All from Authentic Documents.* (Philadelphia: Benjamin Franklin Bache, 1793); A. A. E. correspondance politique, États-Unis, vol. 37, fol. 22–23, 4 January 1793, Genet's plein pouvoirs and fol. 59, January 1793, his instructions. Also see A. A. E., correspondance politique États-Unis, vol. 37, fol. 20 report on mission of citizen Genet, fols. 22–23 Genet's *plein pouvoirs*, fol. 59, Instructions from Conseil exécutif provisoire of 17 January 1793.
126. B. L., Add. Mss. 59084, fols. 25–28, Grenville to Hammond, 12 March 1793.
127. Library of Congress, Manuscripts Division, British Collection, copies P.R.O., FO 5, vol. 1, fol. 247, 10 August 1793, Hammond.
128. Conrad L. Donakowski, *A Muse for the Masses: Ritual and Music in an Age of Democratic Revolution 1770–1870* (Chicago: University of Chicago Press, 1977), 45. Singing would "arose and reinforce enthusiasm." Laura Mason, *Singing the French Revolution: Popular Culture and Politics, 1787–1799* (Ithaca, NY: Cornell University Press, 1996), 109. See also Chap. 4.
129. A. A. E., États-Unis, CP vol. 41 1794, part I fol. 10 and fol. 12, 14 floréal, an II; Ammon, *The Genet Mission*, 56–57.
130. A. A. E., États-Unis, CP vol. 37, fol. 450, Genet to Jefferson, 22 June 1793.
131. John Adams and John Quincy Adams, *Selected Writings*, ed. Adrienne Koch and William Peden (New York: Alfred Knopf, 1946), 238.

132. Genet was "[h]ot headed, all imagination, no judgment, passionate, disrespectful & even indecent towards the President." Genet, he concluded, was "incapable of correcting himself." Thomas Jefferson, *The Writings of Thomas Jefferson*, edited by Paul Leicester Ford, 6 vols. (New York: G. P. Putnam's Sons, 1895), 6: 338–339, To James Madison, 7 July 1793.
133. Thomas Jefferson, *Papers of Thomas Jefferson*, ed. Julian Boyd, 35 vols. (Princeton: Princeton University Press, 1995), 26: 464, conversation with Genet, 10 July 1793.
134. A. A. E., CP, États Unis, vol. 37, fol. 279–281 George Hammond to Secretary of State, also fols. 283–289, Edmond Randolph to Secretary of State; fols. 313–316, Genet's response of 28 and 29 May to Jefferson; fols. 316–323, Jefferson's response.
135. Library of Congress, Manuscripts Division, British Collection, copies P.R.O., FO 5, vol. 1: fol. 198, Hammond, 1 July 1793.
136. P.R.O., FO 5/1, Philadelphia, 7 July 1793.
137. P.R.O., FO 5/1, fol. 241–245, Philadelphia, 10 August 1793.
138. Library of Congress, Manuscripts Division, British Collection, copies P.R.O., FO 5, vol. 1, fol. 244, Hammond, 10 August 1793.
139. P.R.O., FO 5/1, 17 September 1793, Philadelphia, Hammond. Also see P.R.O., FO 881/1552, Hammond to Jefferson, Philadelphia, 8 May 1793, fol. 3, also see Jefferson to Hammond, 5 June 1793; P.R.O., FO 881/1552, Hammond to Grenville, Philadelphia, 7 July 1793, fols. 8–9; P.R.O., FO 881/1552, fol. 16, Hammond to Grenville Philadelphia, 19 August 1793. Also see Thomas Jefferson, *Calendar of the Correspondence of Thomas Jefferson, part I, Bulletin of the Bureau of Rolls and Library of the Department of State*, #6 (Washington: Department of State, 1894), letters from Jefferson, 176–177, also see 201–204.
140. A. A. E., CP, État Unis, vol. 38, fol. 190, Jefferson to Genet, 16 August 1793.
141. P.R.O., FO 5/1, fol. 355, Hammond, 10 November 1793.
142. George Washington, *The Writings of George Washington*, 12 vols. (Boston: Hilliard, Gray, and Co., 1836), 10: 355–356, George Washington to Thomas Jefferson, Philadelphia, 11 July 1793.
143. Adams and Adam, *Selected Writings*, 237.
144. De Conde, *Entangling Alliance*, 289.
145. A. A. E., CP, États-Unis, vol. 38, fol. 219–231, Jefferson to Genet. For Genet's conduct see Jefferson, *Calendar of the Correspondence of Thomas Jefferson. part I*. #6, 292. to Madison, Philadelphia, 11 August 1793; 292, to Madison, Philadelphia, 25 August 1793. Also see 292, 330, 381, and 531, a detailed conversation with Genet, 10 July 1793.
146. *Greenleaf's New York Journal and Patriotic Register*, 8 January 1794. See also 11 January 1794 and 4 January 1793.

147. Irving Brant, *James Madison* (Indianapolis: Bobbs-Merrill, 1948), 3: 348.
148. Childs, "The Hauterive Journal," 72.
149. Ibid., 71.
150. Ibid., 73.
151. University of Virginia, Alderman Library, Special Collections Thomas Jefferson papers, Thomas Jefferson to James Madison, 14 July 1793.
152. Jefferson, *Writings*, 4: 20, Jefferson to Monroe, 14 July 1793, and Madison to Jefferson, 5 August 1793, where he remarked that Genet's folly "would almost beget suspicions of the worst sort." James Madison, *The Writings of James Madison*, ed. Gaillard Hunt (New York, 1906), 6: 139n. For Genet, also see *Calendar of the Correspondence of Thomas Jefferson. part II*, #8, 262–264, letters from Genet about French privateers; 289–290 letters from Hammond; 402 from James Monroe, 21 August 1793; 403, from Monroe, 4 December 1793; 567 from George Washington, 11 July 1793, 25 July 1793, 31 July 1793. For concern about the privateers, also see The Historical Society of Pennsylvania, 1454 Cadwallader Family Papers, Series 5: Phineas Bond papers, box 258.
153. Washington, *Writings*, 10: 386–387, George Washington to Richard Henry Lee, 24 October 1793.
154. Jefferson, *Papers*, 27: 649, Jefferson to Genet, December 1793.
155. Ibid., 26: 685–696.
156. Albert Hall Bowman, *The Struggle for Neutrality, Franco-American Diplomacy during the Federalist Era* (Knoxville, TN: University of Tennesse Press, 1974), 95.
157. Childs, "The Hauterive Journal," 79.
158. P.R.O., FO 5/1, fol. 296, Philadelphia, Hammond, 17 September 1793.
159. Paul Mantoux, "Le Comité de Salut public et la mission de Genet aux États-Unis," *Revue d'histoire moderne et contemporaine*, 13 (1909): 5–35.
160. A. A. E., Correspondance politique, États-Unis, vol. 39, Report to National Convention in the name of the Committee of public safety by Robespierre, 27 brumaire.
161. Maximilien-Marie-Isidore Robespierre, *Rapport fait à la Convention Nationale au nom du Comité de salut public par le citoyen Robespierre, membre de ce comité, sur la situation politique de la république* (Paris: Imp nationale, s.d.), 11.
162. P.R.O., FO 5/4, fol. 148, Philadelphia, 15 April 1794, Hammond.
163. Turner, ed. *Correspondence of the French Ministers to the United States 1791–1797*, 2: 770, 18 August 1795.
164. F. A. Aulard, ed. "Lettres de Noël à Danton." *La Révolution française*. 24 (1893): 463, Noël to Danton, Venice.
165. P.R.O., FO 5/4, fol. 43, 53, from Hammond, Philadelphia, 22 February 1794.

166. A. A. E., CP, États-Unis, vol. 47, part 6, fol., 406–408 par M. Otto Consideration sur la conduite du gouvernement des États-Unis ... 1789–1797. For Jean Antoine Joseph Fauchet's views see A. A. E., CP, États-Unis, vol. 43, part VII, fol. 504 undated.
167. A. A. E., CP, États-Unis, vol. 40, fols. 386–389.
168. Childs, "The Hauterive Journal," 81.
169. A. A. E., CP, États-Unis, vol. 46, fol. 181–184, and fols. 420–421. Minister of Navy and the Colonies to the Minister of Foreign Affairs, Paris, 11 frimaire, an V.
170. A. A. E., CP, États-Unis, vol. 47, part 6, fol. 404–406 par M. Otto Considération sur la conduite du gouvernement des États-Unis ... 1789–1797.
171. Hagley, W3–298, Victor to his father, 23 September 1796.
172. Kidner, "The Girondists and the 'Propaganda War' of 1792," 281–282.
173. Colucci, ed., *La Repubblica di Genova e la rivoluzione francese*, 1: 58.
174. Ibid., 1: 86, 128, 142–143, 182.
175. Ibid., 2: 102, 117. Saint-Just, *Oeuvres complètes*, 2: 347.
176. Ibid., 2: 183–184, Bocarrdi note of 13 June 1795 and 190, Committee of Public Safety to Boccardi, 24 prairial, an III.
177. Chapuisat, *La Suisse et la Revolution française*, 129.
178. John P. McLaughlin, "The Annexation Policy of the French Revolution 1789–1793," unpublished Ph.D. thesis, University of London, 1951, 354–355.
179. Patricia Chastain Howe, *Foreign Policy and the French Revolution: Charles-François Dumouriez, Pierre Lebrun and the Belgian Plan* (New York: Palgrave Macmillan, 2008), 75.
180. Napoleon, *Memoirs*, 271–272.
181. Boulot, *Le Général Duphot (1769–1797)* (Paris: Plon Nourrit et cie, 1908), 197–199; Frey, and Frey, *A History of Diplomatic Immunity*, 309–310. Also see Montaiglon and Guiffrey, eds., *Correspondance des directeurs de l'Académie de France à Rome*, 17.
182. Pingaud, *Jean de Bry* 141.
183. Quoted in Jeremy Black, "Anglo-French Relations in the Age of the French Revolution, 1787–1793," *Francia: Forschungen zur westeuropäischen Geschichte* 15 (1987): 407.
184. R. R. Palmer, "A Revolutionary Republican: M. A. B. Mangourit," *William and Mary Quarterly* 9 (October 1952): 496.
185. Burke, *Burke's Politics*, 422–423.
186. Ibid., 424–425.
187. Burke quoted in Chapman, *Edmund Burke: the Practical Imagination*, 186.
188. Burke, *Burke's Politics*, 458–460 and 465–466.

189. William Cobbett, *The Parliamentary History of England* (London: T. C. Hansard, 1817), 30: 280–281.
190. A. H. L. Heeren, *A Manual of the History of the Political System of Europe and Its Colonies* (London: Bohn, 1846), x. It was first published in Göttingen in 1800.
191. Ibid., xi.
192. Hagley, Winterthur Ms. Group 2 box 34W 2, 5626, Memoirs of Joseph Fouché, 5 August 1815.
193. Vivenot, *Zur Geschichte des Rastadter Congresses*, 153–156, Thugut to Dietrichstein, Vienna, 5 April 1798.

References

Adams, John, and John Quincy Adams. *The Selected Writings of John and John Quincy Adams*. Edited by Adrienne Koch and William Peden. New York: A. A. Knopf, 1946.
Ammon, Harry. *The Genet Mission*. New York: W. W. Norton & Company, Inc, 1973.
Archives parlementaires de 1787 à 1860. Series 1: 1789–1800. Vol. 15: Assemblée nationale constituante du 21 Avril au 30 Mai 1790. Edited by M. J. Mavidal and M. E. Laurent. Paris: Paul Dupont, 1883.
Ardant, Philippe. "Chinese Diplomatic Practice During the Cultural Revolution." In *China's Practice of International Law: Some Case Studies*, edited by Jerome Alan Cohen, 96–128. Cambridge, MA: Harvard University Press, 1972.
Aulard, François-Alphonse, ed. *Recueil des actes du Comité de salut public avec la correspondance officielle des représentants en mission et le registre du conseil exécutif provisoire*. 27 vols. Paris: Imprimerie nationale, 1889–1923.
———, ed. "Lettres de Noël à Danton." *La Révolution française* 24 (1893): 448–467.
Bailleu, Paul, ed. *Preussen und Frankreich von 1795 bis 1807. Diplomatische Correspondenzen*. Osnabrück: Otto Zeller, 1965.
Barthélemy, François. *Papiers de Barthélemy, ambassadeur de France en Suisse, 1792–1797*. Edited by Jean Kaulek and Alexandre Tausserat-Radel. 6 vols. Paris: Alcan, 1886–1910.
———. *Mémoires de Barthélemy, 1768–1819*. Paris: Plon-Nourrit et Cie., 1914.
Basdevant, Jules. *La Révolution française et le droit de la guerre continentale*. Paris: L. Larose, 1901.
Black, Jeremy. "Anglo-French Relations in the Age of the French Revolution, 1787–1793." *Francia: Forschungen zur westeuropäischen Geschichte* 15 (1987): 407–434.
Blackwell, William L. "Citizen Genet and the Revolution in Russia." *French Historical Studies* 3, no. 1 (Spring, 1963): 73–92.

Blakemore, Steven. *Burke and the Fall of Language: The French Revolution as Linguistic Event*. Hanover, NH: Published for Brown University Press by University Press of New England, 1988.

———. "Revolution in Language: Burke's Representation of Linguistic Terror." In *Representing the French Revolution: Literature, Historiography, and Art*, edited by James A. W. Heffernan, 3–23. Hanover: University Press of New England, 1992.

Boulot, Georges. *Le Général Duphot (1769–1797)*. Paris: Plon Nourrit et Cie, 1908.

Bowman, Albert Hall. *The Struggle for Neutrality, Franco-American Diplomacy During the Federalist Era*. Knoxville, TN: University of Tennessee Press, 1974.

Brant, Irving. *James Madison*. Indianapolis: Bobbs-Merrill, 1948.

Browning, Oscar, ed. *England and Napoleon in 1803: Being the Despatches of Lord Whitworth and Others*. London: Longmans, Green, and Co., 1887.

Burke, Edmund. *Burke's Politics: Selected Writings and Speeches on Reform, Revolution and War*. New York: Alfred A. Knopf, 1970.

Callières, François de. *On the Manner of Negotiating with Princes*. Translated by A. F. White. 1963. Reprint. Washington, DC: University Press of America, 1963.

Chapuisat, Édouard. *De la Terreur de l'annexation: Génève et la république française, 1793–1798*. Geneva: Edition ATAR, 1912.

———. *La Suisse et la Révolution française: Épisodes*. Geneva: Editions du Mont-Blanc, 1945.

Childs, Frances S. "The Hauterive Journal." *New York Historical Society Quarterly Bulletin* 33 (April, 1949): 69–86.

Cobbett, William. *The Parliamentary History of England*. London: T. C. Hansard, 1817.

Cohen, Raymond. *Theatre of Power: The Art of Diplomatic Signaling*. London: Longman, 1987.

———. *Negotiating Across Cultures: Communication Obstacles in International Diplomacy*. Washington, DC: United States Institute of Peace Press, 1991.

Colucci, Giuseppe, ed. *La Repubblica di Genova e la rivoluzione francese. Corrispondenze inedite degli ambasciatori genovese a Paregi e presso il congresso di Rastadt*. Rome: Tip. delle Mantellate, 1902.

Criste, Oscar. *Rastatt: L'Assassinat des ministres français*. Paris: Librairie Militaire R. Chapelot et cie, 1900.

De Conde, Alexander. *Entangling Alliance: Politics and Diplomacy Under George Washington*. Durham, NC: Duke University Press, 1958.

Derry, John W. *William Pitt*. London: B. T. Batsford Ltd., 1962.

Donakowski, Conrad L. *A Muse for the Masses: Ritual and Music in an Age of Democratic Revolution, 1770–1870*. Chicago: University of Chicago Press, 1977.

France. Commission des Archives diplomatiques au ministère des affaires étrangères. *Recueil des instructions données au ambassadeurs et ministres de France depuis les traités de Westphalie jusqu'à la Révolution française*. Vol. 28.

États Allemands, part 1: *L'Electorat de Mayence*. Edited by Georges Livet. Paris: Centre National de la recherche scientifique, 1962.

———. Commission des Archives diplomatiques au ministère des affaires étrangères. *Recueil des Instructions donnéees aux ambassaduers et ministres de France depuis les traitées de Westphalie jusqu'à la Révolution française vol. 9: Russie*, part 2: 1749–1789. Edited by Alfred Rambaud. Paris: Félix Alcan, 1890.

Frey, Linda, and Marsha Frey. *The History of Diplomatic Immunity*. Columbus, OH: Ohio State University Press, 1999.

Fugier, André. *Histoire des relations internationales. Vol. 4: La Revolution française et l'empire napoléonien*. Paris: Hachette, 1954.

Gentz, Friedrich von. *Friedrich von Gentz, Staatschriften und Briefe*. Edited by Hans von Eckardt. 2 vols. Munich: Drei Masken Verlag, 1921.

Goetz-Bernstein, Hans Alfred. *La Diplomatie de la Gironde, Jacques-Pierre Brissot*. Paris: Librairie Hachette et cie, 1912.

Great Britain, Historical Manuscripts Commission. *The Manuscripts of J. B. Fortescue, esq., Preserved at Dropmore*. 4 vols. London: Eyre and Spottiswoode, 1892–1905.

Greenleaf's New York Journal and Patriotic Register. New York: Thomas Greenleaf, 1794–1800.

Guyot, Raymond. *Le Directoire et la paix de l'Europe: Des traités de Bâle à la deuxième coalition, 1795–1799*. Paris: Félix Alcan, 1911.

Heeren, A. H. L. *A Manual of the History of the Political System of Europe and Its Colonies*. London: Bohn, 1846.

Henri-Robert, Jacques. *Dictionnaire des diplomates de Napoléon, histoire et dictionnaire du corps diplomatique consulaire et impérial*. Paris: Henri Veyrier, 1990.

Howe, Patricia Chastain. *Foreign Policy and the French Revolution, Charles-François Dumouriez, Pierre LeBrun and the Belgian Plan, 1789–1793*. New York: Palgrave Macmillan, 2008.

Hüffer, Hermann, ed. *Quellen zur Geschichte des Zeitalters der französischen Revolution. Teil 2: Quellen zur Geschichte der diplomatischen Verhandlungen. Erster Band: Der Frieden von Campoformio*. Innsbruck: Wagner, 1907.

Iiams, Thomas M. *Peacemaking from Vergennes to Napoleon: French Foreign Relations in the Revolutionary Era, 1774–1814*. Huntington, NY: Robert E. Krieger Publishing Company, 1979.

Jefferson, Thomas. *The Writings of Thomas Jefferson*. Edited by Paul Leicester Ford. 10 vols. New York: G. P. Putnam's Sons, 1892–1899.

———. *The Papers of Thomas Jefferson*. 35 vols. Edited by Julian Boyd. Princeton: Princeton University Press, 1950–.

Kidner Jr., Frank L. "The Girondists and the "Propaganda War" of 1792: A Reevaluation of French Revolutionary Foreign Policy from 1791 to 1793." Unpublished Ph.D. Diss., Princeton University, 1971.

Kittstein, Lothar. *Politik im Zeitalter der Revolution: Untersuchungen zur preussischen Staatlichkeit 1792–1807.* Wiesbaden: Franz Steiner Verlag, 2003.
La Harpe, Frédéric-César de. *Correspondance de Frédéric-César de la Harpe sous la République helvétique.* Neuchâtel: Baconnière, 1982.
Madison, James. *The Writings of James Madison: Comprising His Public Papers and His Private Correspondence, Including Numerous Letters and Documents Now for the First Time Printed.* Edited by Gaillard Hunt. New York: Putnam's Sons, 1900–1910.
Mallet du Pan, Jacques. *Correspondance inédite de Mallet Du Pan avec la cour de Vienne, 1794–1798.* Edited by André Michel. 2 vols. Paris: Librairie Plon, 1884.
Mantoux, Paul. "Le Comité de Salut public et la mission de Genet aux États-Unis." *Revue d'histoire moderne et contemporaine* 13 (1909–1910): 5–35.
Marc, Peter. *Genève et la Révolution.* Geneva: Kundig, 1921.
Marie-Caroline, Queen of Naples. *Correspondance inédite de Marie-Caroline, Reine de Naples et de Sicile avec le marquis de Gallo.* Edited by M.-H. Weil and Marquis C. Di Somma Circello. 2 vols. Paris: Émile-Paul Editeur, 1911.
Marshall, Dorothy. *The Rise of George Canning.* London: Longmans, Green and Co., 1938.
Mason, Laura. *Singing the French Revolution: Popular Culture and Politics, 1787–1799.* Ithaca, NY: Cornell University Press, 1996.
Masson, Frédéric. *Les Diplomates de la Révolution: Hugou de Bassville à Rome, Bernadotte à Vienne.* Paris: Charavay frères, 1882.
Mazon, Albin. *Histoire de Soulavie.* Paris: Fischbacher, 1893.
McLaughlin, John P. "The Annexation Policy of the French Revolution 1789–1793." Unpublished Ph.D. Diss., University of London, 1951.
Menning, Ralph. *The Art of the Possible: Documents on Great Power Diplomacy.* New York: McGraw Hill, 1996.
Mercier, Henri. "La Suisse et Congrès de Bade." *Anzeiger für Schweizerische Geschichte* 15 (1917): 1–31.
Metternich-Winneburg, Clemens Wenzel Neopomuk Lothar, Fürst von. *Memoirs of Prince Metternich.* Edited by Prince Richard Metternich. 5 vols. New York: C. Scribner's Sons, 1880–1882.
———. *Mémoires: Documents et écrits divers laissés par le Prince de Metternich, chancelier de cour et d'état.* 2 vols. Paris: E. Plon et Cie., 1881.
Miles, William Augustus. *The Correspondence of William Augustus Miles on the French Revolution, 1789–1817.* Edited by Charles Miles Popham. 2 vols. London: Longmans, Green, and Company, 1890.
Miot de Melito, Andre F. *Memoirs of Count Miot de Melito, Minister, Ambassador, Councillor of State.* Edited by Wilhelm August Fleischmann. New York: Charles Scribner's Sons, 1881.
Montaiglon, Anatole de, and Guiffrey, Jules-Joseph, eds. *Correspondance des directeurs de l'Académie de France à Rome.* 17 vols. Paris: Charavay, 1887–1908.

Napoléon I. *Napoleon Bonaparte: Memoirs, Dictated by the Emperor at St. Helena to the Generals Who Shared His Captivity*. Edited by Somerset De Chair. London: Soho, 1936.

Ochs, Peter. *Korrespondenz des Peter Ochs (1752–1821)*. Edited by Gustav Steiner. 3 vols. Vol. 1: Basel: Hermann Opperann. Vols. 2 and 3: Basel: Emil Birkhauser & cie., 1927–1937.

Palmer, R. R. "A Revolutionary Republican: M. A. B. Mangourit." *William and Mary Quarterly* 9 (October, 1952): 483–496.

Pecquet, Antoine. *De l'Art de négocier avec les souverains*. The Hague: Jean Van Duren, 1738.

Pingaud, Léonce. *Jean de Bry (1760–1835)*. Paris: Librairie Plon, 1909.

Rain, Pierre. *La Diplomatie française*. 2 vols. Paris: Plon, 1943, 1950.

Robespierre, Maximilien. *Rapport fait á la Convention Nationale au nom du Comité de Salut Public par le citoyen Robespierre, membre de ce comité, sur la situation politique de la république*. Paris: Imp. nationale, s.d.

Roider, Karl A. *Baron Thugut and Austria's Response to the French Revolution*. Princeton: Princeton University Press, 1987.

Saint-Just, Louis de. *Oeuvres complètes de Saint-Just*. Edited by Charles Vellay. 2 vols. Paris: Librairie Charpentier et Fasquelle, 1908.

Schlitz, Graf Hans von. *Denkwürdigkeiten des Grafen Hans von Schlitz*. Edited by Albert Rolf. Hamburg: Rudolph's Verlags-Buchhandling, 1898.

Simioni, Attilio. *Le origini del risorgimento politico dell'Iitalia meridionale*. 2 vols. Rome: Giuseppe Principato, 1925–1930.

Sorel, Albert. *L'Europe and la Révolution française*. 8 vols. Paris: E. Plon Nourrit et cie, 1897–1904.

Thompson, J. M. ed. *Napoleon Self-Revealed*. New York: Houghton Mifflin Company, 1934.

Thugut, Franz Maria, Freiherr von. *Vertrauliche Briefe*. Edited by Alfred Ritter von Vivenot. 2 vols. Vienna: Wilhelm Braumüller, 1872.

Tocqueville, Alexis de. *The Old Regime and the French Revolution*. Translated by Stuart Gilbert. Garden City, NY: Doubleday, 1955.

Turner, Frederick Jackson, ed. *Correspondence of the French Ministers to the United States, 1791–1797*. 2 vols. 1903. Reprint. New York: Da Capo Press, 1972.

Vivenot, Alfred Ritter von. *Zur Geschichte des Rastadter Congresses*. Vienna: Wilhelm Braumüller, 1871.

Washington, George. *The Writings of George Washington*. 12 vols. Boston: Hilliard, Gray, and Co., 1834–1840.

Weil, Maurice-Henri. *Un Agent inconnu de la coalition, Le Général de Stamford d'après sa correspondance inédite (1793–1806)*. Paris: Payot and Cie., 1923.

Winter, Otto Friedrich. *Repertorium der diplomatischen Vertreter aller Länder seit dem Westfälischen Frieden*. Vol. 3. Graz: Verlag Hermann Böhlaus Nachf., 1965.

Zweig, Stefan. *Joseph Fouché: The Portrait of a Politician*. Translated by Eden and Cedar Paul. New York: Blue Ribbon Books, 1930.

CHAPTER 8

Conclusion: Return to the Old

> The cabinet of the government is not the portico of Athens. Virtue does not consist in depriving ourselves of advantages. The republican diplomacy, always open and pure, ought, however, to yield to the force of circumstances.[1] —Ange-Elisabeth-Louis-Antoine Bonnier

The revolutionaries' attempt to change the face France projected on the international scene reflected a larger vision of a new international order. In his diplomatic encounter with Napoleon Metternich certainly understood that. He saw Napoleon staging a scene "unlike anything that had occurred in diplomatic circles up to this time." Metternich grasped the larger purpose behind the scenario: "he wished to speak to me but not alone; he wished to do it in the face of Europe."[2] The international agenda of the revolutionary regime underscores the validity of Durkheim's observation that "these conflicts which break forth are not between the ideal and reality, but between two different ideals, that of yesterday and that of to-day, that which has the authority of tradition and that which has the hope of the future."[3] The consciously crafted language and deliberately deployed symbols of the French diplomats reflected the attempts of the revolutionaries to create that elusive entity, a revolutionary identity, to define and forge a revolutionary community, and to challenge the assumptions of the international order. While they were re-envisaging the French community, they were also attempting to forge a new international one, or even change the rules of that game. That moment of creation and definition illumines another aspect of what Furet called the "symbolic universe of the Revolution."[4] Within the international framework, these tales from the revolutionary woods raise questions of how the international system of the day adjusted to a challenge flung by a revolutionary state. In the eyes of a number of contemporaries, including Burke, the French undercut "the secret, unseen, but irrefragable bond of habitual intercourse" that binds men together.[5] The struggle over symbols was part of that challenge, then and now. In the aftermath of that struggle, Bassville's fate verified the truth of Machiavelli's dictum that "all armed prophets have conquered, and the unarmed ones have been destroyed."[6]

Furet argued that the French obsession with discourse reflected the revolutionaries' "illusion of politics," namely, their belief that "all personal problems and all moral or intellectual matters have become political" and hence "amenable to a political solution." Furet asked us to step outside of "this game of mirrors where the historian and the Revolution believe each other's words literally." He enjoined us not to take the revolutionary discourse at face value. For "what if the discourse about a radical break reflects no more than the illusion of change?"[7]

In July 1793, Johann Schiller would have agreed: I am "very far from believing that a political regeneration had begun; indeed, present events rob me of all hope that this will ever come to pass for centuries."[8] Many in revolutionary France, however, still entertained hopes of revolutionary change. By altering ceremony, etiquette, speech, language, and dress the diplomats reaffirmed their revolutionary credentials to an audience at home and proclaimed the revolutionary agenda to those abroad. The revolutionaries sought an international society liberated from the constraints of public ceremony and one not guided by the common rules established by law and usage. The political culture of the revolution deliberately undermined the system of norms established by the *ancien régime*. Many of the revolutionaries suspected and often correctly that the diplomats of the *ancien régime* would undermine the revolutionary agenda. Witness, for example, Cardinal Bernis, who "subtly altered the tenor" of his instructions on the Civil Constitution of the Clergy.[9] Unlike the Second Republic (1848–1851), which dispatched aristocrats as ambassadors,[10] the First Republic rejected them as too entwined in the old order. The Directory did, however briefly, send three aristocrats abroad. The dismissal or resignation of most who had served the *ancien régime* and their replacement by true patriots, however defined, did not resolve the basic contradiction between their role and their instructions. The mission of a number of diplomats provides a window into the ambiguous position of these men; they were at least theoretically integrated into the hierarchical international society that was "habituated to solve problems by negotiation," and yet simultaneously they had to conform to the principles advocated by a revolutionary order.[11] The international society and diplomatic interchange was based on the continuity of treaties and or usage. While questioning the validity of positive law and turning to natural law, they nonetheless did not hesitate to cite positive law when it aligned with their goals and reject it when it did not and to use natural law as a weapon to be wielded at home and abroad.[12] The novelty of the revolutionary dictates inevitably contradicted the internal prescriptions of the international order.[13] The function of a diplomat inevitably entailed a culture of mediation postulated on shared customs and norms. Those sent abroad exploited diplomatic interactions but tore aside the expectations that had facilitated that interaction. They never attempted to resolve the tensions between revolutionary ideas and diplomatic usage but instead unilaterally rejected the traditional norms. These diplomats felt obliged to reject diplomatic usage (and not coincidentally the norms of international law). Instead of crossing the bridge of diplomatic etiquette, they tended to breach it and alienate their hosts, even the democratic Americans (and one as Francophilic as Jefferson). The revolutionaries upended the ceremonial and protocol that had traditionally played an important role in the diplomatic network. They found themselves sacrificing the substance of diplomacy for the symbolism of revolutionary simplicity.

Confrontational diplomacy proved to be an oxymoron. In order to act within the European international system, they increasingly accommodated themselves to it. Moreover, they wanted the trappings associated with great power status. Diplomats were still useful and access still vital. The revolutionaries, in particular after Thermidor, found themselves treading "the tortuous paths of traditional diplomacy" and violating previously declared principles.[14] As Tocqueville argued so brilliantly: many of the "administrative methods which were suppressed in 1789 reappeared a few years later, much as some rivers after going underground re-emerge at another point in new surroundings."[15] As Professor Bély has maintained, despite the revolutionary pronouncements, the same concepts organized international relations,[16] just as they dictated the same geostrategic concerns. Despite public posturing and protestations against the old arrangements of "cunning and conveniences, artificial balances and indemnities"[17] and against the "length and vexations of the old diplomacy,"[18] the committees inserted secret articles and even demanded indemnifications. In a letter of 24 brumaire, an IV (1795), the minister of foreign relations requested foreign representatives to draft "as soon as possible a *mémoire raisonné* that was to be kept separate from their ordinary dispatches." They were to include a discussion of the members of the court and of the government and agents of foreign powers with particular notice of their age, character, influence, and so on; the attitude of the court and government; and the public spirit of the nation. They were to assess the economic status of the country, including its agriculture, commerce, finances, and industry and its military strengths, land and sea, and the advantages and disadvantages of its alliances and commercial relations with other states. They were to evaluate the state of the arts and sciences and list the names of the men who excelled, and so on. A particular section dealt with foreigners and travelers.[19] This directive eerily echoed that of the *ancien régime* and the *relazioni* required by the Venetian Senate. It also signaled a break from the isolationist policy of the Terror.

The new instructions sent to its agents reflected the more pragmatic emphasis of the Directory. The rules of conduct were to ensure that the great character of the French nation would be "esteemed, loved and respected." The representatives were still enjoined to maintain "the dignity of the French nation" and to offer an example of purity of morals, but the circular urged them to "respect the political, civil, and religious laws of the country" and avoid any difficulties about etiquette. Each nation, it emphasized, found happiness in its "own way" and had "more or fewer advantages toward the perfection of the social order." In that search they "should only be instructed by mutual respect."[20] This tolerance, although not universally observed, signaled a marked departure from the revolutionaries' earlier disdain of, if not hostility toward, *ancien régime* practices and monarchical government. Still John Hampden-Trevor, 3rd Viscount Hampden (1748–1824), the former British envoy in Turin from 1783 to 1798, may have voiced the skepticism of many when he noted that the French government had stopped irritating and insulting his Sardinian majesty. This "new line of conduct" demonstrated to him that the Directory was "as artfull [sic] as it [was] audacious … in order to lull and disarm the animosity."[21]

The revolutionaries also found themselves more concerned with protocol and form. Under the Thermidoreans as early as 6 fructidor, an II (1794), the National Convention had provided that the representatives of foreign powers would not be heard until after the reading and acceptance of their letters of *créance*.[22] In some cases principle had to bend to expediency. For example, in 1793 the Committee of Public Safety ordered the executive council to empower the Republic's agents in Sweden to concede on the matter of usages in order to facilitate the negotiations. The agents were to eliminate any difficulties which arose over questions of etiquette. They could even use the title "Swedish Majesty."[23] When the Directory sent Dominique-Catherine de Pérignon (1754–1818), a moderate, in 1796 to Madrid, the British ambassador found the "great splendor and magnificence" of the embassy "extraordinary."[24] A law of 4 floréal, an III (23 April 1795), established the procedure to be followed in diplomatic audiences. In discussing the measure Merlin de Douai noted that the question of etiquette had not arisen for residents, ministers, and chargés. Only fraternity guided them; protocol was improvised. The difference between those officials and ambassadors whose character is more elevated demanded that the revolutionaries draw certain distinctions. These distinctions may seem minute but they indicated the degree of respect they should be accorded. For example, they should be seated in an armchair and be able to speak sitting.[25]

The simple ceremony created by that law was soon supplanted by a considerably more elaborate etiquette, one stipulated by the decree of 28 brumaire, an IV (18 November 1795). The Directors even held receptions for diplomats as they did for the Prussian representative David Alphons, baron von Sandoz-Rollin (1740–1809), in December 1795 and donned formal attire. A longer report on etiquette, submitted to the Directory on 14 germinal, an IV (24 March 1796), more precisely regulated the presentation of ambassadors. The Genevan representative to France in 1797, Michel Micheli, thought the new rank of presentation "places things in a convenient order without derogating from the principle of diplomatic equality." He noted the full-dress uniform of the French officials and the presence of the cavalry and infantry under arms accompanied by the beating of the drums.[26] Another representative had a different impression. In 1797, Harris found that the French "have not revolutionized (as M. Delacroix told me that they had done) all diplomatic forms and ceremonies, but that on the contrary they are desirous of adhering to them with the strictest punctuality." He found indeed "strong indications of a disposition to revert to the established forms of negotiation." Still he noted the "extravagant pretensions" of the French who insisted on "points of insignificant form."[27] Burke did not see a major shift during the Directory. He saw only a new form assumed by "a succession of anarchical tyrannies." Despite the changes in form, such as in pomp and ceremony, the same principles persisted. Burke argued that the momentum of the revolution, not a change in government or the wishes of the revolutionaries, determined its policy. Only the destruction of the Revolution would make peace possible.[28]

Despite Burke's reservations, further indication of the new direction was Barras' suggestion that his colleagues adopt the elaborate ceremonial dress designed by David, a large red cloak with a lace collar, a sword *à la romaine*, and a hat decorated with immense plumes.[29] This custom led the Parisians to ridicule the Directors, calling them "*gueux plumés*" or "feathered scoundrels.[30] Other critics impugned the Directors for the "extreme magnificence" of their costume; this splendor "constituted not only a violation of equality, but a pernicious attempt to warp the ideas of the masses, more accustomed to be influenced by sentiment than by reason." Furthermore, such a policy involved a "subjection" to the customs of foreign governments, who preferred "splendor to simplicity" and "wealth to virtue." In short, the Directors had abandoned a "too republican sympathy." We can see here how a debate over gold braid raised larger issues of republican identity. Barras, for one, thought the debate undermined the government. Ironically enough, he also realized that in dressing, undressing, and re-dressing officials, one treated them like puppets or children.[31]

The Directory often found themselves making exceptions to rules they had only recently adopted. In deference to the formalistic spirit of the Turks, the Directory agreed to replace an envoy extraordinary to Turkey with an ambassador *en titre* and to reestablish the old ceremonial for the reception of the Ottoman ambassador.[32] Charles Delacroix, the foreign minister, had emphasized that the ambassador would take offense if the grandeur of his audience did not equal that accorded the French representative at the Porte. The French had told the Ottomans that the pomp of yesterday had been suppressed, but the Ottomans insisted that any change would diminish the glory accorded their state. The Directors adopted a pragmatic policy; they conceded and restored the traditional pomp, including ten cannon salvoes. The French tried to schedule the festivities to coincide with a national celebration, initially with the anniversary of the taking of the Bastille, but later with another anniversary, the fall of Robespierre. After much debate the reception was regulated down to the smallest detail in an attempt to replicate as exactly as possible the ceremonial observed at Constantinople. The irony of a republican regime imitating a Turkish despotism struck many. The revolutionaries deployed a detachment of 40 cavalrymen for the procession plus an additional 50 cavalrymen in the courtyard of the Ministry of Foreign Affairs. After seemingly endless quibbling about such matters as armchairs and who could or could not "cover" their heads, issues which echoed those of the *ancien régime*, the reception was finally arranged. In order to ensure that the march would not be interrupted or crossed, infantry was placed at the corner of every street. Befitting the occasion, the Directors were ornately attired in white satin vests and culottes, blue sashes, embroidered red cloaks, swords, and huge hats with tricolor plumes. State messengers accompanied them in costumes *à la Van Dyck*.[33] As one of the Ottoman ambassadors wrote, "By the grace of God, the ceremony of the *lettres de créance* was executed with the greatest respect."[34] Was that relief? An opposition journal disagreed; the writer found the pomp shabby, the music barbaric and disagreeable, and the ceremony neither brilliant nor majestic. In short, the revolutionaries had borrowed all the forms of the old regime, except richness and magnificence. One editor argued that the most brilliant participant in all the festivities and who best supported the honor of the Ottoman court was definitely—the horse.[35]

The Directors tried to reconcile the often conflicting demands of republican simplicity and contemporary practice. When questioned by their representatives abroad, they usually responded by citing usage and reciprocity. In 1798, Bernadotte at Vienna, for example, only returned visits to his colleagues who were accredited as ambassadors, a consciousness of rank at odds with republican pretensions. He was so sensitive about his prerogatives that he followed rules that the aristocratic courts no longer used and thereby earned a reputation as both ill-informed and tactless.[36] Still an astute observer, Miot de Melito, who returned to Paris in 1798 after a three-year absence, noted the change: "To the too simple manner, to the coarse language of the Republic under the Convention, had succeeded politeness in speech, and elegance in manners and dress. Thee and thou were no longer used; *carmagnoles* were no longer worn ... Not that the luxury and magnificence of a court had as yet been restored; we still have some steps to take before returning to those. Our habits were still tinged with the roughness we were leaving behind us, and with the contempt for the social conventions that we had so long professed."[37] We see in this picture a republic caught between the old and the new.

The concern with protocol and form was even more pronounced under the Consulate and the Empire.[38] In 1801 Sir George Jackson, on a special mission to Paris, noted that the "the parade of this Republican General was a right royal one, & on a small scale, an unrivaled display of the 'pomp and circumstance of war.'" He noted the splendid uniforms, elaborately embroidered with gold and silver, boots with gold inlays and gold spurs. In short, "a very grand affair." Not incidentally, he also reported the rumor that the inscription *République française* on the palace "may vanish."[39] The pomp of the reception signaled a larger shift. In 1802 Charles Whitworth, the British ambassador extraordinary and plenipotentiary, described at great length the ceremonial of his presentation to the First Consul, remarking that such detail was necessary "as it may from its novelty be thought curious."[40] Another individual supports that point. Miot de Melito, who returned to France in 1802, found everywhere "monarchical customs" instead of "austere republican forms." The Tuileries and Saint-Cloud were no "longer the seat of government, the abode of the first Magistrate of a Republic, but the Court of a Sovereign."[41] He admitted that "the first impression made on me by the novel pomp and display was disagreeable and painful." His irritation only increased when he had to return, as he sarcastically remarked, "to pay my court." He resented that access to this "punctilious Court" was rendered almost impossible because of the "rigid etiquette." Miot noted that the First Consul "diverged from Republican manners by small degrees, imperceptible at first, but becoming every day more marked." "Austere Republican forms had disappeared. Gorgeous liveries, sumptuous garments, similar to those worn in the reign of Louis XV, had [displaced] ... military fashions." Boots, sabers, and cockades were "replaced by tights, silk stockings, buckled shoes, dress swords and hats held under the arm." He thought "the change was still more apparent in the reality of things than in their outward appearance ... everything except the name of *Consul* was monarchical."[42]

Once the Empire was proclaimed, the ceremonial became more elaborate. In a note of 16 March 1805 Napoleon underscored that he would be in "grand costume," "on my throne, surrounded by my grand officers."[43] The law of 3 nivôse provided for uniforms for the members of the assemblies and those of the government. Napoleon appointed a Grand Master of Ceremonies, Ségur, who published *Etiquette du palais impériale* in 1805. In asking the grand master of ceremonies to draw up a report on the reception of ministers and ambassadors, he wanted to know what had been done at Versailles, and what was being done at Vienna and St. Petersburg but noted that "Mon règlement adopté, il faut que tout le monde s'y conforme."[44] A statement the sun king would have applauded. In 1807 Napoleon looked back not to the Revolution but to the *ancien régime* when he underscored the importance of regulating the ranks between the great number of foreign princes and the princes of his family with the caveat that "the armchair is uniquely reserved for the emperor and the empress."[45] In a note tinged with irony, Metternich wrote from Paris that Napoleon wanted the marriage ceremony in 1810 to be observed with great *éclat* and to follow the etiquette and protocol used for the marriage of Marie Antoinette, adding that "we know by experience how much the Emperor of the French thinks of these details."[46] Along with the new etiquette went new titles, "My Lord" and "Serene Highness," new denominations, the abolition of "citizen" and the restoration of "monsieur,"[47] and a return to the Gregorian calendar in 1806. As he explained, he intended to impress foreign powers "by the spectacle of my power," which renders every negotiation easier.[48] Could Louis XIV have said it better?

This obsession with the *accoutrements* of a court society extended to diplomats abroad. In 1802 Napoleon told the French ambassador at Constantinople that he must "recapture, by all means, the supremacy that France had for two centuries in this capital." His house must be the most beautiful. He must rank above the other ambassadors. He should always be surrounded "with a numerous suite and only march with grand pomp." He was to "seize all occasions to fix the eyes of the Empire on the ambassador of France."[49] Napoleon continued to assert the precedence of France in other areas. "Pre-eminence," he wrote to Maret in 1812, "is due to my ministers at Naples."[50]

Did the revolutionaries compromise not just on what they called "vain points of etiquette" but also on points of honor? The French did not hesitate to use diplomatic technicalities to achieve their ends or to resort to extortion as the two republics, the United States and France, slid into the quasi-war. The French rejected the credentials of Charles Cotesworth Pinckney (1745–1826) as US minister to France. In an internal memo the question was raised: "Do we want to refuse to receive Pinckney?" There could be many plausible reasons for not doing so; the nomination may not be complete until the Senate confirmation and the *lettre de créance* was "problematic."[51] Adams had sent Pinckney as part of a three-man commission to France, where he was then involved in unsavory negotiations with Talleyrand. The XYZ affair, in which Talleyrand had "requested" a gift of 50,000 pounds sterling from the American commissioners, illustrated only too publicly the sordid corruption in the Directory.[52] The Americans regarded it as an affront to American honor, refused to pay, and broke off negotiations. Pinckney and another member of the commission were deported to the United States; the third member remained but accomplished nothing. The outraged Americans had refused, but others did not. The Prussian representative suggested a gift of 300,000 francs for Talleyrand plus other gifts to various members of the government. The Prussian government did not contest this rather moderate sum, moderate in contrast to that demanded of others. Portugal paid 8,000,000 francs (with Talleyrand receiving 7,000,000 of the total). According to one estimate (and it can only be that), from 1797 to 1804 Talleyrand received more than 30,000,000 francs in "gifts" from various foreign powers. Talleyrand at this time was beginning to accumulate the tremendous fortune that would eventually be his. As Chateaubriand acerbically noted: "Talleyrand, when he is not conspiring, is bargaining."[53] Nor was bribery the only problem. Diplomats of the Revolution proved as subject to other temptations as their predecessors, such as the use of the ambassadorial seal to smuggle goods and exploitation of the exemption of embassy goods from taxation.[54] Pierre Claude, marquis de Poterat, had wanted the new diplomacy to have "this character of malice, of persiflage, of depth and of gaiety which so often rendered the French nation redoubtable to strangers."[55] In too many ways his wish had been fulfilled.

The revolutionaries also made major changes in policy. After 5 September 1793 foreign relations had virtually ceased; the French recalled all their representatives except those accredited to other republics. Subsequent revolutionary governments were forced to abandon the policy of virtual isolation. As Miot de Melito noted: "We were then endeavoring to emerge from the abyss of anarchy." He thought the committee was trying to "restore order, and to restore France ... to Europe, whence she had been in a manner exiled."[56] Under the Thermidoreans, the reception of Barthélémy at Basel in January 1795 with all the former courtesies marked the end of the diplomatic ostracism imposed by Europe since Valmy.[57] On 9 February 1795 the first representative of a monarchical power, Carletti from Tuscany, presented his credentials to the Convention.[58] Prussia, Sweden, Sardinia, Spain, Hesse-Cassel, and others as well resumed relations. The Prussians condemned the diplomatic practices of the Directory as opportunism, if not worse: France uses "guile with powers they still fear a little and arrogance with those they believe subjugated." France proceeded by expediency alone. That meant one could not predict what the revolutionary government would do.[59] In 1796 the British diplomat James Harris noted that "the conduct of this country toward persons vested with public character was perfectly new." The ministers of Modena and Geneva "have been sent away ... without assigning any reason to justify so unprecedented a measure."[60] As Miot de Melito saw it, the Directors were trying to "renew our foreign relations, so far as the isolation in which the coalition of all Powers against France had placed her rendered it possible to do so." They sent consuls to all countries where they thought they would be received.[61] That strategy also meant appointing additional diplomats and even reviving the diplomatic traditions associated with the former monarchy.[62] During the Consulate in 1800 Napoleon instructed Talleyrand to tell Alquier, then ambassador in Spain, that he did not approve of him inviting only ministers of other republics to a celebration of 14 July. He wanted all of the diplomatic corps invited.[63] That directive explicitly abandoned the policy of the Terror that isolated both France and its representatives.

The criteria for appointment had also shifted. The Committee of Public Safety during the Terror recalled its agents, such as Genet, who were jeopardizing France's relations with neutral states because of their zealous republicanism. "In short, although the French Republic had not abandoned all of its ideological principles, its policies in 1793–1794 were a striking departure from the lofty visions that had driven France to war in 1792–1793."[64] Martin notes another shift; in the autumn of 1794 the Thermidoreans implemented a "republican" diplomacy, which purportedly differed from the "revolutionary" diplomacy of the Terror. The Thermidoreans abandoned the "inordinate bellicosity" and the "passionate propaganda" of the revolutionary diplomacy which had alienated so much of Europe.[65] In the area of personnel, just as Robespierre had earlier ordered Genet to return, so later the Directors recalled ardent republicans who had antagonized the host government such as Villars, the minister to Genoa (1794–1796) and an outspoken Jacobin.[66] In order not to alienate other powers, the Directors initially avoided appointing to permanent posts any former member of the Convention who had voted for the death of the king. In an attempt to conciliate other powers, the Directors selected either career diplomats or those of moderate opinions. For example, in 1796 they sent to Spain General Dominique Catherine de Pérignon, a sincere republican, but also a former noble of the robe.[67] Such measures were designed to secure respect for France and instill confidence in the regime. After fructidor, that policy shifted and a number of regicides such as Siéyès were sent. On 5 germinal, an VIII (26 March 1800), in the first months of the Consulate, Talleyrand outlined the qualities a diplomat should have: circumspection, discretion, an inclination to study political relations, a certain elevation of sentiments, a breadth of ideas, and an ability to deal with affairs. Conspicuously missing was the revolutionary agenda of the earlier governments.[68] Aristocrats did not play a significant role in the revolutionary diplomatic corps until Napoleon, who also ennobled a number of men who had served the Directory. Under the Empire, in 1808 Napoleon advised Jerome, king of Westphalia, that if he wanted to send someone to Russia he had to be distinguished, "important for his birth and his education." If he could not find such a person, send no one.[69] The contrast with the early revolutionary governments could not have been more obvious.

The gales of revolution, often of tornadic force, also swept through the ministry of foreign affairs. The number of French legations abroad reflected the revolutionary currents. In 1792 the French had 23 legations; by January 1793, 7; by July, 6; and by the end of 1793, 3. Within the ministry in early 1792 about half of the officials were over 50 years of age and predictably were related. Both the personnel and the basic organization would soon be transformed. As the ministers changed, so too did the ministry of foreign affairs. From 1792, successive purges, "qui avaient jeté sur le pavé tous les ancient serviteurs," devastated the ministry.[70] In 1792 Dumoriez radically modified the dual divisions inherited from the old regime into six different bureaux, only appointing as heads men he personally knew and selecting about half the *commis*. Under Dumouriez, Bonne-Carrère vaunted that the department would be "cleansed in the fire of patriotism."[71] After the Revolution of 10 August, the bureaux were reduced to four. The fall of the Girondins meant further change and the guillotining of Mendouze, Baudry, and Jozeau. Only the fall of Robespierre saved Otto, Colchin, Reinhard, and Rouhière. When Delacroix came to power in 1795 he established ten divisions and, following the recommendations of the Commission des Dix-Sept, fired 40 individuals, four of whom were reinstated. Under the Directory employment was "more precarious, favoritism more audacious and ignorance more brazen."[72] Under Reinhard in 1799 the dual division again emerged. A very few officials did cling on, imparting at least minimal continuity. In ten years the ministry had been transformed; the number of officials increased as did the number of regulations.[73] In 1790 the Department of Foreign Affairs had employed 46; in 1793, 74; and in 1795, 94. In that same period, the expenses had more than doubled from 235,100 livres in 1793–1794 to 505,000 livres in 1795–1796. In 1796–1797, France spent almost three times more on foreign affairs than did any other European power.[74] From 1797 to 1807 the bureaus and exterior posts were reorganized, personnel reduced and regrouped.[75] Talleyrand wanted to change the name from *affaires étrangères* which dated from April 1794 to the *ancien régime* denomination of *relations extérieures*. That request was denied and the name did not change until after the fall of the Empire.[76] Talleyrand at the foreign office did change the republican salutation, "salut et fraternité," in 1801 to "Je vous salue," and in 1803 to "J'ai l'honneur de vous saluer."[77] There were now new "Bastilles of words."

Just as the leaders of France turned against revolutionary internationalism, so they returned to the old and well-trodden paths of traditional diplomatic practice—and power politics. As early as 1792, after the fall of Jemappes, Lebrun suggested that Austria should break with Prussia and be compensated in Silesia for the loss of the Netherlands.[78] *Realpolitik* drowned out the "new diplomacy."[79] In 1797 at the Peace of Campo Formio, revolutionary France turned part of the ancient republic of Venice over to Austria, another part to the Cisalpine Republic, and part to France. "This was old regime diplomacy *redivivus*," as one historian has noted.[80] Even Talleyrand had opposed Napoleon's move: "We are not in Italy to become traffickers in nations."[81] France shucked aside the mask of liberator and revealed the face of conqueror. Venice was traded for other lands. An uprising against the French and the bombardment of a French ship caused Napoleon to remark to a Venetian that "you have called me Attila and I will show you that I am capable of acting like him."[82] When the French envoy criticized the treaty, Bonaparte scoffed. "There is no treaty between the French Republic and the municipality of Venice which obliges us to sacrifice our interests and advantages to those of the Committee of Public Safety or of anyone else in Venice. The French Republic has never made it a matter of principle to fight for other nations." He continued in even blunter terms: "No doubt it comes easily enough to a few chatterboxes, who only deserve the name of fools, to call for a universal Republic. I should like to see these *messieurs* undertake a winter campaign. In any case there is no such thing as a Venetian nation. Effeminate, corrupt, split up into as many divisions as there are towns and as false as they are cowardly, the Italians, especially the Venetians, are quite unfit for liberty."[83]

One wonders what Reybaz, the "simple citizen" from Geneva, thought when the French partitioned Venice and still later when they invaded republican Switzerland in 1798. In the betrayal of Venice and of Switzerland, and other instances, expediency triumphed over ideological commitment. Did Talleyrand recall his condemnation of territorial expansion in 1792? "We now have learned that the only true, useful and reasonable superiority, the only one which is worthy of free and enlightened men, is that of being master of one's own nation and of never making the ridiculous claim that one is master of other nations."[84] The shifts in revolutionary diplomatic practice can be illustrated by Talleyrand's advice to the French minister at Rastatt: "You will have the advantage over Metternich," he wrote. "He has to abandon the gothic forms of German diplomacy." "He forgets that opinion has changed on this point as on many others. If his ideas on European affairs are not better than those he has of the situation in Paris, he will leave himself open to taking more false steps and to reversing his position often."[85] Metternich, the man nauseated by the culinary tricolor, had taken the sugar for the substance.

As Sorel argued: "The revolutionaries used the procedures of the *ancien régime* and made them serve the purposes of the Revolution. They did not break with the traditions of this regime, they simply took them over. They did not innovate, they continued the same practices,"[86] thus imperiling not the old system, but the new. In the words of the historian Paul Viollet: "The heart of the past continued beating and living."[87] Nor were just procedures endangered. More fundamentally, the revolutionaries abandoned their own principles. Not surprisingly given the nature of geopolitical realities, their policies bore a striking resemblance to those of Bourbon France. Bertrand de Jouvenel argued that "the city of command still stands. All that we have done has been to drive out the occupant of the palace and put the representatives of the nation. The new arrivals will quickly find in their newly conquered habitation the memories, the traditions, the symbols, and the means, of domination."[88] We cannot know for certain if the revolutionaries ever realized how ironic their actions were. Sliding down the slippery slope of compromise, the revolutionaries' fervor blinded them to the divergence between their ideals and their actions. Consciously, at least a Genet, a Soulavie, a Bernadotte did not acknowledge the contradiction between the tenets of revolutionary ideology and actual practice. Perhaps they should have heeded the words of Edward Gibbon: "From enthusiasm to imposture the step is slippery and perilous." He was discussing "how a wise man may deceive himself, how a good man may deceive others, how the conscience may slumber in a mixed and middle state between self-illusion and voluntary fraud."[89]

"The reign of the charlatans was over,"[90] but the charlatans of Bourbon France had been replaced by the charlatans of the new revolutionary order who engaged in much the same type of behavior they had earlier denounced. They too seized others' territories, they too fought unjust wars, and they too quibbled over issues of precedence, address, or dress. Style mattered as much to revolutionary France as it had to the *ancien régime*. Like the calendar and the festivals, the new diplomatic style reflected the republican ideology. It reinforced the republican code just as the old had the aristocratic one. The importance of style and the recurrence of certain common territorial and strategic concerns tended to diminish the differences between the old and the new. Indeed, the new diplomacy increasingly resembled the old as the revolutionaries found themselves making compromises with the demands and practices of the old diplomacy.

We can glimpse here, albeit briefly, how at least one revolutionary coped with the blatant discrepancy between avowed ideals and actual practice. Ange-Elisabeth-Louis-Antoine Bonnier, chief of the Diplomatic Bureau, justified just such policies when he argued that "the cabinet of the government is not the portico of Athens. Virtue does not consist in depriving ourselves of advantages. The republican diplomacy, always open and pure, ought, however, to yield to the force of circumstances." That meant not rejecting "expediency in these types of negotiations." We should, he concluded, be able to operate successfully "without compromising ourselves"—an argument a minister of the *ancien régime* would have understood only too well.[91] He would also have understood the earlier actions of Dumouriez, the advocate of an open diplomacy, who had initiated a secret correspondence with Louis XVI, and of Talleyrand, who had scattered an army of secret agents across Europe. Some such as Du Pont in Charleston, found themselves troubled by the ministerial instructions. He found the instructions "as iniquitous as the letters of *cachet* of the old regime and as the mandates of arrest and judgments for execution of a minister of Robespierre." He found himself placed in an unenviable position "between the desire to execute with zeal and exactitude the order transmitted and the fear of being a passive instrument of an arbitrary act."[92]

Ineluctably the revolutionaries found themselves enmeshed in the diplomatic imbroglios of old and though they would not have admitted it, their policies illustrated "the perdurability and resilience of the old regime."[93] Only too soon the French found themselves playing the same role in the international theater of power. Geopolitical concerns and strategic considerations enmeshed them in traditional diplomatic practice and power politics. "The patterns of war as the revolutionaries waged it arrestingly recalled the patterns of competition in the *ancien régime*."[94] The struggle with Austria impelled the revolutionaries to tread the familiar path to the East. The republican regime that publicly courted only republican regimes sent agents to conduct secret negotiations with the Turkish Empire.[95] Moreover, the Committee of Public Safety still cherished the notion of invading Britain, the modern Carthage.[96] As Stone has argued: "When Robespierre or Bertrand Barère or one of the other Jacobins wielding power in the Terror banged the deafening drums of patriotism in the National Convention over the supposed turpitude of the British, what were they doing if not resurrecting (and manipulating) the Anglophobia of the old regime?"[97] In 1783 Lafayette remarked, "Without having the self-conceit to treat them as personal enemies, I cannot forget that they are enemies of French glory and prosperity."[98] In 1797 La Harpe tellingly remarked: "'Delenda est carthago' is in the mouth of all here."[99] Bell remarks that "the massive propaganda campaigns against foreign enemies … dwarfed anything seen previously … In fact they literally re-discovered the war propaganda of the 1750s." They recycled old poems just as Rouget de Lisle borrowed lines for the *Marseillaise*. Those who did not welcome the French were to be treated like Carthage.[100]

An anonymous bureaucrat in the Ministry of Foreign Affairs articulated the agenda in 1794: "The Netherlands were to be 'ruined,' Spain was to be stripped of its royal house, and Prussia was to be conquered."[101] The Directory continued the *ancien régime's* policy of weakening Austria and counteracting English power.[102] The so-called *tournant diplomatique* of the Directory entailed only changes in form such as the reception of ambassadors and the return of more ceremonial.[103] The regimes had changed, but the enemies had stayed the same. The continuity is underscored by historians who dub the period from 1688 to 1814 the Second Hundred Years' War. The British saw the aggression of revolutionary France as a continuation of the traditional rivalry. Dundas at the War Office wanted to humble France "with the view of enlarging our national wealth and security."[104] Note the argument of the diplomat Robert Liston for supporting the British declaration of war with France: "The majority of the nation will approve of our ministry's seizing the occasion that offers to attempt to clip the wings of France. The wars of the last century showed how dangerous she was to her neighbors as an absolute monarchy. The end of the present has proved that she is not less so as a republick."[105] The argument of François d'Ivernois (1757–1842), the Genevan exile and British agent, spoke to many: "who could wish himself into thinking that the French revolution is not another Louis XIV?"[106]

Underlying this Anglo- and Austrophobia was an even deeper current, the conviction that France could and should play a hegemonic role in both maritime and continental affairs. In a letter of 2 January 1794 the Committee of Public Safety contended that France "alone of all European states can and should be a power on both land and sea."[107] "How could 150 years of Gallic pretensions in the world's great affairs have been more effectively summed up?"[108] That statement echoes an earlier one of 1759 of François-Joachim de Pierre, cardinal de Bernis: "The object of [our] politics ... "has been and always will be to play in Europe the superior role which suits [France's] seniority, its dignity, and its grandeur."[109] It could have been written in 1794 or 1800. Nor did the French revolutionaries hesitate to link the destiny of France with "the destiny of humanity" in Robespierre's words or "the fate of the world" in Lacroix's.[110]

This combination of Gallic ambitions and eschatalogical expectations made a dangerous concoction. As Bailey Stone has argued: "as the Revolution furthered the agenda of the old regime, so the Napoleonic era advanced the agenda of both prerevolutionary and revolutionary France."[111] Indeed the revolutionary policy was partly a return to the old regime in both military strategies and diplomatic stratagems with its secret treaties, spies, bribes, requisitions, forced contributions and indemnities but other acts including the organized pillage reflected its new ambitions: defense of the dignity of the republic and propagation of liberty.[112] And yet the mix of ideology with nationalism was a new brew. The contemporary Clausewitz noted the "fury of the oncoming torrent." "The colossal weight of the whole French people ... came crashing down us."[113] Marshal Ferdinand Foch noted the difference: "the wars of kings were at an end; the wars of peoples were beginning."[114] In the words of Victor Hugo, revolutions although "unfinished, bastardized and doctored," "nearly always retain sufficient sanity not to come wholly to grief. A revolution is never an abdication."[115] Fouad Ajami was speaking of the Iranian revolution but it could apply equally to France: "By their very nature revolutions are brief affairs; then the world reconstitutes itself. What emerges is not quite the old world before the storm, but a hybrid, a jumble of old and new realities spawned by the revolutionary situation."[116]

The French revolutionaries challenged the Europeans' assumption of a common diplomatic culture, culture in the sense that Burke defined it as "a system of shared meanings, attitudes and values."[117] That that assumption was widely shared is revealed in a letter to Grenville of November 1792 by the British minister to Turin from 1783 to 1798, John Hampden-Trevor. After analyzing the "present unexampled situation of Europe," he discussed the Abbé de Saint Pierre, who had formulated a project for perpetual peace at the conclusion of the War of the Spanish Succession. He attached a lengthy enclosure by an unidentified correspondent because he felt obliged "not only to think but to act for the benefit of Nations." The anonymous author thought that powers should be obliged to act in concert "against the furor of the new delirium" because Europe is "une grande République," bound together despite their disputes by economic products and reciprocal needs.[118]

This letter was sent as Britain was moving to join the alliance against France in a struggle that would last until 1815. When the rules of that comity broke down, the tensions escalated as seen in Florence. Count Carletti, a Florentine nobleman, noted for his Jacobin sympathies and his hostility to England, insultingly questioned William Wyndham about allied victories. Wyndham, who responded by horsewhipping Carletti, admitted that perhaps his response was "too violent." After a "convivial" dinner, he sent a letter to Carletti, who refused to read it. Instead he sent Wyndham a letter alleging that he was hiding behind the shield of his position as British minister. A duel ensued in which Carletti fired first and missed and Wyndham deloped. The issue was resolved when Carletti wrote Wyndham a letter retracting his earlier statements.[119] In this incident the protagonist resorted to a traditional method to resolve a quarrel, the duel. Note that the rules of engagement were determined by what Burke called "that federative society" or "the diplomatic republic of Europe."[120] Gentz saw it as "an extensive social commonwealth of which the characteristic object was the preservation and reciprocal guarantee of the rights of all its members."[121] The French rejection of that society led Gentz to bemoan "the fatal dissolution of all ties, or all reciprocal attachment and fidelity"[122] or Burke to argue that France should be "expunged out of the system of Europe."[123] That culture created a code of conduct, certain expectations of what and what was not appropriate behavior. The revolutionaries fractured that ideological unity and defied its expectations. Although they continued to espouse revolutionary principles, the dream of transforming the international system remained just that. Eckstein would argue that the anarchic nature of international system inevitably entails competition for power "which soon becomes an end in itself."[124] Even Talleyrand, hardly a starry-eyed idealist, had thought that the "reign of illusions [by which he meant the royal thirst for conquest] is then over for France."[125] He could hardly have been more wrong.

Notes

1. Guyot, *Le Directoire et la paix de l'Europe*, 88.
2. Metternich, *Memoirs*, 2: 235.
3. Emile Durkheim, *The Elementary Forms of the Religious Life: A Study in Religious Sociology*, trans. Joseph Wood Ward Swain (Glencoe, IL: Free Press, 1947), 423.
4. Ibid., 63.
5. Edmund Burke quoted in Chapman, *Edmund Burke*, 186.
6. Niccolo Machiavelli, *The Prince*, ch. 6, in *The Chief Works and Others*, translated by Allan Gilbert (Durham, NC: Duke University Press, 1965), 26.
7. Furet, *Interpreting the French Revolution*, 25–26, 16–17.
8. Schiller's letter of 13 July 1793 in Klaus L. Berghahn, "Gedankenfreiheit: From Political Reform to Aesthetic Revolution in Schiller's Works," in *The Internalized Revolution: German Reactions to the French Revolution 1798–1989*, edited by Ehrhard Bahr and Thomas P. Saine (New York: Garland Publishing, Inc., 1992), 107.
9. Dale Van Kley, "The *Ancien Régime*, Catholic Europe, and the Revolution's Religious Schism," in *A Companion to the French Revolution*, edited by Peter McPhee, 123–143 (London: Blackwell, 2013), 138.
10. Verena Steller, "The Power of Protocol: On the Mechanisms of Symbolic Action in Diplomacy in Franco-German Relations, 1871–1914," in *The Diplomats World*, ed. Mösslung and Riotte, 200.
11. Christian Windler, "Réseaux personnels, perceptions de l'autre et pratique des relations consulaires et politiques dans l'espace méditerranéen" in *Acteurs diplomatiques et ordre international XVIIIe–XIXe siècle*, edited by Marc Belissa and Gilles Ferragu, 73–97 (Paris: Éditions Kimé, 2007), 88.
12. Martin, "Le Comité diplomatique," 18 underscores that "the principles of the *droit des gens* remained entirely subordinated to the exigencies of the national interest."
13. Windler, "Réseaux personnels," 90.
14. Guyot, *Le Directoire et la paix de l'Europe*, 674.
15. Alexis de Tocqueville, *The Old Regime and the French Revolution*, x.
16. Bély, *L'Art de la paix en Europe*, 657.
17. Cambacérès quoted in Sorel, *L'Europe et la Révolution française*, 4: 265.

18. Merlin to Jean Baptiste Lallement quoted in Sorel, *L'Europe et la Révolution française*, 4: 268.
19. A. A. E., États-Unis, CP 44, fol. 385, from Minister of Foreign Relations, 27 brumaire, an 4. See also circular of 5 brumaire, an III (26 October 1794), quoted in Martin, "Les Enjeux diplomatiques," 6–7 and the redefinition of diplomats as not only political agents but also as "a cultural vehicle."
20. Debidour, ed., *Recueil des actes du Directoire exécutif*, 1: 417, instructions to Perignon, ambassador of the republic in Spain, 13 January 1796.
21. B. L., Add. Mss. 59025, John Trevor to Lord Grenville, fol. 92 Richmond, 24 November 1798.
22. France, *Bulletin des lois de la République*, an II, no. 237, 6 fructidor.
23. Aulard, ed., *Recueil des actes du Comité de salut public*, 4: 185–186, meeting of 16 May 1793.
24. Devon Record Office, CP 453, John Stuart, 4th earl of Bute to Drake, Madrid, 5 January 1796.
25. *Moniteur*, 24: 292–293, 4 floréal 1795.
26. Chapuisat, *De la Terreur à l'annexation*, 201–202, 21 prairial, an V.
27. P.R.O., FO 27/49, fol. 248 Harris, 6 July 1797 and fol. 279–282 of 11 July 1797.
28. Marc Belissa, "La Paix impossible?" Le Débat sur les négociations franco-anglaises sous le Directoire et la Consulat," in *Le Négoce de la paix. Les nations et les traités franco-britanniques (1713–1802)*, edited by Jean-Pierre Jessenne, Renaud Morieux, et Pascal Dupuy (Paris: Société des études Robespierristes, 2008), 100.
29. Dry, *Soldats ambassadeurs*, 1: 30–31.
30. Burke, *Works*, 6: 48.
31. Barras, *Memoirs*, 3: 511, thermidor, an VII (July–August 1798).
32. Guyot, *Le Directoire et la paix de l'Europe*, 79 and 92.
33. Maurice Herbette, *Un Ambassade turque sous le Directoire* (Paris: Perrin et cie, 1902), 110–131.
34. Morali Seyyid Alî Efendi and Seyyid Abdürrahim Muhibb Efendi, *Deux Ottomans à Paris sous le Directoire et l'Empire* (Arles: Sinbad, 1998), 86–93.
35. Herbette, *Un Ambassade turque sous le Directoire*, 138, *Le Véridique*.
36. Dry, *Soldats ambassadeurs*, 2: 395–396.
37. Miot de Melito, *Memoirs*, 131–132.
38. See for example, Talleyrand, *Lettres inédites*, 17, 19, 109, 137.
39. Jackson, *Diaries and Letters*, 1: 18–19, 23 November 1801.
40. Oscar Browning, ed., *Being the Despatches of Lord Whitworth and Others* (London: Longmans, Green and Co., 1887), 21–22, 26. On the irritability of the First Consul, triggered by a perceived insult to a French representative in Sweden, see 77–78, Paris, 17 February 1803.

41. Mowat, *The Diplomacy of Napoleon*, 103.
42. Miot de Melito, *Memoirs*, 161, 247–249, 282.
43. Napoléon, *Correspondance*, 10: 229 to Marescalchi, Minister of Foreign Relations of the Italian republic, 25 ventôse, an XIII (16 March 1805).
44. Palluel, ed. *Dictionnaire de l'Empereur*, 913–914, Paris, 22 September 1807. Title XIII of the imperial decree of 24 messidor, an XII (1814), that regulated public ceremonial dealt with French and foreign ambassadors. *France, Bulletin des lois de l'Empire française*, 4th series, vol. 1, bulletin #10, #110.
45. Palluel, ed. *Dictionnaire de l'Empereur*, 913, Paris, 22 August 1807.
46. Metternich, *Memoirs*, 2: 383–384, Metternich to Schwarzenberg, 19 February 1810.
47. Miot de Melito, *Memoirs*, 337.
48. Madeleine Delpierre, "Les Costumes de cour et les uniformes civils du Premier Empire," *Musée Carnavalet*, 11 (November 1958): 2–22.
49. Napoléon, *Correspondance*, 8: 69, Saint Cloud 26 vendemaire, an XI (18 October 1802).
50. Palluel, ed. *Dictionnaire de l'Empereur*, 58, Paris, 26 janvier 1812.
51. A. A. E., CP, États-Unis, vol. 46, part 4, fols. 427–429.
52. J. F. Bernard, *Talleyrand: A Biography* (New York: G. P. Putnam's Sons, 1973), 205.
53. Ibid., 205–207.
54. Grandmaison, *L'Ambassade française en Espagne pendant la Révolution (1789–1804)*, 125.
55. Dard, *Un Épicurien sous la terreur*, 235.
56. Miot de Melito, *Memoirs*, 32.
57. Dry, *Soldats ambassadeurs sous le Directoire*, 1: 26–27.
58. Masson, *Le Département des affaires étrangères*, 348.
59. Kittstein, *Politik im Zeitalter der Revolution*, 136, quotes Jacobi to Sandoz, 18 October 1798, and Jacobi to Sandoz, 4 February 1799.
60. Harris, *Diaries and Correspondence*, 3: 346 Paris, Harris to Grenville, 14 December 1796.
61. Miot de Melito, *Memoirs*, 32.
62. After fructidor 1797, Carnot refuted the charge that he had suggested not sending ambassadors to various courts. He claimed that the Directors on the contrary "by their puerile haughtiness of conduct toward the envoys of foreign courts, expose those of the Republic to humiliating retaliations" and undermine the possibility of peace. *Reply of L. N. M. Carnot, Citizen of France, one of the Founders of the republic, and constitutional Member of the Executive Directory* (London: J. Wright, 1799), 89–90.
63. Napoléon, *Correspondance*, 6: 427, to Talleyrand, Paris, 28 July 1800.

64. Walt, *Revolution and War*, 97.
65. Martin, "Les Enjeux diplomatiques," 5.
66. Guyot, *Le Directoire et la paix d'l'Europe*, 81.
67. Dry, *Soldats ambassadeurs sous le Directoire*, 1: 60–61.
68. Lacour-Gayet, *Talleyrand*, 2: 42.
69. Napoléon, *Correspondance*, 16: 411, Napoleon to Jerome, 11 March 1808.
70. Masson, *Le Département des affaires étrangères*, 495.
71. Ibid., 159.
72. Ibid., 497.
73. Baillou, Lucet, Vimont, Jacques, eds., *Les Affaires étrangères et le corps diplomatique français*, 279–363 and Frey and Frey, *Proven Patriots*, 91.
74. Masson, *Le Département des affaires étrangères*, 384–386.
75. Outry, "Histoire et principes de l'administration française des affaires étrangères," 494.
76. Lacour-Gayet, *Talleyrand*, 2: 42.
77. Ibid., 2: 31.
78. Savage, "Foreign Policy and Political Culture in Later Eighteenth-Century France," 323.
79. Sorel, *Europe and the French Revolution*, 525.
80. Blanning, *The Origins of the French Revolutionary Wars*, 175.
81. Bernard, *Talleyrand*, 197.
82. Lincolnshire Archives, Worsley Papers, 14, fol. 178 Worsley to Grenville, Venice 3 May 1797.
83. Napoléon, *Correspondance*, 3: 399–401, #2318.
84. Bernard, *Talleyrand*, 197.
85. Pallain, ed., *Le Ministère de Talleyrand sous le Directoire*, 188, Talleyrand to Jean Baptiste Treilhard, 5 nivôse, an VI.
86. Sorel, *Europe and the French Revolution*, 526.
87. Paul Viollet quoted in Bertrand de Jouvenel, *On Power: the Natural History of its Growth*, translated by J. F. Huntington (Indianapolis: Liberty Fund, 1993), 242.
88. Jouvenel, *On Power*, 123.
89. Gibbon quoted in ibid., 260.
90. Buchez and Roux, *Histoire parlementaire*, 6: 65, Goupil de Prefeln, 27 May 1790.
91. Guyot, *Le Directoire et la paix de l'Europe*, 88.
92. Hagley, W3–322, Victor Du Pont to Letombe, 21 pluviôse V, [9 February 1797].
93. Mayer, *The Persistence of the Old Regime*, 6.
94. Stone, *The Genesis of the French Revolution*, 238.
95. R. R. Palmer, *Twelve Who Ruled* (Princeton: University Press, 1941), 104.

96. Ibid., 340. Reference to modern Carthage, A. A. E., CP, États-Unis, vol. 44, part III, fol. 253, Adet to Randolph, Philadelphia, 23 thermidor, an III. Also see Adet's reference, it is necessary above all to destroy "this universal Carthage" in A. A. E., CP, États-Unis 44, part 4, fol. 394 Adet, Philadelphia, 29 brumaire, an 4. Or Cloots "C'est en Hollande qu nous détruirons Carthage," in Piers Mackesy, *Statesmen at War* (London: Longman, 1974), 36.
97. Stone, *The Genesis of the French Revolution*, 238. On Anglophobia see Frances Acomb, *Anglophobia in France, 1763–1789: An Essay in the History of Constitutional and Nationalism* (Durham, NC: Duke University Press, 1950).
98. Acomb, *Anglophobia in France, 1763–1789*, 115. Camille Desmoulins remarked that "[w]e shall go beyond these English, who are so proud of their constitution and who mocked at our servitude." Ibid., p. 121.
99. La Harpe, *Correspondance*, 1: 136, 14 floréal, an V, 3 May 1797.
100. Bell, *The Cult of the Nation in France*, 100–101.
101. Ibid., 101.
102. Denis Woronoff, *The Thermidorean Reaction and the Directory*, translated by Julian Jackson (Cambridge: University Press, 1972).
103. Belissa, "'La Paix impossible?'" in *Le Négoce de la paix*, ed. Jessenne, Morieux, and Dupuy, 95–109.
104. Harvey Mitchell, *The Underground War against Revolutionary France: The Missions of William Wickham, 1794–1800* (Oxford: Clarendon Press, 1965), 31.
105. P.R.O., FO 353/64, Robert Liston, London, 29 April 1793.
106. Quoted in Jouvenel, *On Power*, 244. On that same page Jouvenel remarks, "And the war was pursued with the same enemy, the same plans, and the same objects as in the palmiest days of the monarchy."
107. Quoted in Bailey Stone, *The Genesis of the French Revolution*, 238–239.
108. Ibid.
109. Ibid., 29–30.
110. See Robespierre, "Report on the Principles of Political Morality," 5 February 1794, 368–384, and "Discourse by Citizen Lacroix to the Unity Section at the meeting of July 28, 1793," 332–337, quoted in *University of Chicago Readings in Western Civilization*, edited by John W. Boyer and Julius Kirshner vol. 7: *The Old Regime and the French Revolution*, edited by Keith Michael Baker (Chicago: University of Chicago Press, 1987), 370 and 336.
111. Stone, *The Genesis of the French Revolution*, 242.
112. Hervé Leuwers, "Théorie et pratique des relations internationales chez les hommes du Directoire," *La République directoriale* (1998): 944.
113. Karl von Clausewitz, *On War*, 518.
114. Quoted in T. C. W. Blanning, *The French Revolutionary Wars*, 82.

115. Victor Hugo, *Les Misérables*, translated by Norman Denny (New York: Penguin, 2012), 712. Hugo is quoted in Fouad Ajami, "Iran: The Impossible Revolution," *Foreign Affairs*, 1 December 1988. http://www.foreignaffairs.com/articles/43992/fouad-ajami/iran-the-impossible-revolution.
116. Fouad Ajami, "Iran: The Impossible Revolution."
117. Burke quoted in Tim Harris, ed., *Popular Culture in England, c. 1500–1850* (New York: St. Martin's Press, 1955), 1.
118. B. L., Add. 59025, fol. 222, John Trevor to Grenville, November 1792.
119. B. L., Add. Mss. 59031 fol. 18–19, Wyndham to Grenville, Florence, 14 June 1794.
120. Burke, *Works*, 4: 433.
121. Gentz, *Fragments Upon the Balance of Power in Europe*, 60–61.
122. Ibid., 93.
123. Burke, *Speeches*, 3: 456, 9 February 1790.
124. Arthur M. Eckstein," Review: Brigands, Emperors and Anarchy," *The International History Review*, 22, no. 4 (December 2000): 870.
125. Quoted in Schama, *Citizens*, 680.

References

Acomb, Frances Dorothy. *Anglophobia in France 1763–1789; an Essay in the History of Constitutionalism and Nationalism*. Durham: Duke University Press, 1950.

Ajami, Fouad. "Iran: The Impossible Revolution." *Foreign Affairs*, 1 December 1988. http://www.foreignaffairs.com/articles/43992/fouad-ajami/iran-the-impossible-revolution.

Alî Efendi, Morali Seyyid, and Seyyid Abdürrahim Muhibb Efendi. *Deux ottomans à Paris sous le Directoire et l'Empire*. Arles: Sindbad, 1998.

Aulard, François-Alphonse, ed. *Recueil des actes du Comité de salut public avec la correspondance officielle des représentants en mission et le registre du conseil exécutif provisoire*. 27 vols. Paris: Imprimerie nationale, 1889–1923.

Bahr, Ehrhard, and Thomas Saine, eds. *The Internalized Revolution: German Reactions to the French Revolution, 1789–1989*. New York: Garland Publishing, 1992.

Baillou, Jean, Charles Lucet, and Jacques Vimont, eds. *Les Affaires étrangères et le corps diplomatique français. Tome 1: De l 'Ancien Régime au Second Empire*. Paris: Éditions du Centre national de la recherche scientifique, 1984.

Baker, Keith Michael, ed. *The Old Regime and the French Revolution, vol. 7 of University of Chicago Readings in Western Civilization*. Edited by John W. Boyer and Julius Kirshner. Chicago: University of Chicago Press, 1987.

Barras, Paul, vicomte de. *Memoirs of Barras, member of the Directorate*. New York: Harper and Brothers, 1895.

Belissa, Marc, and Gilles Ferrague, eds. *Acteurs diplomatiques et ordre international XVIIIe–XIXe siècle*. Paris: Éditions Kimé, 2007.
Belissa, Marc. "'La Paix impossible?' Le débat sur les négociations franco-anglais sous le Directoire et le Consulat." In *Le négoce de la paix. Les nations et les traités franco-britanniques (1713–1802)*, edited by Jean-Pierre Jessenne, Renaud Morieux, and Pascal Dupuy, 95–109. Paris: Société des études robespierristes, 2008.
Bell, David A. *The Cult of the Nation in France: Inventing Nationalism, 1680–1800*. Cambridge, MA: Harvard University Press, 2001.
Bély, Lucien. *L'Art de la paix en Europe: Naissance de la diplomatie moderne XVIe–XVIIIe siècle*. Paris: Presses universitaires de France, 2007.
Bernard, J. F. *Talleyrand: A Biography*. New York: G. P. Putnam's Sons, 1973.
Blanning, T. C. W. *The French Revolutionary Wars, 1787–1802*. London: Arnold, 1996.
———. *The Origins of the French Revolutionary Wars*. New York: Longman, 1987.
Browning, Oscar, ed. *Being the Despatches of Lord Whitworth and Others*. London: Longmans, Green and Co., 1887.
Buchez, Philippe-Joseph-Benjamin, and Prosper-Charles Roux-Lavergne, eds. *Histoire parlementaire de la Révolution française*. 40 vols. Paris: Paulin, 1834–1838.
Burke, Edmund. *The Speeches of the Right Honourable Edmund Burke, in the House of Commons and in Westminister Hall*. London: Longman, 1816.
———. *The Works of the Right Honourable Edmund Burke*. 12 vols. Boston: Little Brown and Co., 1866–1867.
Carnot, Lazare Nicolas Marguerite. *Reply of L. N. M. Carnot, Citizen of France*. London: J. Wright, 1799.
Chapman, Gerald W. *Edmund Burke: The Practical Imagination*. Cambridge, MA: Harvard University Press, 1967.
Chapuisat, Édouard. *De la Terreur à l'annexation: Genève et la république française, 1793–1798*. Geneva: Edition ATAR, 1912.
Debidour, Antonin, ed. *Recueil des actes du Directoire Exécutif (procès-verbaux, arrêtés, instructions, lettres et actes divers)*. Paris: Imprimerie nationale, 1910.
Delpierre, Madeleine. "Les Costumes de cour et les uniformes civils du premier Empire." *Bulletin du Musée Carnavalet* 11 (November, 1958): 2–23.
Dry, Adrien Fleury. *Soldats ambassadeurs sous le Directoire, an IV-an VIII*. Paris: Plon, 1906.
Durkheim, Émile. *The Elementary Forms of the Religious Life: A Study in Religious Sociology*. Translated by Joseph Ward Swain. Glencoe, IL: The Free Press, 1947.
Eckstein, Arthur M. "Brigands, Emperors, and Anarchy." *The International History Review* 22, no. 4 (December, 2000): 862–879.
France. *Bulletin des lois de la République, an III, 1794–1795*, no. 705.
Frey, Linda, and Marsha Frey. *"Proven Patriots": The French Diplomatic Corps, 1789–1799*. St. Andrews, Scotland: St. Andrew Studies in French History

and Culture, 2011. http://research-repository.st-andrews.ac.uk/handle/10023/1881.

Furet, François. *Interpreting the French Revolution.* Cambridge: Cambridge University Press, 1981.

Gentz, Friedrich von. *Fragments Upon the Balance of Power in Europe.* London: Peltier, 1806.

Grandmaison, Charles-Alexandre Geoffroy de. *L'Ambassade française en Espagne pendant la Révolution (1789–1804).* Paris: Plon, 1892.

Guyot, Raymond. *Le Directoire et la paix de l'Europe: Des traités de Bâle à la deuxième coalition, 1795–1799.* Paris: Félix Alcan, 1911.

Harris, James. *Diaries and Correspondence of James Harris, First Earl of Malmesbury.* 4 vols. 1844. Reprint. New York: AMS Press, 1970.

Harris, Tim, ed. *Popular Culture in England, c. 1500–1850.* New York: St. Martin's Press, 1995.

Herbette, Maurice. *Un Ambassade turque sous le Directoire.* Paris: Perrin et cie, 1902.

Jackson, Sir George. *The Diaries and Letters of Sir George Jackson, K. C. H.* Edited by Lady Catherine Hannah Charlotte Jackson. London: Richard Bentley and Son, 1872.

Jouvenel, Bertrand de. *On Power: The Natural History of Its Growth.* Translated by J. F. Huntington. Indianapolis: Liberty Fund, 1993.

Kittstein, Lothar. *Politik im Zeitalter der Revolution: Untersuchungen zur preussischen Staatlichkeit 1792–1807.* Wiesbaden: Franz Steiner Verlag, 2003.

Lacour-Gayet, Georges. *Talleyrand, 1754–1838.* 4 vols. Paris: Payot, 1928–1934.

La Harpe, Frédéric-César de. *Correspondance de Frédéric-César de la Harpe sous la République helvétique.* Neuchâtel: Baconnière, 1982.

Leuwers, Hervé. "Théorie et pratique des relations internationales chez les hommes du Directoire." In *La République directoriale*, edited by Philippe Bourdin and Bernard Gainot, 2, 937–939. Clermont-Ferrand: Société des Études Robespierristes, 1997.

Machiavelli, Niccolò. The Prince. In *The Chief Works and Others.* Translated by Allan Gilbert. Durham, NC: Duke University Press, 1965.

McPhee, Peter, ed. *A Companion to the French Revolution.* Chichester, West Sussex: Wiley-Blackwell, 2013.

Martin, Virginie. "Le Comité diplomatique: homicide par décret de la diplomatie (1790–1793)?" *La Révolution française: Cahiers de l'Istitute d'histoire de la Révolution française* 3 (2012a): 1–33.

———."Les Enjeux diplomatiques dans le *Magasin encyclopédique* (1795–1799): du rejet des systèmes politiques à la redéfition des rapports entres les nations." *La Révolution française: Cahiers de l'Institut d'histoire de la Révolution française* 1 (2012b): 1–30.

Masson, Frédéric. *Le Département des affaires étrangères pendant la Révolution, 1787–1804.* Paris: E. Plon, 1877.

Mayer, Arno J. *The Persistence of the Old Regime: Europe to the Great War.* New York: Pantheon Books, 1981.
Metternich-Winneburg, Clemens Wenzel Neopomuk Lothar, Fürst von. *Memoirs of Prince Metternich.* Edited by Prince Richard Metternich. 5 vols. New York: C. Scribner's Sons, 1880–1882.
Miot de Melito, Andre F. *Memoirs of Count Miot de Melito, Minister, Ambassador, Councillor of State.* Edited by Wilhelm August Fleischmann. New York: Charles Scribner's Sons, 1881.
Mitchell, Harvey. *The Underground War Against Revolutionary France: The Missions of William Wickham, 1794–1800.* Oxford: Clarendon Press, 1965.
Mösslang, Markus, and Torsten Riotte, eds. *The Diplomats' World, A Cultural History of Diplomacy, 1815–1914.* Oxford: Oxford University Press, 2008.
Moniteur, seule histoire authentique et inaltérée de la Révolution française. 32 vols. Paris: Plon Frères, 1847–1863.
Mowat, R. B. *The Diplomacy of Napoleon.* London: Edward Arnold & Co., 1924.
Napoléon I. *Correspondance de Napoléon I.* 32 vols. Paris: Imprimerie Impériale, 1858–1869.
Outry, Amédée. "Histoire et principes de l'administration française des affaires étrangères." *Revue française de science politique* 3, nos. 2, 3 (1953): 298–318, 491–510.
Palluel, André. *Dictionnaire de l'Empereur.* Paris: Plon, 1969.
Palmer, R. R. *Twelve Who Ruled: The Year of the Terror in the French Revolution.* Princeton: University Press, 1941.
Savage, Gary. "Foreign Policy and Political Culture in Later Eighteenth-Century France." In *Cultures of Power in Europe During the Long Eighteenth Century*, edited by Hamish Scott and Brendan Simms, 304–324. Cambridge: University Press, 2007.
Schama, Simon. *Citizens: A Chronicle of the French Revolution.* New York: Alfred A. Knopf, 1989.
Sorel, Albert. *L'Europe and la Révolution française.* 8 vols. Paris: E. Plon Nourrit et cie, 1897–1904.
Stone, Bailey. *The Genesis of the French Revolution.* Cambridge: Cambridge University Press, 1994.
Talleyrand-Périgord, Prince Charles Maurice de, prince de Bénévent. *Lettres inédites de Talleyrand à Napoleon 1800–1809.* Edited by Pierre Bertrand. Paris: Perrin et Cie., 1889.
Tocqueville, Alexis de. *The Old Regime and the French Revolution.* Translated by Stuart Gilbert. Garden City, NY: Doubleday, 1955.
Walt, Stephen M. *Revolution and War.* Ithaca, NY: Cornell University Press, 1996.
Woronoff, Denis. *The Thermidorean Reaction and the Directory.* Translated by Julian Jackson. Cambridge: University Press, 1972.

Index[1]

A

Adams, John Quincy, 4, 14n14, 237, 238, 249n131, 250n143
Adet, Pierre-Auguste, 77, 79, 80, 83, 89n110, 90n115, 103, 115, 148, 157, 193, 239
Agulhon, Maurice, 4, 5, 14n15, 15n27, 15n31
Aiguillon, Emmanuel-Armand de Vignerot du Plessis- Richelieu, duc d, 190, 208n92
Ajami, Fouad, 275, 282n115, 282n116
Alquier, Charles- Jean-Marie, 235, 269
Ambroise, Louis- Gabriel, 145
Amiens, Congress of, 128n103, 131n165
Andréossy, Antoine- François, comte d, 202
Argenson, René-Louis de Voyer de Paulmy, marquis d, 25, 32, 47n16

Aubert-Dubayet, Jean-Baptiste-Annibal, general, 107
August 10th, 70, 80, 107, 223
Austria, 30–35, 38, 39, 44, 50n76, 207n75, 220, 232, 234, 271, 274
Austrian Succession, War of the, 27, 30, 31, 48n37, 51n76
Avignon, 3, 179

B

Baden, negotiations at, 221
Baecque, Antoine de, 5
Baker, Keith, 142, 161n10, 281n110
Baldwin, George, 90n132, 223, 245n27
Ball, Alexander John, captain, 83, 91n142, 91n143
Barère, Bertrand, 9, 45, 75, 99, 124n22, 142, 162n15, 163n42, 200, 274

[1] Note: Page number followed by 'n' refer to notes.

Barnave, Antoine- Pierre Joseph-Marie, 37, 41, 54n151
Barras, Paul-François- Jean-Nicolas, 76, 88n77, 113, 155, 202, 212n185, 264, 278n31
Barthélémy, François, marquis de, 69, 71, 74–76, 81, 87n70, 107, 125n38, 125n52, 154, 201, 208n94, 212n177, 221–223, 233, 234, 245n31, 248n112, 268
Basel, 75, 88n74, 167n115, 201, 268
Basel, Peace of, 75
Basire, Claude, 146
Bassville, Nicolas-Jean-Hugou de, 157, 178–184, 203n10, 235, 260
Bavaria, 33, 35, 39, 99, 222
Bavarian Succession, War of, 33, 35, 37
Beaumarchais, Pierre-Augustin Caron de, 161n12
Belissa, Marc, 6, 16n42, 16–17n58, 17n64, 47n19, 47n23, 49n44, 49n58, 53n122, 86n40, 124n27, 124n30, 277n11, 278n28, 281n103
Bell, David, 7, 8, 14n6, 16n38, 16n41, 17n59, 55n171, 127n77, 163n41, 207n88, 274, 281n100
Bély, Lucien, 49n55, 52n113, 53n138, 54n148, 56n183, 56n193, 84n15, 105, 124n35, 125n50, 127n73, 127n74, 127n76, 261, 277n16
Berlin, 11, 103, 107, 108, 110, 111, 117, 128n98, 128n99, 129n126, 129n129, 132n191, 158, 192, 201, 202, 207n73, 234, 235
Bernadotte, Jean Baptiste-Jules, 11, 12, 103, 178, 185–189, 220, 234, 265, 272
Bernis, François-Joachim de Pierre de, cardinal, 30, 52n108, 260, 275

Beurnonville, Pierre de Ruel, marquis de, 116, 132n191
Bigot de Saint Croix, Claude, 234
Bischoffwerder, Johann Rudolf von, 6
Blaauw, Jacob, 119
Black, Jeremy, 50n66, 69, 86n45, 87n68, 101, 125n45, 131n174, 198, 208n108, 210n152, 252n183
Blakemore, Steven, 14n5, 161n1, 161n14, 162n17, 162n19, 162n20, 162n22, 162n28, 222, 244n19
Blanc de Volx, Jean, 51n94
Blanning, T.C.W., 7, 16n35, 16n48, 26, 34, 36, 46n1, 48n26, 51n79, 51n86, 51n96, 52n103, 52n114, 52n115, 53n120, 53n130, 53n135, 54n142, 57n210, 105, 127n83, 280n80, 281n114
Böhm, Christian Wilhelm von, 106
Boisgelin, Jean de Dieu-Raymond de Cucé de, 194, 209n120
Boissy d'Anglas, François Antoine, 191
Bonaparte, Joseph, 103, 104, 114, 117, 128n103, 151, 206n56, 219, 224–226, 242, 244n2
Bond, Phineas, 83, 91n142, 91n143
Bonne-Carrère, Guillaume, 41, 145
Bonnier, Ange-Elisabeth-Louis-Antoine d'Alco, 114, 159, 226, 259, 273
Bosc d'Antic, Louis Augustin-Guillaume, 73
Bossuet, Jacques-Bénigne, 46n3
Boston, 12, 18n87, 18n88, 18n90, 77, 123n4, 126n61, 126n69, 132n195, 167n107, 250n142
Bourgoing, Jean-François, baron de, 234, 248n90
Bournonville, Charles-François, 77

INDEX   289

Boursault, Jean François, 195
Bray, François-Gabriel, comte de, 99, 124n31
Brinton, Crane, 5, 15n21
Brissot de Warville, Jacques-Pierre, 4, 14n12, 38, 40, 43, 54n152, 54n153, 56n184, 65–68, 74, 84n7, 84n17, 85n21, 86n41, 87n66, 108, 109, 125n37, 128n102, 128n110, 146, 150, 152, 162n30, 164n55, 166n90, 200, 211n160
Broglie, Charles François de, marquis de Ruffec, 34
Brûlart de Genlis, Charles-Alexis, marquis de Sillery, 39
Brumaire, coup of, 1, 75, 88n80
Brune, Guillaume-Marie-Anne, general, 116
Brunswick, Frederick William, duke of, 226
Bruyère, Jean de la, 65, 84n4, 99
Bry, Jean de, 109, 226
Buchot, Philibert, 200
Bukovina, 35
Burke, Edmund, 2, 5, 9, 14n5, 15n22, 18n90, 18n91, 85n34, 98, 123n6, 123n13, 123n17, 123n18, 123n19, 123n20, 124n21, 129n131, 133n212, 171n180, 252n187, 277n5

C
Cabot, George, 193
Cacault, François, 76, 77, 183, 211n162, 234
Caillard, Antoine-Bernard, 107, 108, 201
Calais, 111, 129n134
Callières, François de, 99, 124n28, 127n81, 142, 145, 161n12, 244n12

Cambacérès, Jean-Jacques-Régis de, 42, 194–196, 277n17
Cambon, Pierre-Joseph, 201
Campo Formio, Peace of, 186, 271
Canada, 31, 39, 239
Canary Islands, 80
Canning, George, 224
Caribbean, 30
Caritat, Marie-Jean-Antoine-Nicolas, marquis de, 29, 56n176
Carletti, Francesco Xaverio, comte, 119, 268, 276
Carnot, Lazare, 74, 79, 148, 228, 279n62
Carra, Jean-Louis, 33
Castiligione, Baldassare, 105
Castries, Charles-Eugène-Gabriel de La Croix, maréchal de, 37
Catherine II of Russia, 235
Caulaincourt, Armand-Augustin-Louis, de, 145
Ceremony, 97–99, 105, 109, 111, 115, 118–120, 122, 124n29, 124n33, 156, 227, 260, 263–265, 267
Chambonas, Victor-Scipion-Charles-Auguste de La Garde de, 68
Charles Emmanuel IV, king of Sardinia, 51n76
Charleston, 12, 70, 76, 77, 86n50, 89n106
Charleston, Antoine, 80, 131n179, 131n182, 157, 237, 241, 273
Chateaubriand, François-René, viscount of, 268
Chauvelin, Bernard-François, marquis de, 74, 108, 130–131n164, 144, 150, 192, 193, 201, 222, 223, 232, 233
Chazal, Jean-Pierre, 196, 209n126, 209n134
Chesterfield, Philip Stanhope, 4th earl of, 69

Chinard, Joseph, 179
Choiseul, Étienne-François, duc de, 68, 192
Cisalpine Republic, 186, 271
Clarke, Henri-Jacques- Guillaume, general, 199
Clausewitz, Carl Philipp Gottfried von, 8, 16n55, 275, 281n113
Cloots, Anarchasis, 42, 281n96
Cobb, Richard, 152, 167n117, 167n119, 168n127
Cobenzl, Johann Karl Philipp von, 103, 117, 118, 126n63, 132n197, 132n199, 219, 224, 225, 244n3, 245n39, 246n46
Coblentz, 82
Cohen, Raymond, 106, 118, 128n90, 132n198, 171n179, 244n7, 244n8
Cologne, 35, 79
Committee of Public Safety, 3, 41, 45, 69, 71, 75, 77–80, 87n69, 87n70, 89n94, 89n110, 99, 114, 116, 119, 120, 133n204, 133n206, 144, 146, 147, 151, 156, 163n42, 165n72, 191, 194–196, 200–202, 212n177, 233, 239, 240, 242, 248n101, 251n160, 252n176, 263, 269, 271, 274, 275
Condillac, Étienne Bonnot de, 146, 164n59
Condorcet, Marie- Jean-Antoine-Nicolas de Caritat, marquis de, 29, 42, 56n176, 56n178, 106, 127n84
Constantinople, 77, 78, 88n90, 100, 118, 132n202, 149, 156, 166n87, 178, 264, 267
Cornwallis, Charles, Earl of Cornwallis, 128n103
Corsairs, 35, 237, 241

Corsica, 38, 116
Couthon, Georges, 196
Custine, Adam-Philippe, comte de, 41, 43, 55n166, 86n43

D

Dalmatia, 82
Danton, George, 40, 55n161, 73, 211n172, 247n77
David, Jacques-Louis, 154, 156, 180, 264
Deane, Silas, 38
Debry, Jean-Antoine-Joseph, 108, 226
De Conde, Alexander, 167n106, 167n107, 250n144
Deforgues, François-Louis-Michel Chemin, 66, 68, 75, 87n70, 166n86, 200, 233, 248n101
Degelmann, Sigmund Ignaz Freiherr, baron von, 76, 88n74, 132n196, 188, 223, 245n29
Delacroix, Charles, 67, 89n106, 111, 112, 147, 148, 197, 198, 223, 228, 245n30, 245n31, 263, 264, 270
De las Casas, Simón, 189
Delhorme, Barthélemy-Albin-Fleury, 75
Derché, Antoine Liébaud, 159
Derrida, Jacques, 164n62
Desch, Michael C., 11, 17n74
Descorches, Marie-Louis-Henri, marquis de Sainte-Croix, 77–79, 89n94, 149, 178, 191
Deshacquets, François, 242
Desportes, Félix, 72, 242
Devocelle, Jean-Marc, 153, 168n122, 168n128, 168n141, 169n146, 169n150, 170n158
Diderot, Denis, 27, 49n43, 49n44
Digne, Joseph, 182

Diplomatic Committee, 14n13,
    55n171, 67, 80, 128n101,
    166n85, 192
Diplomats, attack on, 29, 65–83
Directory, 3, 71, 73, 76, 77, 79, 81,
    83, 103, 104, 110, 116, 118,
    121, 147, 149, 150, 154, 156,
    185, 186, 188, 189, 197–199,
    201, 202, 211n169, 222, 224,
    227, 229–231, 240, 260,
    262–264, 268, 270, 274
Dorset, John Frederick Saville,
    3rd duke of Dorset, 35
Douai, Merlin de, 120, 133n209, 263
Dress, 1, 2, 4, 5, 11, 98, 99, 112, 118,
    131n165, 141–160, 195, 221,
    225, 230, 260, 263–266, 273
Dubois-Crancé,
    Edmond-Louis-Alexis, 69
Dubois, Guillaume, cardinal, 84n2
Duclos, Charles Pinot, 25, 47n20, 78
Duhem, Pierre Joseph, 195, 209n127
Duindam, Jeroen, 97, 122n4,
    125n46, 125n48
Dumouriez, Charles-François du
    Périer, 6, 45, 66, 68, 72,
    85n20, 192
Dundas, Henry,
    1st viscount Melville, 274
Duphot, Léonard, general, 242
Du Pont de Nemours, Pierre Samuel,
    6, 16n45, 29
Du Pont, Victor, 6, 12, 16n46,
    18n83, 18n84, 18n85, 18n88,
    18n89, 70, 72, 76, 77, 80,
    86n48, 86n49, 86n50, 87n57,
    88n76, 88n83, 88n84, 88n85,
    88n86, 88n87, 88n88, 88n89,
    89n106, 89n112, 90n114,
    115, 131n177, 131n179,
    131n180, 131n181, 131n182,
    157, 166n88, 170n156,
    241, 273, 280n92
Duprat, Annie, 5
Durkheim, Emile, 178, 203n4,
    259, 277n3

E
Edelstein, Dan, 8, 17n63, 17n64
Eden, Treaty of, 36
Eden, William, 1st Baron Auckland,
    82, 150, 222
Eggers, Christian Ulrich
    Detlev von, 226
Elias, Norbert, 122n1, 123n7,
    123n15, 124n23, 124n24
Elliot, Hugh, 221, 244n15
Eschasseriaux, Joseph, 44
Etiquette, 4, 11, 97–122, 141,
    178, 183, 225, 228, 230,
    232, 260–263, 267
Executive Provisionary Council, 66
Expilly de la Poipe,
    Louis-Alexandre, 80

F
Fabre d'Eglantine, Philippe-François-
    Nazaire, 144, 178
Fagel, Hendrik, 150
Faipoult de Maisoncelle,
    Guillhaume-Charles, 74
Falklands, 33
Fauchet, Joseph, 72, 81–83, 90n116,
    90n121, 90n122, 115, 131n178,
    147, 165n67, 165n68, 167n109,
    200, 240, 252n166
Fénelon, François, archbishop,
    24, 124n22
Fernán Nuñez, Carlos José Gutiérrez
    de los Ríos y Rohan Chabot,
    conde de, 191, 208n100
Fersen, Hans Axel von, 225
Finckenstein, Karl Wilhelm
    Finck von, 107, 110

Fisher, Glen, 220, 244n9
Fitzgerald, Lord Robert, 9, 17n66
Fitzherbert, Alleyne, 124n33
Floréal, coup of, 74, 155, 169n146, 263
Florida, 34, 237, 238, 240
Floridablanca, José Moñino y Redondo, conde de, 37
Flotte, Jean Charles de, 180–182, 184
Foch, Marshal Ferdinand, 275
Fonspertius, Antoine-Louis, 12, 80, 81
Forster, Georg, 1, 6
Fouché, Joseph, duc d'Otrante, 228, 243, 253n192
Francis II, Holy Roman Emperor, 104, 199
Franco-Austrian Alliance of 1756, 32, 33, 223
Franklin, Benjamin, 155
Frédéric, Jean, 71
Frederick William II, King of Prussia, 26, 37, 47n24, 49n43
Fructidor, coup of, 3, 74, 76
Furet, François, 5, 7, 8, 15n28, 16n49, 16n56, 99, 146, 147, 165n70, 260, 277n7

G
Galicia, 35
Garardin, René-Louis, marquis de, 41
Garat, Dominique-Joseph, 151, 167n103, 229–231, 247n77
Geertz, Clifford, 4, 14n16, 14n17, 14n18
Genet, Edmond Charles, 12, 71, 77, 81, 82, 102, 115, 193, 235–242, 249n125, 250n132, 250n134, 250n145, 251n152, 269, 272
Geneva, 11, 71, 72, 75, 79, 119, 121, 178, 201, 211n162, 233, 269, 272

Genoa, 71, 73, 76, 80, 101, 116, 189, 194, 241, 242, 269
Gentz, Friedrich von, 13, 18n92, 245n40, 276, 282n121
George III, 192, 204n24, 206n55, 236
Gestures, 2, 5, 98, 99, 106, 115, 116, 118, 151, 160, 177, 187, 219, 221, 246n68
Ginguené, Pierre-Louis, 154, 229, 230, 247n77
Girodet de Roussy-Trioson, Anne-Louis, 153, 179, 181, 183, 204n12, 204n23, 204n27, 205n38, 205n49
Girondins, 2, 12, 71–73, 76, 102, 190, 197, 239, 240, 247n77, 270
Gordon, Daniel, 143, 161n5, 161n11, 162n21, 203n4
Goupil de Préfelne, Guillaume-François-Charles, 40
Goya, Francisco, 158
Gravier, Charles, comte de Vergennes, 33
Great Britain, 9, 31, 34, 38, 66, 68, 76
  See also London
Grégoire, Henri-Jean-Baptiste, abbé, 44, 102, 141, 143–145, 153, 156, 162n22, 162n29, 163n33, 163n46, 168n129
Grenada, 31
Grenadines, 31
Grenville, William Wyndham Grenville, Baron, 9, 10, 13, 17n66, 17n71, 18n93, 83, 90n127, 90n128, 90n130, 90n131, 90n132, 90n133, 90n134, 91n135, 91n136, 91n137, 91n138, 91n139, 91n140, 108, 111, 113, 116, 128n95, 129n133, 130n138, 130n139, 130n140, 130n141,

131n166, 154, 166n93, 166n95,
    166n96, 166n98, 167n102,
    168n137, 170n163, 170n170,
    192, 193, 198, 201, 205n47,
    206n72, 207n83, 207n84,
    207n85, 207n86, 208n107,
    209n117, 210n144, 210n145,
    210n146, 210n147, 210n149,
    210n150, 222, 232, 244n21,
    244n22, 244n23, 244n24,
    245n41, 246n68, 247n70,
    248n96, 248n114, 249n126,
    250n139, 276, 278n21, 279n60,
    280n82, 282n118, 282n119
Guerini, Alvise, 121
Guerini, Paolo, 228
Guibert, Jancques-Antoine-Hippolyte, 8
Guidi, Domenico, 180
Guillemardet, Ferdinand Pierre Marie Dorothée, 109, 158
Guiomar, Jean-Yves, 7, 16n47

H

Hague, The, 47n19, 73, 82, 122, 144, 159, 201, 222
Hammond, George, 115, 193, 236–239, 249n125, 249n126, 249n127, 250n134, 250n135, 250n138, 250n139, 250n141, 251n152, 251n158, 251n162, 251n165
Hardouin, comte de Châlon, 79
Harris, James, Earl of Malmesbury, 109, 111–114, 121, 129n132, 129n133, 129n134, 129n135, 129n137, 130n138, 130n139, 130n140, 130n141, 130n144, 130n145, 130n146, 130n147, 130n152, 130n153, 130n154, 130n156, 130n161, 130n162,
    131n165, 131n168, 131n170,
    152, 154, 159, 167n116,
    168n136, 168n137, 170n172,
    197, 198, 210n144, 210n145,
    210n146, 210n147, 210n148,
    210n149, 210n150, 210n151,
    263, 269, 278n27, 279n60
Haugwitz, August Heinrich Kurt, Graf von, 110, 129n126, 158, 167n115
Hauterive, Alexandre Maurice Blanc de Lanautte, comte d, 86n56, 132n191, 238, 239
Heeren, Arnold Hermann Ludwig, 243, 253n190
Heidrich, Kurt, 6
Helvetic Corps, 71
Hénin de Cuvillier, Étienne Félix d, 78, 79, 88n90, 88n93
Hérault de Séchelles, Marie-Jean, 201, 248n92
Hermann, Jean Frédéric, 196
Hertzberg, Ewald Friedrich, Graf von, 36
Hervey, Frederick Augustus, 4th Earl of Bristol, 227
Holbach, Paul-Henri Thiry, baron d, 26
Holy Roman Empire, 24, 31, 32, 225
Hosdan, Emmanuel de Maulde, 82, 150
Hugo, Victor, 275, 282n115
Hunt, Lynn, 5, 15n27, 15n29

I

Images, 4–6, 11, 142, 144, 155, 157, 159, 177–203
India, 30, 31, 34
Italy, 12, 71, 184, 186, 188, 226, 271
Ivernois, François d, 275

J

Jackson, Francis James, 113, 114
Jackson, Sir George, 72, 87n59
Jay, John, 115
Jefferson, Thomas, 66, 84n10, 98, 104, 126n70, 148, 160, 193, 209n113, 236–239, 241, 249n130, 250n132, 250n133, 250n134, 250n139, 250n140, 250n142, 250n145, 251n151, 251n152, 251n154, 261
Jemappes, fall of, 271
Jerome, King of Westphalia, 270, 280n69
Johann I Joseph, Field Marshal, Prince of Liechtenstein, 117
Johnson, Samuel, 69
Jolivet, Nicolas Michel, 242
Joseph II, Holy Roman Emperor, 23, 32, 33, 35, 36, 39
Joseph, Jean Antoine, 72, 147
Jouvenel, Bertrand de, 48n34, 272, 280n87, 280n88, 281n106

K

Kant, Immanuel, 43
Kaunitz-Rietberg, Wenzel Anton, prince von, 38
Kutchuk-Kainardji, Peace of, 35
Kutzleben, Freiherr von, 232

L

Lacombe, Saint-Michel, general, 116
Lafayette, Gilbert du Motier, marquis de, 34, 274
La Forest, Antoine-René-Charles-Mathurin, comte de, 72
La Harpe, Frédéric-César de, 142, 146, 227, 246n64, 274, 281n99
Lallement, Jean Baptiste, 81, 83, 158, 278n18
Language, 4, 5, 11, 13, 66, 67, 71, 76, 98, 106, 123n8, 141–160, 177, 191, 219, 222, 229, 230, 237, 259, 260, 265
La Révellière-Lépaux, Louis-Marie de, 74, 197
Las Casas, Simon de, 189
La Vauguyon, Paul-François de Quelen de, 67
Le Blanc, Georges-Pierre, 90n116, 240
Lebrun, Charles-François, 68, 70, 72, 102, 115, 116, 164n55, 179–181, 183, 184, 201, 211n170, 232, 236, 271
Lebrun-Tondu, Pierre-Henri-Hélène Marie, 164n55, 190
Lee, Richard Henry, 251n153
Le Hoc, Louis-Grégoire, 73
Leibniz, Wilhelm, Baron von, 24, 46n6, 47n12
Lessart, Claude-Antoine de Valdec de, 68, 148
Létombe, Philippe-André-Joseph de, 18n84, 77, 80, 88n84, 88n85, 88n89, 89n106, 90n114, 149, 166n88, 193
Lévis, Pierre-Marc-Gaston de Lévis, duc de, 8
Liège, 77, 108, 231, 242
Lille, negotiations at, 10, 112, 159
Linguet, Simon-Nicholas-Henri, 84n15
Liston, Sir Robert, 149, 166n87, 274, 281n105
London, 8, 68, 73, 74, 81, 150, 192, 198, 200–202, 222, 232
Lorraine, 24, 38
Lotman, Yuri, 15n23
Louisbourg, 31
Louis XIV, 23, 24, 39, 47n15, 97, 99, 101, 105, 180, 267, 275

Louis XV, 23, 25, 29–33, 38, 39,
    52n108, 178, 266
Louis XVI, 23, 29, 33, 36, 38, 39,
    70, 192, 194, 231, 273
Louis XVIII, 88n80, 186
Loustalot, Elysée, 143, 145, 162n16
Luc, Charles-Felix René
    de Vintimille, du, 221
Luzerne, César Henri,
    comte de la, 72, 222

M

Mably, Gabriel Bonnet de,
    25, 47n19, 66
Machiavelli, Niccolò, 260, 277n6
Mackau, Armand Louis, baron de,
    157, 184, 204n34, 234
MacLeish, Archibald, 3, 14n10
Madison, James, 104, 193
Madrid, 12, 74, 77, 82, 109,
    128n95, 131n166,
    159, 191, 201, 221,
    234, 248n90, 263
Magra, Perkins, 223, 245n26
Mainz, 1, 149, 193, 234
Mallet du Pan, Jacques, 34, 247n86
Malouet, Pierre Victor Baron, 39
Mangourit, Michel-Ange-Bernard,
    12, 70, 77, 80, 109, 159,
    242, 252n184
Manners, *see* Etiquette
Mann, Golo, 129n122, 129n124
Manuel, Pierre, 207n88
Marat, Jean-Paul, 3
Marbois, Barbé, 85n31, 114, 212n186
Maret, Hugues-Bernard duc de
    Bassano, 112, 267
Maria Theresa of Austria, 50n76
Marie Antoinette, queen of France,
    32, 52n100, 52n111, 231,
    234, 235, 267

Marie Caroline, queen of Naples and
    Sicily, 116, 132n188, 184,
    206n54, 235
Marseilles, 179
Martens, George Friedrich, 125n44
Martin, Virginie, 12, 14n8, 16n50,
    55n171, 85n23, 85n30, 86n53
Marwitz, Friedrich August
    von der, 158
Marx, Karl, 8, 16n57
Mastrilli, Marzio, 75
Mattingly, Garrett, 13, 18n94
Maure, Nicolas-Sylvestre, 144
Maurepas, Jean-Frédérie Phélypeaux
    comte de, 32
Maximilian Franz, Archduke, 35
Menning, Ralph, 219, 244n1
Mercier, Henri, 244n13
Mercy-Argenteau, Florimond Claude
    comte de, 131n183
Merry, Anthony, 104
Merveldt, Maximilian Graf von, 155,
    224, 245n38
Metternich, Klements Wenzel, Fürst
    von, 114, 117, 141, 156, 159,
    160, 220, 221, 225, 226
Meyer, Casparus, 119
Micheli, Michel, 263
Miles, William, 127n87
Miot de Melito, André-François,
    81, 87n64, 90n117, 144, 157,
    163n37, 165n76, 169n154,
    170n159, 228, 229, 235,
    247n71, 249n118
Miquelon, 31
Mirabeau, Honoré-Gabriel Riqueti
    comte de, 6, 34, 67, 68, 110,
    178, 221, 244n15
Moldavia, 35, 39
Monroe, James, 102, 119, 120, 122,
    126n55, 133n204, 133n205, 152,
    155, 167n110, 167n113, 251n152

Montbreton d'Urtubise, Auguste marquis de, 106
Montesquieu, Charles-Louis de Secondat, baron de Brède et de, 26, 48n29, 48n33, 48n34, 48n37, 50n75, 164n58
Montmorin, Armand Marc comte de, 37, 54n147, 85n28
Montreal, 31, 83
Morieux, Reynaud, 8, 17n62, 278n28, 281n103
Moritz, Christian, 232
Morque, Jacobin, 232
Morris, Gouverneur, 151, 152
Moustier, Eléonor-François Elie comte de, 68, 150
Moutte, banker in Rome, 182, 183
Mouysset, Guillaume, 190, 208n93
Mozard, Théodore- Charles, 12, 13, 18n88
Muir, Edward, 14n19, 123n14, 127n78

N

Naples, 77, 116, 126n68, 132n188, 157, 179, 181, 183, 184, 206n54, 229–232, 234, 242, 248n114, 267
Napoleon, 15n26, 69, 81, 104, 116–118, 122n3, 126n62, 132n187, 155, 160, 184, 185, 187, 189, 193, 194, 199, 202, 203, 207n79, 209n118, 210n154, 212n196, 220, 227, 242, 259, 266, 267, 269–271, 279n43, 279n49, 279n63
Narbonne-Lara, Louis comte de, 68
Natural Law, 8, 9, 26, 261
Netherlands, *see* United Provinces
New York, 73
Noailles, Emmanuel-Marie-Louis marquis de, 70, 149, 234
Noël, François-Joseph-Michel, 73, 239
Nootka Sound Controversy, 2, 221
North America, 30
Novale, 78

O

Ochs, Peter, 152, 167n115, 227, 246n63
O'Kelly Farrell, Jean-Jacques, 193
Oresko, Robert, 100, 124n34, 125n41, 125n42
Otto, Louis Guillaume, 71, 120, 221, 240
Ozouf, Mona, 15n27

P

Pacte de famille, 2, 37, 38
Paget, Sir Arthur, 83, 91n136, 91n137, 91n138, 91n139, 91n140, 194
Paine, Thomas, 84n5, 141–160
Paris, Peace of, 33
Paul I, Emperor of Russia, 154
Payan, Claude-François de, 75, 87n69, 154, 233
Pecquet, Antoine, 100, 221, 244n14
Pelet, Jean, 196
Perignon, Dominique-Catherine de, 77, 82, 107, 148, 170n162, 263, 269, 278n20
Perrochel, Henri Maes de, 74
Pétion de Villeneuve, Jérôme, 39, 57n199, 208n89
Petry, Jean-Baptiste, French consul, 240
Peysonnel, Charles de, 33
Philadelphia, 72, 77, 80, 236, 237, 239
Pichon, Louis-André, 98, 123n16

INDEX 297

Pickering, Timothy, 126n61
Pinckney, Charles Cotesworth, 122, 267, 268
Pitt the Younger, William, 67
Poland, 34, 39, 44, 77, 201
  partitions of, 33
Polignac, Melchior de, 23, 154
Politeness, see Etiquette
Pondicherry, 31
Popilius, 197
Portugal, 79, 268
Poterat, Pierre-Claude marquis de, 75, 76, 201, 223, 245n28, 245n30, 268
Prairial, coup of, 74
Precedence, 11, 28, 97–122, 186, 267, 273
Protocol, 101, 102, 109, 116, 120, 261–263, 265, 267
Prudhomme, Louis Marie, 65, 84n3, 184, 205n50
Prussia, 30, 31, 34, 35, 44, 158, 232, 268, 271, 274

Q
Quebec, 31

R
Randolph, Edmund, 115, 147, 250n134
Rastatt, Congress of, 159
Ratter, Ildephonse, 179
Raynal, Guillaume-Thomas-François, 44, 49n52
Rayneval, Gérard de, 32
Redondo, José Moñino y, 37
Resnier, Louis-Pierre, 178
Reubell, Jean-François, 45, 76, 113, 122, 228
Revellière-Lépeaux, Louis-Marie de la, 73, 197

Reybaz, Étienne Salomon, 45, 75, 121, 272
Robespierre, Maximilien, 43, 70–72, 75, 87n69, 114, 119, 144, 149, 191, 196, 200, 208n95, 233, 240, 241, 247n77, 251n160, 251n161, 264, 269, 270, 273–275, 281n110
Roche, Daniel, 141, 168n124, 168n141
Rochefoucauld, François Jeanne Manon duc de la, 105, 127n79, 127n80
Roland, Jeanne Manon, 154
Rome, 8, 11, 65, 68, 76, 116, 153, 154, 157, 178–184, 189, 197, 235, 242
Rossbach, battle of, 30, 51n80
Rouget de Lisle, Claude-Joseph, 274
Rousseau, Jean-Jacques, 27, 28, 46n6, 49n52, 49n54, 49n57, 49n59, 49n62, 50n65, 98, 123n8, 123n10, 143, 146, 162n16, 247n77
Rovigo, Anne-Jean-René Savary duc de, 116
Russia, 5, 34, 35, 37, 44, 82, 103, 107, 116, 124n33, 126n68, 145, 154, 155, 234, 235, 270
Russo-Austrian War against Turkey, 35

S
Sackville, John Frederick, Duke of Dorset, 35, 53n128, 53n138, 54n145, 85n34, 245n36
Saint André, Jeanbon, 43, 67
Saint-Just, Louis-Antoine, 3, 86n44, 86n54, 142, 161n8, 196, 209n122, 211n174, 222, 244n20, 252n175
Saint-Maur, Verninac de, 118
Saint-Pierre, Charles-Irénée Castel de abbé, 23, 46n6, 46n7

Saint Simon, Louis de Rovroy, duc de, 23
Saladin, Jean Baptiste Michel, 190
Sandoz-Rollin, Alphonse von, 130n143, 227, 228, 246n66, 263
Sardinia, 230, 241, 262, 268
Savary, Anne-Jean-René Rovigo, duc de, 116
Savoy, 51n76, 101, 124n34, 125n42, 231, 232
Scheldt, 33, 39
Schiller, Johann, 243, 260, 277n8
Schroeder, Paul, 34, 52n117
Second Hundred Years' War, 274
Secret diplomacy, 190, 195
Ségur, Louis-Philippe comte de, 30, 31, 35–37, 68, 234, 266
Sémonville, Charles Louis Huguet marquis de, 78, 100, 157, 231, 232, 234, 241, 248n89
Senegal, 31, 34
Seven Years' War, 30–32, 34, 51n78, 52n98
Short, William, 84n10, 126n70, 191, 208n101
Sicard, secretary of French legation at Genoa, 242
Sicily, 114, 116
Sieyès, Emmanuel-Joseph, 38, 103, 110, 111, 158, 202
Solothurn, 74, 233, 234
Sorel, Albert, 7, 46n3, 48n25, 50n74, 51n77, 52n116, 56n180, 56n190, 57n208, 84n2, 86n52, 89n94, 132n196, 170n166, 171n176, 206n58, 208n106, 249n116, 272, 277n17, 278n18, 280n79, 280n86
Soulavie, Jean-Louis-Giraud, 75, 201, 233
Souza Botelho, Maria José de, 227

Spain, 31–34, 37–39, 50n76, 67, 106, 108, 109, 148, 151, 158, 222, 242, 268, 269, 274, 278n20
See also Madrid
Staël-Holstein, Anne-Louise-Germaine Necker, baroness, 132n192
Staël-Holstein, Erik Magnus, baron, 119
Stewart, John, third Earl of Bute, 107
Stites, Richard, 5, 15n20, 165n69
Stone, Bailey, 47–48n24, 50n66, 50n69, 51n83, 51n86, 51n87, 51n95, 52n108, 53n123, 53n132, 53n139, 53n141, 274, 275, 281n96, 281n97, 281n107, 281n111
Strasbourg, 24, 25, 221, 222
Sweden, 35, 73, 76, 116, 119, 151, 194, 263, 268
Swiss, 71, 107, 121, 142, 152, 154, 179, 227, 231, 233
Symbols, 5, 101, 106, 155, 160, 177–203, 229, 259, 260, 272

T
Talleyrand-Périgord, Charles-Maurice de, prince of Benevento, 210n154, 211n163
Ternant, Jean Baptiste, 115, 131n176, 193
Terror, 2, 3, 8, 17n63, 70, 72, 73, 75, 86n56, 107, 144, 196, 223, 235, 240, 247n77, 262, 269, 274
Thermidor, 15n25, 68, 72, 73, 75, 87n69, 107, 109, 118–120, 148, 149, 200, 233, 247n77, 261
Thibadeau, Antoine-Claire, 196
Thionville, Merlin de, 121, 166n86, 197
Thucydides, 142

Thugut, Johann Amadeus Franz de Paula, Freiherr von, 75, 87n71, 88n74, 117, 126n63, 132n196, 132n197, 132n199, 186, 188, 220, 221, 223, 224, 226, 243, 244n3, 244n5, 245n29, 245n37, 245n38, 245n39, 248n109
Thuriot de la Rosière, Jacques-Alexis, 146
Tilly, Jean, 11, 189, 241, 242
Tocqueville, Alexis de, 23, 40, 46n2, 55n159, 146, 165n64, 247n83, 261, 277n15
Tolentino, Treaty of, 184–185
Torcy, Jean-Baptiste Colbert, marquis de, 101, 125n49
Tournon, Antoine, 146, 147
Transylvania, 35
Treilhard, Jean-Baptiste, 109, 114, 129n114, 199, 207n76, 210n157, 225, 226, 280n85
Trevor, John Hampden, 3rd Viscount Hampden, 207n86, 223, 244n25, 262, 276, 278n21, 282n118
Trier, 88n90, 234
Tronson du Coudray, Guillaume-Alexandre du, 198, 210n148
Trotsky, Leon, 2, 13n2
Tunis, 116, 223
Turin, 81, 154, 223, 229–231, 234, 262, 276
Turks, 27, 32, 34, 35, 39, 71, 79, 116, 149, 194, 232, 264
Turreau, Louis Marie, 193
Tuscany, 119, 268

U

Udine, negotiations at, 224
United Provinces, 150, 222
United States (U.S.), 12, 45, 71–73, 77, 80, 81, 83, 84n10, 86n56, 98, 102–104, 115, 120, 147–150, 155, 157–159, 191, 193, 194, 200, 211n164, 222, 235–242, 267, 268
Utrecht, Congress of, 23

V

Valais, 71, 242
Varennes, 2, 67, 70, 194, 234, 235
Vattel, Emerich de, 25, 26, 47n21, 47n23, 101, 103, 125n40, 126n57
Vauban, Sébastien Le Prestre de, marquis de, 23
Vellinghausen, battle of, 30
Venaissin, 179
Venice, 28, 71, 73, 79, 81, 83, 88n90, 101, 116, 120, 121, 151, 158, 189, 191, 194, 201, 224, 239, 271, 272
Vergennes, Charles Gravier, comte de, 26, 33, 36, 37, 48n25
Verninac Saint-Maur, Raymond de, 79, 118, 149, 232
Victor, Amadeus III, king of Sardinia, 231, 241, 252n171
Vienna, 11, 12, 31–33, 38, 70, 75, 103, 104, 116, 149, 155, 178, 185–189, 194, 201, 221, 224, 225, 234, 235, 265, 266
Villars, Baptiste-Dorothée, 73, 76, 77, 149, 221, 234, 242, 269
Vincent, François-Nicolas, 153
Viollet, Paul, 272, 280n87
Voltaire, François Marie Arouet de, 27, 105, 146, 164n58

W

Washington, George, 193, 238–240, 250n142, 251n152, 251n153
Whitworth, Charles, 166n87, 227, 266
Wicar, Jean-Baptiste, 179, 181
William V, 36

Wilmington, 73
Wittgenstein, Ludwig, 9, 17n70
Woolf, Stuart, 7, 16n53
Worsley, Sir Richard, 83, 90n119, 90n132, 90n133, 90n134, 91n135, 167n102, 170n163, 207n83, 207n84, 207n85, 224, 245n27, 245n33, 245n34, 246n68, 280n82
Wyndham, William, 9, 243, 245n34, 276, 282n119

X
XYZ affair, 267

Z
Zante, 82
Zelada, Francesco Saverio de, cardinal, 181
Zinzendorf, Karl Christian, Graf von, 225, 246n47
Zweibrücken, 72, 242

Printed in the United States
By Bookmasters